Cultures of Sustainable Peace

Full details of all our publications can be found on https://www.channelviewpublications.com, or by writing to Multilingual Matters, St Nicholas House, 31–34 High Street, Bristol BS1 2AW, UK.

Cultures of Sustainable Peace

Conflict Transformation, Gender-Based Violence, Decolonial Praxes

Edited by
Hyab Teklehaimanot Yohannes, Alison Phipps and Tawona Sitholé

MULTILINGUAL MATTERS
Bristol • Jackson

DOI https://doi.org/10.21832/YOHANN8356
Library of Congress Cataloging in Publication Data
Names: Yohannes, Hyab Teklehaimanot, editor. | Phipps, Alison, editor. | Sitholé, Tawona, editor.
Title: Cultures of Sustainable Peace: Conflict Transformation, Gender-Based Violence, Decolonial Praxes/Edited by Hyab Teklehaimanot Yohannes, Alison Phipps and Tawona Sitholé.
Description: Bristol, UK; Jackson, TN: Multilingual Matters, 2025. | Includes bibliographical references and index. | Summary: "With an emphasis on addressing gender-based violence and the role of women and cultural work in peacebuilding, the chapters in this book represent the fruit of collaborative work across borders, between artists, activists and academics, bringing a wide range of disciplinary perspectives to bear on situations of violence and precarity" – Provided by publisher.
Identifiers: LCCN 2024024873 (print) | LCCN 2024024874 (ebook) |
  ISBN 9781800418349 (paperback) | ISBN 9781800418356 (hardback) |
  ISBN 9781800418370 (epub) | ISBN 9781800418363 (pdf)
Subjects: LCSH: Women in peace-building. | Gender-based violence – Prevention. | Decolonization – Social aspects.
Classification: LCC JZ5578 .C85 2025 (print) | LCC JZ5578 (ebook) |
  DDC 327.1/72082--dc23/eng/20240802
LC record available at https://lccn.loc.gov/2024024873
LC ebook record available at https://lccn.loc.gov/2024024874

British Library Cataloguing in Publication Data
A catalogue entry for this book is available from the British Library.

ISBN-13: 978-1-80041-835-6 (hbk)
ISBN-13: 978-1-80041-834-9 (pbk)
ISBN-13: 978-1-80041-836-3 (pdf)
ISBN-13: 978-1-80041-837-0 (epub)

Open Access

Except where otherwise noted, this work is licensed under the Creative Commons Attribution-NoDerivatives 4.0 International License. To view a copy of this license, visit http://creativecommons.org/licenses/by-nd/4.0/ or send a letter to Creative Commons, PO Box 1866, Mountain View, CA 94042, USA.

Multilingual Matters
UK: St Nicholas House, 31-34 High Street, Bristol, BS1 2AW, UK.
USA: NBN, Blue Ridge Summit, PA, USA.

Website: https://www.multilingual-matters.com
X: Multi_Ling_Mat
Facebook: https://www.facebook.com/multilingualmatters
Blog: https://www.channelviewpublications.wordpress.com

Copyright © 2025 Hyab Teklehaimanot Yohannes, Alison Phipps, Tawona Sitholé and the authors of individual chapters.

All rights reserved. No part of this work may be reproduced in any form or by any means without permission in writing from the publisher.

The policy of Multilingual Matters/Channel View Publications is to use papers that are natural, renewable and recyclable products, made from wood grown in sustainable forests. In the manufacturing process of our books, and to further support our policy, preference is given to printers that have FSC and PEFC Chain of Custody certification. The FSC and/or PEFC logos will appear on those books where full certification has been granted to the printer concerned.

Typeset in Sabon and Frutiger by R. J. Footring Ltd, Derby, UK.

For Refaat Alareer

Our Colleague in Creating Cultures of Sustainable and Inclusive Peace
Brilliant Decolonial Thinker
Gentle Human
Fierce Critic of Violent Colonialism
Poet of Peace

Assassinated in a targeted Israeli airstrike on 6 December 2023

And for the women killed in violence 2019–2024

Contents

Figures and Tables	xiii
Contributors	xv
Acknowledgements	xxv
I Am You	xxvii
Un-Foreword	xxxi

Introduction   1
Hyab Teklehaimanot Yohannes, Alison Phipps and Tawona Sitholé
    Part 1: Towards Cultures of Conflict Transformation   5
    Part 2: Popular Arts and Everyday Culture Meet Gender-
        Based Violence   5
    Part 3: Reflexivity, Dilemmas and Safeguarding with
        Grassroots Organisations   5

Part 1: Towards Cultures of Conflict Transformation

1   Three Moroccan Women's Liberation Journeys   9
    Rajaa Essaghyry and Aadel Essaadani
    Context   9
    Methodology   13
    Three Women. Three Tempers. Three Strategies.   14
    Liberation Tactics – Echoes of Emancipation   24
    Conclusion   25

2   High School Women in the Face of Violence During the
    COVID-19 Pandemic: Towards the Production of Spaces of
    Prevention and Sisterhood   30
    Angelica Lucia Damian Bernal, Maria Veronica Ibarra
    Garcia, Eva Citlali Jiménez Rodríguez, Violeta Torres Carroll
    and Paola Cueto Jimenez
    Introduction   30
    Feminist Geography as a Theoretical and Methodological
        Framework   33
    Discussion   40
    Concluding Remarks   48

3   Narratives of Change: Young Palestinian Women's
    Engagement with Short Stories to Promote Dialogue for
    Peacebuilding   52
    *Taghreed El Masry, Fatma Abubaker, Hana El-Badri and
    Eman Alzaanin*
        Introduction   52
        Unpacking the Notions of 'Conflict' and 'Peace':
            A Transformative Approach to Peacebuilding   54
        Research Design and Recruitment   58
        Discussion of Findings: The Transformative Power of
            Dialogue in Understanding Conflict, Peace and
            Peacebuilding   62
        Conclusions and Lessons Learnt   70

4   Creative Corridors: Peace, Inclusivity and Engagement with
    Persons with Disabilities   75
    *Chipo Basopo, Simbarashe Mudhokwani and Rashiwe
    Chipurunyenye*
        Introduction and Chapter Structure   75
        Stories   78
        From Stories to Research   90
        Findings   92
        Concluding Remarks   94

5   A Tale of Two Cities: Recovering Community Spaces for
    Peacebuilding in Medellín and Acapulco   96
    *Evelyn Arizpe, Sinéad Gormally, Nohora Niño Vega,
    Jerónimo Castillo Muñoz, Manuela Suárez Rueda, Javiera
    Donoso Jiménez, Alejandro Bahena-Rivera and Sergio
    Hernández Mendoza*
        Introduction   96
        Cultural Intervention and Everyday Peace   98
        Methodology: Mapping Cultural and Peacebuilding
            Initiatives   99
        Two Cities: Medellín and Acapulco   100
        Recovering and Sustaining Community Spaces   108
        Conclusion   114

Part 2: Popular Arts and Everyday Culture Meet Gender-Based Violence

6 Popular Arts as Communication Tools for the Eradication of
 Gender-Based Violence and Child Marriage in Ghana 121
 Adwoa Sikayena Amankwah, Hasiyatu Abubakari and
 Abigail Opoku Mensah
  Introduction 121
  Background: The Kusaas and the Kusaal Language 122
  Theoretical Framework 125
  Methodology 127
  Results 128
  Main Themes of *Googi* Performance and Docudrama on
   Child Marriage and Teenage Pregnancy in Kusaug 130
  Discussion: Cultural Motivations for Child Marriage and
   Popular Art as a Tool for its Mitigation 134
  Conclusions 135

7 Resilient Palestinian Women Facing Gender-Based Conflict in
 the Gaza Strip 138
 Mahmoud O. Jalambo, Nazmi Al-Masri, Somaya M. Sayma
 and Azza Al-Sahhar
  Introduction and Background 138
  Methodology 141
  Results 142
  Discussion 153
  Conclusion and Recommendations 154

8 Popular Culture and Gender-Based Violence in an Evolving
 COVID-19 Context in Zimbabwe 158
 Manase Kudzai Chiweshe, Sandra Bhatasara and Gareth James
  Introduction 158
  Gender, Sex and Violence in Zimbabwean Popular Culture 159
  Methodology 162
  Findings and Discussion: Popular Culture as a Vehicle for
   Normalising and Combating GBV 164
  Conclusions and Recommendations: Harnessing Popular
   Culture to Combat GBV in a Post-COVID Recovery
   Context 172

9 Promoting Women's Participation in Social Transformation
   Through Popular Arts in Kusaal-Speaking Communities
   in Ghana   179
   Hasiyatu Abubakari, Adwoa Sikayena Amankwah and
   Abigail Opoku Mensah
       Introduction   179
       Methodology and Design   181
       Findings   184
       Analysis and Discussion of the Interviews   187
       Results and Discussion of Feedback from the Interviewees   192
       Conclusion and Recommendations   195

Part 3: Reflexivity, Dilemmas and Safeguarding with Grassroots Organisations

10 Decolonial Praxes: Metaphors, Mediation and Writing
   in Motion   201
   Rocío Elizabeth Muñoz Santamaría and Carlos Eduardo
   Arias Galindo
       Introduction   201
       Praxes as a Methodological Approach   202
       Exploring Intersectional Realities   206
       Decolonial Praxes: Metaphors, Narratives and Knowledge
           Praxes Through the Mediation of Reading   213
       Conclusions   223

11 Contextualising Safeguarding in International Development
   Research: Requirements and Challenges   227
   Maria Grazia Imperiale, Giovanna Fassetta and
   Fatma Abubaker
       Introduction   227
       First Conundrum: The Opacity of Safeguarding   229
       Second Conundrum: Vulnerability and Safeguarding 234
       Third Conundrum: Contextualising Safeguarding
           in Research   239
       Final Reflections and Unsatisfying Conclusions 244

12 Between Success and Failure: Researching with Grassroots
   Organisations Involved in Conflict Transformation   248
   Julie E. McAdam, Cristina Amescua and Evelyn Arizpe
       Introduction   248
       Introducing Conflict   249
       Methodology   251
       Conclusion: Making Space for New Possibilities When
           Working with *Colectivas*   262

13 The Many Twists and Turns in the Pathways to Peace:
    Reflections on the Bright Sadness of Decolonising and
    Structuring Cultural Work   265
    Alison Phipps
       Introduction   265
       Reflecting Back   267
       Tears and Triumphs   272
       Concluding with Bright Sadness   274

Index   277

Figures and Tables

Figures

2.1	Map created collectively in geography class by ENP high school students, 2021	43
2.2	Collective counter-cartography elaborated in the classroom by high school students	44
2.3	First example of individual counter-cartography elaborated from home by a high school geography student	45
2.4	Second example of individual counter-cartography elaborated from home by a high school geography student	46
3.1	A visual prompt for the pre-enrolment creative writing task	59
3.2	The creative writing workshops	59
3.3	A digital depiction of the short story 'The story of Watan'	65
3.4	A digital depiction of the short story 'Talent creates opportunity'	66
3.5	Conflict tree tool	67
3.6	Scenes from 'Dim light'	69
3.7	Conflict transformation through narrative storytelling	71
4.1	Provincial distribution of the study sample across Zimbabwe	93
5.1	Perception of safety survey conducted in Medellín: Percentages of responses to the survey item 'Please rate how safe the neighbourhood where you live was in the following decades'	102
5.2	Cultural actors identified in Medellín before 1980. Credit: Fundación Ideas para la Paz	103
5.3	Density of cultural actors identified in Medellín during the period 1990–1999. Credit: Fundación Ideas para la Paz	104
5.4	Photographs of Comuna 13 and the street art promoting reading, education and literature, taken by Gormally on a trip to Medellín, April 2022	109
5.5	Photographs of the escalator beside the steep steps going up through Comuna 13, taken by Gormally on a trip to Medellín, April 2022	111
6.1	Map of the Kusaug (Abubakari, 2022)	122

12.1	Timeline of events from March 2020 to October 2022	249
12.2	Opening up spaces of new possibility using a Greimas square	255
12.3	Overview of the relationships between the named organisations and the *colectivas*	259
13.1	Launch of our project and our small grants. It was a wonderful event with participation of a 'live drawing' artist who documented our work for us and gave a pictorial representation of the processes ahead	269
13.2	Letter from the Global Challenges Research Fund (GCRF) confirming funding cuts	270
13.4	Artwork by a Gazan clinician who prefers to remain anonymous	275

Tables

7.1	The top 14 forms of GBC among Palestinian women as identified by the first focus group and then ranked by the second focus group	144
7.2	The other forms of GBC among Palestinian women identified by the first focus group	145
9.1	Findings from the interviews with Kusaal-speaking participants in Ghana	189

Contributors

Hasiyatu Abubakari is a Senior Research Fellow and the Head of the Language, Literature and Drama Unit at the Institute of African Studies, University of Ghana. She holds a PhD (Summa Cum Laude) in African Studies (Languages and Literatures) from the University of Vienna, Austria (2018). As an interdisciplinary researcher, her interests span linguistics and language documentation, folktales and cultural studies, popular culture, language and gender, language and education, language and environment, and onomastics, among others. She is a fellow of the American Council of Learned Societies (AHP, 2019–2020) and a Carnegie Corporation Emerging Scholar Fellow (2023). She has received several grants and has published widely. Additionally, she serves on the editorial boards of several prestigious journals.

Fatma Abubaker is an Associate Tutor and researcher at the School of Education, University of Glasgow, where she instructs in the MSc TESOL programme. Her doctoral degree in educational studies, obtained from the University of Glasgow, centres on teaching literature within language classrooms and advancing arts-based methodologies and literary creativity. Her research is dedicated to crafting programmes and multimodal pedagogies that blend media, literature and short fiction through response-based and arts-centred approaches. Her academic pursuits encompass the utilisation of literature in English language teaching (ELT), reader-response theory, curriculum design, reading in EFL/ESL, the integration of digital technologies in EFL classrooms and, more recently, conflict transformation through the arts.

Nazmi Al-Masri is an Associate Professor of English Language Teaching at the Islamic University of Gaza. He is an Honorary Fellow in the School of Education at the University of Glasgow. He has served as a Principal Investigator and Co-investigator for various international research projects, including Disabled Voices from Gaza, Disability under Siege, Culture for Sustainable and Inclusive Peace (CUSP), Researching Multilingually at the Borders of Language: The Body, Law and the State, Welcoming Languages, and eTraining FinPal.

Azza Al-Sahhar is a Monitoring and Evaluation Specialist at Mazars Chartered Accountants and Consultants on USAID-funded projects in the

Gaza Strip. She previously worked as a Business Developer and Projects Coordinator for multiple international projects at the Islamic University of Gaza (IUG). She holds an MA in business administration (2020), a bachelor's degree in business administration (2016) and a bachelor's degree in financial and banking sciences (2017) from IUG. She also completed her master's thesis on enhancing the role of the International Relations Department at IUG-PMO, aligning with existing experiences and international practices. It was the first of its kind and garnered the interest of the university's decision-makers. Importantly, she led the Gaza team for a USAID-funded outcome learning study of the Positive Youth Engagement (PYE) project implemented by Mercy Corps and its sub-partners in Gaza.

Eman Alzaanin is Assistant Professor of Applied Linguistics in the English language programme at the Faculty of Languages and Translation – King Khalid University. Her areas of interest include language pedagogy and teacher education, teacher emotion, curriculum design and programme evaluation.

Adwoa Sikayena Amankwah is a Senior Lecturer of Media and Communications and Head of the Communication Studies Department at the University of Professional Studies, Accra, Ghana. She holds a PhD in communication science from the University of South Africa and has pedagogical, research and industry experience in training journalists and communications scholars, as well as in project execution. As an affiliate researcher with the Global Risk Journalism Hub (an international communications network consisting of 33 countries), her interests are intertwined with the interstices of journalism, digital media, health, politics, and the interface between language and communication. By exploring the nexus between these subjects and contemporary issues, her research aims to provide pragmatic solutions to challenges confronting communications and society. She has many publications in peer-reviewed journals to her credit, is a reviewer for a number of them and has presented research papers at international conferences.

Cristina Amescua is a professor and researcher at the National University of Mexico's Regional Center for Multidisciplinary Research. Some of her work has received awards from national institutions in Mexico. Since 2018 she has been the holder of the UNESCO Chair for Research on Intangible Heritage and Cultural Diversity. She has published seven books as editor or co-editor, as well as 30 chapters in books and articles.

Evelyn Arizpe is Professor of Children's Literature at the University of Glasgow. She has published widely and worked on research projects funded by the Arts and Humanities Research Council (AHRC) and the British Academy. She is past president of the International Research Society for Children's Literature (IRSCL) and has been on the jury for the Hans C. Andersen Award. See https://childslitspaces.com.

Alejandro Bahena-Rivera has done PhD research that analysed the psychosocial outcomes associated with fear of crime and victimisation. He has gained experience in quantitative and qualitative methods through projects on aesthetics, place-making and clinical interventions in the UK and Mexico. His current research includes mixed methods to understand the psychological impact of art and ancient manuscripts.

Chipo Basopo is a writer, arts administrator, actress and arts trainer in Zimbabwe. She is dedicated to empowering children and young adults through the arts. Currently, she serves as the Executive Director of Precious Children's Arts Organisation (PICA) and the chairperson of the interim committee of ASSITEJ Zimbabwe. She holds a diploma in media arts from Midlands State University and has previously worked as a director at CHIPAWO Trust. Throughout her career, she has led and developed various projects on arts education, gender, children's rights and child counselling in both rural and urban areas. She has also had the opportunity to travel to numerous countries with children and youth performing groups and has acted in several theatre productions. She has initiated national campaigns, such as 'My Story Our Story' and 'Creative Corridors', which focus on children with disabilities. Additionally, she has actively participated in national events, such as education curriculum development planning, children's events, workshops and training in Zimbabwe. She is happily married and a proud mother of three.

Angelica Lucia Damian Bernal is a professor at the Faculty of Philosophy and Letters, National Autonomous University of Mexico (UNAM), School of Geography. She obtained her doctorate in geography from the UNAM, where she currently teaches in both the undergraduate and the graduate geography programmes. She is a member of the Researchers for Mexico programme (CONAHCYT) and her project is titled 'Production of Spaces Free of Violence for and with Women with Disabilities: Intersectional Cartography for Social Inclusion'. Her research focuses on feminist geography, access for women to spaces free of violence, feminist cartography and the political participation of women with disabilities in legislative spaces.

Sandra Bhatasara is Senior Lecturer in the Department of Social and Community Development, University of Zimbabwe. She has published widely in the field of gender studies and women's rights. Her current research interests include land and natural resources governance, globalisation, global and local environment and sustainability, rural development and poverty alleviation, indigenous knowledge, climate change, adaptation and mitigation, gender, HIV and AIDS.

Violeta Torres Carroll is an operations manager at a school in California. She is affiliated with the National Autonomous University of Mexico (UNAM) through research projects and also studied there. She holds a bachelor's degree in geography from UNAM. Her research focuses on identifying spaces of vulnerability and gender-based violence, utilising embodied geographies and feminist theories and methods. She is currently a member of the research project 'Geographic Scales: Local Spaces for Processes of Change, Prevention, and Attention of Gender-Based Violence Against Women' in the Faculty of Philosophy and Literature at UNAM.

Rashiwe Chipurunyenye, born and raised in Zimbabwe, holds a degree in applied media arts, which she completed in 2021. Her passion for development led her to participate in the YALI Regional Leadership Centre Southern African Programme in South Africa in 2023. She has actively engaged in national campaigns on children with disabilities, including the 'My Story, Our Story' campaign with UNICEF, where children showcased their talents. She has also contributed to the 'Creative Corridors' project with the University of Glasgow in the UK and the *Vana Vanotamba* television show. As a co-producer, she has worked on a docudrama that explores the causes and effects of eloping and child marriages in marginalised areas of Zimbabwe. She is a member of CHIPAWO Trust, a prominent arts organisation for children and young people in Zimbabwe. In this role, she has organised arts education programmes, television shows, projects, festivals and exchange programmes. Her work primarily focuses on project management, training primary school teachers and local artists in performing and media arts education, and organising community performing arts festivals.

Manase Kudzai Chiweshe is Senior Lecturer in the Department of Social and Community Development, University of Zimbabwe, and winner of the 2015 Gerti Hesseling Prize for Best Paper Published in African Studies. His research focuses on the sociology of everyday life in African contexts. Through an approach that promotes African epistemologies, his work examines gender studies, identity, sport, leisure and livelihoods as they relate to the lived experiences of African communities. His work carries multiple policy dimensions informed by on-the-ground realities. He is a frequent presenter at international conferences; his scholarship has been widely published and provides invaluable insights into lifeworlds often overlooked in academic literature yet critically shaped by socioeconomic and political dynamics on the continent.

Hana El-Badri is an Associate Professor and currently holds the position of Dean in the Faculty of Languages at the University of Benghazi. Her doctoral degree in educational studies was obtained from the University of Aberdeen. At the university, she teaches a range of literature courses, including American literature and literary stylistics. Her research endeavours concentrate on teaching literature to English as a foreign language (EFL) learners, incorporating interactive reading into ELT, language assessment, and exploring cultural and intercultural communication.

Recently, her research has delved into assessing online learning and fostering learner autonomy through student self-assessment mechanisms.

Taghreed El Masry is a researcher currently working as a lecturer at Israa University in Gaza, Palestine, where she instructs English language and literature within the Faculty of Arts. With extensive experience in English as a foreign language (EFL) education, she has engaged with students throughout Gaza, actively contributing to curriculum development and teaching. Additionally, she holds a supervisory role at the Palestinian Ministry of Education, dedicating efforts to youth programmes centred on language and creative skills to foster educational reform within Palestine. She also fulfils a part-time teaching position at the Islamic University of Gaza. Her academic interests span language pedagogy, teacher training, curriculum development, and assessment, with a focus on integrating arts-based methodologies into language instruction.

Aadel Essaadani holds a diploma in urban sociology from the University of Tours, France, with a specialisation in 'Spaces, societies, and cities in the Arab world'. He also has a master's degree in urban and country planning from the University of Perpignan, France. His doctoral research focused on studying behaviours and attitudes in the public space of Casablanca, as well as self-presentation and social interactions. He is a cultural policy consultant and technical scenographer, and has conducted various training and consulting initiatives for cultural projects and policies in France and Morocco. Currently, he serves as the Director at Racines Aisbl, an international non-profit organisation dedicated to integrating culture into human, social and economic development policies in Africa and the MENA region.

Rajaa Essaghyry is a cultural studies researcher who specialises in the aesthetics of emancipation in cinema, particularly during Morocco's 'Year of Lead'. She holds a diploma in cultural project management and currently works as a programme officer at Racines Aisbl. In this role, she has made significant contributions to the production of a series of short documentary films that address critical issues such as gender-based violence, migration and forced displacement, the Turkey–Syria earthquake and the challenges faced by the LGBTQIA+ community in Morocco.

Giovanna Fassetta is Senior Lecturer in Social Inclusion in the School of Education, University of Glasgow. Her research focuses on inclusion in education of children and young people from refugee backgrounds and on refugee education in general, particularly the role of languages and cultures in the process of integration. She has led several projects working with partners in the Gaza Strip and other low- and middle-income countries, including the Welcoming Languages projects. She teaches on several master's degree programmes with a focus on inclusion in relation to cultural and linguistic diversity, gender identity and sexuality, and socio-economic backgrounds. She currently co-convenes the Glasgow Refugee, Asylum and Migration Network (GRAMNet).

Carlos Eduardo Arias Galindo studied marine biology and has been working for more than seven years on the mediation of culture and children's and young people's literature, with a focus on their interactions with science. Currently, he is studying for a postgraduate degree in philosophy of science, specialising in science communication. His areas of interest include cognitive science, epistemology and social studies of science and technology.

Maria Veronica Ibarra Garcia is a professor at the Faculty of Philosophy and Letters at the National Autonomous University of Mexico (UNAM), School of Geography. She holds a doctorate in geography from UNAM and currently works as a professor in the SUAYED programme in geography in the Faculty of Philosophy and Literature. She is also a member of the National System of Researchers (SNI, Mexico). Her research focuses on feminist geography and political geography. She is the coordinator of three books: *Geografías Feministas de Diversas Latitudes* (2016), *Megaproyectos en Mexico una Mirada Critica* (2016) and *Mexico visto desde una Geografia Politica* (2020).

Sinéad Gormally is Professor of Community Development and Youth in the School of Education, University of Glasgow. She has worked in the UK and abroad with a range of communities and young people. Her research focuses on social justice and equality, analysing how youth and community practitioners can create positive social change. She also looks at the impact of violence and conflict on individuals and communities.

Maria Grazia Imperiale is a lecturer in adult education in the School of Education (University of Glasgow). Her research interests focus on language education for adult refugees and migrants, multilingualism and intercultural education. She has conducted research in several contexts, including Palestine, Lebanon, Ethiopia, Ghana, Italy and Scotland. She has also worked as a language teacher and a teacher trainer. She is a member of the Glasgow Refugee, Asylum and Migration Network (GRAMNet) and part of the Network's steering committee.

Mahmoud O. Jalambo is Assistant Professor of English Language at Dhofar University. He holds a bachelor's degree in TEFL, a bachelor's degree in English literature, a postgraduate diploma in professional translation, an MA in linguistics and English language studies and a PhD in curriculum and methodology. He is a certified trainer for IELTS and PCELT from World Learning/SIT. He has contributed to international projects with the University of Glasgow and the University of Birmingham. He has published several papers in international journals. His primary research interests include teaching and training, gender studies and conflict transformation, and disability studies.

Gareth David James is a research fellow in the Division of Urban Studies at the University of Glasgow. He holds a PhD in African studies from the University of Edinburgh and is primarily interested in rural and urban land reform, as well as the everyday lived experiences of rural and urban dwellers in Zimbabwe and Southern Africa more generally.

Eva Citlali Jiménez Rodríguez is a professor at the National Preparatory School (ENP) and the Faculty of Philosophy and Letters at the National Autonomous University of Mexico (UNAM), as well as the Modern American School. She is currently a candidate for a PhD in geography at UNAM. She also works as a consultant for pedagogical strategies in distance learning for high school students. She has contributed to the creation of study guides for admissions to the ENP and has been involved in several commissions aimed at updating the curriculum and programme of the ENP. At present, she is Professor of Geography at the ENP, teaching courses on economic geography, political geography and the geography of Mexico at middle school, high school and undergraduate levels.

Javiera Donoso Jiménez is an independent researcher and consultant in Mexico who has worked in universities and organisations on a range of projects on security, justice and children's rights, focusing on violence, sexual exploitation and, more recently, the search for disappeared persons.

Paola Cueto Jimenez is a professor at the National Preparatory School (ENP) and Faculty of Philosophy and Letters, National Autonomous University of Mexico (UNAM). She is a geographer and has completed master's studies in digital technologies for education. With 29 years of teaching experience, she is a professor in the National Preparatory School System (ENP). She has enhanced her education by participating in numerous courses, seminars, certificates and congresses that focus on new pedagogic strategies. Currently, she holds the position of chair of the geography programme at the Escuela Nacional Preparatoria (UNAM). During the 2015–2018 Curricular Modification Project in the ENP high school, she served as a coordinator for the revision and updates made to the geography curriculum. Additionally, she has coordinated various academic development activities for geography high school students from the ENP and has led two INFOCAB projects within the same institution.

Julie C. McAdam is Senior Lecturer in Language and Literacies at the University of Glasgow. She is the current president of the Scottish Education Research Association (SERA) and has worked on research projects funded by the Arts and Humanities Research Council (AHRC) which explore the role played by children's literature in supporting mediators working with children in precarity. See https://childslitspaces.com.

Sergio Hernández Mendoza has worked as a policy adviser and research assistant, specialising in planning, monitoring and evaluation of public policies for social development with international organisations and the public sector in Mexico. He recently worked with the UNESCO Institute for Lifelong Learning Glasgow City Council and is currently Education and Skills Policy Adviser for the Institution of Mechanical Engineers in the UK.

Abigail Opoku Mensah holds a PhD in industrial and organisational psychology. She is an associate professor in the Department of Business Administration at the University of Professional Studies, Accra (UPSA). She is currently the Director of the Centre for International Education and Collaboration (UPSA). At the University, she serves on a number of boards and committees and actively participates in a number of external services within the University and beyond. Her research interests include workplace diversity and knowledge management, work–family conflict, employee work attitudes, employee efficiency and effectiveness, and social issues in management. She has published extensively in international peer-reviewed journals and as chapters in books and presented numerous academic papers at conferences, both locally and internationally. She is an alumna of the DAAD/DIES training course on 'Management of Internationalisation' (Germany) and is a Work Family Researchers Network–USA Early Career Fellow.

Simbarashe Mudhokwani is an experienced researcher and monitoring and evaluation (M&E) specialist in the culture and creative industries in Zimbabwe. He has over 13 years of experience in data collection, tool development, qualitative and quantitative analysis, and report writing. He holds a bachelor of arts honours degree in African languages and culture from Midlands State University and a postgraduate diploma in development studies from the National University of Science and Technology (NUST). He has received specialised training in social accountability monitoring and research ethics. He has managed projects funded by the European Union, securing grants totalling €3 million to support the creative sectors in Zimbabwe and the SADC region. He has collaborated with development financiers such as Sida, EU, Hivos, UNDP and DANIDA, managing budgets exceeding US$1 million annually. His interactions with stakeholders, including individual artists, arts education institutions and national arts councils, have allowed him to contribute to initiatives like the Sound Connects Fund for SADC countries and the Arterial Network–Zimbabwe mapping exercise. As a consultant, he has supported research studies for organisations like the Zimbabwe Applied Arts and Crafts Association and has made contributions to UN frameworks for the creative sector.

Jerónimo Castillo Muñoz is Area Director at the Fundación Ideas para la Paz in Colombia. His work focuses on citizen security and the relationship between the private sector and the criminal justice system, working as a researcher and director of government entities, cooperation agencies and private enterprises.

Rocío Elizabeth Muñoz Santamaría has a professional background that spans public policy, research and social programme design. She is particularly committed to issues of inequality, justice, anti-punitivism and human rights. Her work covers a wide range of topics, including gender violence, education, children, migration, refugees, intersectionality and restorative justice. Through various roles in education, consultancy and project coordination, she has actively contributed to initiatives aimed at promoting community networks and fostering peacebuilding efforts.

Alison Phipps is the UNESCO Chair in Refugee Integration through Languages and the Arts at the University of Glasgow and Professor of Languages and Intercultural Studies. She is Co-Convener of Glasgow Refugee, Asylum and Migration Network (GRAMNet). She was Distinguished Visiting Professor at the Waikato University, Aotearoa New Zealand, 2013–2016, Thinker in Residence at the EU Hawke Centre, University of South Australia in 2016, Visiting Professor at Auckland University of Technology, Visiting Professor at Otago University, New Zealand and Principal Investigator for the Arts and Humanities Research Council Large Grant 'Researching Multilingually at the Borders of Language, the Body, Law and the State' and now a co-director of the Global Challenge Research Fund South–South Migration Hub. She is an academic, activist and published poet.

Manuela Suárez Rueda worked as a researcher at the Fundación Ideas para la Paz in Colombia. She now works in sustainable agriculture and farming.

Somaya M. Sayma is a scholar with a PhD in educational administration. She currently teaches at the Education Faculty of the Islamic University of Gaza (IUG). She leads the Women's Studies Center at IUG and plays a vital role in developing an early childhood education programme as part of a Norwegian project team. Additionally, she serves as an advisory member in the 'Culture for a Sustainable and Comprehensive Social Peace' project. She has published numerous papers and actively participates in conferences and workshops focusing on gender equality and early-childhood education.

Tawona Sitholé, better known as Ganyamatope Dzapasi, is inspired by his ancestral family name to connect with other people through creativity and the anticipation to learn. He is a poet, Mbira player, storyteller and playwright. He is a co-founder of Seeds of Thought, a non-profit arts group; a research associate for MIDEQ Global Migration Hub; and a UNESCO artist in residence at the University of Glasgow. As he continues to write, teach and perform, he most appreciates his work for the opportunity it provides to meet many inspiring people.

Nohora Niño Vega is a National Council for Science and Technology (CONACYT) researcher at the Children's Research Observatory (ODIN), El Colegio de Sonora, Mexico. Her areas of research include children and youth in armed violence contexts, forced displacement, human security, gender and peacebuilding processes in Colombia and Mexico.

Hyab Teklehaimanot Yohannes is a researcher with the UNESCO Chair in Refugee Integration through Languages and the Arts at the University of Glasgow. His work involves conducting research and synthesising findings to provide insights into theoretical, methodological and policy-related questions. Recently, he co-edited a special issue on 'Intercultural Knowledge Production' for the *Journal of Language and Intercultural Communication*. Additionally, he has signed a contract with Routledge for his upcoming book entitled *The Refugee Abyss*. His research interests include decoloniality, cultures of peace, political theories and (b)ordering (physical, onto-epistemic, spatio-temporal, juridico-political, etc.).

Acknowledgements

Acknowledgements are a place for expressing gratitude. Gratitude is vital in the work of peacebuilding and conflict transformation. It helps us move forward from stuckness or hollowness or anger or blame into a place of hope. Our gratitude as editors must go first to the lands in which our work took place and must go foremost to each contributor to this book. We are grateful to all who participated in the research and the cultural work as well as attending and supporting the art which grew from the collective endeavour. We acknowledge that this is a collective, human ecological work, woven of water, and masks, and virus, and violence overcome. We acknowledge this work is one of *sumud*, tenacity, resilience and sharp intellect. We acknowledge the critics and detractors, and we acknowledge the many strong disciplines and fields and writings with which we contend, especially in the field of security studies and international relations, where our work parts company. We know we need rigorous academic freedom to sustain visions which will enhance us all.

We must acknowledge our funders. It is a condition of our work. We do so knowing that the civil servants who devised the scheme worked diligently to do so and had a strong vision, a good one, despite all the neoliberal difficulties of funding in Global North contexts and in higher education and in the arts and humanities. We struggled to have the cuts restored that were made to our project by the UK government, through UK Research and Innovation (UKRI), and became locked in a bitter and public argument; dialogue and trust were eroded. We acknowledge that this brought personal sadness to professional relationships. We are grateful for the quiet, personally professional meetings after the fact, where acknowledgements could be made, bread broken together again, and we could find a peace after so much anguish and suffering. We celebrate our success in surviving the cuts, the COVID-19 pandemic and the plausible genocide against the Palestinian people living in Gaza.

We acknowledge that this work was funded by the UK Arts and Humanities Research Council under the Culture for Inclusive and Sustainable Peace (CUSP N+) Grant Scheme (AH/T007931/1).

Importantly, we acknowledge the Principal of the University of Glasgow, Professor Sir Anton Muscatelli, whose response, an outlier in the sector, when the cuts to our project were announced, was to find ways of enabling payments to continue and the work to be restored, and some trust to be repaired. This was at no small cost to the institution and has enduring ramifications.

Finally, our thanks to Anna Roddick at Multilingual Matters for her faith in this project and care in its development.

I Am You

Two steps: one, two.
Look in the mirror:
The horror, the horror!
The butt of your M-16 on my cheekbone
The yellow patch it left
The bullet-shaped scar expanding
Like a swastika,
Snaking across my face,
The heartache flowing
Out of my eyes dripping
Out of my nostrils piercing
My ears flooding
The place.
Like it did to you
70 years ago
Or so.

***

I am just you.
I am your past haunting
Your present and your future.
I strive like you did.
I fight like you did.
I resist like you resisted
And for a moment,
I'd take your tenacity
As a model,
Were you not holding
The barrel of the gun
Between my bleeding
Eyes.

***

One. Two.
The very same gun
The very same bullet
That had killed your Mom
And killed your Dad
Is being used,
Against me,
By you.

***

Mark this bullet and mark in your gun.
If you sniff it, it has your and my blood.
It has my present and your past.
It has my present.
It has your future.
That's why we are twins,
Same life track
Same weapon
Same suffering
Same facial expressions drawn
On the face of the killer,
Same everything
Except that in your case
The victim has evolved, backward,
Into a victimizer.
I tell you.
I am you.
Except that I am not the you of now.

***

I do not hate you.
I want to help you stop hating
And killing me.
I tell you:
The noise of your machine gun
Renders you deaf
The smell of the powder
Beats that of my blood.
The sparks disfigure
My facial expressions.
Would you stop shooting?
For a moment?
Would you?

***

All you have to do
Is close your eyes
(Seeing these days
Blinds our hearts.)
Close your eyes, tightly
So that you can see
In your mind's eye.
Then look into the mirror.
One. Two.
I am you.
I am your past.
And killing me,
You kill you.

Refaat Alareer

https://thisisgaza.wordpress.com/2012/11/01/i-am-you

Un-Foreword

Refaat was the lead investigator on one of our small grant awards from our Culture for Inclusive and Sustainable Peace project, as an English literature scholar and brilliant decolonial thinker in the context of Palestine, especially with regard to the violent effects of all settler colonialism, not least that stemming from the Balfour Declaration.

He was beloved by his students, whom he taught to become writers, poets, story-writers and journalists. He was passionate about poetry and folktales and ensuring the survival of the intangible cultural heritage of Palestine.

I addressed his students via remote links on a number of occasions through the course of our collaborations and after one such address he wrote me the email below.

> Dear Alison,
>
> It was really heart warming and soothing to listen to you talk about story-telling and stories for children. I loved your experiences and loved the connections you made with our situation and how stories can help us connect and heal and grow. It was very moving.
>
> I particularly loved your stories about your Mom, daughter, and granddaughters. The similarities with the Palestinian situation is uncanny.
>
> I'd love to share this poem of mine that I wrote a few years ago. I hope you love it.
>
> I have written just a few minutes, but in my university classes I always urge and coach students to write poems. I have collected hundreds, and I already started short listing the best of them hoping to publish a volume of poetry asap. Maybe when that materialises we could ask you to write us a blurb or a foreword.
>
> Looking forward to hearing from you!
>
> Best regards
>
> Refaat

I never got to write that foreword but hope that these words here, in a different foreword, dedicated to our colleague, can do a little justice to

Refaat's request, before the utter darkness of the plausible risk of genocide engulfed so many of our colleagues. Refaat saw intently the structures and cycles of violence. That we are one. That in 'killing me, you kill you'.

We dedicate this volume, a work resulting from the project he was an integral part of, to Refaat, and we offer his words, in the poem mentioned in the email ('I Am You'), as a guide to futures of sustainable and inclusive peace.

Alison Phipps

Introduction

Hyab Teklehaimanot Yohannes, Alison Phipps and Tawona Sitholé

Peacemaking is ordinary work, for ordinary people, in ordinary ways and through ordinary yet enduring institutions, when it is sustainable. This is the story that the chapters in this volume set out to describe and analyse in a range of different contexts. It does so through a focus on research and practice-led peacebuilding activities which have focused on women and on the role of culture and the arts, in ordinary communities visited by multiple forms of violence. As such, it focuses on cultural rights alongside the right to gender equality as key constituents in the work for sustainable peace in communities. Thus, cultural rights and intercultural and inter-epistemic work are critical but receive very little support to connect to sustainable and regenerative peacebuilding work. Achieving sustainable, regenerative and restorative infrastructure of peace requires what Lederach (2012: 13) calls 'crucial characteristics and commitments': (a) 'an infrastructure must have a long-term vision and assured support that invests in resources emergent in, close to and responsive to local contexts'; (b) 'an infrastructure approach must commit to continuous learning that tests both practice and theory in order to innovate and adapt'; and (c) 'an infrastructure must have a vision and commitment to systemic change that requires cooperative and engaged relationships beyond their immediate offices, projects or mandates'.

However, aside from the work of Lederach on peacebuilding, practical, large-scale research led by intercultural practice, with exegetical criticism and a coherent series of examples, is yet to be undertaken. While arts are present in the literatures on peacebuilding, cultural work is muted and either assumed or barely articulated. Most of the research on international relations concerns itself with what might be termed 'liberal peacebuilding' (Berg, 2020), where economic development is the core aim, not the social and cultural work of ensuring intercultural relations. In particular, the intersectionality of gender has not been foregrounded in scholarship either intercultural or with regard to peacebuilding and conflict transformation. The recent publication by Holmes and Corbett (2022), *Critical Intercultural Pedagogy for Difficult Times: Conflict, Crisis, and Creativity*, offers a useful basis for widening the field of intercultural communication into questions of practice, cultural work and sustainable peace. That book is distinctive in that it also works primarily with examples from the Global South and with decolonising and restorative paradigms to create sustainable cultures of peace using arts. It does so in order to demonstrate the ways the instituting of the cultural practices of everyday life (Certeau, 2013) through the work of women and full participation of women can be enabled through cultural work and the arts, though this is also prevented by hardened institutional structures.

Drawing together expertise from a range of disciplines (i.e. theatre studies; art practice; languages, literature and cultural studies; gender studies; anthropology; sociology; geography; postcolonial studies), this book builds on and expands established academic and non-academic collaborations with a range of partners based in fragile contexts and contexts of conflict and protracted crisis. The book distils the work carried out by the Culture for Inclusive and Sustainable Peace Network Plus (CUSP N+). Supported by the UK Arts and Humanities Research Council, CUSP N+ collaborated with arts and cultural institutions in low- and middle-income countries (LMICs) using a conflict transformation approach, with a specific focus on ensuring the full and equitable participation of women and girls. The project aimed to strengthen LMIC arts and cultural institutions so that they could identify and address social conflicts, including gender-based violence, coercion and injustice. The project consisted of three interconnected strands: (a) original research conducted with core partners; (b) commissioning research from new partners; and (c) synthesis of insights and knowledge exchange. The project was led in context, not remotely, trusting those present in and familiar with the nuances, cultures, communicative challenges and needs of those fragile contexts, who knew how to devise and develop their cultural work for peace.

The first strand involved conducting research to achieve the project objectives, focusing on integrating conflict transformation strategies into artistic and cultural practices, utilising decolonial praxes for collaborative work, and exploring how artistic and cultural organisations in LMICs can become influential. The second strand built upon the insights from the original research. It involved collaboration in creating and sharing funding calls, as well as assessing applications with external reviewers. This strand resulted in over a dozen small grant projects, with a focus on developing locally grounded practices for sustainable peace at a micro level. In the third strand, all CUSP N+ partners synthesised outputs based on the main themes that emerged from the first two strands. The aim of these outputs was to inform policy and practice in the field of conflict transformation through arts and cultural work. This book is just one of the various outputs from the project. Those outputs also include a special issue of the journal *Language and Intercultural Communication*, titled *Intercultural Knowledge Production: Against Gender-Based Violence and Towards Epistemic Justice* (Yohannes et al., 2023), as well as other publications by individual researchers and project reports.

Geographically, the book covers research and decolonial praxes that have emerged from various contexts, namely Ghana, Gaza, Zimbabwe, Mexico, Morocco and interdisciplinary work in Scotland. In relation to Ghana, the book draws on work with young performers and researchers who use dance as a means to overcome disadvantaged backgrounds, deprivation, marginalisation and, in some cases, domestic violence. In the Gaza Strip, we collaborated with educators and artists, who responded creatively to the lack of employment opportunities in a collapsing economy and the constant threat of military violence. Unfortunately, as we finalise this book, there is an ongoing Israeli war on Gaza, with the International Court of Justice warning against the risk of genocide. In fact, the Special Rapporteur on the situation of human rights in the Palestinian territory, Francesca Albanese, presents credible evidence of genocide in her report *Anatomy of Genocide* (Albanese, 2024). It deeply saddens us to write here that some of our partners were killed in the war, and many have lost multiple members of their extended family. In particular, we honour the work with CUSP N+ of Professor Refaat Alareer. In Zimbabwe, we worked with artists and writers who find strength in theatre and literature despite the extremely fragile and volatile political, economic and material environment. In Mexico, we supported mediators and other professionals who use books and the arts to assist children and young people displaced by poverty and violence. These partners worked in collaboration with grassroots collectives, whose work informed this book through decolonial praxes. In Morocco, we collaborated with cultural actors to revitalise civic values and promote democratic engagement through the production, dissemination and consumption of arts for all. In the UK, we worked with early to mid-career researchers who specialise in safeguarding and conducting research in contexts of conflict, and young people who work in theatre and with people seeking asylum.

Drawing from intercultural and interdisciplinary work, the book offers original conceptualisations and theorisation of the methods used to sustain cultures of peace across these different contexts, using arts and advocacy to destitute violence. Our starting point is the insight that 'fighting violence' or 'smashing gender-based violence', as the policy discourse suggests, is to fail to care for words and to enable a conceptualisation that aims at peacebuilding in its formulations. Instead, by destituting violence, the examples and case studies in the book seek to remove the power to produce violence by using approaches which are restorative, and even beautiful in their formulations and forms.

It provides examples and exemplars of how this is undertaken in contexts of extreme violence and precarity in the Global South, where the Global South is not a geographical vector but a metaphor for the cultural work for building sustainable peace (Imperiale & Phipps, 2022). The book offers an intercultural and inter-epistemic framework for theorising peace work outside the framework of international relations, and on the home territory and in the vernaculars of those working to produce cultural work sustainably themselves (e.g. in the language of Joy and *Sumud* in the context of occupied Palestine). In fact, each community and context has produced its own reflexive praxis in which peace is understood as neither the reduction nor the management of conflict but as a restorative and regenerative praxis of destitution of violence and conflict. This book distils the intersubjective, intercultural, inter-epistemic, and multilingual relationships and partnerships between communities across borders, genders and cultures. Its purpose is to initiate peacebuilding and healing through knowledge-sharing and the arts, when approached critically and with acute awareness of the nuanced and contextualised use of cultural data and artistic practices within the field of arts.

Theoretically, the book utilises an approach that recognises the complex and dynamic nature of conflict, its potential as a catalyst for change, and the iterative nature of peacebuilding processes through cultural institutions and community work.

Critically, the ways in which the dominant frameworks of conflict transformation and peacebuilding have been located within Global North notions of liberal peacebuilding are questioned and alternatives are derived from the contextualised contributions. The findings demonstrate the importance of meso-level thinking; of the multiplication of 'edges' from which to engage in reciprocal, agentic, intercultural dialogue, and the critical role the arts play within this work. This book offers a range of examples of work with meso-level institutions engaging in forms of cultural work and in such a way as to build on the insights that women and girls are key bearers of the work for peace. It draws together the ways in which those in the Global South understand conflict and are able to pursue peace through conflict transformation and destitution of violence.

Methodologically, it is tailored to the theory and emergent practice in conflict transformation and works with gender/feminist and decolonial methodologies. It uses practice-led artistic methods, participatory methods and methods that have proven to be productive in gender-based research, as approaches to conflict transformation. Importantly, these methods are not deconstructive to the point of oblivion, and not critical to the point of abyss, but instead work to devise new approaches within the abyss of violence and fragility, knowing that there are no perfect routes into or out of fugitive spaces. It is also strategic in highlighting the structural conflicts experienced by women and girls, identifying wider tensions within cultural institutions and their importance for ensuring sustainable peace. It builds its knowledge through case studies that draw on local cultural policies and procedures. Thus, the book offers innovative insights into the decolonising potential of adopting conflict destitution strategies in participatory partnership working.

Structurally, the chapters in the book span borders, genders and cultures through an interdisciplinary and intercultural approach. The book is organised into 13 chapters, which are further organised into three parts, as follows.

Part 1: Towards Cultures of Conflict Transformation

The first part of the book focuses on the use of arts and artistic methods for conflict transformation. The stories shared highlight the experiences and insights of women and girls in Morocco, Palestine, Zimbabwe and Mexico. By drawing from these lived experiences and their narratives of change, Part 1 offers a conceptualisation of spatiotemporal spaces that are crucial not only for understanding gendered conflicts within sociocultural contexts but also for transforming them to ensure social justice and challenge patriarchal traditions. It also examines the high levels of crime and drug-related urban violence in Medellín and Acapulco, exploring the struggles of communities in these cities to recover and maintain peaceful spaces that contribute to social transformation. Additionally, Part 1 examines the realities faced by persons with disabilities in Zimbabwe and their contributions to inclusive cultures of peace. In the face of systemic, exclusionary and gender-based violence, the scholarship presented emphasises the importance of creating spaces for prevention, sisterhood and sustainable cultures of peace through arts-based decolonial approaches.

Part 2: Popular Arts and Everyday Culture Meet Gender-Based Violence

Part 2 explores the intersection of popular culture, the arts and stories in understanding, raising awareness of and transforming violence against women, particularly gender-based violence, in the Gaza Strip in Palestine, Zimbabwe and Morocco. Palestinian women, especially those living in the Gaza Strip, face constant Israeli bombardment, and those living in the West Bank face displacement by settlers, which poses ongoing challenges to their lives and dignity. Their pursuit of self-determination is continuously hindered by the actions of Israel as the occupying power. The stories of resilience they share offer unique observations, insights and strategies in the fight against toxic masculinity and gender-based violence within the context of perpetual conflict. In the case of Ghana and Zimbabwe, Part 2 critically examines the role of popular culture and the arts both in perpetuating violence against women, including child marriages, and in combating and transforming such violence through intercultural, arts-based approaches.

Part 3: Reflexivity, Dilemmas and Safeguarding with Grassroots Organisations

This part begins by exploring decolonial praxes for fostering shared experiences, transformative dialogues and the development of a society that thrives on interculturality and informed understanding. It then addresses the challenges and requirements for safeguarding, as well as the successes and failures of conducting research with grassroots organisations across borders, genders and cultures. Finally, this part and the book conclude by reflecting on the 'Many Twists and Turns in the Pathways to Peace'. The last chapter emphasises the importance of restorative thinking, the creation of multiple edges for engaging in reciprocal, proactive, intercultural dialogue and the critical role that the arts play in peacebuilding work.

References

Albanese, F. (2024) *Anatomy of a Genocide*. Report of the Special Rapporteur on the situation of human rights in the Palestinian territories occupied since 1967. United Nations Human Rights Council.

Berg, L.-A. (2020) Liberal peacebuilding: Bringing domestic politics back. In H.F. Carey (ed.) *Peacebuilding Paradigms* (pp. 77–93). Cambridge University Press.

Certeau, M. de (2013) *The Practice of Everyday Life*. University of California Press.

Holmes, P. and Corbett, J. (2022) *Critical Intercultural Pedagogy for Difficult Times: Conflict, Crisis, and Creativity*. Routledge.

Imperiale, M.G. and Phipps, A. (2022) Cuts destroy, hurt, kill: A critical metaphor analysis of the response of UK academics to the UK overseas aid budget funding cuts. *Journal of Multicultural Discourses* 17 (1), 61–77.

Lederach, J.P. (2012) The origins and evolution of infrastructures for peace: A personal reflection. *Journal of Peacebuilding and Development* 7 (3), 8–13.

Yohannes, H.T., Phipps, A., Fernandes, F. and Silva, J. (eds) (2023) Intercultural knowledge production: Against gender-based violence and towards epistemic justice. Special issue of *Language and Intercultural Communication* 23 (6).

Part 1

Towards Cultures of Conflict Transformation

1 Three Moroccan Women's Liberation Journeys

Rajaa Essaghyry and Aadel Essaadani

Context

In 2019, the Moroccan government's High Commission for Planning (HCP) reported that 8 out of 10 women in Morocco have been subjected to at least one act of violence in their lives. It also noted that 'the marital setting remains the living space most severely afflicted with violence', with a prevalence rate of 46.1%, which means that 5.3 million women in Morocco are victims of psychological, economic or sexual violence (Haut Commissariat au Plan, 2019). According to the same source, 13% of women are assaulted in public spaces, representing 1.7 million women – 16% in urban areas and 7% in rural areas. Violence is most prevalent among women between the ages of 15 and 24 (22%), unmarried women (27%), women with a high level of education (23%) and employed women (23%), and violence against women within public spaces covers sexual harassment (49%), psychological violence (32%) and physical violence (19%).

Official communications present Morocco as one of the few countries in the Middle East and North Africa (MENA) region to have undertaken significant measures to counter violence against women and redress gender inequalities. This was prompted to some extent by pressure exerted since the 1980s by women's rights movements, which have mobilised to promote gender equality and the elimination of all forms of gender-based violence. Actions (studies, campaigns, protests, etc.) have resulted in legislative reforms and heightened public debate on violence against women (VAW) within Morocco. A first step was achieved in 2004, with the amendment of the Moudawana, or 'Family Code' (Morocco Code Pénal, 2004), which for many years had been widely deemed as discriminatory against women.[1]

After his accession to the throne in 1999, the King of Morocco was determined to promote the idea of a modern and progressive kingdom in which women are fully emancipated and have full rights as citizens:

'the reform of the Moudawana appears to be the beginning of a legal and social revolution consecrating the equality between men and women and improving women's rights within the family structure' (Murgue, 2011: 15). The Moudawana reform enabled, among other things, the raising of the minimum age for marriage, and the amendment of divorce procedures, children's custody arrangements and conditions for polygamy. However, non-governmental organisations (NGOs) working for women's rights considered these reforms to be ineffective and merely theoretical. Sadiqi (2008: 336) declares that even if this reform 'strengthens the position of women in the private and the public sphere, the issues of implementation of the law and religion still remain'. Clearly, she claims, 'the impact of patriarchy, tradition, illiteracy and ignorance' continues to hinder women from reporting crimes and claiming their rights. This is especially relevant given that there are still several uncertainties and gaps in the legal framework that keep many women marginalised.

Over the years, a series of reforms and measures to advance women's rights have been adopted. The 2011 constitutional reform, triggered by the Arab Spring uprising, devotes significant attention to gender equality and women's rights at large. The reform stands out for its incorporation of the term 'woman' as an entirely independent category on a number of occasions as well as the term 'citizen' (in its female form in French and Arabic), previously unused in prior texts, which brought the constitution up to universal terminological gender standards, which is itself a major step forward (Sabbar, 2014). The 2011 constitution's preamble states that 'The Kingdom of Morocco is committed to banning and combating all discrimination against anyone on the grounds of sex, colour, creed, culture, social or regional origin, language, disability or any other personal circumstance whatsoever' and the constitution itself features a fuller articulation of the concept of gender equality than was present in the 1996 constitution.[2] Article 19 asserts that:

> The man and the woman enjoy, in equality, the rights and freedoms of civil, political, economic, social, cultural and environmental character, enounced in this Title and in the other provisions of the Constitution, as well as in the international conventions and pacts duly ratified by Morocco and this, with respect for the provisions of the Constitution, of the pillars [*constantes* in French] of the Kingdom and of its laws. The State works for the effective implementation of parity between men and women. An Authority for parity and the struggle against all forms of discrimination is created, to this effect.

Some other examples illustrate similar commitments and efforts undertaken by the Moroccan parliament, including labour code reforms prohibiting gender-based wage discrimination (2003), changes to the Citizenship Code allowing Moroccan women married to foreigners the right to transmit their citizenship to their children (2007) and the adoption of law no. 11-15, reorganising the High Authority for Audiovisual Communication (HACA) to combat – among other things – all forms of discrimination and stereotyped images that undermine the dignity of women (2016).

Furthermore, 2018 was another significant year, as the government passed law no. 103-13, which criminalised VAW, describing it as 'any material or moral act or abstention based on discrimination on the grounds of sex resulting in physical, psychological, sexual or economic harm to the woman'. Women's rights groups regard this law as 'a modest step forward [...] which does not comply with international norms' (Assouli, 2018)[3] in the sense that it does not recognise marital rape as a crime and contains considerable vagueness regarding the measures to be undertaken for victims of domestic violence. According to Kasraoui (2020), international human rights lawyer Stephanie Willman Bordat states that law no. 103-13 is 'vaguely formulated and does not set up any concrete measures for protecting women subjected to violence'.

With regard to its international commitments, Morocco has, since its independence in 1956, ratified and adhered to several international human rights instruments, including the International Covenant on Economic, Social and Cultural Rights (ICESCR) in 1979, the International Covenant on Civil and Political Rights (ICCPR) in 1979, the Convention on the Elimination of All Forms of Discrimination against Women (CEDAW) in 1993, the Beijing Platform for Action (BPfA) in 1995, with its 12 axes, the Millennium Development Goals (MDGs) and the Sustainable Development Goals (SDGs). It should be noted that on 8 April 2011, Morocco withdrew its reservations to the CEDAW concerning article 9 (transmission of nationality to children) and article 16 (equality in marriage and divorce).[4]

The general approach adopted by successive Moroccan governments has been to assimilate international law, particularly in the field of human rights, with colonialism, and in its reservations against international conventions the Moroccan government contests the universality of human rights, seeing them more as a matter of Western hegemony (Glacier, 2015). Yet, civil society organisations involved in women's rights continue to criticise enacted laws as being insufficient, since they contain numerous ambiguities and are open to arbitrary interpretations by judges, who do not always find in favour of women.

There are other criticisms regarding the gaps in communication and in women's knowledge about the provisions of laws, as many women are unaware of their rights and therefore unable to claim them. Civil servants themselves are not often properly trained on new legislation nor on the appropriate procedures to be adopted when dealing with a woman subjected to violence. The reforms, described as promising and progressive in the literature, also appear to be limited in scope given that the dominant laws regarding the Civil Code (marriage, inheritance, divorce, etc.) in Morocco are largely Sharia-based.[5] Civil society organisations argue that these efforts remain a work in progress, full of good intentions. More steps are needed to ensure greater efficiency (e.g. trained staff, clearer texts, a detachment from religion, a considerable awareness-raising operation and, above all, genuine application of the laws). Gagliardi (2018) considers that reforms initiated over the past 20 years by the Moroccan government have not substantially addressed structural inequalities for women (see also Assouli, 2018).

As for civil society and its role within these reforms, the early feminist movements came primarily from the political left and were organised in the 1980s (Alami M'Chichi Houria, in Naciri, 2014). Drawing largely on CEDAW's provisions, the movements raised awareness among decision-makers and the general public of the injustices and violence suffered by women, and advocated for gender equality. The first feminist association to be founded was the Association Démocratique des Femmes du Maroc (ADFM, 1985), followed by the Union de l'Action Féminine (UAF, 1987), the Association Marocaine des Droits des Femmes (AMDF, 1992), the Ligue Démocratique des Droits des Femmes (LDDF, 1993) and Joussour-Forum des Femmes Marocaines (1995) (Naciri, 2014).

Gradually, there has been a shift in the approach of feminist organisations, moving from indignation towards a more sustainable and effective approach through strong advocacy (Naciri, 2014). As a result, new forms of mobilisation have been introduced (Naciri, 2014), such as drafting parallel reports alongside the government reports on the implementation of the CEDAW in 1997 and 2003. These alternative reports brought together a number of feminist and human rights organisations to elaborate a common analysis and suggest recommendations, re-appropriating public space by organising demonstrations (Garçon, 2000) and organising large-scale communication campaigns, in particular the 'Printemps de l'égalité' ('Springtime for Equality').[6] They do so through media involvement and by handing out documentation and flyers at railway stations, the exits of government offices and schools, and setting up and expanding listening, information, and legal assistance centres for women subjected to violence, and so on.

Nowadays, with the advent of social media, an entirely new generation of intersectional feminist activists has emerged. They are organising themselves and carrying out their advocacy campaigns mainly, and sometimes exclusively, through social networks, thus engaging with a wider audience, to advocate for gender equality, to apply pressure for laws to be changed or enforced, or simply to act as a resonating box for stories and realities, thus shifting the prevailing dominant narratives.

Methodology

The following account stems from field work conducted by Racines (an international non-profit association working for the integration of culture in public policies for human, social and economic development) within the CUSP N+ (Culture for Sustainable and Inclusive Peace Network Plus), which involved engaging with three different groups of women in three different regions in Morocco in order to collect testimonies on VAW in the country.[7] The action was developed using an arts-based participatory project intended for gathering testimonies of women, triggering discussion on the issue of VAW and promoting a shift of perspectives and raising awareness of the issue in Morocco. Forum theatre was adopted as an arts-based methodology to collect data from women, and the initial questions raised concerned the way some Moroccan women perceive or experience violence and in various settings (both public and private), the way they express it and, most importantly, the means by which they deal with it.

On site, teams conducted three forum theatre workshops, each taking place in one of three Moroccan cities (Casablanca, in central Morocco; Tiznit, in the south; and Al Hoceima, in the north) – ensuring an equitable geographical balance between participants from urban and rural areas. Each workshop was conducted over three days and gathered around 20 women aged between 15 and 60. Participants were approached through Racines' existing network, with a view to establishing a climate of trust between potential participants and the workshop leader. Some of the participants were women from the arts and crafts sector who had previously been – either directly or indirectly – cooperating with Racines on different projects, while others were contacted directly by Racines' local partners, providing an outreach function and inviting women to attend the workshops. Criteria for selecting participants were designed to involve a diverse group of women, particularly in terms of age, social class, profession, level of education, ethnicity and urban/rural geographical location.

The choice of having only female participants was driven primarily by the observations arising from previous experiences, particularly ones involving mixed-gender participants. Usually, when women are in equal numbers with men in a gathering, they tend to restrain their answers while watching out for men's reactions, whereas in the case of women being a substantial majority, participants are more likely to forget about the male presence altogether and to respond without self-surveillance. For many women, this gives them a rare opportunity to express themselves openly and, more importantly, the women participants usually realise in these kinds of gatherings that they are not alone.

As a means to reach out to potential participants, teams drew up a call for participation to the workshop using a poster for each region, which was available in French and Arabic, and circulated it through Racines' networks, using WhatsApp groups to gather regional partners of civil society organisations, alongside newsletters, posts on social media and printed flyers delivered by post to Racines' partners across Morocco. Each workshop required over a week of recruitment, and the workshops were conducted between February and April 2021.

The workshops were led by Maha El Boukhari, a Moroccan actress well known in the country. The three workshops followed a common structure and approach. The first day consisted of ice-breaking sessions between the women and a brief forum theatre training session. On the second day, women were actively invited to speak about their own perceptions of VAW and share personal stories drawing from their experiences. On the last day, the facilitator called on the participants to perform short scenes/roles drawing from their testimonies and, during these scenes, the participants played their own role in life along with that of their oppressor, whether it was the father, the civil servant, the older brother, the mother-in-law, the husband, the employer and so on. Mitigation measures were taken to address potential situations that might cause participants to feel vulnerability, embarrassment or a violation of privacy. During the process of sharing personal stories on day 2, the team asked the men who were present at the workshop to leave the venue altogether, to provide a safe space where women could express themselves freely. Moreover, throughout the workshop, participants were constantly reassured that the video-recording of the session could be stopped at any point if they were uncomfortable with it.

Following the workshops, 14 follow-up semi-structured interviews were conducted with participants, selected on the basis of their willingness and availability to engage more widely with the project. Interviews were conducted in person, all of them in Moroccan Darija – except one, which was held in Amazigh. Some were on site, while others took place at the women's workplaces or in their private homes.

Three Women. Three Tempers. Three Strategies.

Three women in three local variations of the same patriarchal context in three Moroccan regions (north, south and central) showed the same determination in a hostile environment, despite the initial shortcomings, with almost identical strategies of struggle and self-assertion: awareness, refusal to believe in the normality of patriarchal, male domination, desire for emancipation and, finally, strategies and actions for liberation.

Dikra from Al Hoceima (north), Souad from Casablanca (central) and Fatima from Anzi (south) were kind enough to describe their situations to us in more detail. These striking examples follow individually in order to show three variants of the struggle of Moroccan women who had decided to emancipate themselves from the patriarchal carcass. The aim was to pinpoint the triggers and determine each woman's strategy and the convergences between the three approaches. The three women did not speak spontaneously, out of modesty, fear or shyness. It took 'theatre of the oppressed' workshop sessions to get them to speak freely, one group per region. The participants were artists (theatre and visual arts) and craftswomen or workers in the fields of textiles, jewellery or cooking.

The 'theatre of the oppressed' workshops were moments during which the women played, in addition to their own roles, the roles of those who oppressed them: father, brother, boss, colleague and so on. The playful aspect of the theatre workshops acted as a disinhibitor and a space for confession and psychological release, with some workshops ending in tears, while drawing sessions and interviews with some of the participants helped to verify information and clarify details.

Dikra was born in a village a few kilometres from Al Hoceima. As a young girl, she helped her father, a shepherd, to look after the livestock, and she helped her mother with the household chores. From an early age, she was responsible both for the herd and for her younger brothers and sisters when at home. Dikra, while continuing to talk about the moments of freedom she had had during her adolescence, pointed to the Spanish islet less than two kilometres from the headquarters of the association at which she was currently employed. She told us that when she was young, she used to swim to the island, but she quickly came back to reality, remembering that this period was, unfortunately, too short for her. Dikra comes from a Rifian society with quasi-insular characteristics, and the regular repression of its inhabitants and the long banishment by King Hassan II have kept the region on the social and economic margins. Its confinement has accentuated the reputation of its inhabitants as tough and stubborn people.

This form of marginality is based on a past of which the Rifians are very proud, and the Rif war in particular, together with Abdelkrim Khattabi's short-lived Republic of the Rif (1921–1927). It is also a very conservative region, with its diaspora in the Netherlands and Belgium influenced by rigorous and even Salafist Islam. The Rif is a region where women have long been marginalised and discriminated against, particularly in rural areas. Today, a large number of community organisations focus on the issues of girls' access to education and of underage marriage and on running advocacy campaigns and making their voice heard through public and digital spaces.

Souad was born in Casablanca. She had a brilliant education up to the baccalaureate and spent two years at university. With a degree (bac+2) in economics in her pocket, she worked in an import/export company, then, after a period of unemployment, some friends suggested that she join a social economy association in a neighbourhood on the outskirts of Casablanca. At first glance, her fairly conventional life path showed no signs of patriarchy, domination or violence, but it was during the interviews and especially during the theatre workshops that additional life events full of violences surfaced: 'violences' in the plural, actual or insidious, in the family, at school, in society and in the workplace. Souad chose to work in the social and solidarity economy because, she said, it allowed her to rehabilitate the sense of solidarity that she felt society had lost. It was a way of campaigning for a better society. She lives in Casablanca, the economic capital and largest city in Morocco, and the birth of the modern city corresponds to the creation of its port in 1913. It is a cosmopolitan and progressive city and has been the cradle and scene of several political liberation movements. Women generally have more freedom and opportunities in Casablanca than elsewhere in the country.

Fatima was born in Anzi 35 years before the study and was married with two children. Her liberation started the day she decided to break free from the yoke of male exclusivity in the jewellery market, taking over the family business from her father and uncles, who made silver jewellery. She learnt the business with her father and began marketing her products with her neighbour, who later became her husband and was in the same field.

Fatima was born and lives in the southern region, where the Soussis (Amazigh people from the South of Morocco) have adopted orthodox Muslim beliefs and practices, which they have used to support a dedication to hard work, frugality and austerity. The largest Soussi villages are made up of separate hamlets that were originally small, autonomous political units.

In Morocco, some women are the lowest bargaining chip. From the moment they are born, they are insidiously indoctrinated into a process that prepares and perpetuates their domination, and throughout their lives these women internalise a series of norms. Resistance to the established order is severely punished and breaking conventions is heavily penalised within society.

Patriarchal systems deploy a variety of mechanisms, tactics and tools to hinder women's emancipation and keep them firmly in a submissive status. Dikra's, Fatima's and Souad's life stories are a close-up look at the way these insidious mechanisms are manifested in everyday life.

'It all started at school' - socialisation into heteronormative codes of masculinity

> A 'true woman' is a graveyard of desires, failed dreams and illusions.
>
> Les chimères collective

From an early age, young girls are socialised into heteronormative codes of masculinity that force them to internalise the idea that their rightful and most natural environment is the household, while the outside world belongs exclusively to men. Women seem to be destined to bear children, cook and take care of endless domestic chores, thus being deprived of opportunities for personal fulfilment, and they are also expected to obey orders and accept punishments without questioning them. An effective first patriarchal tool that sets the stage is to prevent some girls' access to education, pulling girls out of school as soon as possible or, 'better yet', never sending them to school in the first place. Dikra recounted:

> My father said that girls do not need to study. My older sister was top of her class. After her final year of secondary school, my father would not let her go to the high school in a neighbouring village, despite the insistence of the teacher who believed in my sister's potential.

In order to ensure the normalisation of this masculine structure, multiple official institutions present women with a set of emotional and religious predicaments as undeniable facts and truths. Despite these, the three women's stories attest that motherhood is the most honourable and highest form of labour, and that women guarantee the continuity of human existence. In the *Encyclopaedia of Women*, Doctor Monsarrat sarcastically states, as cited by Chollet (2018: 79), that educating girls:

> [...] must be done in the most altruistic sense. A woman's role in life is to give everything around her – comfort, joy, beauty – while keeping a smile on her face, without looking like a martyr, without bad temper, without apparent fatigue. It's an onerous task; our daughters need to be trained in this perpetual and happy renunciation. From the very first year, she must spontaneously know how to share her toys and sweets, and give what she has around her, especially what she values most.

Despite the progress observed by the Moroccan High Commission for Planning, girls' schooling remains a major challenge in Morocco. In rural areas, the challenge is aggravated by enrolment rates continuing to be very low. According to official statistics, 6 out of 10 girls living in rural areas do not receive any formal education (Chaker, 2021). It is worth pointing out that Morocco has undertaken many measures in this area, and access to schooling for all citizens without discrimination is underlined in article 31 of the constitution (Secrétariat Générale de Gouvernement, 2011). Similarly, the national education charter has always been considered a reference document for education system reform and was adopted by national consensus in 1999 with the objectives of combating gender disparities in basic education and encouraging girls' enrolment in schools in rural areas. However, the disparities between promises, stated intentions and lived realities continue to be glaringly apparent, and these disparities can be partly linked to the dominance of a patriarchal mentality, hierarchising individuals on the basis of their gender and seeking to limit women's functions to domestic, marital and motherly ones, while keeping them away from any activity that falls beyond the domestic arena. This was echoed by another participant in the workshops, Rachida:

> I grew up in an environment where women cannot express themselves, cannot choose, cannot have friends, cannot go to school and cannot dress the way they want. They also cannot go out and work. Everything is forbidden. The boys didn't go through the same thing at all. When I graduated from primary school, I had to move to a different school and neighbourhood, which meant I had to take a bus. That's when my father forced me to abandon school, telling me, 'In our family, girls don't take buses. It's either you learn *Harfa* ["a profession"] and work at home or forget about learning anything altogether'. I grew up in a very strict environment; I was not allowed to laugh or talk. And even when I got married, I did not know how to express myself or my feelings. It is not easy when you have never expressed yourself from an early age. It is only recently, when I joined the association, that I gradually started to speak up.

Similarly, Souad shed light on the fact that male domination starts with parental favouritism in raising boys:

> Girls are expected to do everything: to do well at school, to take care of household chores, not to have demands and certainly not to request anything, to dress appropriately, to be respectful and modest, not to go out.... As for the boy, even when he comes home at three in the morning, parents think that at least he did not spend the night out. When he is violent, they say he is just pissed off and that he will get over it.

She also explained that, in Morocco, women may benefit from their rights when they belong to upper social classes; however, most women of a lower social status are subjected to oppression and denied their rights.

Maryam related childhood memories which corroborate this gendered vision of patriarchy and which, in an insidious way, perpetuate the alienation of women and deprive them in the most ordinary matters:

> From childhood, everything is forbidden.... Unlike boys ... I experienced this differentiated treatment with my brother, because we weren't treated the same. I used to tell my family: the only reason you don't treat us the same is because I am a girl. I noticed over the years that even the most educated parents did not treat girls and boys the same.

Underage marriage and patriarchy

One of the most common forms of VAW, and the one that impacts teenage girls in Morocco, is underage marriage. From childhood, some young girls internalise the idea that they should fulfil their marital and maternal duties as soon as possible; they are taught that their body is not their property and that they should safeguard their virginity for the sake of their husband-to-be. Not surprisingly, many girls in this situation do not get to choose their partners; instead, their families do so.

Fatima testified:

> It happened in 1990. On a beautiful sunny winter morning. I was preparing my homework, peacefully, when my father told me that I will have to quit school to marry a man he met in the village's weekly market. The next day, we headed to the *Adoul* office in Inezgane (southern Morocco).[8] I had no choice but to accept this fate chosen by my father. The *Adoul* asked me if I consented to this marriage. I did not answer. Everyone was looking at me in the room. Basically I wanted to shout 'No – I don't want to get married; it's not my choice. I want to go to school. I'm only 14 years old!' But, I could not say it and I remained silent. This long moment of silence prompted my father to remind *Adoul* of the popular proverb 'Who does not say a word consents'. Within a month, I was told that I was going to get married; we signed the marriage certificate; we had the wedding celebration and I moved to another city with my husband. My brain was anaesthetised; I did not understand what was happening around me. Marriage was an unknown word for me. It was literally as if I was stepping into a void. I had a child the first year. My husband beat me up almost every day; I was not allowed to leave the house. My missions were household chores and raising my child. This situation lasted for years.

Underage marriages symbolise a girl's allegiance to her family, and particularly to her father. Prompted by economic circumstances, a married girl means having one less person to feed, although the reason is not always economic. Sometimes, it is a 'legitimate' handover of power; once the father no longer intends to control his daughters, but remains concerned about the family's honour, he passes on this authority to another man through the process of marriage. Zeina pointedly reflected on this point, stating:

> I was barely 16 at the time; I was a little bomb with uncontrollable curiosity. I couldn't imagine myself sitting at home all the time, and I was a little rebel, asking outrageous questions. I had a different mentality compared to those around me. I had the impression that I belonged somewhere else and wished I had been born in a European country. I could not see the difference between a boy and a girl. To me, both were the same and were supposed to be treated the same. My father, confronted with this situation, came up with a brilliant idea to get rid of me and my potential problems: withdraw me from school and force me to get married.

In Moroccan society, the belief that a pubescent girl is a woman and thus ready for marriage is as prevalent as ever, but this does not necessarily imply that she is physically and mentally capable of overcoming the repercussions of pregnancy. The World Health Organization (2011) states that the leading cause of death among women aged 15–19 is complications during pregnancy and delivery. Premature marriage deprives young girls of their adolescence, and consequently of an important phase in their personal and physical development. Added to this, forced sexual relations and premature motherhood have a considerable impact on girls, whether psychologically, economically or socially. The practice of underage marriage generally leads young girls to drop out of school, to devote themselves fully to their new role. As a result, early-married girls find themselves trapped within the marital prison, with no prior knowledge of motherhood, which adversely impacts children born within this type of marriage.

As for Moroccan law, there are several gaps and insufficiencies. While article 19 of the Family Code (Morocco: Penal Code, 2004) sets the age of majority at 18 – 'matrimonial majority is acquired, for boys and girls, at the age of eighteen' – article 20 of the same code authorises families to request a derogation at the age of 15 and, depending on the circumstances and motives for the union, judges may grant one. Civil society organisations claim that this derogation is being used by the courts on a massive scale. In 2020, over 13,000 derogations were issued, out of nearly 20,000 requests (*Le Monde* & AFP, 2022). Certain families, having seen their requests rejected by courts, circumvent the law simply by marrying off their minor daughters using the *Fatiha* (customary marriage),[9] a bypass that confronts judges with a *fait accompli*, forcing them, basically, to legally recognise customary marriages. In this specific case, it should be recalled that in 1993, Morocco ratified the International Convention on the Rights of the Child, adopted by the United Nations General Assembly on 20 June 1989, which sets the age limit for childhood at 18.

Several women internalise specific rules, many of which they consider to be normal. The various mechanisms of patriarchy – strongly rooted in Moroccan society and legitimised by religious and political structures – lead young girls to be convinced that their ultimate role is to be mothers, spouses and housewives, while women who seek a different path are labelled selfish, treacherous and 'sluts'.

Fatima's story resembles hundreds of life accounts from other Moroccan women. All these stories have the same pattern; in patriarchal societies, a woman is first her father's property, and then her husband's, or her brother's if she has one and is unmarried. Within families, a hierarchy is naturally established in that fathers retain decision-making authority, given that they wield economic power, although there are cases where daughters endure family oppression despite contributing considerably to the family's finances, if not assuming full financial responsibility. Clearly, girls' financial independence on its own is not sufficient to stand up against the status quo. Some girls and women prefer marriage, believing it to be an escape route from parental prison and an opportunity to obtain freedom, before they realise that this is merely a matter of shifting prison settings. As Dikra stated, 'Many girls have resigned themselves to their situation while waiting for a husband to rescue them'.

Women's domestication

> Within the family, men are the bourgeoisie while women are the proletariat.
>
> Friedrich Engels

The women's stories highlight a set of findings. A common denominator is how society is not fundamentally against women working, under the right conditions. The majority of women taking part in the workshops were craftswomen, making silver jewellery, sewing and cooking, for example. They had been introduced to the professions by their families, starting in childhood, and work often took place in the family home's workshop, generally situated in a basement, on a terrace or in separate areas of garden courtyards. The products created by women are sold to retailers and storekeepers, as women are never allowed into the markets.

Working constitutes a many-sided burden for women. They not only work hard in the shadows, but also receive no decent remuneration for their efforts. As Rachida testified:

> Even though we worked every day and all the time at the workshop, my father wouldn't pay us, claiming that the money went into the family savings and, if we ever needed something, he would buy it for us. Consequently, we have never actually received any money, although we wanted to be independent and purchase whatever we wanted. Meanwhile, my brothers, who worked with us, were always walking around with money. Our financial independence terrified my father.

Another major constraint raised by women was their difficulty in accessing markets and selling their products, as Mina indignantly recounted:

> Our village [Anzi] is very conservative and women are under constant surveillance. I have spent most of my life in the workshop, designing jewellery, in all kinds of styles, designs that people really liked. I wanted to be in direct contact with sellers, the people who purchase, and be able to talk about my pieces and the creation process and all the stories behind them. This wasn't an obvious thing to do; as soon as I raised this topic with my father and suggested going with him to the market, he always responded exactly the same way: 'Women of good families do not talk to men who are not relatives; they do not bargain on prices. The market is a man's domain. If you go there, you will bring dishonour upon the whole family.'

Fatima, a native of the same village, added more contextual details and, more importantly, her own thoughts on this difficulty, which she deemed unjustified and unfair:

> We have always worked with my sisters in the workshop at home, while my father and my brother were in charge of selling products in the market. The front door was our boundary. It was strictly forbidden to go to the market and talk to the owners of jewellery stores. If we did so, we would be banned from our family and the village for the rest of our lives. Our village is very conservative; for example, we cannot go to a public administration office on our own without a male relative, nor can we take public transport on our own. This means that going to a market – as a woman – and socialising with men is simply not possible, which I consider to be very unfair towards us.

According to women's accounts, those who do access markets and establish contacts with sellers experience yet another sort of difficulty: their credibility and know-how are questioned by sellers. Fatima commented:

> When I finally had access to the market, the sellers doubted that it was me who created the jewellery, using the pretext that it takes a huge physical effort to make them, and manipulating fire is very dangerous for women. They said: 'How do you expect me to believe you? Women are not capable of doing dangerous tasks like that!'

Mina echoed this, pointing out that it is because women are extremely rare in markets that sellers can afford to lower prices or refuse to buy from them. One seller told her:

> I have never bought from a woman; I do not believe you made this jewellery item. This market is a place where men buy and sell. Your prices are high. Why would I give so much money to a woman?

The villages are usually small and almost everyone knows each other. Sellers already have a pejorative attitude towards women who transgress family rules. Therefore, in markets, they either avoid buying from them out of fear of being considered accomplices in women's subversion or take advantage of the context to reduce prices while discrediting the women.

Souad raised another key point, that of housework, which she considered to be the most arduous part of a woman's life:

> Women work hard. First, they work in the sewing workshops or agricultural land, but once they return home, another heavy labour awaits them, that of the endless household chores, looking after the children and their every need. And for this work there is no remuneration. Imagine if a man hires a domestic maid, he will have to pay her a fortune, and when it is his wife, that's by default. If she dares to complain, she is immediately accused of being an unworthy wife and mother.... This is a task assigned to women simply because they are women.

It seems that household chores are not deemed worthy of compensation. Engels' statement in *The Origin of the Family, Private Property and the State* that 'Within the family, men are the bourgeoisie while women are the proletariat' (Engels, 1884: 39), reminds us that women, by doing housework, generate an added value which is not acknowledged by the dominant economic regime, and that assigning them to housework, with all its associated duties, only keeps them within class exploitation. Gisèle Halimi (1992: 166) argues that:

> The housework done by women at home, i.e. cooking, is considered the most alienating and degrading household chores, which cut women off from reality and shut them in, and are considered to have no exchange value. In order for this to continue, for women to continue to be what Engels calls 'the first servant' within the family, they have to be excluded from social production. This is what the family has been used for, and how it oppresses women. The man in the forum, the woman at home. By riveting her to alienating and unpaid tasks, we almost certainly ensure her complete dependence.

Souad's testimony supports this quote by referring to the potential logic behind the entire setup:

> I believe that by overwhelming women with work and responsibility, the idea is to prevent them from having their heads free to rethink the world and to minimise any attempts at subversion. You know, it happens in all social classes, even a woman who can afford to have household help, she simply assigns these tasks and acts as mediator, but ultimately she remains the primary person responsible *vis-à-vis* her husband, when it comes to cleaning the house, providing food, looking after the children….

This once again points to a mentality that seeks a single unified model, namely that of an obedient woman who never questions the status quo, works uncomplainingly and settles for a life made up of minimum needs and rights with no demands.

A significant part of patriarchy remains firmly established by law. It is still current, given that the reform of the Family Code (the Moudawana) continues to be a matter of debate. For instance, women are entitled to half a man's inheritance. Polygamy is still permitted by law, although recently the legislator brought the obligation of consent from the first wife into law.

Patriarchy is synonymous with violence; it runs against women's emancipation or their right to pursue an education when the decision is taken by the father or the husband. Besides its insidious nature, this violence is structural since it is still legally authorised.

Liberation Tactics – Echoes of Emancipation

> If not me, then who? If not now, then when?
> José Balmès

Insidious violence is deliberately kept out of sight. It places women in extremely vulnerable positions. The consequences of such violence may not always be obvious, nor is being a victim of it sufficient to grasp it. These forms of violence are deeply rooted within social structures. Each of the three women has chosen a different path to face the alienation and discrimination she experiences.

Dikra, who has always felt she was missing out on something, relates her problems, from the smallest to the biggest, directly to the fact that her father would not allow her to go to school. She realises that, if she solves this issue, her whole life will be much more fulfilling. After her teenage years, Dikra's life was full of resolutions. She assiduously attended literacy classes to learn to read, write and count. She realised that being illiterate reduced her participation in the world, because she did not understand what was around her. She gave examples as simple as reading traffic signs, the names of shops or writing the articles for the association she later set up: 'the day I learned to read and write, I felt like a different person'.

In the same quest for emancipation, Dikra obtained her driving licence. She needed independence, the freedom to move around. She set herself up as a caterer for events, companies, weddings and so on. She says she uses the cooking her mother taught her, not as a tool for her husband to enslave her but to turn into a profession. Her husband now helps her with the preparations and deliveries, and Dikra is now president of an association that runs cookery classes for young girls in her town.

Fatima, for a long time outraged by the restrictions on her access to the jewellery market, decided one day to penetrate it and confront all those male sellers, convinced she was doing the right thing: 'One day, I took my merchandise and went to the silver jewellery market in Tiznit. No one had ever seen me in the *souk* [market] or even in the corner shop.' She traces her liberation to the day she decided to break free from the yoke of male exclusivity in the jewellery market, and she expresses her emancipation in two words: *dert boom*. In Moroccan *Darija*, this literally means 'I exploded' and 'I hatched', in the figurative sense.

Maryam made an extremely sharp statement in saying that the war against patriarchy begins with a war against ourselves and by unlearning what we have absorbed over the years:

> My emancipation upset a lot of people, including my family. To name me, they say 'the slut who left her household'. At the beginning, it bothered me. Afterwards, to resist and provoke people, I began to present myself as the slut who decided to emancipate herself. If emancipation is synonymous with being a slut, I would rather be a slut than an oppressed girl from a good family.

She has taken up all these vulgar terms used against her, to further provoke those who fail to recognise her fight and oppose her emancipation.

Fatima, meanwhile, no longer wants to wait for someone to come and rescue her:

> Patriarchy chooses to dismiss our emancipation. Women who aspire to freedom are considered traitors, selfish and sluts. Time flies. I won't wait for associations to come to defend me or for laws to be changed so that I can be free.

The testimonies of these women present the insidious violence exerted on women in Morocco and the strategies deployed by women to escape their dominated condition. Fatima recalled numerous dramatic episodes from her own past, before outlining the path she followed:

> I was taken out of school when I wanted to become a doctor. I was forcibly married when I was only 14 years old. I was imprisoned at home, when I wanted to discover the world. I was never able to put on the clothes I wanted. I have never been able to express my opinion freely. This suffering lasted 35 years. Then I decided to end it. To be free and happy again. I got divorced, started working and I moved to another city. It is funny when I think about it. It was a movie that sowed this idea of freedom in my head – *The Open Door* – particularly when Faten Hamama challenged the misogynist mentality and archaic traditions.[10]

Fatima and Maryam became aware of their condition and transformed their anger into indignation and resisting the status quo. Fatima's trigger was Faten Hamama; Maryam's trigger was anger. After years of suffering, she decided to end the injustice she was encountering. Just like Fatima, Mina too had chosen a life partner who also supported her fight against patriarchy. He was an accomplice and an ally in every decision she made and a constant companion.

Conclusion

Souad provides the conclusion as she made it her mission to work towards empowering other women in her district by offering learning, and thus work opportunities, and by organising sorority clubs where women can get together in a safe space and speak out:

> Among the negative consequences of such violence against women is an unbalanced society. A shaken, impulsive and hopeless generation. It is often said that mothers are schools, but how can they be when they have been humiliated? The problem is right there. When society demeans women, it inevitably produces unbalanced children after 10 or 15 years, who will themselves be harmful to their surroundings. Governments

could implement policies brought in from abroad, designed by experts. It would not work, because there is no one to implement it. Because when you humiliate women, you undermine their dignity and you treat them as second-class citizens. That is when we, as a society, are going to pay the price, and society is already paying the price for this degrading treatment inflicted on women. You forbade women from going to school, so maybe their children will be educated to a certain level. But imagine if we allowed those same women to have access to education, imagine what their children would be like.

Not to mention the delinquency that is directly linked to the fact that if women do not have access to all their rights, society pays heavily for it. And we are paying heavily. Just look at the people living in extreme vulnerability; they have reached an unimaginable bottom. So, let us put a stop to it!

And Myriam said:

There are no miracles. I had to do a lot of research to accumulate the arguments and kill the unfounded opinions given by people, including my family. Today, I succeeded in imposing certain rules inside the house: collective vote on decisions, freedom of expression for all members, mansplaining is not allowed, and encouraging women to speak. It took me a while, but I noticed that I managed to install new habits that would not have been possible back in the day.

The liberating triggers shared by these women recall once again that change must originate from people themselves, and understanding acts of systemic violence, and articulating them using the right wording, contribute greatly to deconstructing patriarchy. In the words of the character Shams in the book *Soufi mon amour*, 'I learned by unlearning everything I knew' (Shafak, 2011).

Social stability is essentially based on equal opportunities and democracy shaped by emancipated citizens. This will never be achieved as long as half of society (women) is excluded by discriminatory laws and long-established traditions and is being treated as second-class citizens. Society's wellbeing is assessed by the way in which its women and girls are treated and, more fundamentally, how different minorities live and whether they genuinely perceive themselves to be fully fledged citizens. In their own way, these women epitomise 'shards of radical potential buried in the sedimentation of the political present' (Kramer, 2019: 12).

Beyond any attempt at conceptualisation or generalisation, this text is based on three accounts from bearers of valuable insights who bring together observations, formulations, behaviours and strategies that we saw and heard from a number of women during our tour of the three regions. Although their contexts are similar to a certain extent, with regional variations, no woman is representative of the others. Their struggle for emancipation is first and foremost an individual one, even if the three women have had allies who have supported, helped and encouraged them. Our role, as civil society, is to propose forms of collective organisation to better structure the action and amplify the impact.

Notes

(1) For instance, under the old Family Code, husbands had every right to divorce their wives without recourse to the courts, which was a flagrant injustice to women. The 2004 reform put an end to this violence, as stated in article 78: 'Divorce is the dissolution of the marital pact exercised by the husband and wife, each according to the conditions to which they are subject, under the control of justice and in accordance with the provisions of the present Code'.
(2) The 1996 constitution merely emphasised that 'all Moroccans are equal before the law' and that 'men and women enjoy equal political rights'.
(3) President of the Fédération des ligues des droits des femmes, interviewed by the TAFRA Center research team.
(4) Article 9 (2): 'States Parties shall grant women equal rights with men with respect to the nationality of their children.'
Article 16: 'The same rights and responsibilities as parents, irrespective of their marital status, in matters relating to their children; in all cases the interests of the children shall be paramount.'
(5) The term 'Sharia-based' references the religious directives with which Muslims comply.
(6) 'Springtime for Equality' (Printemps de l'égalité) is a coalition created in 2001 by nine feminist organisations to monitor the work of the commission in charge of reforming the Moudawana (Family Code). The coalition subsequently grew to include 26 associations working in the field of democratic advancement throughout the country (Naciri, 2014).
(7) The project also included: (1) a mapping of VAW in Morocco, illustrating how actors dealing with violence are geographically located, what sort of violence they tackle and their legal status and contacts; (2) a study providing an overview of gender-based violence in Morocco, in terms of the legislative framework, statistical data relating to this issue and a description of the various forms of violence prevalent in Morocco; and (3) individual interviews with actors involved in the field, in order to complement the documentary research.
(8) *Adoul* are traditional religious notaries hold the duty of writing authenticated certificates in areas relating to personal status and real estate affairs.
(9) Al-Fatiha is the opening sura of the Quran. Composed of seven verses, it emphasises God's sovereignty and mercy. It is used to declare marriages granted and blessed by God.
(10) Faten Hamama is an Egyptian film and television actress and film producer. *The Open Door* is an Egyptian film directed by Henry Barakat, which follows the life of a young Egyptian girl from a middle-class family. Laila, the main character, has been appointed to symbolise both oppression and struggle, and the events of the film unfold alongside the political circumstances of Egypt's past, from the revolution of 1952 to the Tripartite attack on the country. According to the film, political circumstances have impacted Laila and guided her pursuit of freedom in a patriarchal repressive society.

References

Assouli, F. (2018) Violences envers les femmes: Des avancées de papier ? [Violence against women – Progress made on paper?]. *TAFRA*, interview. http://tafra.ma/violences-envers-les-femmes-des-avancees-de-papier (accessed 20 August 2023).

Chaker, H. (2021) Éducation des filles: Le défi de la scolarisation des filles rurales [Girls' education: The challenge of educating rural girls]. *Journal L'opinion*, 21 October. https://www.lopinion.ma/Education-des-filles-Le-defi-de-la-scolarisation-des-filles-rurales_a19909.html (accessed 15 July 2023).

Chollet, M. (2018) *Les sorcières* [The witches]. Éditions Zones.

Engels, F. (1884) *Origin of the Family, Private Property, and the State*. Resistance Books.

Gagliardi, S. (2018) Violence against women: The stark reality behind Morocco's human rights progress. *Journal of North African Studies* 23 (4), 569–590. https://www.tandfonline.com/doi/full/10.1080/13629387.2017.1363649 (accessed 20 August 2023).

Garçon, J. (2000) Les islamistes défilent à Casablanca, les 'modernistes' à Rabat [Islamists march in Casablanca, 'modernists' in Rabat]. *Journal Libération*, 13 March. https://www.liberation.fr/planete/2000/03/13/les-islamistes-defilent-a-casablanca-les-modernistes-a-rabat-au-maroc-les-femmes-reveillent-la-rue-l_318528 (accessed 11 August 2023).

Glacier, O. (2015) *Les droits humains au Maroc: Entre discours et réalité* [Human rights in Morocco: Between discourse and reality]. Tarik Éditions.

Halimi, G. (1992) *La cause des femmes* [The women's cause]. Éditions Gallimard.

Haut Commissariat au Plan (2019) Note sur les violences faites aux femmes et aux filles [Note on the violence against women and girls]. Blog. https://www.hcp.ma/Note-sur-les-violences-faites-aux-femmes-et-aux-filles_a2627.html (accessed 10 August 2023).

Kasraoui, S. (2020) Moroccan courts handle 17,000 cases of violence against women annually. *Morocco World News*. https://www.moroccoworldnews.com/2020/03/295690/moroccan-courts-handle-17000-cases-of-violence-against-women-annually (accessed 20 August 2023).

Kramer, S. (2019) *Excluded Within: The (Un)intelligibility of Radical Political Actors*. Oxford University Press.

Le Monde and AFP (2022) Au Maroc, la 'tragédie' des mariages de mineures [In Morocco, the 'tragedy' of underage marriages]. *Le Monde*, 7 March. https://www.lemonde.fr/afrique/article/2022/03/07/au-maroc-la-tragedie-des-mariages-de-mineures_6116439_3212.html (accessed 16 July 2023).

Morocco: Code Pénal (2004) *Loi No 70-03 portant code de la famille* [on the Family Code]. http://idpbarcelona.net/docs/recerca/marroc/pdf/nor_loi_70_03.pdf (accessed 19 August 2023).

Morocco: Code Pénal (2016) *Loi No 11-15 portant réorganisation de la Haute autorité de la communication audiovisuelle* [on the reorganisation of the High Authority for Audiovisual Communication]. https://www.wipo.int/edocs/lexdocs/laws/fr/ma/ma071fr.pdf (accessed 20 August 2023).

Murgue, B. (2011) La Moudawana: Les dessous d'une réforme sans précédent [La Moudawana: The underside of an unprecedented reform]. *Les Cahiers de l'Orient* 102 (2), 15–29. https://www.cairn.info/revue-les-cahiers-de-l-orient-2011-2-page-15.htm (accessed 15 August 2023).

Naciri, R. (2014) Le mouvement des femmes au Maroc [The women's rights movement in Morocco]. *Nouvelles Questions Féministes* 33 (2), 43–64. https://www.cairn.info/revue-nouvelles-questions-feministes-2014-2-page-43.htm (accessed 11 August 2023).

Sabbar, M. (2014) Les apports de la constitution 2011 en matière des droits de la femme [The contributions of the 2011 constitution in terms of women's rights]. *PJD* [blog]. https://www.pjd.ma/fr/news/les-apports-de-la-constitution-2011-en-mati%25c3%25a8re-des-droits-de-la-femme (accessed 16 August 2023).

Sadiqi, F. (2008) The central role of the family law in the Moroccan feminist movement.

British Journal of Middle Eastern Studies 35, 325–337. https://www.researchgate.net/profile/Fatima-Sadiqi/publication/308673837_The_Central_Role_of_the_Family_Law_in_the_Moroccan_Feminist_Movement/links/57ea806408aed3a3e08aa662/The-Central-Role-of-the-Family-Law-in-the-Moroccan-Feminist-Movement.pdf (accessed 11 August 2023).

Secrétariat Générale de Gouvernement (2011) *Moroccan Constitution*. http://www.sgg.gov.ma/Portals/0/constitution/constitution_2011_Fr.pdf (accessed 15 July 2023).

Shafak, E. (2011) *Soufi mon amour* [Sufi, my love]. Éditions 10-18.

World Health Organization (2011) Prévenir les grossesses précoces et leurs conséquences en matière de santé reproductive chez les adolescentes dans les pays en développement [Preventing early pregnancy and its reproductive health consequences among adolescent girls in developing countries]. https://www.who.int/fr/publications-detail/9789241502214 (accessed 10 July 2023).

2 High School Women in the Face of Violence During the COVID-19 Pandemic: Towards the Production of Spaces of Prevention and Sisterhood

Angelica Lucia Damian Bernal, Maria Veronica Ibarra Garcia, Eva Citlali Jiménez Rodríguez, Violeta Torres Carroll and Paola Cueto Jimenez

Introduction

COVID-19, which was first detected at the end of 2019, spread throughout the world, becoming a global pandemic by March 2020, impacted the generations of the second half of the 20th century and beginning of the 21st in unprecedented ways. Everyday life as we knew it was disrupted when the first state lockdowns were implemented as a means of confronting the virus, mirroring the social distancing and quarantine measures implemented to face the bubonic plague roughly 700 years ago. Only activities deemed essential for social reproduction continued 'normally': namely, the health, security, food supply and garbage collection sectors. The scientific and technological advances of the 21st century provided important elements for facing a global pandemic in ways that were unavailable to the world in the decades and centuries before (Carhuachín, 2021; Spinney, 2018).

Scientific and technical developments meant pharmaceutical companies swiftly started trials to create a vaccine. Furthermore, the technological advances of the so-called Fourth Industrial Revolution had developed systems of virtual communication such as Zoom and Google Meet, among others, that were used massively throughout the world in unprecedented ways and were taking off to their full potential, transforming, perhaps irreversibly, social patterns and space, while virtual spaces assumed a dominant role in society. By virtue of the technological developments of the 21st century, many economic activities were able to transition to socially distanced ways of organising, particularly in the education, administration, sales and government sectors. This transition marked a new space-time, where mass communication made possible through the internet changed the dynamics across diverse spaces. Domestic space became the workspace, the educational space and the recreational space all at once. Firstly, the private space became the workplace as the 'home office' became the new norm. Secondly, education was also confined to private space with distance learning and instruction. Finally, even recreational activities were adapted using technologies – reunions of friends and family were taking place in everyone's own homes simultaneously. Even doctor and therapy appointments went online. All these activities were still able to take place, but not in the physical realm that involves commuting, taking up public space and placing bodies outside of their homes. This interconnectivity transformed not only humankind's physical experience but also the psychological experience in the midst of a new reality that no one had ever experienced.

Education was set to distance learning and teaching, with this change in the traditional classroom setting revealing inequalities such as differentiated access to internet services, overcrowded conditions in some families' living spaces, the lack of privacy in homes as well the different violences that are created in domestic spaces. Online classes broke a 'fourth wall', much like in the theatre, and looking into private homes showed the different conditions students were in – privilege, or lack of, was on camera, not only for students but also for teachers.

One of the main problems that was evident when different realms and activities of human life were condensed into the domestic space was gender-based violence (GBV). The domestic sphere had been identified before the COVID-19 pandemic as a realm in which girls and women experience GBV; however, during the pandemic families had to adapt to staying indoors at all times. Unemployment coupled with emotions of anxiety, uncertainty and everyday social interactions confined in the home space created tension within the domestic space in which care work has historically been feminised. In this way, different aspects of life clashed together inside homes, exposing women and girls in some extreme cases to male family members from whom the women and girls experienced domestic violence and which caused a longer exposure to their aggressors.

Monroy (2020) reported that, according to Olga Sánchez Cordero, the former Secretary of the Interior in Mexico, violence against women and girls increased by 120% during the state of emergency confinement due to the COVID-19 virus, while 9 out of 10 people who experienced domestic violence were women, and 66% experienced physical violence and 22% psycho-emotional violence. According to the Pan American Health Organization (2020: 2), 'access to basic sexual and reproductive health services, including those aimed at women who experience violence decreased in the pandemic'. Moreover, 'the provision of other services, such as telephone help lines, centers for crisis care, shelters, legal assistance and protection services were affected, which further reduced access to the few support services that women in a relationship of abuse have access to' (2020: 2). The lack of access to services meant an increased vulnerability for women and girls who were experiencing domestic violence before and during the pandemic.

The research presented in this chapter draws from a series of pedagogic interventions from a feminist geographical lens implemented with the aim of identifying violence that students experienced before and during the COVID-19 pandemic in remote and in-person school contexts. The classroom research took place in three different high schools: (1) Escuela Nacional Preparatoria (ENP 2, Mexico City), the oldest high school in Mexico, incorporated with the National Autonomous University of Mexico (UNAM); (2) a private Catholic high school in the city of San Luis Potosi; and (3) a high school located in the mountainous region of the Tehuantepec Isthmus in the south of Oaxaca. Geography is a core subject in all three high schools, and economic geography and political geography are also taught at these schools as electives. Students ranged between 15 and 19 years old, in classrooms with 15- and 16-year-old students and others with 17- to 19-year-old students.

From a feminist geographic perspective, we approach how the COVID-19 pandemic shed new light on the GBV which was already present in educational spaces prior to the global lockdown and how it transformed during and after confinement. This is examined through the viewpoint of feminist geography, as we are a group of geographers involved in research that intersects gender and space. The specific aims of our research project were to identify the presence of GBV in domestic, school and digital spaces, to trace the experiences and participation of adolescent women in producing spaces free of GBV during the confinement, and to propose methodologies to prevent GBV that young women face in high school, steering towards the long-term elimination of GBV in domestic, educational and digital spaces.

In this chapter, we detail the research that we undertook to demonstrate the shift of everyday life in physical space to virtual space as an implication of the global COVID-19 pandemic and how it greatly affected students' ability to create safe spaces and adapt to the new conditions of the pandemic that greatly changed society, starting in the year 2020. The chapter deals with the following research questions:

- In what ways did violence manifest itself in the lives of young women during their everyday confined lives, and did the COVID-19 pandemic act as a catalyst?
- Drawing from their experiences, did they find solutions to create spaces that prevented violence and foster networks of sisterhood?
- How do the experiences of young women contrast as they relate to diverse spatial settings (rural/urban)?

These questions filled knowledge gaps because they allowed us to explore the experiences of young adolescent girls coming of age during the COVID-19 pandemic, to propose ways to prevent GBV, and to gain a better understanding of inequalities in different educational contexts. This chapter is divided into three main sections. The first details how we incorporate feminist geography into our study as the main methodological and theoretical framework through which the research was conducted. The second section describes the outcomes of the methodologies that were implemented, and the third section makes some concluding remarks and summarises the horizons that were identified as a result of this study.

Feminist Geography as a Theoretical and Methodological Framework

Feminist geography is concerned with identifying different spatial patterns produced by the patriarchal system that place women in conditions of subordination, invisibility and violence. Feminist geographers have dedicated research to denouncing the physical and symbolic violence that women face in every social space, understanding the causes and looking to transform spatialities to guarantee access to freedom and justice (Diaz *et al.*, 1995; Fluri & Piedalue, 2017; Johnson, 1994; Katz, 2009; Valentine, 1992). Doreen Massey (2007) spoke during a conference at the Central University of Venezuela about how social space is a product of actions, relationships and social practices, and therefore open to politics, understanding that if we produce space, we can equally transform it. According to Damian and Ibarra (2020), feminist geography assumes that both space and GBV are socially produced through actions as well as legal, political, social, cultural and economic omissions; thus, GBV can be addressed and ultimately eliminated with actions articulated at different scales in the aforementioned areas.

In the regional context of Latin America, studies of GBV have been carried out across diverse disciplines, which means there is a rich interdisciplinary field concerned not only with studying but also eradicating violence against women and girls. Within geography, we add the feminist lens to our studies by engaging concepts of positionality and situated knowledge, understanding how our contexts affect our research and the non-neutral role we have as researchers (Baylina *et al.*, 2008). Thus, we can say that the feminist perspective has gained traction in Latin American geography over the past two decades, given the need to adopt a gendered view of a wide range of social problems (Ibarra García & Escamilla-Herrera, 2016).

In the case studies that we focused on, violence in educational spaces was brought to light mainly at the high school and university levels. More specifically, the research project itself was started within the confinement of the COVID-19 pandemic, which placed a marker both in our own experience as researchers as well as in the contextual time frame of our study and the effect of the pandemic on the lived experiences of the youth involved in the research project.

In geography, space is identified as a fundamental category of analysis, understood as a social product that manifests relations of power at different scales. In this way, educational spaces were specified in this study in order to identify how academic contexts can also be territories where violence against girls and women is normalised. The spatial concepts of diffusion and transmission are of utmost importance when analysing the transition of physical spaces in the midst of the COVID-19 pandemic to virtual spaces where multiple activities took place. The specificity of virtual space is that it allows for interconnection through electronic devices that require, as geographer Milton Santos (2000) defines, fixtures and flows, where fixtures constitute fibreoptic networks that connect humans through modems that send wireless signals through mobile devices such as tablets and phones or desktop computers. This virtual space is socially constructed and thus presents inequalities, power dynamics and unequal access to scientific and technical development.

This interconnected cyberspace expanded through networks can contain, on the one hand, violent spatialities and, on the other, places of solidarity; creating empathy and indifference, digital space has become a double-edged sword. Because of this, digital space has increasingly been subject to regulations since it has been used as a place to inflict emotional violence, sexual harassment, bullying and slander, and has affected the emotional integrity of members of society. In this sense, regulations, laws and statutes have been established to sanction practices like cyberbullying and online sexual harassment.

Given this context, the concept of sisterhood was placed at the centre of our research, as we believe that within it lies an important key for reconstructing solidarity among women, in effect transforming the spaces that we move in, are influenced by and socially build. Sisterhood is a way of relating to other women in political solidarity; it must be actively and consciously knit with the understanding that the division of women and the concept of women's worth in relation only to men hinders the possibilities of girls and women upholding each other and the feminist movement collectively (hooks, 1984). In this sense, we uphold sisterhood not as a romanticised view of women's sameness but as an element that bridges diverse female experiences intertwined in systems of oppression, such as gender, class, race, ethnicity, marginalisation and spatial exclusions. Sisterhood has exceeded the interpersonal level and can be viewed within the feminist movement locally and globally; it has furthered legislature, public policies and agendas spearheading laws. The executive order commonly known as Ley Olimpia officially added modifications (amid the COVID-19 pandemic) in June 2021 to the Ley General de Acceso de las Mujeres a una Vida Libre de Violencia by addressing, categorising and criminalising digital gender violence (Diario Oficial de la Federación, 2021). This is especially relevant to our research since it legally attends to GBV in digital spaces.

When introduced to the concept of *cuerpo-territorio*, students are able to understand how everyday life and politics, specifically relations of power, are embodied. From this concept, we understand that human experience is not outside of our bodies but rather directly felt and lived through them. In this way, being able to identify how bodies are sexualised and racialised within neo-extractivism and capitalist dynamics, we move away from normalising expressions of these dynamics such as racism, machismo, classism and ableism, among other marginalising practices and beliefs. This can be especially transforming in the experiences of young women, as they can take back their bodies as their own spaces of both resistance and lived experience: where they might identify a variety of emotions, fears, wounds but also dreams and aspirations. In Latin America, it is evident that fears of not returning home from daily routines or activities of leisure are affecting girls' and women's everyday life, which further demonstrates how female bodies are controlled, excluded and put in situations of vulnerability because of their gender.

Expressions of these fears can be found in the digital space, with public digital condemnation such as on social media platforms like Facebook and Instagram, where hashtags like #SiMeMatan (#IfTheyKillMe) denounce the revictimisation of victims of femicide and slogans such as 'La policia no me cuida, me cuidan mis amigas' ('The police don't take care of me, my friends do') show that women have felt that the overwhelming impunity that characterises the institutions that should be guaranteeing their safety have failed them. Instead, women of all ages have created their own safe practices by doing things like sharing their live location on WhatsApp groups in order to feel safer while transiting public space and making the phrase 'avisame cuando llegues' ('let me know when you get home') a pillar of collective self-care. Offline, massive feminist protests and demonstrations such as the 8M marches have flooded the streets of Latin America with chants and slogans that contextualise the violence lived in women's bodies. 'Señor, señora, no sea indiferente, Se matan a las mujeres en la cara de la gente' (roughly translated: 'Mister, miss, don't be indifferent, women are being killed right in front of our people') can be heard as well as the emblematic 'Ni Una Menos' slogan that demands action from state officials to prevent femicide.

Cuerpo-territorio is a concept that originates in Latin American community-based feminism outside of academia, within contexts of territorial struggles against patriarchal, colonial extractivism of land and resources. It has also found its place and been incorporated within feminist geographic studies and research in recent years. As such, students were introduced to the idea that their bodies constitute the first space from which they experience the outside world and given the multiple interlocked power dynamics that our bodies are contextualised within, such as gender, race, class and sexual orientation, among others, it can be understood as a territory. We find the concept of *cuerpo-territorio* a rich framework for introducing, identifying and transforming structural violence.

According to Lorena Cabnal (2010: 22):

> This approach is taken on first as a political slogan, to then give it life through contents that weave a community-based feminist outlook from xinka women. It implies consciously reclaiming our body-territory, as an emancipatory political act, aligning with the thought that 'the personal is political', 'what is not named, does not exist'. Assuming individual corporality as a territory that is unique and personal allows for the strengthening of the sense of self, affirming one's existence and right to be in the world. In this way, self-awareness emerges which allows one to understand how this body has lived its personal, particular and temporal history as well as the different manifestations and expressions of patriarchies and all of the oppressions derived from them. Reclaiming the body to defend it from the historic structural onslaught that has attacked bodies, becomes an indispensable everyday battle, because the body-territory has been a territory of dispute by patriarchies for thousands of years in order to guarantee the sustainability through and above the bodies of women. Reclaiming and defending the body also imply a conscious way of provoking the dismantlement of masculine pacts that we live with; it implies questioning and provoking how we think of our feminine bodies in order to gain liberty. (Translated)

Taking these concepts, theories and experiences into the classroom, our methodologies were applied in three educational contexts located in different states in Mexico. Digging deeper into identifying the violence that was lived during the pandemic, we identified some characteristics of the contexts in which students lived their day-to-day lives in both private and public spaces. Three high schools participated in this study: one in Mexico City, one in San Luis Potosi and another in Oaxaca. The three high schools were either incorporated or have partnerships with the National Autonomous University of Mexico (UNAM), which the researchers in this project are all affiliated to.

The methodologies that were implemented were considered 'interventions' in the sense that students would first have to understand and name GBV and the different ways and spaces in which it might arise. Moreover, we understood that these topics could cause emotional tribulations in students and therefore establishing a safe space of dialogue and respectful listening and exchange was essential for this classroom dynamic. In this way, our first intervention was based on teaching within the context of the subject of geography where and how GBV could appear. Students were first introduced to the types and modalities of violence and geared towards understanding how identifying a problem is the first step to addressing and transforming spaces. In the classroom, this meant an introduction to the Mexican federal law pertaining to gender-based violence passed in 2007 called the Ley General de Acceso de las Mujeres a una Vida Libre de Violencia (LGAMVLV; General Law of Access for Women to a Life Free of Violence, 2007).

An important note is that the students involved in the research had been previously introduced to concepts of space as a social construct because geography is a core subject in Mexican high schools. As feminist geographers, we emphasise the importance of geography as a core subject in schools as it is a field of knowledge that can aid in developing critical thought in students as they incorporate theories that explain their spatial contexts. The concept of *cuerpo-territorio*, which is informed by decolonial feminist thought and practice, was introduced to students as a precursor to the three phases of the methodology that followed, which were focus groups, collaborative cartographies and counter-cartographies.

The high school in Mexico City is incorporated into the Escuela Nacional Preparatoria (ENP) high school system that has a total of nine campuses and a student population of around 52,000 adolescents, which means there is a plurality of experiences. The ENP is one of the most prestigious high schools in the country because of its high academic level and, therefore, the admission process is very competitive. The students who were part of this research project attended the ENP 2 campus, which is located in the east of Mexico City; many students commute from surrounding neighbourhoods within Mexico City as well as from localities in Estado de Mexico that are mainly highly populated and do not have adequate transportation services. This means long journeys to and from school. This campus has the particularity of being part of a university pathway programme that reflects in the development of strong research capabilities and formation of its students.

The high school located in San Luis Potosi is a private Catholic school located in the central plateau region. San Luis Potosi is a colonial city where mining was one of the most prolific economic activities during the 16th and 17th centuries. In the last 15 years, however, there has been an upsurge in the presence of drug trafficking cartels. The school is located in the old town of the city, where the students are mostly upper-middle class.

The third high school is located in Lagunas, Oaxaca, and is much smaller than ENP. It was created by the Cruz Azul cement cooperative with a mission statement that reads 'education inspired in collective wellbeing'. Many of the students who attend this school have parents who work at the Cruz Azul cement plant.

We also used focus group discussions in classrooms to create a space for opinion that captured the feelings, thoughts and lives of the students. The discussion was guided based on questions that we had previously established. This method was useful for opening up the conversation about experiences of violence before, during and after the COVID-19 pandemic. This strategy produced collective knowledge; when testimonies were shared, students were able to mirror their experiences with others' and see how everyone was affected by the confinement measures of the pandemic, albeit not in the same ways. Hence, our focus groups discussed: (1) whether the confinement caused by the COVID-19 pandemic increased violence in the domestic, educational and digital spheres; (2) the types and modalities of violence that participants faced when they were attending in-person classes; (3) the types and modalities of violence that victims faced in their daily lives during the COVID-19 pandemic; (4) whether the participants' families managed to keep their jobs and work from home; (5) whether families continued to maintain work, educational or family activities in the same space; and (6) the potential solutions that participants found or built to create spaces free of violence, promoting prevention and sisterhood.

The second methodological instrument applied during another class session was collaborative cartography. Students were divided into groups and the lesson plan was created based on the 'spaces of fear' methodology developed by the Argentinian geographers Diana Lan and Heder Rocha (2020). In this class activity, students utilised geographic information systems (GIS) to pinpoint diverse spaces of fear that they identified on their way to and from school. Spaces of fear were described to students as places that caused anguish, anxiety or heightened senses of the need for self-defence, given real or imagined dangers in public space emanating from a feeling or perception of distrust. Cartography is utilised in geography as a tool that creates spatial representations; following this line of thought, students created maps that reflected the types of violence that they collectively perceived. Students were asked to identify five places where they had heard of or seen violence on their way to school. The types of violence that were considered for this cartographic activity were sexual harassment, sexual abuse, prostitution, human trafficking, drug sales/consumption, theft, femicide and other violence.

Lastly, the methodology of counter-cartography again called for the incorporation of the concept of *cuerpo-territorio* to create embodied representations of violence through a sensory exercise that graphically traced feelings and emotions. Critical geography has incorporated counter-cartographies into its research to highlight how traditional cartography has been historically used as a tool to maintain power and oppression when it excludes and does not represent marginalised communities or their interests. As André Mesquita (2018: 26) puts it:

> Counter-cartographies are understood as maps that break with the scientific tradition of specialization of cartography as well as its mere technical or essentially positivist view of the world. This type of transgression goes against official geopolitical maps while exposing relations of domination over and exploitation of a territory as well as revealing concealed networks of power.

We implemented the counter-cartography exercise by having students create their own body maps. For this activity, students were asked to trace their body's outline and prompted to think of how their bodies are at the centre of their experience. To guide their counter-cartographies, we presented a series of questions and asked students to create a body map of their personal experiences of violence, fear and pain, but also those that they might have heard. We suggested that they create a symbology and use different colours to represent different feelings. The participants were asked the following questions based on Lan and Rocha's (2020) methodology:

(1) How do you experience places identified as violent in your body?
(2) Where do we feel insecure? In what part of our body are violence, pain and anger perceived?
(3) What part of the body do you feel when you hear about a case of femicide?
(4) When you go through areas where there are robberies, what part of your body registers fear?
(5) When have you seen bullying or experienced it, where can you record it in your body?
(6) What about family violence? From a teacher? Digital violence? Psychological? Economic?

The answers to these questions were heterogeneous in terms of the parts of the body where students identified violence. However, the most common body parts were hands, intimate areas, the brain (related to thoughts) and the heart (related to feelings). Danger for women was often felt in the legs, chest and intimate parts; anger was drawn in the fists; and pain was depicted in the head as well as in the heart. Fear of physical aggression or assault was portrayed mostly in the chest, as a feeling of oppression that also reflected feeling powerless and the anger of being attacked.

According to testimonies about violence within families or in school settings and about psychological and/or economic violence, these were traced mainly in the arms and the mouth, perhaps reflecting the feeling of being powerless in the face of something that cannot be changed.

These methodological frameworks were our paths to responding to our research questions. Every classroom setting created diverse collective knowledge and also called for different adaptations of each exercise. Although the spatial contexts of our research were diverse, it was interesting to note how many experiences are comparable and, as Teresa De Lauretis (1987: 5) writes, we noted the 'cultural construction of sex into gender and the asymmetry that characterizes all gender systems cross-culturally (though each in particular ways) are understood and how they are systematically linked to the organization of social inequality'.

The research team met up in order to compare the counter-mapping representations and see similarities in terms of the violences that came up and the ways students portrayed them. As for the focus groups, we listened to the recordings of the sessions in order to compare the experiences students had had during the COVID-19 pandemic. In terms of the participatory cartography exercise, we observed the diverse points that were identified by the students to search for patterns. We had originally planned to add a layer with official homicide data; however, we were not able to get this information in time to add this to the exercise. These methodologies were enriching for the students, and they have great potential for identifying and preventing GBV in the diverse spaces that are taken up by youth, both private and public. The results of these classroom activities allowed us to identify the concepts that should be incorporated into the curriculum to create a culture of GBV prevention.

Discussion

The increase in the use of information and communication technologies (ICT) during the COVID-19 pandemic revealed the imbricated relationship between public and private spaces and the fallacy of the division between them; following Cabnal (2010, as quoted above), we evoke the phrase 'the personal is political'. Ash *et al.* (2018: 7) understand the concept of the digital turn in geography as 'a set of ontics, aesthetics, logics and discourses' that have become increasingly intertwined in society. Moreover, these authors urge the need to 'think critically about the relationship between geography and the digital, thinking of "digital geographies" as a turn towards the digital as object and subject of inquiry in geography, and as a simultaneous inflection of geographical scholarship by digital phenomena' (Ash *et al.*, 2018: 7). In this way, we engage the digital space in our feminist geographic understanding of the GBV present in experiences inside and outside of private space. The use of ICT has imbricated the domestic/public spatial division by constituting a spatio-temporal compression. What is evident is that even when violence is experienced online, it is always territorialised in the body. In this sense, the use of digital communication tools made the articulation of the corporal, local, regional, national and global scales clearer.

Another point to consider in the case of Mexico is the inequalities in access to both internet services and infrastructure (computer, tablet, phone). In our research, we found that many families shared a single computer, especially those in Mexico City and in Oaxaca, which contrasted with students from San Luis Potosi, who had more access to devices. A large array of differences between students based on socioeconomic variations in semi-rural spaces and urban localities came to light during the focus groups. The spectrum was very broad; while some students had parents with professional backgrounds with larger homes and access to different coping mechanisms during the COVID-19 pandemic, others lived in close quarters with extended family and did not have access to a room of their own for their daily educational activities. In San Luis Potosi, a variety of students shared that they had housekeepers and because of this they were able to focus on their classes while their parents worked from home. In Oaxaca, many students alluded to the fact that gender roles dictated their day-to-day activities during the pandemic. In Mexico City, due to high population density, students and their families had to figure out how to manage their activities in smaller spaces.

During the focus groups, we were able to verify that students from these three contrasting high school contexts had identified parallel experiences with diverse violence, such as physical, digital, sexual, psychological, family and educational, which varied in intensity. One of the parallel experiences that were noticed during the focus groups was that the first time students had experienced GBV was actually before high school, during middle school, between the ages of 12 and 14 years. Another pattern was that the lockdown meant every family member was taking up domestic space all day, whereas before the pandemic students and their parents left the home, which meant less interaction; this caused many tensions, heightened by unemployment.

Violence during the COVID-19 pandemic was most often experienced in the private domestic space, with economic, digital and family violence being the most talked about during the focus groups. Students across the board shared that with everyone being confined to their homes, there were reduced spaces for stress relief or outlets, and father figures oftentimes had misogynistic attitudes like disputes about space, lack of shared household chores, intolerance of noise and control of spending. A few families identified these forms of violence during the pandemic and looked for support.

At the beginning of the focus groups, many students initially responded that they had not experienced violence but they started recognising it when the conversation had taken off. Students in all three settings identified that the pandemic forced every family to make certain arrangements for co-living and organising work, domestic and school activities all at once. They also narrated how gender roles were more evident at the beginning of the lockdown but also modified to cope with economic struggles like fathers losing their source of income and mothers finding jobs, in that traditional gender roles were inverted.

On the other hand, digital violence proliferated during the COVID-19 pandemic lockdown. Many students shared that it was easy for people to 'hide behind their devices' and they either had experienced or knew of instances where intimate pictures had been disseminated, or knew about fake pictures, fake profiles or cyber-bullying. Fake profiles were used either to impersonate someone or to harass others online. Many students spoke about fake content, where erotic pictures would be edited with other students' faces and the perpetrator remained anonymous. There were also many testimonies of online harassment through social media such as Facebook and Instagram, like receiving unwanted advances, sexual content or having pictures taken of them without them knowing and sent through chat groups. Extortion and blackmail also presented themselves, as students knew of or had experienced threats of publishing intimate pictures. These cases were expressed especially when students learned about digital violence according to the Ley General de Acceso de las Mujeres a una Vida libre de Violencia, which brings us to highlight the importance of including aspects of legislation within the geography curriculum.

During the focus groups, students also shared that they had experienced feeling uncomfortable after comments by male teachers about the way they were dressed. It was interesting to hear that sexual harassment was something they had heard of outside of their school settings. They talked about other schools where teachers had been reported for sexual misconduct and how some of these teachers were still working. In response, they noted there were several protests and mobilisations in the context of International Women's Day, 8 March. On another note, the physical education class was mentioned at various times as a space where girls feel uncomfortable with the way they are looked at and excluded from playing sports. Moreover, girls who are athletic also received unwanted comments or bullying. This sexual violence can escalate into physical violence when girls and women do not feel free to take up certain spaces.

Some unexpected comments were shared during the focus groups that we did not think of beforehand. Some of the experiences shared had to do with the depression, sadness, anxiety and anguish that students experienced during confinement. At first no one wanted to mention it but as soon as someone had the courage to talk about their experience, many other testimonies were shared. In the 'post-pandemic' time we are currently living in, it is important that young students have access to mental health services to make sense of what they might be feeling now. That is, the COVID-19 peak may be over but what of the emotional effects of long COVID?

With all this in mind, the ways students organised to confront GBV were generally limited and scarcely reflexive. Some solutions they found were to not do things alone – always take up space with someone else. Others shared that they should not gossip about people. However, an interesting element that can be considered is the identification of a larger feminist movement in public spaces across Mexico and Latin America. Students mentioned that there should be more GBV awareness campaigns in their high schools, or that they should organise protests and larger movements to prevent violence. This means that young students do identify the feminist movement as a place for violence prevention and as a social referent. The focus groups were wrapped up with some final considerations from the teacher in charge about violence being a social problem, how respect for everyone's body is essential and that bridges can be built between classmates to collectively confront injustice. Students were also reminded that there are laws that protect them against GBV both in physical and virtual space: namely, the Ley General de Acceso de las Mujeres a una Vida Libre de Violencia and Ley Olimpia in Mexico.

The concept of *cuerpo-territorio* was also reintroduced to students to remind them how the violence that they had talked about regarding offensive comments about their bodies is unacceptable. The teachers emphasised that every body is perfect as they are and that everyone deserves respect; no one should permit verbal violence about women's or men's bodies. It was also an important moment to identify the multiple ways that bodies are culturally produced and consumed through networks of mass communication like music, television series, telenovelas, commercials, social media, movies and so on, and how they spread certain body stereotypes that have a clear patriarchal imprint simultaneously intersected with racism, colonialism and capitalism, which assigns an unrealistic 'beauty' standard.

We were able to introduce collaborative cartography activity in only one high school, because it was necessary to have knowledge of GIS. Students in the ENP 2 were the only ones who produced a map, given their broader background in geography. These students had previously taken several classes, such as political and economic geography, and they had experience of using GIS. The map that they collaborated on showed how the most common type of violence that they experience is sexual harassment in public spaces, where the majority of students said they

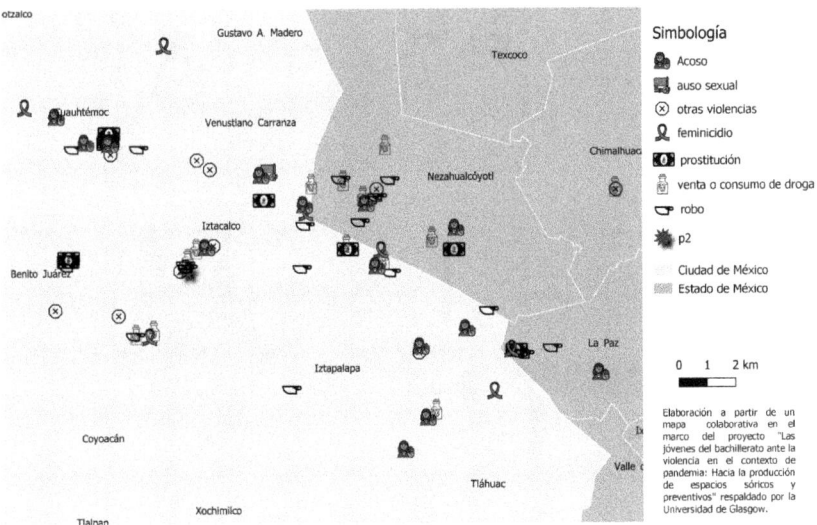

Figure 2.1 Map created collectively in geography class by ENP high school students, 2021

had experienced it directly and a few had only known others who had experienced it. Spatially, it was interesting to note that the frequency of sexual harassment was more common around the school campus, as seen in Figure 2.1.

The counter-cartographies activity was well received among students and also represented a rich exercise for analysing violence on the body scale. (Due to the different stages of the COVID-19 pandemic, some counter-cartographies were elaborated in person and others were online.) We found that when students did this activity, either in an environment where they felt comfortable or from their homes, they produced more elaborate body mappings. On the one hand, doing this activity in a mixed-gender group in San Luis Potosi created tensions among students, and when the teacher implementing the activity realised students were not comfortable, they changed the dynamic and created groups of students so that they could do a collective counter-cartography. In cases where this activity was done in mixed-gender classrooms, they were not so detailed, although still informative.

The collective counter-cartography shown in Figure 2.2 has many layers. Students drew several violent circumstances that they had witnessed: a girl crying because her ex-boyfriend shared her intimate photos; two

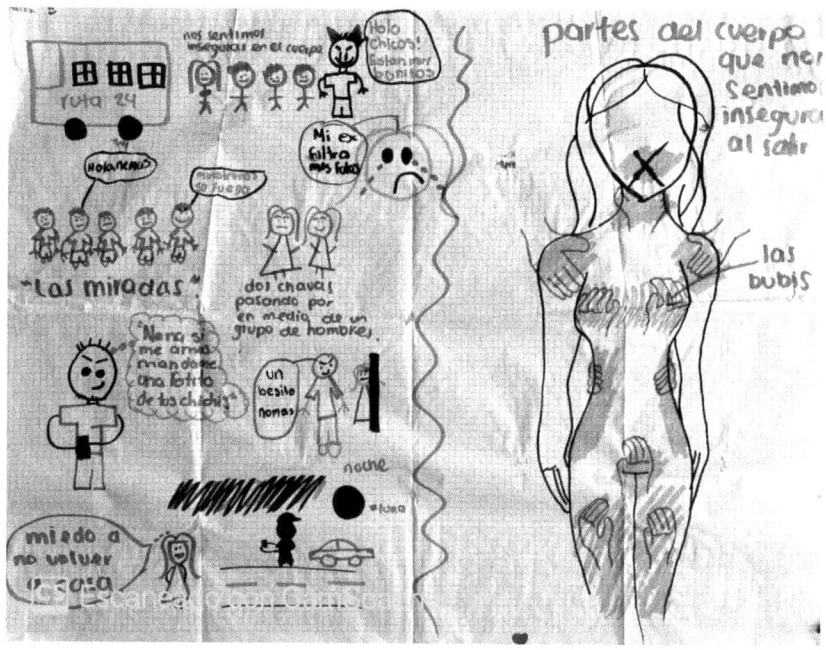

Figure 2.2 Collective counter-cartography elaborated in the classroom by high school students

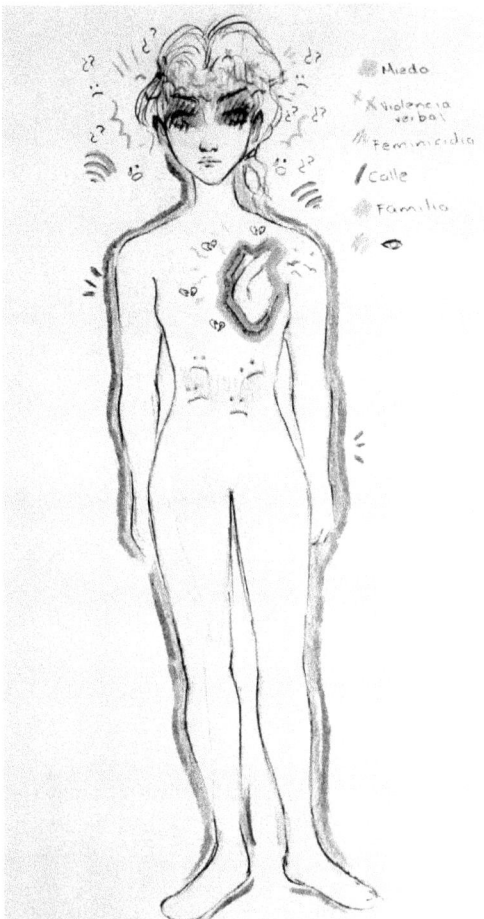

Figure 2.3 First example of individual counter-cartography elaborated from home by a high school geography student

girls feeling uncomfortable because they are walking by a group of men; a girl hiding while a boy says 'just a little kiss'; a girl scared that she will not come home; a man texting a girl requesting sexual content; the night as a time of danger; their bodies as places where they do not feel secure. On the other hand, they drew the silhouette of a woman and the parts of their bodies that they identify as places of violence; as their text says, 'we don't feel safe when we go out'.

Figures 2.3 and Figure 2.4 show individual counter-cartography produced when students were asked to elaborate their body mappings from home. We believe this allowed them to have the space and time to draw their counter-cartographies without feeling the pressure of being

46 Part 1: Towards Cultures of Conflict Transformation

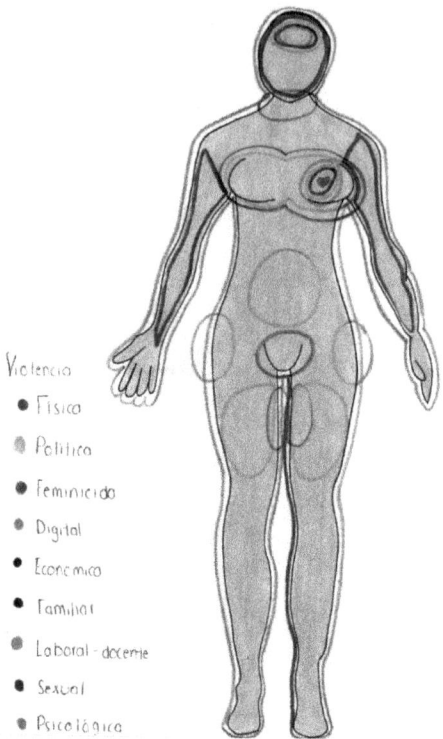

Figure 2.4 Second example of individual counter-cartography elaborated from home by a high school geography student

seen or judged by others. After seeing how the activities unfolded in different contexts, we understood that this exercise can be done in-person or from home, with diverse results.

With each exercise, the students described what they had represented. The student who produced Figure 2.3 described how her eyes are drawn over because she has seen things online she did not ask to see, and it is noticeable how multiple violences can be found in one body part and simultaneously all over the body. The student who produced Figure 2.4 explained how she outlined her whole body because 'you never know what and where something could happen to you'.

The following explanation was written by the student who created the counter-cartography shown in Figure 2.3:

> I represented fear in my head, my ears and my stomach, the things that are happening around me make me afraid, nervous and make me think about how horrible gender violence is. I put verbal violence with an x in my head, because people have insulted me and said rude things, when I have treated those people with respect and it bothers me. The green

colour represents the feelings of fear, doubt and nervousness from hearing about cases of femicides, rapes and the situations that are currently being experienced [in the country]. I highlighted my body in purple, because when I go out on the street, I am very afraid that something will happen to me, because like many of the women I have received harassing comments, but fortunately not beyond that. In pink I have highlighted my heart and my head because I am worried that something could happen to my family, like my mother, sister, etc. Finally, the colour orange in my eyes represents violence I have experienced through social media networks as I have been sent photos that I did not ask for.

The counter-cartography shown in Figure 2.4 was described by the student in the following way:

Physical and femicide violence
I surrounded the whole body because you really don't know where they will attack you, your whole body is in danger and fear is present in your mind. Political violence: I selected the mind and heart from knowing that a man is in a better position or rank than you, because you are a woman, which is stressful and gives you a feeling of anger.

Digital violence
I selected the stomach, the mind and the heart, because the fact that something intimate can be distributed without your permission turns your stomach, gives you a feeling of anger and sadness, which you feel in your heart and mind.

Economic violence
I surrounded the heart and mind, because the fact that a man earns more than you, when they do the same job, gives you a feeling of anger, frustration and sadness.

Family violence
I selected the face and arms because I remember that I read that the main actions or aggressions are slaps and pinches or pushes; however, your whole body is at risk. Also, the heart is important here, because the fact that someone from your own family assaults you is sad and difficult.

Work-teacher violence
I assumed that this violence can take place in front of several people since it is not very common to be alone with your attacker, so I selected the hip because someone could touch you either as a 'hug' or something like that. Also, the breasts and the legs, because you can get stared at, and if you wear a skirt you can get touched or looked at.

Sexual violence
I selected the buttocks, vagina, bust, neck and mouth, because it is where you are commonly attacked and where you are most at risk.

Psychological violence
I put the mind because, as the name indicates, violence is psychological.

The guide to these homework assignments were the questions outlined in the methodology section taken from Lan and Rocha (2020). Although not all the questions were answered specifically, each student was able to depict diverse violences in their counter-cartographies and describe the feelings and thoughts that they provoked. Most violences were depicted in the head, intimate parts, legs and stomach area, while sexual harassment in public spaces was placed in their ears, as they had heard obscene comments as they walked down the street. The eyes and ears were also pointed out when the students were asked about violent experiences on social media.

With the representations of the body as a territory we were able to achieve results that we believe help empower young women as they are able to identify a range of their emotions and experiences; some had been named for the first time within the educational context. This led to a collective catharsis of sorts that simultaneously upheld sisterhood as a repertoire of safe spaces and horizontal relationships where young women's subjectivities are mirrored between each other's parallel experiences. Moreover, their subjectivities were revindicated in the identification of the possibility to create safe spaces of solidarity.

In Mexico, the first cartographies regarding femicide were part of a national research endeavour that made way for the Ley General de Acceso de las Mujeres a una Vida Libre de Violencia (2007), which names not only the different types of GBV but also the modalities which meant being able to locate the spaces where it manifests. Once these maps were made public, GBV could be understood as a public health issue that must be attended to by the government in order to prevent, sanction, eradicate and repair damages caused. Being able to understand what was happening nationally created space to analyse GBV on local and body scales. In this sense, the products presented here as counter-cartographies and focus groups are part of a historical feminist movement that we can see in academia.

Concluding Remarks

Some of our classroom interventions revealed things that had been covered up in a sense; many students said they had never had the space to talk about these topics at school, while others said they did not know about the laws that exist. Many students expressed that they had never had a space like this, and their silence came with shame and distrust. Some things came to light, like the fact that some of the students might have experienced sexual harassment not only from other students but from teachers and this shows the importance of creating safe spaces for talking about and denouncing violence (Barffusón *et al.*, 2010).

We sustain the recommendation of incorporating the gender perspective starting in middle school and through university since students involved in this study identified their first experiences of GBV before they entered high school. The new education plan of 2024 implemented by the Mexican government has included the mainstreaming of the gender perspective in education. Although we can recognise this as an important step, we were able to determine during our research that teachers generally lack a formal background in feminist topics and therefore seldom incorporate a gendered lens into their curriculum. In this sense, there is a risk that this public policy currently being put in place will stay on paper and not be solidified in the classroom.

On another note, we believe that GBV prevention must be understood through the elements that constitute space. In this way, schools should be understood also as spaces built through social relations which can be transformed in order to guarantee access to justice and the creation of cultural and ethical principles that defy patriarchal traditions within education. In this sense, we believe that feminist geography is a rich field of knowledge, not only for identifying characteristics that create violent spatialities but also for dismantling elements that uphold injustice. Feminist geographic theories and methodologies aid in creating spaces where sisterhood and prevention of violence can grow.

Introducing students to the local legislature on matters of GBV is central for creating consciousness of their rights. Simultaneously, including the concept of *cuerpo-territorio* in order to understand the body as a space has proved to be essential in preventing violences. Understanding violence as a social and systemic construct, guided through a geographic framework, is an essential component in students' critical thought formation. Students were able to see that GBV does not happen because of where they are or how they are dressed but, rather, it exists within the confines of systems of power.

Some of the activities were done in mixed-gender groups, but we found that girls are more likely to share their experiences when they have a safe space with other girls. As a result, we believe that the methodologies should be adapted by dividing classrooms by gender identity so that students can feel more comfortable and understand their experiences first collectively with other girls before expanding their knowledge in mixed-gender groups. This adaptation should be considered in future interventions to create restorative praxis.

An important final point in this research is that although the students involved in this research came from diverse socioeconomic backgrounds, there was not one female student who had not experienced GBV, which supports the fact that, on the one hand, geography can be used to teach and empower young students to take accountability for their actions as active social builders of space and, on the other, to know that their body is a territory that deserves respect and to live a life free of violence. The violence that students identified ranged in intensity and modality but was present across the board, which means it affects everyone in society and it must be addressed. The collective knowledge that was shared and created showed the relevance of geographic methodologies for creating spaces of sisterhood and the prevention of GBV. Classroom interventions like the ones carried out in this research are fundamental for uncovering violence and power dynamics, and for teachers to contribute to an education with a gender perspective that helps students to become citizens who know their rights but also their active roles in creating a social context where gender equity is central for social and intercultural development of infrastructures that create places of peace.

References

Ash, J., Kitchin, R. and Leszczynski, A. (2018) Introducing digital geographies. In J. Ash, R. Kitchin and A. Leszczynski (eds) *Digital Geographies* (pp. 1–10). Sage.

Barffusón, R., Revilla, J. and Carrillo, C. (2010) Aportes feministas a la educación. *Enseñanza e Investigación en Psicología* 15 (2), 357–376. https://www.redalyc.org/pdf/292/29215980008.pdf (accessed 2 July 2024).

Baylina, M., Ortiz, A. and Prats, M. (2008) Conexiones teóricas y metodológicas entre la geografía de género y la infancia. *Scripta Nova* 12 (270), 41.

Cabnal, L. (2010) *Feminismos Diversos: el feminismo comunitario*. Calameo. https://www.calameo.com/books/002488953253b6850c481 (accessed 2 July 2024).

Cámara de Diputados del H. Congreso de la Unión Secretaría General, Secretaría de Servicios Parlamentarios (2023) Ley General de Acceso de las Mujeres a una Vida Libre de Violencia.

Carhuachín, C.G. (2021) Lutero y la peste en Wittenberg. *Ciencia Nueva, revista de Historia y Política* 5 (2), 100–118. https://revistas.utp.edu.co/index.php/historia/article/view/24913 (accessed 2 July 2024).

Damian, A. and Ibarra, M. (2020) La violencia feminicida: Abordaje desde la geografía feminista. *Tlalli revista de investigación en Geografía* 4, 31–52. http://www.revistas.filos.unam.mx/index.php/tlalli/article/view/1366 (accessed 2 July 2024).

De Lauretis, T. (1987) *Technologies of Gender: Essays on Theory, Film, and Fiction*. Indiana University Press. https://www.jstor.org/stable/j.ctt16gzmbr (accessed 2 July 2024).

Diario Oficial de la Federación (2021) Decreto por el que se adicionan diversas disposiciones a la Ley General de Acceso de las Mujeres a una Vida Libre de Violencia. https://www.dof.gob.mx/nota_detalle.php?codigo=5619905&fecha=01/06/2021#gsc.tab=0 (accessed 2 July 2024).

Díaz, M., Rodríguez, J. and Sabaté, A. (1995) *Mujeres, Espacio y Sociedad. Hacia una Geografía del Género*. Editorial Síntesis

Fluri, J. and Piedalue, A. (2017) Embodying violence: Critical geographies of gender, race, and culture. *Gender, Place and Culture* 24 (4), 534–544. https://doi.org/10.1080/0966369X.2017.1329185.

hooks, b. (1984) *Feminist Theory: From Margin to Center* (pp. 43–65). South End Press.

Ibarra García, V. and Escamilla-Herrera, I. (eds) (2016) *Geografías feministas de diversas latitudes*. Instituto de Geografía, UNAM.

Johnson, L. (1994) What future for feminist geography? *Gender, Place and Culture* 1, 103–114.

Katz, C. (2009) Social systems: Thinking about society, identity, power and resistance. In N. Clifford, S. Holloway, S. Rice and G. Vallentine (eds) *Key Concepts in Geography*

(2nd edn, pp. 236–250). Sage. https://www.researchgate.net/publication/287102661 (accessed 2 July 2024).

Lan, D. and Rocha, H.L. (2020) Feminist methodologies for mapping oppressed geographies in Argentina. *Geopauta* 4 (4), 46–67. https://doi.org/10.22481/rg.v4i4.7552 (accessed 2 July 2024).

Massey, D. (2007) Geometrías del poder y la conceptualización del espacio. Lecture given at the Central University of Venezuela, Caracas, 17 September. https://ecumenico.org/geometrias-del-poder-y-la-conceptualizacion-del-es (accessed 2 July 2024).

Mesquita, A. (2018) Counter-cartographies – The insurrection of maps. In Kollektiv Orangotango+ (ed.) *This Is Not an Atlas: A Global Collection of Counter-cartographies* (pp. 26–36). Transcript Verlag. https://doi.org/10.1515/9783839445198-002 (accessed 2 July 2024).

Monroy, J. (2020) Segob: Violencia intrafamiliar aumentó 120% desde la emergencia del Covid-19. *El Economista*, 16 April. https://www.eleconomista.com.mx/politica/Segob-violencia-intrafamiliar-aumento-120-desde-la-emergencia-del-Covid-19-20200416-0111.html (accessed 2 July 2024).

Pan American Health Organization (2020) COVID-19 y violencia contra la mujer. https://iris.paho.org/bitstream/handle/10665.2/52034/OPSNMHMHCovid19200008_spa.pdf?sequence=1&isAllowed=y (accessed 2 July 2024).

Santos, M. (2000) *La naturaleza del espacio. Técnica y tiempo. Razón y emoción.* Ariel.

Spinney, L. (2018) *El jinete pálido. La historia de la epidemia que transformó el mundo.* Crítica.

Valentine, G. (1992) Images of danger: Women's sources of information about the spatial distribution of male violence. *Area* 24, 22–29.

3 Narratives of Change: Young Palestinian Women's Engagement With Short Stories to Promote Dialogue for Peacebuilding

Taghreed El Masry, Fatma Abubaker, Hana El-Badri and Eman Alzaanin

> Peace cannot be kept by force; it can only be achieved by understanding.
> Albert Einstein

Introduction

Too often, we hear about war and conflict, but not enough stories about peace or the dialogues that promote it. While many of these conflict stories often justify the presence of violence and, at times, even injustice, being exposed to new stories, which are rooted in the realities of the people who experience this violence and injustice, might provide a better version of reality and, in turn, offer a pathway to peace (Vermeersch, 2023). Dialogue can be a classical means of dealing constructively with such conflicts (Ropers, 2004). What forms this constructive process in any dialogue is the interaction and communication that take place between those taking part in it, which, through reflection, can generate a change in perspectives (Ropers, 2004).

Recently, arts-based works have emerged as a paradigm in approaching peace and peacebuilding (Hunter & Page, 2014). Many studies have explored the role of art in peacebuilding, including music, dancing, rituals, theatre, youth culture and storytelling (e.g. Anyeko & Shaya Hoffmann, 2020; Coburn, 2011; Hunter, 2005; Hunter & Page, 2014; Jeffrey & Pruitt, 2019; Premaratna & Premaratna, 2018; Senehi, 2008; Stobbe, 2011). Artistic approaches have unique qualities, such as the ability to touch emotions, transcend verbal language barriers and promote creativity (Knight, 2014). Nevertheless, limited research has focused on the use of literature as a medium, particularly storytelling, in understanding and dismantling concepts such as 'peace' and 'peacebuilding' and its potential as a tool for generating dialogue on issues relating to these concepts.

The concepts of dialogue for social transformation proposed by Lederach (1997) and Freire (1996) suggest that art acts as a form of dialogue, which, as we will argue in this chapter, can take the form of storytelling. This research study focuses on a group of young Palestinian women from Gaza, a society which considers verbal dialogue and storytelling valuable approaches for social and cultural change. Scholars have argued for the role of storytelling in helping people living in war zones deal with trauma. In the Palestinian context, storytelling can help young women discuss trauma, and explore conflict and peacebuilding in greater depth.

A report published in 2022 by the Palestinian Central Bureau of Statistics (PCBS) shows that women represent nearly half of the Palestinian population (49%, or 2.63 million) (see Awad, 2022). For some time, Palestinian women have suffered from being in a hostile environment that deprives them of their right to live in dignity, security and peace due to the Israeli occupation. Disturbed by the harsh reality of the occupation that has taken their homeland from them, many have ended up killed, displaced or imprisoned. As a result, Palestinian women have lost their families and spouses and have suffered psychologically, emotionally and economically. Moreover, they continue to suffer after each violent attack in which they see the loss of their homes and loved ones. Women have also been directly subjected to these violent attacks over the last few years. For example, 184 women were arrested and 48 martyred during the Israeli attack on the Gaza Strip in 2021 (Awad, 2022). These violent attacks have resulted in further armed conflict between Israelis and Palestinians, leaving even more women vulnerable and at risk.

The aforementioned report also highlights these women's experiences of living in a patriarchal society, where there are many restrictions on their actions and their efforts to follow their dreams and achieve their goals. Given all the societal injustices that Palestinian women have to endure, it is a challenge for them to attain high levels of success. Only 17% of adult women have access to decent jobs and active participation in the workforce, where their role in decision-making is very limited. For example, women account for only 11% of Palestinian ambassadors, 2% of the heads of local councils and only one woman holds the position of governor (among 16 male governors). In the education sector, only 61% of female graduates complete their higher degrees. Early marriage is still prevalent in Palestinian society: 13.4% of women aged between 20 and 24 had married before they were aged 18. Violence against women mainly involves psychological abuse (58.2%), physical abuse (18.5%) and sexual abuse (9.4%). Generally speaking, Palestinian women face many conflicts in their daily lives, both personally and at the societal level, leaving them more vulnerable.

As we set out on our research endeavour, we were driven by our contemplation and enquiry into the Palestinian situation. Our team of researchers from Gaza, Saudi Arabia, Libya and the UK recognised the significant impact of our varied backgrounds and perspectives on our research approach and analysis. By blending our local insights with broader global perspectives, we aimed to delve into themes of peace, gender and culture within the realm of creative arts amid prolonged crises. So, we pondered the potential outcomes if young Palestinian women were encouraged to take part in conversations revolving around fictional narratives concerning conflict, peace and peacebuilding. What if they were prompted to reflect on their personal histories to envision various avenues through which they could contribute to fostering peace and societal change? What could result from these women, with their diverse experiences, sharing their stories, thoughts, aspirations and dreams with the global community through storytelling? Could such creative endeavours shape and perhaps redefine their perceptions of peace and peacebuilding? If so, in what ways?

Unpacking the Notions of 'Conflict' and 'Peace': A Transformative Approach to Peacebuilding

What is conflict and how does it relate to peace and peacebuilding?

According to peace and conflict scholar Johan Galtung (1969), violence is built into the very structure of societies. Viewing conflict as a future orientation towards creating change, Lederach (1997, 2003) distinguishes between conflict resolution and conflict transformation, arguing that conflict resolution is a short-term approach to solving problems with no potential for creating transformative change. He argues that conflict resolution without transformative change does not allow for a humanistic approach (Maslow, 1954; Rogers, 1995) that emphasises human responsibility and free will, nor does it fulfil human psychological needs, as it takes a negative approach to pursuing change.

An approach based on conflict transformation, on the other hand, asserts that individual conflicts are influenced by larger cultures, structures and systems, and is therefore directed towards creating change. 'The goal of conflict transformation is peace: the capacity to handle conflict creatively and non-violently' (Galtung, 2000: 5). Yet, conflict transformation does not view peace as the absence of conflict, but rather as a continuously evolving and developing quality of relationships (Lederach, 2003: 22). Peace requires an intentional perspective and attitude, a willingness to create and nurture a horizon that provides direction and purpose.

Galtung (1976), taking a rather transformative approach to conflict, introduces the concept of 'peacebuilding', which promotes harmony between people through justice, respect and inclusiveness. He believes that, to achieve sustainable peace, the root causes of violence needed to be addressed, including inequalities, negative attitudes and exclusion. This means that memory and reflection are crucial in identifying causes, and that critical thinking and evaluation regarding the situation are of vital importance. Maiese (2003) and Mitchell (2003) advocate for a holistic view of peacebuilding, which involves both individuals and society as a whole (including its materialistic, sociopolitical, cultural, philosophical, local, international and institutional components). Mitchell (2003) considers peacebuilding to be a future-oriented and intentional process, one that is generated by real or imaginary hope. This view has been criticised for its idealism and hope, since it tends to ignore the political and cultural constraints and imbalances that exist in conflict-divided contexts, thereby maintaining the status quo (Bekerman, 2012). However, some scholars (Gill & Niens, 2014) argue that it can foster a positive pedagogical approach to peacebuilding structured around the idea of creating a shared humanity among societies, thus making the world a better place. Taking a transformative stance, Lederach (1997) views peacebuilding as a process of constructing relationships between all parties involved, with importance given to dialogue and communication. While issues of power might be of concern in certain circumstances (especially in relation to language, dominance and identity), for Galtung (2000), one of the main goals of peace activists in such situations is to facilitate and amplify the voices of those who are not being heard. Whatever the circumstances, dialogue is key to creating peace.

A dialogic approach to peacebuilding and conflict transformation

Taking peacebuilding as a strategy for creating change and, eventually, for promoting peace, we emphasise the opportunities that certain under-represented groups (including young Palestinian women) leverage when it comes to initiating or maintaining dialogue around conflict and the violence resulting from it and argue for its power in creating change.

When it comes to peace studies, dialogue has been heralded as a potential means of resolving social conflict for its ability to communicate across differences and allow the co-creation of new ways of understanding (Bakhtin, 1984). However, the 'ideal of dialogue' is challenged (Burbules, 2000: 1) when the conversation is thwarted by a power imbalance (Freire, 1996). In her influential essay 'Can the Subaltern Speak?', Spivak (1988) argues that the economically dispossessed cannot speak due to the inability of the colonial oppressor to hear or to understand knowledge and perspectives other than through the lens of the oppressor's own Western consciousness and values. This is probably one of the main concerns regarding dialogues that take place in contexts where political and cultural power dynamics seem to be in favour of a particular group, as in the case of the Palestinian–Israeli situation, where the views of the dominant group (the Israelis) are more heard across the world.

In a situation where oppression and unequal power dynamics are deeply ingrained, engaging in meaningful dialogue between the oppressor and the oppressed presents significant challenges, yet it remains crucial for achieving reconciliation and lasting peace. But, for such dialogue to be meaningful, both parties must sincerely commit to confronting uncomfortable realities, acknowledging historical injustices, and collaborating towards a common goal of justice, equality and mutual respect. Certainly, prioritising the exchange of personal experiences initiates a process of introspection and mutual comprehension. Through the open sharing of individual stories, people can gain insight into differing viewpoints, cultivating empathy and a deeper understanding of intricate issues and a more holistic (and realistic) view of the overall narrative around the issue. This fosters the development of trust and empathy, fundamental prerequisites for meaningful conversation and productive efforts towards resolving conflicts and achieving reconciliation. In circumstances such as these, empowering the marginalised and less influential group to express themselves becomes essential for fostering peacebuilding. Promoting agency then becomes the catalyst for instigating change, operating on both individual and collective scales.

This brings us to the central question: what exactly do we mean by 'dialogue'? And which forms of dialogue are we endorsing in this study? While our research is not inherently political, we recognise its political implications and advocate for a human-centred approach to meaningful dialogue. This approach prioritises individual human experiences to catalyse collective change, even within the minds of oppressors. It is an interactive process that emphasises the significance of the conveyed message and its role in sparking reflection and exchange of ideas between both the communicator and the audience. Dialogue, in essence, can manifest in diverse forms and evolve through various stages, including the kind that shapes and reshapes our perspectives – a transformative process culminating in shared understanding and meaning-making. It necessitates critical introspection (of one's reality) and a commitment to actively contribute to creating change through different means.

Critical dialogue for peacebuilding

There has long been debate surrounding power and discourse, particularly in relation to dialogue. Gadamer (1997) suggests that dialogue can both promote prejudices and expand perspectives, while Habermas (1979), on the other hand, argues that dialogue can lead to distortions of meaning, given the nature of words and the meanings that are often attached to them, which can disadvantage weaker groups. Habermas (1984) emphasises the importance of language as a medium for action. For Freire (1996), an ideal dialogue, also known as the 'ideal speech situation' (Habermas, 1979), involves 'conscientisation', whereby both individual consciousness and community consciousness are raised in order to reconceptualise prior perceptions which have come to be understood as 'normal' or inevitable. Furthermore, Freire's *Pedagogy of the Oppressed* (1996) advocates for dialogue through reflection and action. This assumes an approach that values language, whether oral or written, in the production of ideas that capture the realities of the oppressed in ways that promote an expansion of perspectives. What makes this a transformative approach is the fact that it is the oppressed who take on the responsibility of creating their own discourse by voicing their own realities to the rest of the world.

Freire's dialogic pedagogy also raises questions about the role of education in promoting peace and whether it can serve as a transformative tool for peacebuilding. This suggests that young learners can contribute to future strategies for change, since the way adults use this tool will ultimately have an impact on how change in society is construed. By acknowledging the communicative power of art, especially narratives, to connect people and encourage joint meaning-making, storytelling can also become an important dialogic tool for creating change.

Storytelling as a form of artistic dialogue

Narratives are 'storied ways of knowing and communicating' (Jupp, 2006: 186) that can create dialogue because they are a reflection of our reality. They allow for cognitive and emotional growth and the construction of new realities as we connect between the past and the present. Our ability to make such connections can help us reimagine memories of the past and reconstruct more positive futures (Flaherty, 2012). Through storytelling, people can communicate those realities (both real and imaginary) with others, fostering a deeper connection with and understanding of their emotions relating to those memories.

Storytelling allows people to voice their thoughts and ideas. It gives the underrepresented recognition and spreads awareness, eventually starting up conversations around particular topics. Stories usually draw on the different complex issues that humans experience and engage with, including conflicts, past traumas and the consequences of war and violence. Drawing on intellect and emotion, stories offer a creative means for making sense of the world around us (Vygotsky, 2004). Responding to stories allows us to reflect on issues, problems and conflicts, eventually leading to the reconstruction of our views and understandings. Hence, stories and storytelling have been used as an approach to peacebuilding (Flaherty, 2012).

In 2005, Lederach wrote about the need for 'restorying', which goes beyond the simple instrumental use of popular reinterpretations of a conflict to create breakthroughs in mediation. Restorying, as Lederach explains, is an attempt to find a 'deep narrative' or a 'deeper social story and meaning, not just of what happened, but how stories are connected to a more profound journey of discovering what these events mean for who we are as both local and global communities' (Lederach, 2005: 147). In contexts like Palestine, where war and violence are perpetuated, understanding the reality of conflict, peace and peacebuilding becomes a social story, and attempts to communicate this story are of great importance not only for communication ends but also for starting a dialogue that can eventually lead to mutual understanding between teller and receiver.

Research Design and Recruitment

Guided by the notions of constructivism, this project explores the role of the dialogic approach in understanding conflict, peace and peacebuilding among young Palestinian women. It investigates how the participants reconceptualise these constructs and transform their knowledge through stories. As a qualitative study, it focuses on how meaning is constructed through reflection and discussion of past experiences (Cohen *et al.*, 2000; Merriam, 2009).

Russell and Kelly (2002) argue that the goal of research is to raise consciousness, which sometimes requires educating participants to empower them to become critical thinkers. Hence, our main goal in this project was to find 'creative ways to change the story being told, which may trigger internal changes in perception' (Knight, 2014: 92). Our aim was to get the participants to validate their knowledge, personal experience and feelings, and to examine how artistic expression, through story writing, could be useful for reconceptualising their understanding and improving their self-agency as communicators. Moreover, any generalisations, even within the same context, are open to scrutiny, as knowledge and how we make sense of it are constantly changing because of how we interact with and respond to it and the people around us (Lincoln & Guba, 2013).

The project involved a variety of activities, including workshops on conflict, peace and peacebuilding; creative writing; group discussions; written reflections; and focus group interviews.

Participant recruitment

The research participants were a group of female graduate and undergraduate students majoring in English language at Al-Israa' University, aged between 20 and 24. They were all invited to submit a piece of creative writing for assessment. They were provided with a visual prompt and asked to write a story of 300–500 words. Participants were prompted to consider elements such as the setting, characters, plot and resolution. One image depicted a boy walking past a war-damaged building (Figure 3.1), while another showed a young man celebrating triumphantly on a football field. Following an evaluation of the students' writing samples, 12 individuals were chosen to participate in the study. These selected participants

Figure 3.1 A visual prompt for the pre-enrolment creative writing task

were given an information sheet outlining the research's purpose and were asked to sign a consent form before taking part in the study.

Data generation

To gather data for the study, a total of eight three-hour workshops were delivered over two months (December 2022 and January 2023), which included both group and pair work (Figure 3.2). Participants were required

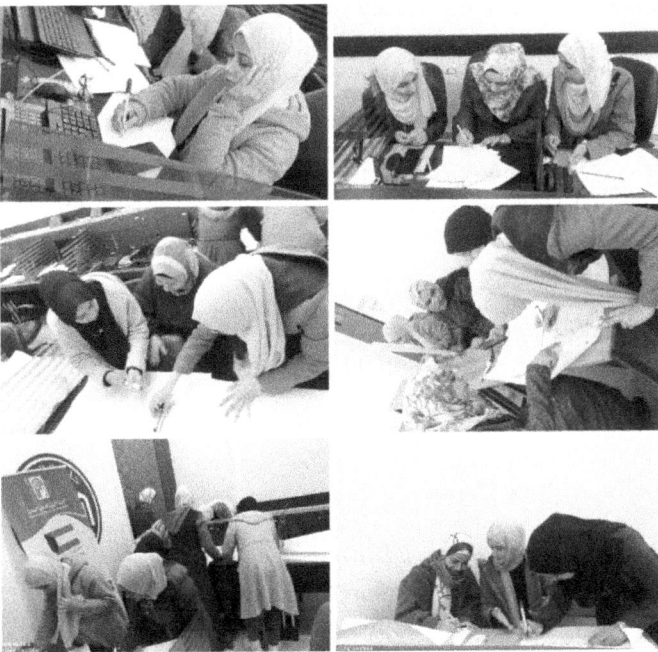

Figure 3.2 The creative writing workshops

to provide personal responses to texts, describe personal experiences and offer opinions to build on each other's views and collectively construct meaning. Field notes and written reflections were made during the first seven workshops. The following is a description of the eight workshops:

Workshop 1: 'Peace begins with us: Defining conflict, peace and peacebuilding'

The introductory workshop was aimed at building a community of learning in which individual responses and the taking on of different perspectives were welcomed. The discussion started with the eliciting of a basic understanding of the concepts of 'conflict', 'peace' and 'peacebuilding', and establishing the relationship between conflict and peace.

Workshop 2: 'I fill my mind with peace: War is never a good idea!'

This workshop focused on the effects of war and violence on people in general, especially women. Participants read the short story *Peace of Mind*, which is about a 12-year-old Syrian girl named Nour. The story, posted by Peace Direct on 12 May 2022, shows how war can destroy people's lives, homes and communities. Participants explored in greater depth issues relating to conflict and peace, and considered ways of taking a transformative approach. A set of activities were assigned that included conflict transformation and peacebuilding tools.

Workshop 3: 'Compassionate action: Responding to stories of war'

Workshop 3 focused on reading and analysing a short story called *An Episode of War* by Stephen Crane, which deals with war and the everlasting effects it leaves behind. After analysing the main elements of the story and the writing style, we discussed aspects of compassionate action and how to turn trauma into a powerful tool for positive change and healing. The discussions were aimed at inspiring and fostering an understanding of how people could find paths of compassionate action and, hence, the role of storytelling in working towards peace.

Workshop 4: 'Women and conflict'

Workshop 4 concentrated on the effects of war and conflict on women in particular, and how women can show resilience by finding inner peace. We discussed how to organise ideas in a coherent way by drawing on a story entitled *Dates and Bitter Coffee* written by a young Palestinian woman, Donia Elamal Ismaeel.

Workshop 5: 'Creative writing I: Starting to write'

In the fifth workshop, we explored differences between fact and fiction, and how the two types of literature can be interlinked. Then, we examined characters and characterisation, how to develop characters and how to start writing. The workshop also emphasised the importance of keeping a notebook to take notes and prepare ideas for writing to share and discuss with others in the following workshop.

Workshop 6: 'Creative writing II: Developing a writing habit'

In the sixth workshop, participants were invited to think more about what inspires them to write in order to create an interesting storyline. They talked about the stories they intended to write, their initial ideas and ways to move forwards. This workshop also introduced the concept of group writing, and explored how shared ideas can be useful in developing a storyline. Participants were given three weeks after this workshop to prepare and write the first drafts of their stories.

Workshop 7: 'Writing is editing'

This workshop was devoted to getting participants to review and reflect on their writing. It was an opportunity for them to exchange feedback with their peers and open up horizons for their imaginations. Some participants found themselves stuck at points in the middle of their stories or did not know how to end them. Others needed suggestions regarding symbols they could use in their stories, and how to integrate dialogue and descriptions.

Workshop 8: The focus groups

The workshops utilised a dialogic approach to explore participants' experiences and thinking relating to conflict, peace and peacebuilding. These dialogues also intensified our constructive process, and developed our ability to make meaning of the research and what it was intended to achieve – a constructive process that ultimately led to a transformation in our thinking. The questions were aimed at gathering participants' imaginative stories, lived experiences and personal views relating to their realities and those of Palestinians. The main topics discussed included their initial understandings of peace and peacebuilding, the value of dialogues in shaping their thinking, meaningful transformation in Gaza, the participants' roles in the process and the writing process itself. In addition, the participants assessed the writing process and sought feedback on their stories and themes. They also discussed the benefits of storytelling in developing their understandings of higher-level morals in relation to peace and peacebuilding, and whether storytelling could connect them with the world and showcase the unique experiences of young Palestinian women.

Data analysis

All workshops, including the focus groups, were recorded audio and transcribed verbatim for subsequent analysis. The data were then thematically organised by grouping related topics and linking the issues raised. These included: existing perceptions of conflict, peace and peacebuilding;

factors influencing societal change; the significance of dialogue in redefining these concepts; the role of storytelling in addressing and conveying ideas related to conflict analysis, resolution and transformation; and how these connect to peacebuilding efforts. All participants' real names were substituted with pseudonyms to ensure anonymity and confidentiality of their responses. The ensuing discussion is informed by our observations from the project and is grounded in the written narratives, comments and feedback obtained from the workshops.

Discussion of Findings: The Transformative Power of Dialogue in Understanding Conflict, Peace and Peacebuilding

Analysis of the data revealed that the dialogues played an effective role in understanding the concept of peace and engaging the participants in a reflective process. One of the main themes that emerged from the data was the shift in participants' conceptualisations of conflict, peace and peacebuilding due to the dialogic exchanges in this study. Initially, participants perceived 'conflict' as connoting war and violence due to the recurring Israeli military attacks on Gaza and the West Bank (the main Palestinian geographical communities). The participants highlighted the countless restrictions on Palestinians' lives, like the continuous siege of their borders, trade and industry. For Layla, '"Conflict" refers to violence, tension, attacks that may culminate in war, like when the Israeli occupation attacks us and bombards our houses' (workshop 1).

The young women agreed that the destruction of a person's will and power to look to the future was a major issue resulting from armed conflict. Layla believed that 'conflict and war disrupt our daily routines, making us feel unsafe, depressed, uncertain and worried' (workshop 1). Sara also reflected on her own personal experiences, explaining how, as a result of such conflict, 'people's dreams and hopes are shattered because of the continuing attacks'. She stated that this prevents them from living in peace and achieving their full potential (workshop 1). Participants also stressed the material and affective dimensions as part of the devastating impacts of conflict and violence on people's lives and wellbeing. They associated conflict with trauma, displacement, loss of loved ones and psychological distress. Rawan lamented: 'With every attack, hundreds of people in Gaza lose their homes and move to live in tents or temporary housing. How can individuals focus on achieving their dreams and goals when they keep suffering from displacement and the loss of their loved ones?'

Participants recognised the role of power dynamics when talking about conflict and peace. As Zinab explained, 'When you live in a country colonised by a tyrannical foreign regime, you are deprived of all your rights to develop and grow as a country. The coloniser will make sure that you surrender to them, no matter what' (workshop 1). In the case of the Israeli–Palestinian conflict, it is crucial to acknowledge the power imbalance as Israel has vast military and economic superiority, while Palestinians have lived under decades of occupation, discrimination and violence. This power imbalance makes any justice or lasting peace difficult, as the weaker are often dominated and marginalised, and their needs and rights are not fully addressed. This confirms the arguments made by Freire (1996) and Spivak (1988) that such power imbalance leads to an asymmetrical view of what peace is and how it can be constructed. Hence, it is crucial that the oppressed have opportunities to express their views about peace and peacebuilding.

In the discussion, Sara referred to a rather narrow view of external conflict and peace. The participants generally agreed that external peace cannot be found in Gaza because of the occupation. Sara noted: 'Peace isn't easy to find; we have to undergo many struggles to find it'. For others, peace can only be found in nature. Rawan stated: 'But we can find it in the sea and flowers, when we look at the colour blue and the many colours in flowers'. As the teacher continued the discussion, she noticed how engaging participants in respectful, open dialogue led to deeper understanding of different perspectives and experiences and developed nuanced and empathetic views of these complex issues.

After the third workshop, different meanings of conflict, peace and peacebuilding started to emerge that deviated from ideas related to war to include wider social and psychological aspects, encompassing every element of the participants' lives, including their mental states, interactions with others and overall wellbeing. As Hiba observed, 'If conflict includes wars, daily obstacles, restricting social traditions and norms and psychological impediments, then peace has a wider meaning than we had previously understood' (workshop 3). Layla described how the workshops had changed her perspective, as follows:

> I realised that peace is a much broader concept. It is related to every aspect of our lives, including our thoughts, interactions with others and our mental state. We need to think peacefully to see peace in all aspects of our lives. Now, I realise that peace is related to concepts such as dignity, love, harmony, absence of hostility and wellbeing. (Workshop 8)

Hence, peace is not just the absence of war or violence but, rather, a positive and proactive process that involves addressing inequalities and promoting social justice, which means targeting the poverty, discrimination and human rights violations that can fuel conflict and contribute to social unrest (Cantle, 2018). This supports the view proposed by Lederach (2003) and Galtung (1976) that peace encompasses wider social and cultural components.

It was clear from the discussion that personal responses and communication were essential for understanding peace. Increased interaction built bridges of thoughts, allowing participants to consider new ideas and possibilities. The dialogic approach, which requires the use of skills like listening, turn-taking, negotiation, reflection and collaboration, can help build trust, reduce tensions and create more peaceful and collaborative communities (Joseph, 2015). In a constructive environment, the participants sought transformative peace, oriented to the future and resulting in stability and prosperity, rather than the immediate absence of war.

Initially, the participants' understanding of peacebuilding tended to include more temporary notions relating to conflict, where the main focus was on the immediate damage resulting from problems. Sara, taking a more static approach to peacebuilding that views peace as the 'end state', argued that if war and conflict were absent, peace would be inevitable. All of the participants thought that a way out of such uncertainty, fear and loss of hope was an unrealistic dream. This resulted from their firsthand experiences of the destruction and death caused by conflict. Rabab believed they were 'helpless and incapable of inducing any changes' (workshop 2) in their context.

However, later on in the project, participants framed peace as multidimensional and peacebuilding as a comprehensive strategy to encourage lasting peace. Their experiences and knowledge of these concepts and their needs, both internal (as individuals) and external (as Palestinians), influenced their collective understanding of peace. These views resonated with the ideas put forward by Lederach (2003) and Freire (1996) that frame peacebuilding as a transformative tool that addresses injustices, helping people who are longing for dignity, human rights and, more importantly, transforming personal conflict and difficulties into something positive.

Analysis of the focus group data from workshop 8 also revealed the effectiveness of the reflective process in which learners engaged during their dialogic exchanges, as it enabled them to develop an understanding of peace and their role in peacebuilding. Sanaa noted: 'When we listened to the others and to their opinions, that changed our opinions. We understood some aspects that we hadn't thought of or didn't even know about.' Fatima's opinion of the process was that 'Overall, it can be a powerful way to develop ideas and shape thinking. By fostering open and respectful dialogue, we can learn from one another and work towards a more nuanced and informed understanding of any topic'. As Zinab commented, dialogues enabled them to build trust and foster mutual understanding and respect.

Zinab summarised the impact of the dialogues as follows: 'I guess that now we have a different understanding of conflict, then we will approach resolving it and its causes differently' (workshop 7). Similarly, Israa observed:

> Initially, I thought that peacebuilding was difficult to achieve. But now, I realise that peacebuilding is a process that can be applied to every aspect of our lives. It involves how we raise our children, how we observe and accept the struggles we face, how we interact with our communities, and how

we create opportunities despite facing difficulties. It's not impossible to achieve peacebuilding since it's related to our everyday lives. (Workshop 7)

One participant suggested that conflict transformation involves using conflict to create something positive and different, while others emphasised the role of tragedy or difficult situations, which can serve as incentives or motivation to work hard to improve one's life. As Lederach (2003) explains, this form of motivation is what truly characterises conflict transformation, separating it from other concepts like 'conflict resolution'. Despite the participants perceiving war as causing disruption and preventing their pursuit of rights, they aimed to challenge such conditions. With this mindset, they showed resilience and willingness to challenge the status quo and seek change in their circumstances. As Hiba argued, 'Women's participation in peacebuilding processes can contribute to greater gender equality, improved governance and long-term stability' (workshop 8). Such an understanding was reflected in the participants' short stories about different types of young women who managed to transform their lives. Those women emerged from their struggles stronger and more determined to succeed (see Figure 3.3).

These young women viewed themselves and their roles in creating change and transforming conflict from a position of power that involves collaboration between men and women. Their view is especially important given that many conflicting issues are socially situated and culturally maintained (Taylor & Miller, 1994). Indeed, as Fatima commented, 'Young Palestinian women face a variety of difficulties. They have limited access to education and employment opportunities, but they are strong, resilient and determined to make a positive impact in their communities' (workshop 8).

One participant believed that conflict transformation includes character development and the resolution of conflicts within one's life. Such transformation involves deep exploration of one's internal conflicts, values and beliefs. It also entails empathising with others, challenging assumptions and finding creative solutions to complex problems. Sara

Figure 3.3 A digital depiction of the short story 'The story of Watan'

Figure 3.4 A digital depiction of the short story 'Talent creates opportunity'

stated, 'If I don't have any opportunities regarding what I study, I will search for something different. I will change everything to make an impact' (workshop 8). This new realisation was reflected in one of the participants' short stories, 'Talent creates opportunity' (Figure 3.4). The protagonist in this story, Amal, used her talent for painting, instead of her study major, to overcome unemployment and build a successful career with the help of a charitable organisation.

Rafeef, the protagonist in a story called 'Dim light', lost her parents in the war and became disabled. However, she managed to overcome societal perspectives (e.g. constant pity and sympathy) to start up her own foundation. Another story ('On the path of Salam') was about a girl called Salam (which means peace), who lost her father and was forced into early marriage with a rich husband. With all that she had gone through, Salam kept focused on her future and was able to pursue her dream of studying abroad, and then come back home to set up a foundation to help vulnerable women. Similarly, the story 'Gaza: The beauty and the pain' depicts a young woman who was forced into marriage, then lost her husband, started a small home-based cooking business and eventually fulfilled her dream of completing her degree and opening her own restaurant and also becoming the founder of a women's support group. Those stories, and others not mentioned here, support the argument put forward by Mitchell (2003) and Maiese (2003) that personal perspectives can promote society's moral growth when both individuals and society work together, thus confirming the holistic nature of peacebuilding.

To sum up this point, the conversations emphasise the complex nature of conflict and personal experiences of finding peace. Conflict and peace are multidimensional concepts, which each person interprets differently. The group's reflections on finding peace within oneself are insightful, confirming Danesh's (2006) integrative theory of peace (ITP), which views peace as a psychological, social, political, ethical and spiritual state. This concept is relevant to various human aspects and relationships.

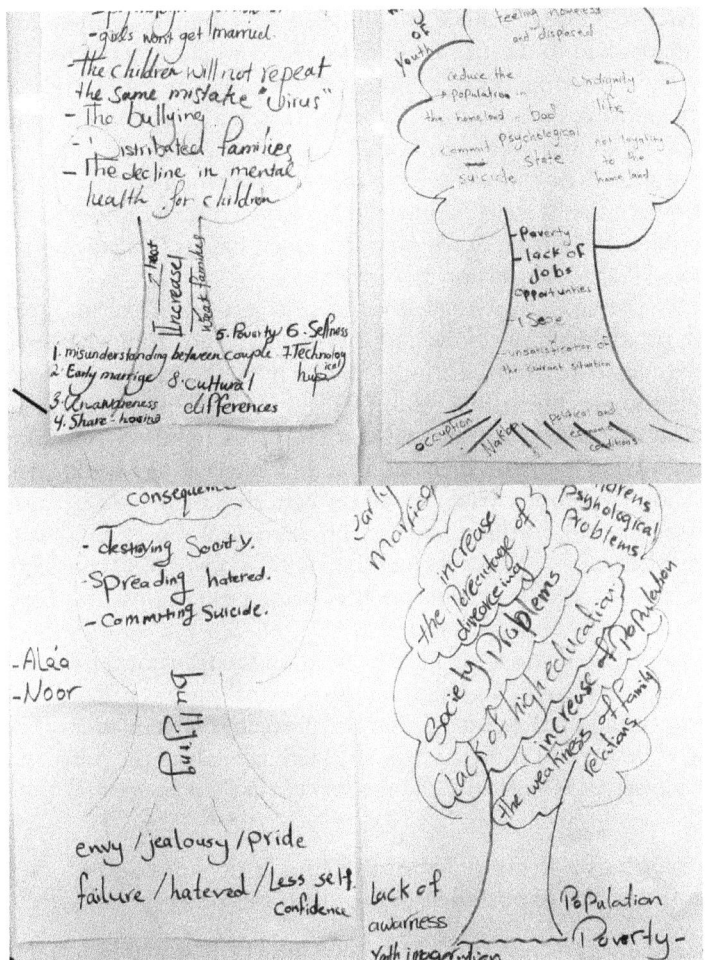

Figure 3.5 Conflict tree tool

The research highlights the importance of education in promoting peace and peacebuilding, challenging preconceived notions and expanding understanding. The participants' experiences during the project led to a deeper and more comprehensive understanding of peace and peacebuilding. As Maryam noted in workshop 8, 'This project has been a life-changing experience.... I have moved from a naive conceptualisation to a deeper and more comprehensive one.' Continuous learning and engagement with diverse perspectives are crucial for a more nuanced understanding. Empowering participants to be agents of change and creating comprehensive and effective initiatives for peacebuilding can lead to a more comprehensive and effective approach. Reflecting on a conflict analysis activity in which participants had to use the 'conflict tree tool' to identify the root causes, effects and consequences of conflicts (see Figure 3.5), Hiba said: 'What I liked the most in the sessions is learning the strategy of conflict resolution through the conflict tree tool. It made me reflect on my personal conflicts and recognise their true underlying causes' (workshop 7). Another participant thought the strategy had helped her gain a broader understanding of her conflicts by putting down on paper 'their causes, effects and possible solutions' (Sanaa, workshop 3).

This strategy involves self-reflection, introspection and personal growth to address and resolve intrapersonal and environmental conflicts, challenges and tensions. Fatima noted: 'If we continued to have such sessions and, of course, involve other Palestinian young women, I am sure people in our community would start to focus more on bettering their lives by solving many of their internal and external day-to-day conflicts' (workshop 7). People would focus on bettering their lives because they would be able to consume conflict in its natural sense, as a motor for change (Lederach, 2003). Habermas (1997) advocates consciousness-raising so that people reconceptualise prior perceptions that have been understood as 'normal' or inevitable.

In the above section, we have focused on the transformative power of the dialogic approach, highlighting the new realisations of conflict, peace and peacebuilding that emerged in the participants' narratives. The next section is devoted to showing how storytelling enabled the participants to view themselves as potential change-makers in their society.

Storytelling as a strategy for promoting critical dialogue (communicating experiences, emotions and hopes)

The data gathered from the study provided valuable insights into the role of literature in promoting transformative actions in response to conflict. Based on Lederach's (1997) and Freire's (1996) conceptualisations of dialogue, art was given prominence in the project as a means of generating dialogue. Literature has the potential to reflect the diversity and richness of experiences, and can contribute to positive social change and peacebuilding (Cobb, 2013; Lederach, 2005). The participants suggested some possible transformative actions they could undertake, such as writing and publishing literature, that could be used to reflect their experiences and perspectives.

For the participants, women's personal transformation means embracing personal growth, self-acceptance and developing skills to navigate conflicts in a constructive and transformative way. By transforming their conflicts, women can cultivate greater self-awareness, enhance their wellbeing and foster healthier relationships with others (Lederach, 2003), as reflected in the participants' creative writing.

Figure 3.6 Scenes from 'Dim light'

Portrayals of Palestinian women's resilience is to be found in the short stories. The main issues tackled in the stories relate to the challenges Palestinian women face in their everyday lives as a result of the armed conflict and social norms in place in Gaza. The narratives depict the trauma of losing loved ones because of random bombings and the killing of civilians. For example, this can be seen in the story 'Dim light', in which a young Palestinian girl (Rafeef) has her legs amputated after she has survived a violent attack on her home that kills her parents and turns her house into ruins. This causes her to struggle alone in life, both financially and emotionally (see Figure 3.6).

In a story entitled 'On 23rd July', a mother lost her husband to the Israeli occupation. Similarly, Zinab's story ('To my brother') was about a young girl who donated her bone marrow to save her brother's life. Despite being prosecuted by the Israeli authorities, she risked her life to cross the border to the West Bank and undergo a bone marrow transplant procedure but was then arrested and imprisoned without any charges or trial, and later found out that her brother had died. Other stories focused on such themes as early marriage, being a widow in Palestinian society, and immigration due to unemployment and armed conflict.

The participants used literature as a means to express their feelings, thoughts and traumas through storytelling. They focused on universal themes like death, grief and love to envision themselves and empathise with others. This interactive process allowed them to help their international readers better understand their reality as Palestinians. The reader–writer relationship (O'Reilly, 2015; Smith, 2004) is more thorough than intellectual understanding, giving literature its communicative power as a tool for imaginative thinking (Abubaker, 2017; Langer, 1991). By reading about their shared experiences, the participants engaged in critical thinking, questioning their experiences and those of others (Matarasso, 1997).

In the group discussion during workshop 8, the participants observed that storytelling can be a powerful tool for peacebuilding, as it allows them to share their experiences and perspectives, build empathy and understanding, and promote dialogue and reconciliation (Benjamin & Sean, 2015). By encouraging young Palestinian women to write and share their stories, this project was intended to build bridges between communities and to promote mutual respect and understanding. Additionally, by writing these stories, it was hoped that the participants would be given a voice and be able to challenge stereotypes and misconceptions, and promote human rights and social justice.

The participants called for universal efforts to prioritise the wellbeing of Palestinian citizens, urging peace and justice for those affected by the conflict in Gaza and Palestine. They emphasised the suffering of innocent civilians, particularly women, and highlighted the sociocultural conflicts faced by Palestinian women. These include gender inequality, violence, discrimination and lack of access to education. One of the stories focused on early marriage, underlining the emotional challenges faced by young Palestinian women and girls, and the emotional journeys they must undergo as a result of political or social conflict. The focus of these stories was on the emotional journeys undertaken by young women and girls, highlighting the emotional impacts of political or social conflict on their lives and personal identities.

Many of the themes depicted in these stories encompassed notions of hope, resilience and the need to create change by taking action. This action might take the form of civil activism, helping one's community and others in need, pursuing one's dreams (including education), entrepreneurship or, at times, looking for a better life and achieving these dreams elsewhere. Analysing the stories revealed the participants' understanding of the situation faced by Palestinian women and their visions of what women were able to achieve. As Veronese *et al.* (2021) point out, Palestinian women have shown resilience and resourcefulness in the face of adversity, and have formed networks of support and advocacy. Women's organisations and grassroots movements have been instrumental in advancing women's rights and promoting social change. Changes in thinking and self-realisation are necessary for people to create peace (in all its forms) (Lederach, 2003).

Conclusions and Lessons Learnt

The young women in this study initially conceptualised 'peace' from a political perspective, as being the absence of war and violence. However, by engaging in the project's educational and arts-based activities, they came to understand 'peace' in a more holistic way, as including humanistic and individualistic dimensions, such as human relationships, breaking free of cultural norms and stereotypes, personal values, hopes, dreams, wellbeing and reaching one's full potential. The participants saw themselves as ambassadors of peace, with a responsibility for instilling resilience and hope in others and empowering them to seek change.

The project demonstrated that arts-based dialogue, through reading and writing stories, can encourage young people (particularly women) to engage in critical dialogue about issues of conflict, peace and (in)justice.

However, the data do not reveal in depth the extent to which such dialogue can impact peacebuilding practices in society or how to integrate both cultural and educational institutions in that process.

The findings suggest that there is a need for further research on how arts-based dialogue can promote peacebuilding in Palestinian society. The next step would be to involve key community stakeholders to develop a strategy to integrate both cultural and educational institutions in mapping out a transformative approach that draws on artistic potential in addressing peacebuilding issues. Through participatory methods, young women, members of the community and relevant stakeholders could work together to create initiatives that can lead to peace in Palestine, where women can make a difference and become an important part of the peacebuilding process. Although we do not try in any way to provide any guidelines as to how we can create peace in Palestine or any context with similar conditions, we can, nonetheless, say that for narratives and storytelling to have a transformative value we need to make sure that:

- We build collective power by giving people in crises the recognition they need to see themselves and their future possibilities.
- We ensure that we give voice to the voiceless by making sure that narratives of the disadvantaged/marginalised are heard and weaved into the main narrative.
- We have a good strategy in place, one in which educational and cultural institutions work together and collaborate with external partners to promote peace and advocate for peacebuilding initiatives.
- Stories aim for creating change by reaching the right audiences.

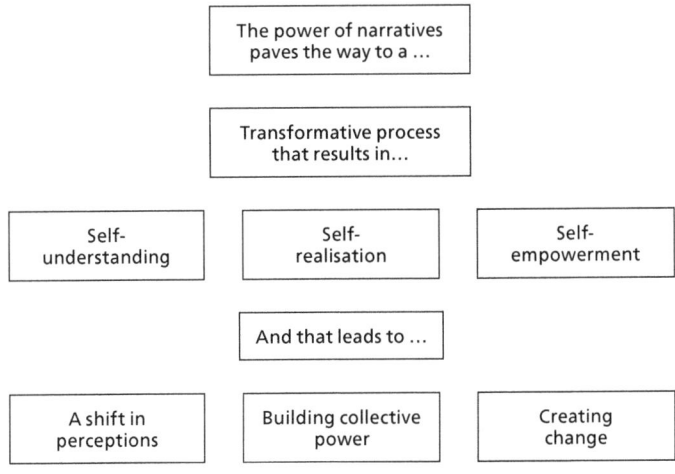

Figure 3.7 Conflict transformation through narrative storytelling

Through this research study we were able to see the power of narratives and their capacity to shift perspectives in a captivating way to change the mindsets of individuals so as to (re)define cultural norms (Figure 3.7). The goal of using narratives was to tell the stories of 12 young Palestinian women as they went through a transformative process of self-understanding, self-realisation and self-empowerment using stories, in order to shift perceptions, build collective power and ultimately create some sort of change. For it is stories that are often said to move people!

References

Abubaker, F. (2017) The road to possibilities: A conceptual model for a program to develop the creative imagination in reading and responding to literary fiction (short stories) in Libyan English as a foreign language (EFL) university classrooms. PhD thesis, University of Glasgow.

Anyeko, K. and Shaya Hoffmann, T. (2020) Storytelling and peacebuilding: Lessons from northern Uganda. In J. Mitchell, G. Vincent, T. Hawksley and H. Cuthbertson (eds) *Peacebuilding and the Arts* (pp. 235–251). Palgrave Macmillan.

Awad, O. (2022) The reality of the Palestinian women on the eve of International Women's Day. *Palestinian Central Bureau of Statistics (PCBS)*, 6 March. https://pcbs.gov.ps/site/512/default.aspx?lang=en&ItemID=4186 (accessed 20 May 2023).

Bakhtin, M. (1984) *Problems of Dostojevskij's Poetics*. Manchester University Press.

Bekerman, Z. (2012) Afterword: Reflecting on critical perspectives of peace education. In P.R. Carr and B.J. Portfilio (eds) *Educating for Peace in a Time of War: Are Schools Part of the Solution or the Problem?* (pp. 271–278). Routledge.

Benjamin, M. and Sean, B. (2015) Peacebuilding and reconciliation through storytelling in Northern Ireland and the border counties of the Republic of Ireland. *Storytelling, Self, Society* 11 (1), 85–110.

Burbules, N.C. (2000) The limits of dialogue as a critical pedagogy. In P. Trifonas (ed.) *Revolutionary Pedagogies: Cultural Politics, Instituting Education, and the Discourse of Theory* (pp. 251–273). Routledge.

Cantle, T. (2018) *Community Cohesion: A New Framework for Race and Diversity*. Springer.

Cobb, S. (2013) *Speaking of Violence: The Politics and Poetics of Narrative in Conflict Resolution*. Oxford University Press.

Coburn, C. (2011) Storytelling as a peacebuilding method. In D.J. Christie (ed.) *The Encyclopedia of Peace Psychology* [online]. Blackwell. https://www.academia.edu/1996602/Storytelling_as_a_Peacebuilding_Method (accessed 25 April 2022).

Cohen, L., Manion, L. and Morrison, K. (2000) *Research Methods in Education* (5th edn). RoutledgeFalmer.

Danesh, H.B. (2006) Towards an integrative theory of peace education. *Journal of Peace Education* 3 (1), 55–78. https://doi.org/10.1080/17400200500532151.

Flaherty, M. (2012) *Peacebuilding with Women in Ukraine: Using Narrative to Envision a Common Future*. Lexington Books.

Freire, P. (1996) *Pedagogy of the Oppressed*. Penguin Books.

Gadamer, H.G. (1997) *Truth and Method* (2nd edn). Continuum.

Galtung, J. (1969) Violence, peace, and peace research. *Journal of Peace Research* 6 (3), 167–191. https://doi.org/10.1177/002234336900600301 (accessed 2 July 2024).

Galtung, J. (1976) Three approaches to peace: Peacekeeping, peacemaking, peacebuilding. In J. Galtung (ed.) *Peace, War and Defense: Essays in Peace Research* (pp. 297–298). Christian Ejlers.

Galtung, J. (2000) Conflict transformation by peaceful means (the transcend method). Curriculum presented at United Nations Disaster Management Training Programme. https://www.transcend.org/pctrcluj2004/TRANSCEND_manual.pdf (accessed 22 May 2022).
Gill, S. and Niens, U. (2014) Education as humanisation: A theoretical review on the role of dialogic pedagogy in peacebuilding education. *Compare: A Journal of Comparative and International Education* 44 (1), 10–31.
Habermas, J. (1979) *Communication and the Evolution of Society* (T. McCarthy, trans.). Heinemann.
Habermas, J. (1984) *Theory of Communicative Action* (vol. 1). Beacon Press
Hunter, M.A. (2005) Young people and performance in Australia and New Zealand. *Australasian Drama Studies* 47, 140–158.
Hunter, M.A. and Page, L. (2014) What is 'the good' of arts-based peacebuilding? Questions of value and evaluation in current practice. *Peace and Conflict Studies* 21 (2), 117–134.
Jeffrey, E.R. and Pruitt, L.J. (2019) Dancing it out: Building positive peace. In K. Bond (ed.) *Dance and the Quality of Life* (pp. 475–493). Springer.
Joseph, D. (2015) *Reflective Structured Dialogue: A Dialogic Approach to Peacebuilding.* University of Massachusetts Boston and Collaboration Specialists Project.
Jupp, V. (ed.) (2006) *The Sage Dictionary of Social Research Methods.* Sage.
Knight, H. (2014) Articulating injustice: An exploration of young people's experiences of participation in a conflict transformation programme that utilises the arts as a form of dialogue. *Compare: A Journal of Comparative and International Education* 44 (1), 77–96.
Langer, J.A. (1991) Discussion as exploration: Literature and the horizon of possibilities. Centre on the Learning and Teaching of Literature Report (version 6.3). Unpublished manuscript, National Research Centre on English Learning and Achievement, New York.
Lederach, J.P. (1997) *Building Peace: Sustainable Reconciliation in Divided Societies.* United States Institute of Peace Press.
Lederach, J.P. (2003) *The Little Book of Conflict Transformation.* Good Books.
Lederach, J.P. (2005) *The Moral Imagination: The Art and Soul of Building Peace.* Oxford University Press.
Lincoln, Y.S. and Guba, E.G. (2013) *The Constructivist Credo.* Left Coast Press.
Maiese, M. (2003) Peacebuilding: Beyond intractability. http://www.beyondintractability.org/essay/peacebuilding (accessed 29 September 2023).
Maslow, A.H. (1954) *Motivation and Personality.* Harper & Row.
Matarasso, F. (1997) Use or ornament. *The Social Impact of Participation in the Arts* 4 (2), 34–41.
Merriam, S.B. (2009) *Qualitative Research: A Guide to Design and Implementation* (2nd edn). Jossey-Bass.
Mitchell, G. (2003) Conflict resolution: Ireland and beyond. *Irish Studies in International Affairs* 14, 3–8.
O'Reilly, M. (2015) Why women? Inclusive security and peaceful societies. https://www.inclusivesecurity.org/publication/why-women-inclusive-security-and-peaceful-societies/ (accessed 15 May 2022).
Palestinian Central Bureau of Statistics (PCBS) (2022) https://www.pcbs.gov.ps/default.aspx
Peace Direct (2022) Peace of mind. https://www.peacedirect.org/mental-health-peacebuilding (accessed 13 June 2023).
Premaratna, N. and Premaratna, N. (2018) *Theatre for Peacebuilding.* Springer.
Rogers, C.R. (1995) *On Becoming a Person: A Therapist's View of Psychotherapy.* Houghton Mifflin.
Ropers, N. (2004) From resolution to transformation: The role of dialogue projects. In A. Austin, M. Fischer and N. Ropers (eds) *Transforming Ethnopolitical Conflict.* VS Verlag für Sozialwissenschaften. https://doi.org/10.1007/978-3-663-05642-3_13 (accessed 3 July 2024).

Russell, G.M. and Kelly, N.H. (2002) Research as interacting dialogic processes: Implications for reflexivity. Paper presented at the Forum Qualitative Sozialforschung/Forum: Qualitative Social Research.

Senehi, J. (2008) Building peace: Storytelling to transform conflicts constructively. In J.D. Dennis, S. Byrne, I. Sandole-Staroste and J. Senehi (eds) *Book of Conflict Analysis and Resolution* (pp. 227–240). Routledge.

Smith, F. (2004) *Understanding Reading: A Psycholinguistic Analysis of Reading and Learning to Read* (6th edn). Lawrence Erlbaum Associates.

Spivak, G. (1988) Can the subaltern speak? In C. Nelson and L. Grossberg (eds) *Marxism and the Interpretation of Culture* (pp. 271–313). University of Illinois Press.

Stobbe, S.P. (2011) The Soukhouan ritual: The legacy of Lao women in conflict resolution. *Critical aspects of Gender in Conflict Resolution, Peacebuilding, and Social Movements* 32, 45–73.

Taylor, A. and Miller, J.B. (1994) *Conflict and Gender*. Hampton Press.

Vermeersch, P. (2023) Narratives of change and repair: How the study of storytelling in the social sciences can inspire peacebuilding research. *Peacebuilding* 11 (1), 104–109.

Veronese, G., Sousa, C. and Cavazzoni, F. (2021) Survival and resilience among Palestinian women: A qualitative analysis using individual and collective life events calendars. *Violence Against Women* 27 (6–7), 900–917.

Vygotsky, L.S. (1978) *Mind in Society: The Development of Higher Psychological Process*. Cambridge University Press.

Vygotsky, L.S. (2004) Imagination and creativity in childhood. *Journal of Russian and East European Psychology* 42 (1), 7–97 (original work published 1930).

4 Creative Corridors: Peace, Inclusivity and Engagement with Persons with Disabilities

Chipo Basopo, Simbarashe Mudhokwani and Rashiwe Chipurunyenye

Introduction and Chapter Structure

There are an estimated 1.3 billion people, about 16% of the global population, living with some form of disability (World Health Organization, 2024). The developing nations face more challenges in solving the issues affecting persons with disabilities compared with developed ones (United Nations Department of Economic and Social Affairs, 2024). Though policies exist in African states, their implementation is limited by lack of funding, weak advocacy, corruption, bureaucracy and lack of political will (Moyo, 2023).

The numbers of persons with disabilities are increasing due to the ageing population and a general increase in the prevalence of non-communicable diseases. The United Nations Convention on the Rights of Persons with Disability (UNCRPD) as an instrument became the point of reference for matters to do with rights of people with disabilities (PwDs). The 2030 Sustainable Development Goals (SDGs) framework and its targets explicitly refer to the inclusion of PwDs in the development agenda.

On 29 January 2018, the African Union (AU) adopted the Africa Disability Protocol (ADP), which is meant to bring unique solutions to the issues faced by PwDs within the African continent. These instruments and frameworks have been put in place appreciating that PwDs are more likely to experience adverse socioeconomic, cultural and political outcomes in education, health and employment opportunities, as they face higher poverty rates and stigmatisation.

Africa is lagging behind where respect for human rights and democracy is concerned. This can be traced from the formation of its continental body, the Organization for African Unity (OAU), in 1963. The old system of the African community accorded human rights based on one's responsibility and ability to contribute to community development, without any help. PwDs, therefore, were viewed as incompetent and unable to join with others fully and equally, resulting in their exclusion from participating within the community, especially in decision-making. Societal beliefs that disability is a curse see some families resorting to hiding their PwDs to avoid humiliation and accusations of witchcraft. By way of example, it has been noted in the Tanzanian context (Lapidos, 2009; Rao, 2017) that people with albinism, including children, have been exposed to rituals and brutal killings for wealth; in Tanzania, those with albinism constitute an estimated 1 in 1400 of the population (Lapidos, 2009). According to the UNCRPD Committee on the Rights of PwDs, it is not the disability that comes with an impairment but it is the environment that is not accessible for all, which acts as a barrier to their full participation (Moyo, 2023).

The provision for PwDs in the AU Charter in 2000 and the subsequent introduction of the UNCRPD – which documents the legal human rights of PwDs – and the immediate joining of nations to the Convention has changed the narrative of PwDs within the African continent. There has been a favourable response by nations through the domestication of the protocol into their laws, with three clear aims to promote PwDs' dignity, empowerment and equality.

Around 7% of the Zimbabwean population, or 1.3 million people, live with a disability (Kuper *et al.*, 2015). Zimbabwe was one of the first countries to ratify the UNCRPD, in 2013, and remains one of the few countries in Africa with legislation that specifically caters for PwDs. By domesticating the Convention, the country made disability matters a priority. The national legislative framework to recognise and promote rights of PwDs includes: the UNCRPD; the 2013 Zimbabwean Constitution; the Children's Act; the Mental Health Act; the Disabled Persons Act (2016); the Social Welfare Assistance Act; the State Service (Disability Benefits) Act; the War Victims Compensation Act; the Criminal Law (Codification and Reform) Act; and the National Disability Policy (2021). All these Acts of Parliament acknowledge the existence of disability and call for non-discrimination and criminalisation of the exclusion of 'disabled persons' or 'mentally handicapped people'. The major drawback of the Disabled Persons Act (DPA) is that it follows an outdated, medical model of disability, which locates disability within the person and views PwDs not as rights holders but as objects for clinical intervention.

As enshrined under section 22 of the Zimbabwean Constitution, all government agencies at every level are mandated to develop programmes that support the welfare of persons with physical or mental disabilities, especially work programmes consistent with capabilities. This stance is commendable and is in line with the UNCRPD's objectives and can be read together with article 12 of that Convention, about recognition of equality before the law, and article 17, which emphasises the significance of protecting PwDs' integrity.

The Constitution of Zimbabwe contains a dedicated section on the rights of PwDs. Section 83 states that:

The State must take appropriate measures, within the limits of the resources available to it, to ensure that persons with disabilities realise their full mental and physical potential, including measures to enable them to become self-reliant. (Government of the Republic of Zimbabwe, 2013)

Furthermore, the same section goes on to specify that the state should: enable them to live independently (in line with article 19 of the UNCRPD); enable them to live with their families (article 23) and participate in social, creative or recreational activities (article 30); protect them from all forms of exploitation and abuse (articles 16 and 17); give them access to medical, psychological and functional treatment (articles 25 and 26); provide special facilities for their education (article 24); and provide state-funded education and training where they need it.

PwDs, however, remain vulnerable to discrimination and abuse, and are often denied fundamental rights and freedoms, such as access to information, the right to be heard and participate, freedom of expression, access to roads, the right to be treated equally and fairly, and movement, just to mention a few.

The disconnection between policies and practices on the ground requires evidence to establish effective implementation strategies. It is imperative to generate evidence on how those with disabilities live and the associated precarities, as well as the limitations that exist, on how to use their potential and how to facilitate initiatives for them. This chapter brings to the fore some of the evidence.

Creative Corridors, a project run by the Children's Performing Arts Workshop (CHIPAWO) Trust in partnership with Shangano Arts, was executed by researchers and professionals who have done work with children, with and without disabilities. Field visits were carried out with the following schools and their surrounding communities: Emerald Hill, Above Boundaries, and St Giles (Harare); Jairos Jiri (Kadoma); Copota School for the Blind (Masvingo); Big Tree Primary (Chipinge); and Hwange. The present chapter draws broadly on the experience of PwDs. It reflects on different areas that make PwDs unhappy while expressing their aspirations, hidden talents and capabilities. Their dreams around contributing to socioeconomic, political and cultural development are captured and embedded into the stories. There is much in the way of talent and skills among PwDs and this chapter reflects on some of it. Creative Corridors has worked with children and young people in the cultural and creative spaces to expose and reflect on key matters that affect their lives.

The following section of the chapter presents stories by children and the childhood experiences of older people. The next focuses on research conducted with children and young people with disabilities. The purpose of the research was to understand how children and young people with disabilities survive with their creative skills in the face of limitations.

The chapter presents the contextual outlook, background of the project and key findings of the research. The motivation for the research is to share the findings on the discourse of those with disabilities in order to inform decision-makers. The study was done not only to influence social development practices in various provinces of the country, but also to add to the body of knowledge and influence further studies in academic and non-academic circles.

Stories

We begin with stories of children and childhood as a means of conveying the lived experiences of marginalised people. These stories highlight the sociolinguistic and intercultural upbringing of the participants, ranging from human–wildlife conflict to the sociocultural significance of the participants themselves. Storytelling serves as their method of conducting research and communicating with the outside world, aiming to garner better support and recognition for their contributions. Below, we present 16 stories: 10 stories of children born with disabilities, three stories of human–wildlife conflict, one story of a child who had an accident that led to disability, and two stories of schools and their mission to support differently-abled people with their needs.

Stories of children born with disability

Pseudonyms are used below, in order to anonymise those who provided these lived experiences.

Ndira's story

Ndira was a boy aged 11, still at primary school, born with a physical disability. When he was two years old it was discovered that one leg was longer than the other. He stayed with his grandmother, Ugogo, who contextualised the situation, noting Ndira was two years old before he could walk. 'Ndira took long to walk, and we had to consult doctors.' It was then that his disability was discovered. The grandmother communicated that Ndira went to school and loved taking care of livestock such as goats and feeding chickens, thus assisting her. In terms of arts, he enjoyed playing the *ngoma* (an African drum) and dancing. His grandmother smiled when seeing Ndira going out to engage in cultural activities and dance. She noticed this when CHIPAWO first visited the area in 2020. The young boy reflected his peace of mind and enjoyment of cultural activities such as dance, drumming and traditional instruments such as the marimba.

He exuded traits of being cooperative and understood when being instructed, mentored and taught. Adults listened to him when he spoke, thereby reflecting authoritative characteristics in him even at his young age. The challenge that he faced was finding shoes locally. 'It's not easy here in rural Hwange to get the other shoe: I have to go to Bulawayo to purchase it and it's expensive', his grandmother said. Ndira was open to answering some critical questions. In his words, he faced the challenge of walking to school with his condition and highlighted that some people look down on him.

Kukadzi' story

> Hi! I am Kukadzi. I am a girl aged 21 and a resident of Hwange rural. I live with albinism. I finished my Ordinary Level. Currently I am a regular participant in the arts and cultural events that are hosted by both Shangano Arts Trust and CHIPAWO Trust. I play marimba, which I learnt through their introduction here in Hwange by CHIPAWO in collaboration with Shangano Arts.

At school, some of the children would take Kukadzi's sun hat and run away with it, yet Hwange is typically hot, with clear skies, and direct sunlight is a problem for those with albinism. The heat affects their skin badly. The challenge was not only the scarcity of lotion for skin protection but also its expense.

Kurume' story

Kurume was a 58-year-old multi-talented professional musician and pastor who was currently attached to his former school as a music teacher. He was born blind. Kurume did his primary schooling at Copota after a very controversial incident during his childhood in the late 1950s. Kurume contracted measles at the age of two and his father chased his mother, claiming that she was a witch and refusing to take care of a blind child.

Innocent little Kurume and his caring mother, out of marriage, left home in desperate search for help. In 1965 they went to the Dry Fountain Clinic, which was the nearest healthcare centre under the colonial Smith government. To get the help that the mother needed in Rhodesia (now Zimbabwe), she had to lie that she did not know the identity of her child's father. The clinic accepted the child as an orphan and treated him. For the period between 1965 up to 1970 Kurume regained his sight.

The blindness came back around 1971, when he was eight years old and supposed to start school. The Rhodesian well-wishers told the mother that if she wanted her child to get support with his education, she would need to go to jail for a year, to which she agreed. That is when Kurume was taken to Copota School, where he did his academic and vocational training.

After being chased away, Kurume never heard about his father's whereabouts until late 1975, when his father sent an elder brother to Copota. When his uncle arrived, Kurume did not know him and told his teachers so. Nevertheless, his uncle took him home to his father, who apologised to Kurume and slaughtered cattle in ceremony to cement the need for re-union and the son forgave his father. At the time of his father's death, they had a good relationship.

Even though he had experienced so many conflicts in his life, Kurume had found peace and was able to learn so much. Now he possessed so many talents from the creative space which he then used to positively touch the lives of other children with disabilities. Kurume majored in music and could play most musical instruments, including guitar, saxophone, keyboard, marimba and *mbira*. The trumpet was a bit challenging to him, but he could play it.

As a teacher, trainer and mentor for children and persons with disabilities, Kurume observed that these children have passion inside them and whenever they are shown something they are eager to learn to do it well. More so, artistic expressions, which are mediums of culture, are their area. The observation is that children with disabilities need to be loved; they need people who are patient and friendly with them.

Due to stereotyping, getting employed as a person who lives with a disability is one of the most difficult scenarios. What needs to be done comes from talents. The first thing is the provision of adequate equipment used by PwDs in realising their talents, and books need to be written in braille to accommodate the blind community.

Kubvumbi's story

Kubvumbi was a 22-year-old brilliant girl, living with blindness. She was currently doing her advanced-level (upper 6) in arts at high school after passing ordinary level with flying colours, surpassing many peers without any disability. She was a *mbira* player, a public speaker, poet and a lawyer in the making. Kubvumbi's music was inspired by Chiwoniso Maraire, one of the female *mbira* legends to emerge from Zimbabwe. She was taught *mbira* by Mr Chiteke, and noted: 'I liked the art from there and also love the music by Fungisai Mashava because of her name'. From the Shona language, Fungisai means 'think deeply'.

> I also sing; I like singing so much and when I was growing up, I used to listen to Fungisai and used to sing her songs. One day in church someone told me that I sing like Fungisai and from there I joined the praise and worship choir.

Kubvumbi had realised the need to become an advocate since she had been speaking up for the voiceless even in her youth. Her intention was to specialise in matters regarding disabilities.

She had challenged stereotypes associated with blindness through her singing talent. Kubvumbi was disappointed by other people's attitude, who pity instead of appreciating musical talents of artists with disabilities. Young people and children with disabilities are not given enough ground to express themselves in speaking, acting and cultural matters.

With the exposure that Kubvumbi got, she had attended many public-speaking competitions with local schools – Zimuto High, Victoria High and Gokomere High School. Kubvumbi's loss in all the competitions was viewed as symptomatic of the unfair treatment commonly given to people living with a disability.

Initially, Kubvumbi wanted to enrol in sciences or commercials at Lord MC but the school could not enrol her because they did not have learning materials in braille. What she was currently doing was the best combination that was available at C School. Her dream was to do commercials or sciences at Group A schools (which are better resourced). Her wish was simple: she wanted all schools to give PwDs room to learn just like all other children, for equality.

> My reason for doing arts now is because I want to do law at university and be a voice of the voiceless. I want to initiate and bring change to my fellow friends who are living with a disability out there and will represent them and that will make me feel happy.

With her current studies, there were very few books in braille, limiting her pursuit in art studies and other extracurricular activities. Her wish was to have a personal computer and keyboard at home so that she could read and also pursue her music fully.

Chivabvu's story

Chivabvu was a nine-year-old blind brilliant boy doing his Grade 2 at C Primary School. He was born blind and according to him there were no challenges to talk about. At his young age, he played more than five instruments – marimba, guitar (both lead and bass), *mbira*, saxophone, drums and keyboard. Given the chance, he could even go beyond the music industry.

When we visited his school, Chivabvu was part of the crew that was playing the instruments for two different music sets – in the first one he was playing marimba and in the second one he was on drums. The playing was unique and melodious.

It should be emphasised, however, that he was not the only child who could play all instruments, but his art was above the normal standard. Chivabvu wanted to become a music producer. Looking into the future he intended to do a collaboration with popular local artist, T. Gonzi. According to his music teacher, Chivabvu was exceptionally good and should be counted within the same category of nationally celebrated blind musicians like Paul Matavire and Chamunorwa Nebeta. As well as pursuing music, he was also learning to write and read using braille.

Chikumi's story

Chikumi was a Grade 4 student at JJ Primary school for the blind. He was a brave student with a strong character. He had lost his eyesight in 2022, just when he was about to get into form 3. For him it was a tragic moment, but he had since accepted it and placed his faith in God. He had lived for most of his life with his grandmother because his mother had died when he was only two. Chikumi lost his grandfather in 2019. His father was alive but had married another woman.

In 2018, during the third term, doing form 2, he was at school and started seeing lines in his eyes coming like lightning but there was no rain at all. From there he began to experience deteriorating eyesight. He told his guardians at home, but they did not believe him. They thought that it was just an excuse to avoid going to school, so that he could play with the two other friends who had just finished their O-level.

He remembered, it was after about a week of such experience and still going to school 'my eyes suddenly became red, and people started joking about them tossing me around saying Chikumi at your age you are now smoking weed'. When he told them that he was having challenges with his eyesight, they could not agree. One day when he came to school, he could only see mist along the road. His friends said there was no mist. Chikumi still had to go to school because his family did not believe him. During a commerce lesson he neither saw what the teacher was writing nor what he himself had written in his notebook – everything turned white. Fortunately, the commerce teacher noticed his predicament and told him that he should go home since he could not see anything.

Chikumi was taken to Richard Morris, in Bulawayo, for treatment. The eye doctor told him that his eyes were swollen, and after treatment he regained his sight.

> When I got discharged, I remember buying stationery and came back to my rural village in Zvimba, excited that the following day I would be back in the classroom.

The following morning, however, he woke up with no sight and that was the fateful day. Chikumi was taken to Chinhoyi Hospital, where he believed he was ignored; he was later referred to Norton and finally ended up in Harare, the capital city.

When Chikumi got to Harare, the doctors told his family that he had developed the problem because he was born HIV positive, having contracted the virus from his parents. During surgery on his eyes, there was overheating of the right eye and the vision was completely lost. The last time he went for check-up they said the other eye would be able to see if treated. He was referred to go to Zambia for treatment, but the hospital fees for surgery were beyond his family's reach.

This was not an easy chapter in the life of Chikumi. Back when he could see, he had a considerable number of friends, who would come and take him for soccer and other outdoor activities. Now he no longer had anyone to check on him because of his condition. One time he asked a friend to accompany him to a barber and had to wait from 9 am until 3 pm. That was when he knew he had lost many friends and regarded himself as a burden in people's lives.

Chikumi did not want to go to school to start learning from scratch again; it was going to be painful, but he realised that just sitting at home was not going to help him.

> I must accept and face reality on the ground. Eventually, I made up my mind after one of my grandmother's friends who works at Jairos Jiri came to me and convinced me that she was going to take me to school to learn braille.

He agreed to go and joined in 2021. He was received well and got downgraded to Grade 4.

Chikumi's pain was soothed when he participated in cultural activities. He loved music and could play the *ngoma* and guitar. He was able to manufacture homemade guitars from scratch. He could also cook at home for the family and clean the house better than anyone at home. 'I remember at one point my grandmother left me at home alone, for a week; I would cook, clean, bath and even wash on my own.'

Chikunguru's story

Chikunguru was born in 2005. At a young age, her head started swelling abnormally. Her parents took her to a medical facility for a check-up and the doctors recommended surgery to drain the water in her head. It was during the process of trying to install a shunt in her head that Chikunguru started coughing and the doctor had to abandon the process abruptly. The doctors then gave Chikunguru's parents medication and advised them to treat her from home. The administration of the medical course reduced the abnormal head swelling. Nonetheless, she had a hearing problem until the age of eight. It was not until 2015 that her parents decided to take her to school. The parents took a step by first visiting the department of psychology under the Ministry of Education. They were told that they could enrol her at Big Tree Primary School in Chipinge under Chikowore Mission, where she was currently doing her primary level (Grade 7).

Chikunguru was a slow learner but a peaceful student. She was an artist who liked knitting and sewing. As her teacher, Ms Khosa, narrated, during the COVID-19 period students were granted an opportunity to do projects such as poultry and fashion. Chikunguru managed to impress her mentors and teachers by sewing a scarf. With continued support, she could become a better artist and maker.

Chikunguru's father died and she was currently staying with her mother, who had become a beacon of support. Chikunguru's teacher pointed out that she needed a lot of financial support for her to perform better in the classroom and at home. More was also needed to support her by providing resources needed for her to continue knitting and sewing. The interview with the teacher raised doubts about whether Chikunguru would be able to attend her secondary education, considering the distance (40 km) to get to the nearest secondary school, as well as the requirements.

Chikunguru used sign language and could knit and sew better than students without disabilities. Her current primary school assisted in building sustainable skills in those living with disabilities. Inclusive education means students are treated the same and, in return, they also treat each other with respect and live in peace.

Nyamavhuvhu's story

Nyamavhuvhu was a 24-year-old student at JJ School of the blind. He was born with blindness. He believed it was a condition that did not stop him from dreaming big. 'I am proud to be blind and I am content with that because that is the work of God, and we must accept it.'

He was the only person who lived with a disability in his family and was also a child with one parent because his mother passed away when he was young. The unfortunate part about his early years was that he was under the care of his stepmother, who had little care and was selective. The challenge was, however, addressed when he started staying with his grandmother instead of his stepmother. He was currently doing his O-level at Jairos Jiri, where he kept on believing that he had been born for a purpose and started his musical career.

After he lost his mother, he was ill-treated at one point and suffered verbal abuse because of his condition but decided to maintain peace. He had composed himself and never lost his dream.

Nyamavhuvhu had remained vigilant and never lost hope in his big dreams. He was a talented musician with six studio-recorded tracks. He was looking forward to having a promoter and marketer for his music to go far and inspire fellow friends living with disabilities. His songs reflected on themes of internal family conflicts for children with disabilities. He had survived attacks and now stayed with his grandmother, who was good to him. Good morals taught at school enabled him to play a supportive role in assisting his grandmother in household duties.

He was also an artist, who drew. He believed that children with disabilities should be treated equal to those without disabilities, as a way of enhancing and promoting peace, social cohesion and talent.

Gunyana's story

'I am a 21-year-old blind boy doing my Early Childhood Development at Jairos Jiri school of the blind.' Gunyana explained:

> I think there must be more awareness campaigns about disabilities and to treat people the same despite their condition. The parents of these

children must be encouraged to send their children to school because some are still shy and keep their children away from the public eye, which is not good for the children and their future.

That is all he wanted to say.

Gumiguru's story

Gumiguru was a 20-year-old form 4 student at JJ Kadoma school. He lived with complete visual impairment, but, with experience, was be able to be self-sufficient. Gumiguru had been born into a family of 10, three of whom had a visual impairment. He was the founder member of a school drama club called BMC. As a prefect, he had good leadership qualities. He was also someone who was into Christianity and preached the gospel on Sundays and other midweek services at school.

Gumiguru said:

People should not feel sorry for us because God does his things purposefully and maybe I am loving school because I am blind, and what if God saw that if he gives me sight, probably I was going to be doing evil things out there and die early so I am thankful and okay to be born blind. I can still do what others can do, right? I am a prefect, I do preach, I play soccer and participate with others in day-to-day living. I am also going to school under BEAM (Basic Education Assistance Model), which is a module that pays my school fees and donors come here and there to support us. I am not worried. What I just need is the exposure to the industry and job placement when I finish school.

According to Gumiguru, their drama club is there to demystify disability. The drama club airs how society sometimes neglects PwDs in so many ways, like hiding away children with disability, insulting them and viewing them as a burden. 'We do it for fun and also to educate the community to treat us equally and know that disability is not inability.'

Gumiguru played a crucial role in the drama club, as he was the one who spoke to introduce their plays. He also alluded to the fact that he wanted to become a radio presenter, like Liberty from Radio Zimbabwe, and to him the sky was the limit. He was someone with skills in weaving and poultry, and was passionate about writing books. He admitted to some barriers and lack of financial resources but believed that the presence of barriers should not stop people from pursuing their dreams.

Stories of human–wildlife conflict

Mbudzi's story

Mbudzi is one of the men who had fallen victim to the human and wildlife conflict happening within the conservation areas of Hwange. His story had touched the hearts of many and brought audiences to the realities and predicaments of people living in areas bordering wildlife zones. Mbudzi was in his early 50s with five children and a wife, currently working at Zambezi Gas at the dispatch department based in Hwange. He was a resident of Lukosi in Hwange, an area that is largely rural. These areas do not offer many opportunities.

As Mbudzi finished work in the early hours of 18 October 2017, like every ordinary day, he embarked on the journey of walking back home. He came across a group of elephants (a normal occurrence), enjoying nature and feasting on plants laced with the morning dew. They were on both sides of the road. The people in Hwange live together with animals and know how to safely interact with them. They have always used whistles as one of the ways of getting elephants to move to one side in order to allow free passage and not interfere with them.

> When I blew the whistle all the elephants moved aside and I was about to walk past them, when one huge female elephant failed to locate her calf and charged in anger towards me.

As he tried his best to run away, Mbudzi hit a stump with his left leg and fell to the ground, on his face. Before he picked himself up the elephant had come very close. At this time, he experienced a hallucination for a moment. Before he did anything the elephant had already forked him with its tusk, taking him into the air. He landed some metres away, on hard ground with thorns, stones and stumps. 'At that time, I couldn't feel myself anymore.' Before he could react, the huge elephant was back on him again and he was forked for the second time. The tusks pierced his buttock, penetrating to the other side and through his thigh.

The third time the elephant charged, Mbudzi suddenly heard a voice telling him to instruct the elephant to go away. He uttered the message in local language, 'Heyi wena hamba', and he saw the elephant taking two steps back and he repeated the statement. All of a sudden, the elephant saw her calf coming out of the bush and she took a few steps back and finally left him.

> When I saw that the elephant was gone, I told myself that I needed to run away immediately before it came back. When I tried to do so, I couldn't carry myself. My right leg was now heavy. That's when I noticed that the elephant had harmed me badly. I tried to walk to my phone, but only moved some few metres and fell to the ground. I stood up and continued to struggle over the less than 20 metres distance. When I saw my phone, I had a glimmer of hope which was quickly shattered as the phone was no longer working – the whole touch screen was cracked.

He had wanted to continue with the journey up to the main road. Since his phone was broken, he walked towards a tree that he had seen. He fell on the ground again, with blood trailing behind him. His vision started to become blurred and then darkened. A 500 ml bottle of water that was stashed in his backpack gave him strength. He was eventually able to open his eyes.

The near and distant sounds of bellowing buffalos and antelopes reminded him that he was still alive. Some rays of sunshine struck him. He decided to remove the safety shoes he was wearing and put them in his satchel and began to limp to the main road. At this moment he could not use his right leg to walk because of the growing pain. He found a stick on the side of the road and used it to balance.

As soon as he got to the main road, his body could not sustain the weight, and he threw himself onto the ground. He waved at cars that were passing by, carrying tourists and business people. Mbudzi was able to stop cars only using one hand while lying down on the other side. Brakes were heard being punched by a truck, which eventually stopped close to where he was lying. In hesitation, none of those people in the truck came down, opting to communicate from safety: 'I requested them to pass by my workplace and notify my workmates that I was by the roadside, and I needed urgent assistance.'

His workmates arrived after a while and Mbudzi was taken to hospital for treatment. This ordeal with an elephant left him with a disability. Over the years when Mbudzi had lived in Lukosi, cases of human and wildlife conflicts were rare, but in some areas children were attacked by wild animals on an almost daily basis. For Mbudzi, the trauma limits full enjoyment of cultural rights and distracts from personal peace and interaction with family.

Zvita's story

Zvita was born in 1986. He was a family man, with two children: one boy, who was currently doing his form 1, and a girl, still at primary level. Zvita was a victim of human and wildlife conflict. 'A buffalo attacked me. As you can see, I use one leg to walk.'

Zvita still had vivid memories of 6 May 2013. He went hunting with a friend and they encountered a wounded buffalo sleeping. Assuming that Zvita and his friend were about to attack it, the buffalo rose, engulfed with all the anger from its wounds, and it came faster than anticipated. Zvita tried to climb a tree, but the buffalo managed to use its left leg to press on one of his legs. 'My foot dislocated from the leg', and that was when Zvita started to live with a disability. The friend managed to escape unharmed.

This incident happened around 10 am in the morning, assistance arrived only around 9 pm and Zvita reached the hospital only around 1 am the following day. The doctors finally attended to him. They recommended surgery and amputation of the foot was undertaken. However, after the procedure, they noticed that they had not initially cut from the correct position. Further painful surgery followed, and this all happened within a space of two weeks.

The representatives of the parks department visited him in hospital and on discharge he went to social welfare for assistance with a worn-out artificial leg: 'I am still using it and it's almost five years now, yet it is supposed to work for only three years before being changed'. Zvita's highest level of education was Grade 7, primary level. Surviving without education means one would need an alternative source of income such as farming, hunting or fishing. Zvita lived with his mother, also disabled, who could not support him to continue with his studies. He had to assist her with parental duties as early as 13 before becoming a victim of the circumstances.

Chirimo's story

Chirimo was a boy aged 15. He stayed in St Mary's, Hwange, located some few kilometres away from a dammed lake where people fish, wash and sometimes bathe. 'I am a victim of a crocodile attack and I'm now a disabled person. I'm no longer going to school as there is no other means of travelling to school other than walking which I no longer manage.'

He was attacked by a crocodile while fishing with his friends. Some panicked and ran away while others started throwing stones at the crocodile. As his mother narrated, 'I was home when one resident of Dhiki village where we stay came and broke the news that Chirimo had been attacked by a crocodile'. She rushed to the dam. She nursed the wound in the indigenous traditional way and wrapped the wounded right leg with a piece of cloth. She was assisted to carry her child on her back. She took him to her homestead, where the ambulance met her and carried Chirimo to the hospital for treatment.

The doctors amputated Chirimo's damaged leg. No longer going to school, he still participated in artistic and cultural activities. He was a marimba player and was also involved in various activities chaired by CHIPAWO Trust and its partner Shangano Arts Trust. He was currently awaiting a prosthetic leg from a potential donor and he wished to go to school like other children. Besides the danger posed by crocodiles, other wild animals like elephants and hyenas enter the homestead to eat vegetables and goats.

Stories of children subjected to accidents leading to disability

Matsutso's story

Matsutso was a Chipinge resident from Chikowore Mission born in 1982. He used to work for STD Diamond, a Russian-owned mining company. In 2015, part of an underground mining shaft collapsed and Matsutso's leg was broken. After the incident, he was taken to Mutambara Clinic, where healthcare staff temporarily nursed his leg before transfer to the general hospital at which he was finally treated. The healing of his leg meant Matsutso was in hospital for almost four months, after which he went back to claim his package. When he got his wages, he decided to rest at home and never set foot again at the company. His condition did not allow him to work on any heavy tasks. The company then closed in 2016, a year after the serious injury. 'So, from 2015, I am here at home.'

Despite the fateful incident, Matsutso advised that everyone should remain hopeful and pursue their dreams. He now attended to his livelihood with projects in poultry (keeping of broilers) and crop farming. Matsutso was also a painter and earned some dollars from that creative business.

The inspirational part was that, with a colleague who was a blood brother, he helped children from the local school, Big Tree Primary, to learn painting and drawing. These lessons were offered free of charge and without any condition. Matsutso shared skills and spread peace through art and at times playing *mbira* with physically challenged and deaf children. This work promoted the message of peace within the community, with the inclusion of people living with or without disability.

Stories of schools and their mission to empower the differently abled

Copota School

There is an emotionally touching and interesting history about how this school was started. It reached us through the school's history and narratives from the school elders.

According to the narrative, the school started in 1915 in Chivi, Chizunga area, where a certain family gave birth to a blind child, whose name was Zhizha. Zhizha's father instructed his mother to throw the child in the river as this was the norm in that era. However, the mother refused and took the child to a missionary family at Chibi Mission of the Reformed Church in Zimbabwe. The missionary family decided to 'try' to take care of the child. It is believed that the motto for the school, 'we will try', came from that incident at the genesis of the school in 1915.

It is also believed that the school was registered in 1927 as the first school for people living with disabilities, and it was also the same year that a missionary bought the current school location. Up until that time, it was a farm owned by a German family. Due to accessibility issues, the school was moved to Masvingo in the Zimuto area in 1938. The children were taught to do different projects, mainly practical subjects such as weaving baskets and carpentry.

The missionary family went to South Africa to learn braille so that they could return to teach the children how to read and write using braille. The missionary mother later left the project in the hands of her daughter, who was also passionate about the welfare of people with disabilities. She accommodated them to the extent of giving them land to build their homes on selected parts of the huge school farm. Some of the people who benefited from the skills from Copota school are now residents because they were given land by the mission after their families abandoned them at the school. Some decided to be independent and stay in a community where no one judged them. The school consists of a primary and secondary school and most of the children's fees are paid through the Basic Education Assistance Module (BEAM) scheme and via donors. Some assistant teachers and school workers are paid by the school through donors as well.

Jairos Jiri School

Jairos Jiri School is one of the most popular schools founded for the blind and to house and educate children who live with different disabilities. It is a school that is known for its development of artists and celebrities.

We had the privilege to work with the school and paid numerous visits to see the children. In October 2022 we had a beautiful tour, interviewed the caregivers, school authorities and of course the children in general. The exceptional children were given a platform to share with us their lives, talents and the hurdles they face when trying to put their talent in the spotlight.

Jairos Jiri is no longer for the blind only but for everyone; hence the school embraces inclusive education. We were privileged to interview these children from all angles for a robust analysis and better understanding of their lifestyle and aspirations.

From Stories to Research

Research objectives and questions

While the above stories foreground lived experience as they were recounted to us, it is imperative to systematically understand the realities of PwDs. This section examines the role and experiences not only of PwDs in sociocultural life but also those at the forefront of interventions, assessing effectiveness in addressing the challenges faced by PwDs. It is necessary to influence bodies such as faith-based organisations, human rights civil society organisations (CSOs) and UN agencies like UNICEF to continue the conversation and engagement with children and young people living with disabilities. The goal is to promote peace and include them in different programmes that align with their talents and the sociocultural fabric of society.

The primary objective of this study is, therefore, to ensure that these children and young people are widely mainstreamed in sociocultural life and become part of any work around conflict transformation. Thus, the study aims to build peace while promoting social inclusion through artistic and intercultural communication, freedom of expression and equitable representation. This study focuses on answering the following questions:

- What challenges are experienced by children and young people living with disabilities in rural communities?
- In what form do conflicts exist in rural communities and what are some of the root causes?
- How do those with artistic skills and talents expose themselves to wider society, and how does society perceive and appreciate their skills?
- What are the limiting factors for children and young people living with disabilities to get recognised?
- Is there any discrimination against children and young people with disabilities?

Methodological approach to the study

Methodologically, a participatory mixed-methods approach that utilised both qualitative and quantitative methods of data collection was used. The participatory approach ensured the active involvement and contribution of the children, parents and guardians. The data-collection processes comprised planned visits to specific areas (with planning completed well before any visits were made). The study gathered data from five provinces of Zimbabwe – Harare, Mashonaland West, Masvingo, Matabeleland North and Manicaland. All the provinces were physically visited by the research team, who facilitated the collection of data from the primary beneficiaries. The study covered St Giles and Emerald School for the Deaf in Harare province; Jairos Jiri in Kadoma, Mashonaland West province; Lukosi and Hwange in Matabeleland North; Copota School for the blind in Masvingo province; and Big Tree School in Manicaland province.

The local CHIPAWO and Shangano Arts facilitators coordinated the visits to communities and assisted in the identification of those with disabilities. The study employed in-depth face-to-face interviews and a survey questionnaire to gather primary data. The interviews were undertaken in order to obtain data, opinions and perspectives on people with disabilities, especially children and young people. These were drawn from all the specific areas that were visited. Heads of school, arts education facilitators, cultural professionals, key caregivers and resource persons who worked with those with disabilities were involved in the face-to-face interviews. Admittedly, some of the targeted key informants were not available for discussions due to personal circumstance and some others were slow in communicating, making it hard to complete the interviews with them.

The survey questionnaire was administered electronically using smart phones/devices that had the Kobo Collect application loaded onto them. This is a real-time data-collection application targeted at the population in all the five provinces covered by Creative Corridors project. A total of 89 respondents were interviewed and their responses captured. The used application facilitated the removal of error, strengthening reliability and validity of data.

In addition to the primary data gathering, a comprehensive and rigorous review of all relevant documents retrieved online and offline was carried out. The data from multiple sources was cross-examined and triangulated.

The study used a cross-sectional research analysis design. This created a relatively passive approach to making causal inferences to the research findings. The design facilitated inferences from differences between people with disabilities, subjects or phenomena. The design estimated the prevalence of an outcome of interest because the sample was taken from a specific group of people from the entire community. Even though data were obtained through survey, the use of a cross-sectional design was generally cheap and merged very well with the survey techniques of data collection and gathering. Time spent in the collection of data was not much, given that smart gadgets/devices were used and the process was simplified. Quantitative survey raw data collected through Kobo Collect was downloaded from the Kobo Toolbox central server and saved as a Microsoft (MS) Excel raw data file. Later, it was exported into the SPSS software package for cleaning and analysis. The findings were examined through statistical analysis and a broader analysis of qualitative data was done through thematic analysis techniques.

The work was guided by research ethics as well as the University of Glasgow Code of Good Practice in Research, specifically the four core principles of honesty, rigour, transparency and open communication, and care and respect.

Findings

Data were collected from 76 respondents from across the five provinces in which CHIPAWO and Shangano Arts Trust conducted the Creative Corridors initiative. Children with different disabilities – visual impairments, hearing impairment, physical disabilities – were all engaged. Figure 4.1 shows the distribution of the sample across the provinces. The urban areas of Harare and Mashonaland West (Kadoma) had the largest numbers of research participants, while Hwange (a rural area) had the lowest numbers due to travel difficulties. Zimbabwe's communication and road networks are still underdeveloped, thus limiting the mobility of both children and those with disabilities to attend one central venue and for researchers to visit the homes of prospective respondents.

Demographically, the respondents who were engaged in this research comprised 28 females (37%) and 48 males (63%). The average age of the participants was 17 years; 61% were born with disabilities while 39% had become disabled later on (through diseases, delayed medical attention, as well as a lack of information or awareness).

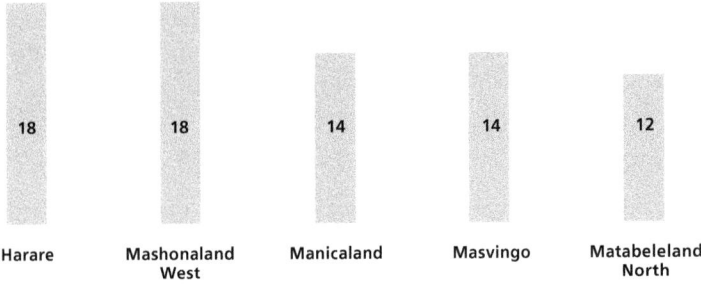

Figure 4.1 Provincial distribution of the study sample across Zimbabwe

Of the interviewed children with disabilities, 82% were going to school and 18% were not. Failure to go to school was mainly due to lack of financial resources, unavailability of educational material support, limited welfare grants, or an unsupportive school infrastructure. Some of the family backgrounds were not effective in supporting their children with disabilities. Some of the parents and guardians who were taking care of these children are disadvantaged, with some themselves possessing different forms of disabilities.

Social conflicts around children with disabilities

The study captured that if children with disabilities get close attention and support, they are persistent and passionate in following their dreams. Their level of focus is high but the children can be shattered by resource constraints, stigma and discrimination. If their requirements are not met, they are driven into deprivation, which potentially leaves them to survive as victims of family and/or community conflicts. Even though some of the disabled are good with their creative talents, some forms of disability limit their full participation, such as quick forgetting and taking time to learn specific concepts.

The children who pursue educational, vocational and/or cultural professions have higher chances of a better life in the future.

The community often ridicules people with disabilities and many people do not accept the condition. Some of the bullying in school disturbs the children's peaceful engagement in education. The research findings also captured that there are some people within the communities who take advantage and steal from those with disabilities. This disrupts the peaceful life and exacerbates social conflicts between children with disabilities and their communities.

The older traditional system that associates disabilities with witchcraft also has a negative impact on those with disabilities. Some of the parents and guardians still have misconceptions (ancient beliefs) that the playing of African traditional instruments such as the *mbira* by children is associated with appeasing the dead, and this can suppress the enjoyment of the children with disabilities who have talent in this music.

Concluding Remarks

There have been many stereotypes, stigmas, myths and forms of discrimination surrounding PwDs. This underscores the importance of storytelling by those who bear these narratives and necessitates research as a means of formulating long-term solutions for them. Through both stories and research, we emphasise the significance of sustained engagement with children who have disabilities yet possess creative talents.

Our research focuses on promoting the capabilities of all children and accommodating the diverse skills possessed by children. We directly engaged with children and young people who have various forms of disabilities to ensure that their voices and insights are incorporated into the cultural context. The study also strives to be as inclusive as possible, acknowledging the work of children and young people, regardless of whether they have disabilities or not.

Supporting these children not only adds value to their lives but also nurtures their artistic and career growth in art, creativity and innovation. This study allows us to discover new insights into the lives of those with disabilities, the social conflicts they encounter and the things that bring them peace. This chapter is significant as it contributes to the development of policies and the overall body of knowledge.

However, neither the stories nor the study is complete. Despite its significant contribution, the chapter remains unfinished and provisional. Further research, orientated towards policy and sociocultural considerations, is essential to address the needs of PwDs.

Acknowledgements

We express sincere gratitude to CHIPAWO Trust and Shangano Arts Trust for placing confidence in this study and spearheading the development of this twofold exercise, which includes researching and compiling stories from children and young people with disabilities in Zimbabwe, specifically in the provinces. The study would not have been possible without the fundamental contributions from the key informants, as well as the children and young people, and the subsequent consent given to the authors by the parents and guardians of these children with disabilities. We acknowledge the contributions made by various representatives, both young and old. Additionally, we extend our appreciation to the numerous artists, partners and communities, whose names we did not list here.

References

African Union (2000) Constitutive Act of the African Union. https://au.int/sites/default/files/pages/34873-file-constitutiveact_en.pdf (accessed 29 April 2024).

African Union (2018) Protocol to the African Charter on Human and Peoples' Rights on the Rights of Persons with Disabilities in Africa. https://au.int/sites/default/files/treaties/36440-treaty-protocol_to_the_achpr_on_the_rights_of_persons_with_disabilities_in_africa_e.pdf (accessed 29 April 2024).

Government of the Republic of Zimbabwe (2013) Constitution of Zimbabwe. https://www.veritaszim.net/node/6427 (accessed 29 April 2024).

Government of the Republic of Zimbabwe (2016) Disabled Persons Act. https://www.veritaszim.net/node/468 (accessed 29 April 2024).

Kuper, H., Smythe, T., Kujinga, T., Chivandire, G. and Rusakaniko, S. (2015) Should disability-inclusive health be a priority in low-income countries? A case study from Zimbabwe. *Global Health Action* 15 (1). https://www.ncbi.nlm.nih.gov/pmc/articles/PMC8928844/#:~:text=These%20commitments%20are%20justified%2C%20as,healthcare%20%5B3%E2%80%935%5D (accessed 29 April 2024).

Lapidos, J. (2009) How many albinos are there in Tanzania? *The Slate.* https://slate.com/news-and-politics/2009/01/how-many-albinos-are-there-in-tanzania.html (accessed 29 April 2024).

Moyo, J. (2023) Friedriech Naumann Foundaton. https://www.freiheit.org/sub-saharan-africa/challenges-and-struggles-faced-persons-disabilities-across-africa#:~:text=Like%20in%20several%20other%20African,%2C%20transportation%2C%20and%20public%20spaces (accessed 29 April 2024).

Rao, P. (2017) Ending albino persecution in Africa. *Africa Renewal.* https://www.un.org/africarenewal/magazine/december-2017-march-2018/ending-albino-persecution-africa (accessed 29 April 2024).

United Nations (2007) Convention on the Rights of Persons with Disabilities and Optional Protocol. https://www.un.org/disabilities/documents/convention/convoptprot-e.pdf (accessed 17 August 2023).

United Nations (2015) The 17 goals. https://sdgs.un.org/goals (accessed 17 August 2023).

United Nations Department of Economic and Social Affairs (2024) Disability. https://gla-my.sharepoint.com/:w:/r/personal/tawona_sithole_glasgow_ac_uk/_layouts/15/Doc.aspx?sourcedoc=%7B0CC2C846-C3D5-45DE-89F7-3631E110BF0D%7D&file=Chipawo%20chapter.docx&action=default&mobileredirect=true (accessed 29 April 2024).

World Health Organization (2024) Disability. https://www.who.int/news-room/fact-sheets/detail/disability-and-health#:~:text=An%20estimated%201.3%20billion%20people,1%20in%206%20of%20us (accessed 29 April 2024).

5 A Tale of Two Cities: Recovering Community Spaces for Peacebuilding in Medellín and Acapulco

Evelyn Arizpe, Sinéad Gormally, Nohora Niño Vega, Jerónimo Castillo Muñoz, Manuela Suárez Rueda, Javiera Donoso Jiménez, Alejandro Bahena-Rivera and Sergio Hernández Mendoza

Introduction

The high levels of crime and drug-related urban violence which made Medellín (the capital of Colombia's Antioquia province) infamous during the 1980s and 1990s were significantly lowered when the city adopted a multi-level strategy that managed to shift policy and transform a range of former spaces of violence into arts and literacy centres, libraries and parks, providing an innovative way to reduce crime rates (Vulliamy, 2013). While the city is not violence-free and the legacy of conflict remains, its successes in reducing its levels of violence have been recognised by a series of prizes and awards, such as the 2016 Lee Kuan Yew World City Prize. Despite criticism of some of these policies and the ways in which the infrastructure has been used, as well as ongoing social and economic challenges, Medellín has made significant progress and was the inspiration for the research project drawn upon in the present chapter.[1] The wider research sought to understand how non-formal and informal education, culture and the arts have helped to achieve progress, both through tracking government policies over several decades and through gathering the experiences and perspectives of those historically and currently involved in peacebuilding work. It also sought to explore whether, and how, these lessons could be adapted for other cities in Latin America suffering from high levels of violence.

Researchers decided to focus on the city of Acapulco, in Mexico, as one of the cities that could 'learn' from Medellín's experience and worked with communities to establish the current context of using arts and culture for peacebuilding. In the 1950s, Acapulco was considered a top tourist destination and refuge for celebrities, but in the past 20 years the resort has changed dramatically, and is currently considered the 10th most dangerous city in the world to live in, depending on the statistics used (based on homicide rates per 100,000 inhabitants). The 'War on Drugs', a militarised approach to tackling the drug cartels introduced by President Calderón in 2006 and supported by the United States, saw a huge increase in urban violence across the whole country. Despite the political rhetoric changing, and successive governments discussing social reform policies, the violence continues. In 2022 Acapulco had the second highest murder rate in the world, at 110.5 per 100,000 inhabitants (Statista, 2022), and in the first six months of 2017 alone there were 12,155 murders in the city (Partlow, 2017), with many of the victims being young people (Solano, 2014). At the beginning of this research, we acknowledged that while serious violence remained, local government authorities were making new attempts to address the situation, and local practitioners were working with victims and perpetrators of the violence in a variety of innovative and progressive ways. This made Acapulco a perfect city to gain local insights and embark on knowledge-sharing processes with practitioners in Medellín.

While there is recognition that the political context and the nature of the conflict differ dramatically in each site, in both cities contemporary citizens' views on the successes and failures of responses to the high levels of violence, obtained through interviews and workshops, serve to illuminate perspectives on what is required for grassroots peacebuilding. The recovery of convivial, community spaces emerged as key, and there was a great amount of interest and will for transformation, with many advocating for artistic and cultural approaches and partnerships as part of this restoration. However, the gathered experiences of those living in these contexts also highlighted the challenges, mostly to do with resources and sustainability, as well as corruption and staff precarity. At the same time, the exchange of stories between grassroots organisations in both countries allowed successful strategies to emerge and a vision of 'The Acapulco We Want' (Cradall, 2022). This vision prefigures new ways of community regenerative peacebuilding for Acapulco through culture and the arts, as well as perspectives on what is needed for these spaces to thrive and be sustainable.

In this chapter, we share the findings of this research by first referencing the relevant literature on cultural intervention for conflict transformation and everyday peace that underpinned this study, focusing on community engagement and the inclusion of local voices. We then detail the methodology we employed to map cultural and peacebuilding initiatives, and provide a brief historical overview of both cities, highlighting the underlying issues but also policies and interventions that have had the most impact in recent decades. The next section summarises some of our findings around the recurrent themes derived from the triangulation of data sources, leading us to a conclusion regarding the most crucial elements required for recovering and sustaining community spaces for peacebuilding, which could be relevant to other countries in Latin America similarly affected by violence.

Cultural Intervention and Everyday Peace

The increasing contribution of the arts to conflict transformation and peacebuilding has been highlighted and examined in a range of publications from around the world (Hunter & Cohen, 2019; Shank & Schirch, 2008; Tovar, 2015). The theoretical basis that has been used to understand cultural intervention for conflict transformation is derived from different disciplines, including the arts and humanities, social and cultural anthropology, safety and mental health studies (Phipps, 2017), and tends to centre on a better understanding of self and others through the cooperative relationships developed during these activities which, as Hyoeun Bang (2016: 357) puts it, can lead to 'more constructive engagement with conflict'. Arts-based projects involving diverse forms of theatre, music, dance and the visual arts have provided the evidence for the impact of the arts on communities living in violent contexts through facilitating intercultural understanding and promoting non-violent pathways for young people (Brody, 2022; Phipps, 2017). Stories collected from around the world show that participation in non-formal education and cultural activities, especially for young people, encourages the creation of 'enabling environments' that help challenge different forms of violence and conflict (Brody, 2022: 130).

Informal participation (Pepper, 2018) in peacebuilding activities can help develop locally engaged, everyday peace practices. MacGinty (2014) explains everyday peace as 'the normal' for those living in conflict, but something that would be deemed abnormal elsewhere. Importantly, acknowledging people's lived experiences and their means of establishing routinised practices to navigate violence facilitates understanding of people's agency and 'creative resistance' to conflict contexts (Ware *et al.*, 2022). Niño (2022: 40–41) notes that 'Everyday peace arises by and for local communities who are the main promoters and connectors, not only of their own lived reality but also of the possibilities of local transformation'. Lederach (2001) notes the importance of local ownership in peacebuilding processes while also highlighting that community engagement can provide a nuanced understanding of peace. The inclusion of local voice and participation in peacebuilding is vital not only to facilitate coexistence but to find creative solutions and tangible alternatives (Pepper, 2018) to violence and conflict.

Writing about how art-centred initiatives can spread and lead to social transformation, Doris Sommer (2014) uses the term 'cultural acupuncture', coined by Antanas Mockus, the philosopher and former mayor of Bogota, Colombia, who became famous for implementing surprising cultural projects for the city which succeeded in promoting collective engagement and reflection around social issues (Yamin *et al.*, 2021). There is thus a consensus that the arts have the potential to support recovery, wellbeing and social transformation. However, to be successful and sustainable, these interventions must have the resources and convivial spaces where participants can safely build relationships of trust, and engage both in dialogue and in the arts-based activities.

Cultural interventions can support the construction of an everyday peace, one that is built from below, with the desires, interests, solidarity and trust that communities have in themselves to collectively build peace actions. The belief that there is capacity to develop local solutions to local problems necessitates listening to local voices (Eversley *et al.*, 2022) and discovering the aspirations of what a peaceful society would look like for practitioners (Gormally *et al.*, 2023), which we sought to do through the voices collected in the document *El Acapulco que soñamos* ('The Acapulco We Want', https://cradall.org/sites/default/files/acapulcowewant.pdf, accessed 29 July 2024).

Methodology: Mapping Cultural and Peacebuilding Initiatives

The research, which involved partnerships with grassroots community organisations, municipal authorities and interdisciplinary researchers, sought to find out about the structural, political and community infrastructure for peacebuilding and to map the cultural organisations in each city to identify existing capacity and gaps as well as the issues around cultural intervention. The first step in our methodology involved reviewing the public policy documents of Medellín's cultural and educational development between 2004 and 2019. As a second step, nearly 90 interviews were conducted across both cities, with a wide range of stakeholders linked to culture and education (e.g. developers of public policy, actors from private companies that invested in these projects, artists, directors of cultural organisations, teachers, artists, librarians, community practitioners). The semi-structured interviews explored participants' knowledge, involvement and experience regarding peacebuilding activities in the cities, and participants were asked to speak about their dreams for their cities.

Participants also helped identify current initiatives, at either government or community level, to map the places where cultural and/or peacebuilding activities were taking place. In Medellín, a survey with 1158 participants from the urban area was also conducted, while in Acapulco, seven focus groups were carried out with a range of these stakeholders, including artists, small business entrepreneurs, community workers and young people, many of them from, or working with, vulnerable groups such as the minority indigenous populations, women, the LGBTQI+ community and victims of violence and disappearances. A cultural intervention was also carried out in a community in Acapulco with 25 children between 3 and 13 years of age in Colonia Llano Largo for a week to gather evidence of how local artists could work with this age group. Finally, a workshop was held in Acapulco which included online presentations and encouraged a dialogue between grassroots organisations in Medellín and in Acapulco.

Ethics approval was granted from the University of Glasgow in 2020, and all ethical procedures and processes were followed. Plain-language forms and consent sheets were provided for participants. All the researchers have worked in violent conflicts before and therefore were sensitive to the potentially distressing nature of discussions. All the researchers had signposting information available, and the right to stop the interviews or be removed from the research was explained to all participants. Data were analysed in multiple ways. Interview data were thematically organised, creating seven large themes and multiple sub-themes covering existing practices and tensions in peacebuilding activities. Policy analysis from Medellín was grouped into five key approaches, discussed below. Mapping data were gathered initially via desk-based review and then subsequently using online participatory mapping with participants using GeoJSON software (see Cradall, 2021). These data highlighted a visual representation of infrastructure gaps in peacebuilding initiatives. Survey data provided graphical depictions of collected views and provided detailed contextual information on Medellín.

Together, these methods helped to provide a broader and more accurate sense of the interaction between the different actors and stakeholders, which helped build an understanding of how each of the cities has been approaching community regenerative peacebuilding. The research project itself acted as a catalyst for people to come together and it reinvigorated discussions about past, current and potential initiatives. After providing a brief context for each city, we summarise some of main points seen by research participants as essential in the recovery and sustainability of community spaces and follow this with a final reflection on what we can learn from these cities' tales in our conclusion.

Two Cities: Medellín and Acapulco

While both cities have a history of violence, much of which is related to drug crime, there are specific political, historical and geographical differences which need to be acknowledged from the start and which have influenced the ways in which communities have been able (or not) to recover spaces for peacebuilding. This section provides some of the necessary background context for understanding the factors that have had an impact on the decreasing level of violence in Medellín, and the increasing level in Acapulco. It also notes some of the main government-led initiatives for peacebuilding through culture and the arts in both cities.

After this section, we look in more depth at the responses of the interviewees from both cities and their perspectives on the success or failure of these initiatives.

Medellín

Medellín is the city with the second largest population in Colombia, a country infamous in the 1980s and 1990s for its drug cartels as well as the complex 50-year conflict between the state, left-wing guerrillas and right-wing paramilitaries, during which atrocities committed by all three groups caused thousands of deaths, including among civilians. The conflict officially ended in 2016, when the FARC (Revolutionary Armed Forces of Colombia) and the government signed a peace deal. Despite peace being declared, the legacy of conflict can have significant, long-lasting impacts. Nevertheless, the country continues to work to sustain peace and has, as mentioned, witnessed a significant reduction in violence. Medellín in the early 1990s was known as the murder capital of the world. During this time there was immigration into the city from other regions of the country, as a result of forced displacement due to violence. However, towards the end of that decade it reinvented itself through industrialisation, urban development and international trade, which seems to have led to a decrease in violence and poverty. Although the current violence figures show that the city still faces important challenges in terms of security and coexistence, various statistics show that there has been a substantial improvement. For example, homicides were down from 232 per 100,000 inhabitants in 1990 to 23 in 2019; armed actions per year were 211 in 1993, down to 96 in 2009; and terrorist actions were more than 50 per year between 1993 and 2000, but down to less than five after 2008. There was also decrease in the reception of displaced population: from 40,000 in 2001 to less than 10,000 in 2017 (Fundación Ideas Para La Paz, 2020). In 2016, the city won the biennial Lee Kuan Yew World City Prize and a few years later, in recognition of its success in promoting an inclusive educational strategy, in 2017 Medellín was named a UNESCO Learning City and in 2019 gained a Learning Cities Award.

This transformation over the last 40 years has been the subject of much political and academic discussion, which has sought to pinpoint the main factors for the significant decrease in the rate of violence, though it seems clear that these factors involve a range of processes, actions and decisions of different actors at different moments in the city's history. These factors include, among other things, the individual and collective demobilisation processes; agreements between criminal groups, police and military strategies; transformations in citizen culture; the generation of employment; incentives to encourage continuity in educational cycles from early childhood to university; support from international cooperation; accompaniment and investment by private enterprise; continuity in

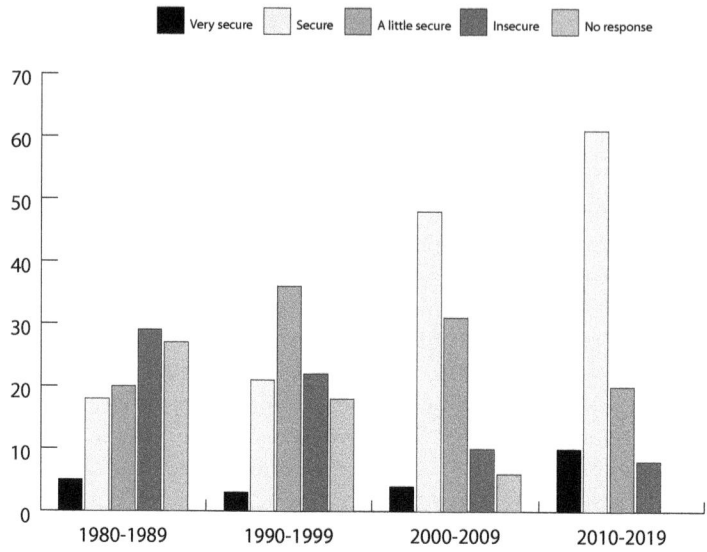

Figure 5.1 Perception of safety survey conducted in Medellín: Percentages of responses to the survey item 'Please rate how safe the neighbourhood where you live was in the following decades'

public policies over several governments; and the generation of cultural and community processes as forms of resistance to violence (Echeverry & Bravo, 2009; Fundación Ideas Para La Paz, 2020). Identifying and determining which of these factors have had the greatest impact on the rates of violence is a difficult task, and one which requires research into public policies and the views of stakeholders and actors who lived through these changes.

In the survey conducted in Medellín to map people's memory of the city over different decades, the perception of insecurity in the neighbourhood decreased from 29% to 8% between the 1980s and 2019 (Figure 5.1). The perception of safety also grew correspondingly (from 18% of people feeling safe to 61%).

Increased feelings of security provide insight into everyday peace in Medellín. Interestingly, there has also been a significant growth in cultural/educational facilities and community organisations over the last 30 years. Figure 5.2 maps community-based organisations prior to 1980 and Figure 5.3 maps them for the period 1990–1999. While these maps cannot guarantee they include the totality of the cultural and educational facilities and organisations, they provide an overview drawn from public records. There is a visible concentration of community and culturally based projects in communities where the highest rates of homicidal

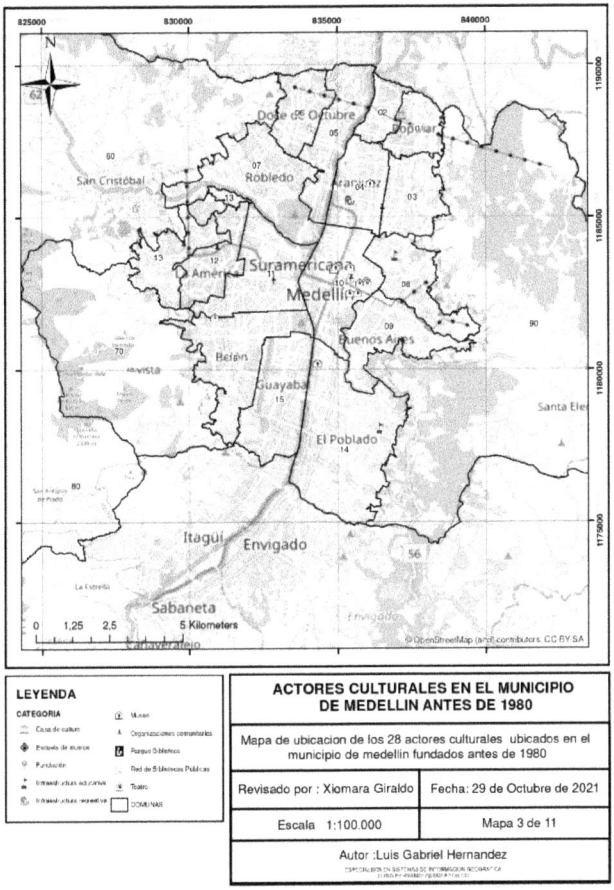

Figure 5.2 Cultural actors identified in Medellín before 1980. Credit: Fundación Ideas para la Paz

violence have historically been recorded in the city. Although the correlation between the concentration of cultural and educational facilities and places with a critical history of violence are not explored in detail in this chapter, it demonstrates the importance of investigating the role of culture and non-formal education in contexts of violence.

In addition, the public policy review carried out for this project indicated some of the main political commitments that have had an important influence on the construction of the community and organisational contexts that supported the social transformation in Medellín. While security and policing strategies clearly had an impact and although the public policies which targeted social and cultural issues were not necessarily aimed at reducing violence, the sustained governmental plan

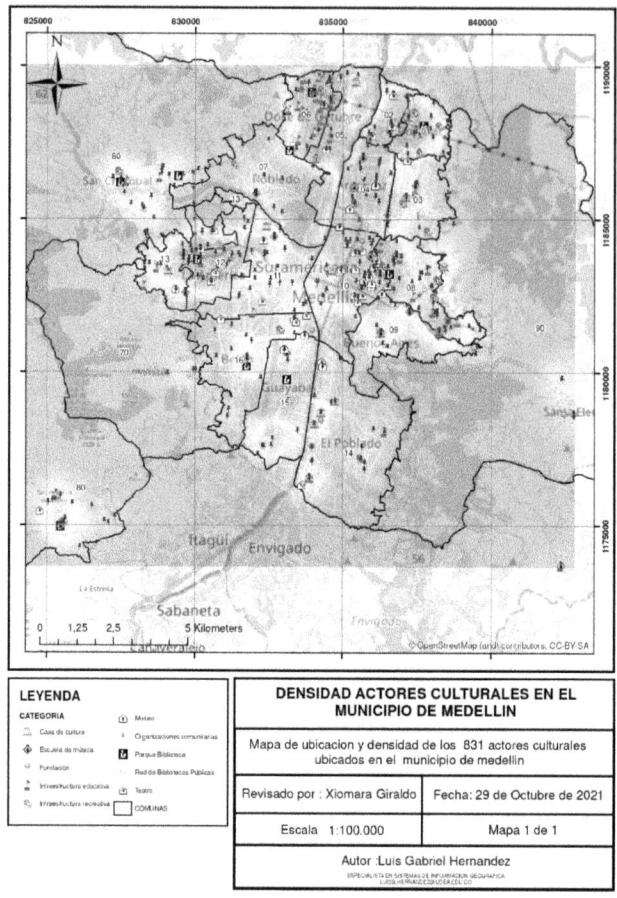

Figure 5.3 Density of cultural actors identified in Medellín during the period 1990–1999. Credit: Fundación Ideas para la Paz

that articulated with the private sector in terms of investment in educational and cultural infrastructure generated organic social and cultural movements and the development of the concept of civic culture linked to the appropriation of public space. This mix of factors seems to have had an enormous impact on the reduction of homicidal violence. These factors can be grouped into five dimensions: policies that consider infrastructure as a tool; policies that guarantee continuity in the educational cycle; citizen coexistence and civic education; culture as an urban marketing strategy and intervention; and articulation between the public and private sectors in the educational sphere. Broadly considered, cultural aspects are linked to all five dimensions because culture and cultural initiatives have benefited from infrastructure; are connected to educational policy;

are used as a marketing tool, as a tourist attraction and for economic development; and, finally, generate interaction and coexistence between diverse population groups.

Several different programmes were implemented to encourage citizen participation in cultural and educational activities and to improve interpersonal trust. The *Manual de Convivencia Ciudadana* (Manual of Citizen Coexistence) (Alcaldía de Medellín, 2013), for example, has been a pedagogical tool to promote peaceful coexistence and respect for norms. Likewise, the Casa de la Memoria Museum, created in 2012, is intended to promote social reconciliation processes and peacebuilding; it also provides lifelong learning opportunities to citizens. One of the most emblematic programmes in Medellín's transformation is the network of *parques biblioteca* (library parks), which comprises 36 information units located at strategic points in 16 *comunas* (neighbourhoods) and five townships in the city. Strategically located in vulnerable areas, the library parks facilitate access to information in an inclusive environment as well as interaction between communities in vulnerable areas, and they host a range of training and cultural events aimed at integral human development and social cohesion. The strategy includes funding libraries, aiming to transfer knowledge and access to information and content, to promote a better-informed citizen to participate in political and social decisions for the city.

Successive government administrations decided to incorporate a cultural perspective into their planning processes because they considered it as an 'indispensable condition for the integral development of the city and the conquest of peace' (Alcaldía de Medellín, 2014). They developed the cultural sector as an axis for the modernisation of Medellín, which meant that cultural resources were conceived as essential to satisfy the vital needs of recreation and citizen integration. According to public management reports, the construction of cultural and educational facilities and infrastructure has facilitated the development of personal, collective and community projects in the city as well as encouraged the circulation of information and the creation of citizen dialogue. As one government official summed it up:

> The policies that the city has today – from the general law of action of the Ministry of Citizen Culture, from the policies that stimulate art and culture, from the networks of artistic practice, of events in the city – [all] point to a society of peace, of innovation and cultural creation [which] looks to promote, through art and culture, relationships in a society which is more respectful of the other.[…] Art, culture and education have provided a great deal towards having a city today that has a focus on creative outlook, but a creativity focused on social development, social transformation and educational transformation to be better citizens, more respectful and peaceful citizens. (Medellín, local government official, male)

At the same time, grassroots activities were also encouraged and helped establish some of the local *casas* (community centres), which also use creative methodologies for engagement. The case of Medellín thus provides evidence for the statement from the Organisation for Economic Cooperation and Development (OECD) that ensuring continuity and transversality in the implementation of public policies, along with the political will to coordinate top-down and bottom-up interventions, is crucial to enabling long-standing peace and sustainable development (OECD, 2020).

Acapulco

According to the 2020 Population and Housing Census conducted by the National Institute of Statistics and Geography (INEGI), the municipality of Acapulco has a total of 779,566 inhabitants. While the seaport has been the most important one on Mexico's Pacific coast for nearly 500 years, from the mid-20th century the city began to rely on tourism as the main economic activity. Its climate and natural beauty attracted national and international travellers, including many celebrities, and in the 1970s and 1980s it was dubbed 'Acapulco Dorado' ('Golden Acapulco'). It also attracted economic migrants from all over the state of Guerrero and the rest of Mexico, lured by the promise of work, who joined other groups living in the city, including Indigenous and Afro-Mexican communities. A complex range of factors has meant that, since then, it has become one of the most violent cities in the world, and it is ironic that the state of Guerrero, in which the city it is located, is also historically known for producing famous revolutionaries and therefore heavy-handed government repression (most recently and notably in the case of the 43 students from Ayotzinapa whose disappearance has never been fully explained) (Solano, 2014).

The resort continues to be famous for its nightlife but also for 'drug tourism', as its advantageous geographical position has made it a strategic corridor for drug trafficking, with fights to control distribution routes heightening gang warfare (Flannery, 2016). During the government of Felipe Calderón (2006–2012), the city was part of the national strategy to fight drug cartels through a 'war on drugs', but this top-down approach, which put military forces on the streets, only escalated the level of violence (Rodrigues *et al.*, 2017), and international tourism significantly decreased year on year due to violence, pollution and general insecurity (Rivera-Gonzales, 2021). Because of its focus on the beach area, with its plethora of expensive hotels and night-life venues, the periphery and surrounding areas of the city tend to be more economically disadvantaged; basic services like water and electricity are often unavailable, and communities experience high levels of drug-related violence (Rodrigues *et al.*, 2017). Statistics from 2010 revealed that 51.6% of the population lived in a situation of poverty in 2010, with 31.6% in extreme poverty (CONEVAL, 2012), in stark contrast to those at the top of the tourist industry and those who come to enjoy the beach-front attractions.

The range of factors that cause and sustain violence in the city include this history of wealth and poverty but also structural corruption along with impunity and a lack of efficient judiciary institutions (UNESCO, 2021). Donoso's research work over several studies breaks these factors down further – as well as their consequences – citing lack of infrastructure, urban segmentation, discrimination and an investment in security that solely covers tourist areas as some of the main issues (see Donoso & del Carmen, 2020; Donoso & Delice, 2018; Donoso & Guerrero, 2021, among others). Despite programmes designed to reduce violence and criminal activity being implemented by successive administrations, homicide numbers continue to increase (Secretariado Ejecutivo del Sistema Nacional de Seguridad Pública, 2023) and in many ways violence has become 'normalised' at all levels, from domestic abuse to theft, kidnapping and femicide. Statistics from the National Institute of Statistics and Geography (INEGI) in 2010 registered the highest homicide index in the country, with 63 homicides per 100,000 inhabitants (more than triple the national average). Violence disproportionately affects young people and women; according to a study from 2015, 46% of deaths were among people between 15 and 29 years of age (Solano, 2014) and, according to Donoso and Delice (2018: 169), their involvement in crime has to do with their being severely marginalised in educational, economic and social terms.

Local and municipal government efforts to counteract the effects of violence have involved sporadically injecting resources into improving social cohesion, along with some peacebuilding activities (Arteaga, 2009). Some have included using culture and art for restoring social cohesion within the cultural centres that exist in a few of the larger neighbourhoods and which also offer sporting facilities and events for young people. Two wider programmes, linked to national strategies to promote culture and arts, stand out: the orchestras for children and young people set up in two marginalised districts; and the Escuela de Iniciación Artística. These programmes were set up in 2012 and 2014, respectively, by the Ministry of Culture for Guerrero and the National Institute of Arts. Due to political tensions and the lack of sustained financial support, both have been affected by frequent periods of uncertainty and closure. The Municipal Development Plan for 2018–2021 (Government of Acapulco, 2018), for example, outlined regulations and guidelines to promote and encourage access to quality education and cultural opportunities in the city. This was under the government of former President Peña Nieto, whose PRONAPRED programme for the prevention of crime seems to have had the most positive impact in terms of promoting peace in the city (Rodriguez, 2020) and was mentioned by several interviewees in the present study.

More recently, at a national level, since 2018, under President López Obrador, the Ministry of Culture has launched activities under a 'Cultural Community' framework which aims to recover public spaces and support cultural rights. While these and other initiatives may be successful for a few years, because outcomes are not consistently documented it is hard to find any evidence of their impact. It also has not helped that each of the three levels of government (municipal, regional and federal) have at times been led by opposing political parties. This has presented challenges of coordination and communication; however, the main issue has been a lack of continuity between administrations because changes every three to four years due to elections usually mean that new authorities cease all programmes linked to the previous administrations, even when they are successful.

There have also been initiatives for peace led by the Catholic Church and other religious groups (El Observador, 2015), though they mainly tend to provide psychological and spiritual victim support (Mendieta & Juárez, 2017). Artistic and cultural activities are more often run by grassroots organisations, but these are often very localised and have short lifespans and there is a lack of knowledge about their impact. The lack of funding, which affects both institutional and grassroots activities, leads to a lack of visibility, of continuity and of building of wider support networks which could help sustainability. Overall, it is not surprising that one participant described most peacebuilding initiatives in Acapulco, especially those set up by government authorities, as offering merely 'un pañito de agua tibia' (a lick of paint) (Acapulco, civil organisation, male).

Recovering and Sustaining Community Spaces

Most interviewees in Medellín were convinced that cultural and artistic activities (many also mentioned sports) provided alternative spaces for young people to move away from involvement in drugs, gangs and crime. They pointed to the network of libraries in the city as an example of the alternative possibilities opened through these spaces:

> ... they became spaces for community coexistence. The community began to see the possibility ... of creating strategies to take young people away from those delinquent gangs and the violent situation they were in. And then the young people also saw that there were possibilities, through theatre, art, reading, anyway, all that this network of libraries generated in those communities. (Medellín, volunteer civil organisation, female)

The survey in Medellín also revealed that participants were aware of, on average, the existence of 35% of the cultural and educational facilities in their neighbourhood, and these were perceived as actions that contributed to the construction of peace in homes and neighbourhood environments. At the same time, more than 53% of those surveyed had

Figure 5.4 Photographs of Comuna 13 and the street art promoting reading, education and literature, taken by Gormally on a trip to Medellín, April 2022

never accessed these facilities. Despite this, as noted above, many felt that the promotion of education, particularly in those areas that had recorded high levels of violence, was a positive move to peace. Figure 5.4 shows four pictures of Comuna 13 and the street art promoting reading, education and literature. While the transformation of community spaces is difficult to correlate directly to the decrease in violence, it undoubtedly was part of a broader approach and set of policies which prioritised alternative opportunities and opening public spaces.

Interviewees in Acapulco also believed that arts and culture had potential for peacebuilding and restoring social cohesion and that the promotion of education and access to cultural and recreational activities could help reduce participation in criminal actions. At the same time, they were vocal about the challenges and barriers to creating, accessing and sustaining cultural interventions, with most of the criticisms aimed at a lack of understanding or consultation, inconsistent investment and corruption at all levels of government. While we recognise the need to address the last, this chapter focuses on more local needs and ways forward; therefore, in what follows, we have highlighted some of the recurrent themes from the triangulation of data sources which identify some of the crucial elements required for recovering and sustaining community spaces for peacebuilding. While most spotlight arts and culture, some also refer more to broader contexts involved in peacebuilding, such as victim support.

Infrastructure that responds to the needs of local communities

All the data sources coincided in the view that the successive investments in infrastructure by Medellín authorities, often in collaboration with the business sector, was a crucial element in the overall transformation of the city. As well as the library park network, projects such as the Metrocable (a gondola lift) and electric escalators (Figure 5.5 shows photographs of the escalator beside the steep steps going up through Comuna 13) were designed to improve the lives of inhabitants of informal settlements by connecting them to the city centre and central resources. However, some interviewees noted that, while well intentioned, these interventions did not always work due to insufficient consultation with the local communities and the assumption that this infrastructure would alleviate more structural problems such as poverty. The result of this is that, for some residents, changes have proved only superficial.

In Acapulco there has been far less investment in permanent infrastructure and neither the business sectors nor the communities tend to be consulted or involved in any decisions about infrastructure, peacebuilding programmes or cultural initiatives. Even when some of the programmes proved successful, no permanent structures were created which would allow them to continue (e.g. building a theatre venue rather than encouraging occasional street performances) and making use of existing physical spaces (e.g. restoring abandoned sites). The need for a diverse range of groundwork projects was also mentioned, not just for the local communities, but also for the development of industry so that Acapulco could move away from its dependence on tourism. However, as one interviewee argued, even more crucial for moving forward with any peacebuilding is ensuring basic public services for all communities:

> ... if there is no transversal, integral, public policy that achieves a better quality of life for these inhabitants, well, then we will continue to repeat the same thing [...] as well as taking culture and healthy entertainment [to poorer neighbourhoods], it is important that the state be present in terms of the areas of medicine, educational areas, the construction of road infrastructure, improvement of drainage, water, etc. (Acapulco, artist, M)

Community Spaces for Peacebuilding in Medellín and Acapulco 111

Figure 5.5 Photographs of the escalator beside the steep steps going up through Comuna 13, taken by Gormally on a trip to Medellín, April 2022

This coincides with the process for peacebuilding recommended by United Nations Peacebuilding (2020) in which investment and the engagement with community leaders are fundamental to creating a visible, sustainable, community-based infrastructure in the city that includes cultural centres and other sites for supporting educational and cultural actions for everyone.

Identity and inclusion

When talking about the importance of feeling a sense of pride in one's city and thus wanting to improve its image as well as reduce violence, the significance of the identity and belonging emerged. 'Paisa culture' was mentioned as an identity which many in the Antioquia region, where Medellín is located, felt part of and which has been promoted by cultural policy and practice. Alongside this strong local identity, there was an awareness of diverse cultural expressions relating to the identity of different social groups, along with attempts to recognise and include them. Others mentioned that the move from an elite understanding of 'culture' to a wider view of it allowed reaching and including social sectors that had historically been excluded as well as considering artists as agents of change:

> culture was reformulated and went from being a vehicle for aesthetics and beauty for one social group to being a motor for development as women and citizens of different social classes who had been denied access to cultural activities, and who, little by little, began to benefit from the distribution of culture in the city. (Medellín, university academic, male)

They also mentioned the importance of having 'buy-in' by all members of the community, including shopkeepers and street vendors; as one interviewee noted, 'with the guy who runs the shop, with the orange juice lady' (Medellín, researcher civil organisation, male).

In contrast, participants in Acapulco lamented the lack of identity, not only of the population (including the loss of the original identities of certain migrant groups) but also of the city itself, due to its history as a port and of extractivist tourism. This lack of identity and sense of belonging was seen as one of the reasons for inhabitants not caring about what was happening in the city:

> ... there is no sense of taking care of the city. They don't feel it is their own, that is, organised crime and violence have taken ownership of the public spaces and the people don't have any interest in recovering it because you are in that same cycle of violence, of repression and insecurity. (Acapulco, social worker, female)

The creation of alternative convivial spaces requires an inclusive focus. While young people were the main concern of many of the projects in both cities, there was a clear sense of the need to include different generations, as well as groups who had immigrated from other regions. It emerged that there has been ongoing work in Medellín to recognise the diversity of its inhabitants and to move away from the stigma attached to certain groups as being more violent or criminal. Some cultural organisations have sought to create community cohesion based on recognising and valuing diversity. In Acapulco, the presence of Indigenous and Afro-Mexicans groups was scarcely mentioned by the interviewees, although when it was mentioned, the recognition and celebration of their diverse cultures and arts was, as in Medellín, considered important for contesting stereotypes. At the same time, negative attitudes among the population in Acapulco – *machista*, misogynist, racist and classist – were cited as working against the attempts at inclusion; as one person noted, over the years these attitudes have been responsible for 'building narratives of marginalisation towards Indigenous peoples, towards women, towards the poor, towards the darker-skinned' (Acapulco, foundation director, male).

Visibility and networks

Unsurprisingly, the process of mapping existing projects highlighted that the number of projects, either institutional or community-based, in Medellín was substantially higher than in Acapulco. In addition to having more visibility, grassroots initiatives, such as in the *casas*, often had a base, however small, in local communities. In Acapulco, while the research also located pockets of cultural initiatives, these were mainly sporadic and had no fixed geographical location. From the interviews, it could be gathered that over the last 10 years, these initiatives tended to be very localised and information between different projects was hardly ever shared. Interviewees were mostly not aware of projects across the city unless they were the immediate beneficiaries or developers.

Yet a lack of articulation and dialogue was also an issue between the community projects scattered throughout Medellín. Stakeholders noted this was partly to do with the fact that art and culture initiatives, together with other forms of non-formal education, do not always require formal recognition (e.g. from an institution or government authority). This situation was said to be more noticeable in the more rural outskirts of Medellín, where a disconnect was perceived between the mayor's office and the organisations that carry out cultural activities. Organisations called for an improvement of the channels of communication and articulation of common goals, so that public facilities could be better used by the communities, as well as supporting a better response to funding calls. Interviewees also mentioned that programmes often remained at the level of government workers or even artists, with no view to include the public in the creation of activities, something which could perhaps lead to a wider development of artistic talents.

In Acapulco, interviewees noted that links are needed across government programmes, most of which tended to concentrate on one topic, such as drug addiction, but did not take a holistic approach: for example, the lack of alternative activities and spaces for young people. Another movement, Todos Por La Paz, attempted to include different sectors of public administration such as culture, health, sport and education, but ineffective communication and lack of remuneration for artists led to issues among participants. One of the most successful *colectivos* (collectives) in the city, Familias de Acapulco en Busca de sus Desaparecidos (Acapulco Families Looking for Their Disappeared), has a wide network of interinstitutional support, from the Archdiocese to news media channels.

Continuity and monitoring

Despite various periods of disruption, the data provided evidence that much of the success of the transformation of Medellín has been due to the continuity of projects by successive government administrations, many of which have supported the arts and culture as routes towards peacebuilding. Long-term investment has been a crucial element of this continuity. However, in the exchanges between grassroots organisations in both cities, those in Medellín pointed out that it was fundamental not to rely solely on government funding and they offered examples of what they had done to obtain funding from other national and international institutions or businesses. Sustaining these grassroots cultural and informal education projects for young people and communities can provide positive alternatives to violence and conflict (Brody, 2022).

Interviewees in Acapulco agreed that it was vital to ensure consistency for participants, especially when young people were involved and that there were no 'quick fix' solutions. Another criticism of the government projects was that many attempts to 'reconstruct the social fabric' through the arts and culture were superficial and, rather than creating the conditions for this reconstruction and healing, they were merely 'bringing in the clowns' as a form of temporary distraction. However, there was also consensus in the experiences recalled that even short projects had a wide-ranging positive impact on participants.

Monitoring was key, according to research participants in both countries, but, according to them, this did not often happen. While there were plenty of stories and examples of success, along with the recognition that measuring peacebuilding is complex, there was an agreement that in any project it is essential to set up monitoring for an evaluation of impact. As one interviewee from Medellín put it:

> [for education] we have the X tests and the Y tests, so that is the way we measure education and, many times, it is transferred to the way we also measure the social investments in that dimension. But when they tell you that culture changes human behaviour and the way you see others, that it helps you have resilience, that it is a way of understanding difference, that it is a way of learning to respect, that it is a community way of thinking, that is very difficult to measure. (Medellín, private foundation, F)

Conclusion

In this tale of how communities in two cities have struggled, and continue to struggle, to recover and sustain convivial spaces that contribute to peacebuilding and social transformation, what emerges is a strong belief in cultural and artistic approaches, as well as in the value of stakeholder partnerships. The gathered experiences show there is clear awareness of the barriers to initiating and sustaining these and other approaches, such as sports and non-formal educational activities. At the same time, these experiences also show that actors such as civil society organisations, artists and young people are finding new and creative ways for getting around these barriers. One such project, Aca En Bici, has been proven successful through establishing a multidisciplinary, collaborative network between urban planners, architects, graphic designers and artists to reactivate the economy through the creation of safe bicycle routes through the city (Aca En Bici, 2020). These restorations build not only on physical infrastructure and resources but also on prefiguring a different vision. One participant in Medellín described the need for this shift: 'there was a consensus […] that we had to generate new imaginaries that would break from the sole focus on the drug culture' (Medellín, university academic, male).

The research in Medellín provided evidence that cultural and educational actors have played an essential role within the vision of development of this city (and the wider regional department of Antioquia) over the last two decades. Led by artists and young people, and supported by civil society organisations, education and culture have become a way of resisting violence and redefining symbols and places related to death and human rights violations. The department of Antioquia and successive political leaders also supported this vision of culture and education as axes of transformation by investing in infrastructure and financing cultural intervention programmes.

However, when we began the research, an overall picture of cultural organisations and connections across them in Medellín was still lacking, and this was also the case in Acapulco. The exercise of geo-mapping locations was shown to help build this picture; it contributed to visibility, creating networks and making a case for recovering community spaces (and requesting funding). The exercise proved that tracking and monitoring of cultural and peacebuilding activities can highlight the positive ways in which spaces are being used, showing there is room for creativity, imagination and collective care, and that these ways can construct a counternarrative to that of violence and move the focus to the stakeholders who are trying to make a difference. While some activities are organic, responsive and short term, and may not have a specific locale, raising their profile within local communities is vital in the day-to-day process of negotiating peacebuilding.

El Acapulco que soñamos (2022) was a document developed from gathering the views of stakeholders that participated in the project and which included the challenges, but also proposed solutions to moving towards everyday peace in Acapulco. These solutions point to the need for cross-sectional articulation and, most importantly, to the need for a trust-based relationship among local government, civil society and private organisations, along with the arts and the cultural sector. There is a strong belief that local communities have the capacity to find and implement solutions, effectively challenge violence and conflict, and offer alternative opportunities. The document points to the crucial issue of supporting these grassroots initiatives by creating long-lasting policy programmes, with adequate resources, that are protected against changes in administration to ensure continuity and transversality. Artistic and cultural approaches and partnerships are seen as part of the restoration of inclusive community spaces, for bringing people together in activities that provide an alternative to living with violence and build peace through encouraging dialogue and a sense of belonging so that all communities in the city can thrive.

Note

(1) The research project was 'Educational Peacebuilding in Medellín and Acapulco: Understanding the role of education, culture and learning in responding to crises', funded by the British Academy, 2020–2022 (ERICC\190110).

References

Aca En Bici (2020) Aca en Bici. https://www.acaenbici.com (accessed 19 March 2021).

Alcaldía de Medellín (2013) Manual de convivencia ciudadana. https://www.Medellín.gov.co/irj/portal/Medellín?NavigationTarget=contenido/1068-Manual-de-Convivencia-Ciudadana (accessed 22 May 2021).

Alcaldía de Medellín (2014) Plan de desarrollo cultural de Medellín 2011–2020. https://www.Medellín.gov.co/irj/portal/Medellín?NavigationTarget=contenido/1081-Plan-de-Desarrollo-Cultural-de-Medellín-2011-2020"https://www.Medellín.gov.co/irj/portal/Medellín?NavigationTarget=contenido/1081-Plan-de-Desarrollo-Cultural-de-Medellín-2011-2020 (accessed 22 March 2021).

Arteaga, N. (2009) The Merida initiative: Security-surveillance harmonization in Latin America. *European Review of Latin American and Caribbean Studies/Revista Europea de Estudios Latinoamericanos y Del Caribe* 87, 103–110. http://www.jstor.org/stable/25676378.

Brody, A. (2022) *Engaging and Empowering Young People Through Arts and Humanities Approaches in the Context of Global Challenges. A Research Report by PRAXIS: Arts and Humanities for Global Development*. University of Leeds.

CONEVAL (2012) Informe de pobreza y evaluación en el estado de Guerrero 2012. https://www.coneval.org.mx/coordinacion/entidades/SiteAssets/Paginas/Guerrero/monyeval/Informe%20de%20pobreza%20y%20evaluaci%C3%B3n%202012_Guerrero.pdf"https://www.coneval.org.mx/coordinacion/entidades/SiteAssets/Paginas/Guerrero/monyeval/Informe%20de%20pobreza%20y%20evaluaci%C3%B3n%202012_Guerrero.pdf (accessed 7 March 2021).

Cradall (University of Glasgow Centre for Research and Development in Adult and Lifelong Learning (CR&DALL)) (2021) Mapping cultural and nonformal education (briefing paper 4). https://cradall.org/content/briefing-paper-4-mapping-cultural-and-nonformal-education (accessed 3 July 2024).

Cradall (2022) 'The Acapulco we want': Unites artists, stakeholders and government in working towards peace. https://cradall.org/content/acapulco-we-want-unites-artists-stakeholders-and-government-working-towards-peace (accessed 27 November 2022).

Donoso, J. and Delice, P.A. (2018) Propuestas de políticas públicas para la prevención de la violencia y el delito en Acapulco, Guerrero 2018. *Inciso* 20 (1), 137–145.

Donoso, J. and Del Carmen, R. (2020) Cartografía y Morfología de la muerte en Acapulco. In J. Acuña and E. Sánchez (eds) *Cotidianidad, Educación y Violencia en el Estado de Guerrero: Otras Prácticas y Quehaceres en un Mundo Turbulento*. Universidad Hipócrates.

Donoso, J. and Guerrero, J. (2021) Diseño urbano desigual, inclusión cultural diferenciada y violencia criminal en Acapulco. In M. Vargas and L. Fuentes (eds) *Violencias, Pobreza y Desigualdad* (pp. 215–245). Ediciones Universidad Nacional Autónoma de México.

Echeverry, M.C. and Bravo, M.V. (2009) Balance plan estratégico de Medellín y área metropolitana. https://www.yumpu.com/es/document/view/15234913/balance-plan-estrategico-Medellín-area-metropolitana-informe-final (accessed 12 March 2021).

El Observador (2015) Inicia proyecto de construcción de paz con jóvenes en Acapulco. *El Observador*, 22 January. https://elobservadorenlinea.com/2015/01/8011/ (accessed 7 March 2021).

Eversley, J., Gormally, S. and Kilmurray, A. (eds) (2022) *Peacebuilding, Conflict and Community Development*. Policy Press.

Flannery, N.P. (2016) From glamour to gunfire: The tourist city of Acapulco torn apart by violence. *Guardian*, 13 December. https://www.theguardian.com/cities/2016/dec/13/gunfire-tourist-resort-acapulco-mexico-torn-apart-violence (accessed 29 July 2024).

Fundación Ideas Para La Paz (2020) *Interim Report for Educational Peacebuilding*. British Academy.

Gormally, S., Arizpe, E. and Bahena-Rivera, A. (2023) What would peace look like in Acapulco? The views of local practitioners and stakeholders. *Journal of Peacebuilding and Development* 18 (2), 195–209.

Government of Acapulco (2018) Plan Municipal de Desarrollo. https://www.scribd.com/document/536956583/Plan-Municipal-de-Desarrollo-2018-2021 (accessed 29 July 2024).

Hunter, M.A. and Cohen, C.E. (2019) Arts and peacebuilding. In M.A. Hunter (ed.) *Oxford Research Encyclopedia of Education*. Oxford University Press.

Hyoeun Bang, A.H. (2016) The restorative and transformative power of the arts in conflict resolution. *Journal of Transformative Education* 14 (4), 355–376.

Lederach, J.P. (2001) Civil society and reconciliation. In C.A. Crocker, F. Hampson and P. Anall (eds) *Turbulent Peace: The Challenges of Managing International Conflict* (pp. 841–855). US Institute of Peace.

MacGinty, R. (2014) Everyday peace: Bottom-up and local agency in conflict-affected societies. *Security Dialogue* 45 (6), 548–564.

Mendieta, J. and Juárez, C. (2017) *Del horror a la esperanza: Aportes del Proyecto de Acompañamiento a Víctimas de las Violencias a la construcción de la paz en Acapulco*. Catholic Relief Services. https://www.crs.org/sites/default/files/tools-research/del-horror-a-la-esperanza-research-study-mexico-peacebuilding-project.pdf (accessed 7 April 2021).

Niño, N.C. (2022) Peacebuilding with youth: Experience in Cúcuta, Colombia. In J. Eversley, S. Gormally and A. Kilmurray (eds) *Peacebuilding, Conflict and Community Development* (pp. 40–58). Policy Press.

OECD (2020) *A Territorial Approach to the Sustainable Development Goals: Synthesis Report*. OECD iLibrary. https://doi.org/10.1787/e86fa715-en (accessed 7 February 2020).

Partlow, J. (2017) Acapulco is now Mexico's murder capital. *Washington Post*, 24 August. https://www.washingtonpost.com/graphics/2017/world/how-acapulco-became-mexicos-murder-capital (accessed 25 March 2022).

Pepper, M. (2018) Ethnic minority women, diversity, and informal participation in peacebuilding in Myanmar. *Journal of Peacebuilding and Development* 13 (2), 61–75.

Phipps, A. (2017) *Research for CULT Committee – Why Cultural Work with Refugees*. European Parliament. https://www.europarl.europa.eu/RegData/etudes/IDAN/2017/602004/IPOL_IDA(2017)602004_EN.pdf (accessed 16 April 2021).

Rivera-Gonzales, O.D. (2021) Factores generadores de la disminución del turismo y afectaciones posteriores, zona costera Acapulco, México. *Revista Geográfica de América Central* 67 (2), 241–273.

Rodrigues, T., Kalil, M., Zepeda, R. and Rosen, J.D. (2017) War zone Acapulco: Urban drug trafficking in the Americas. *Contexto Internacional* 39 (3), 609–631.

Rodriguez, O.H. (2020) Percepción de efectividad del Programa Nacional de Prevención del Delito (PRONAPRED) en Acapulco, Guerrero. https://alacip.org/cong19/471-hernandez-19.pdf (accessed 2 March 2021).

Secretariado Ejecutivo del Sistema Nacional de Seguridad Pública (2023) Datos abiertos de incidencia delictiva, Gobierno de México. https://www.gob.mx/sesnsp/acciones-y-programas/datos-abiertos-de-incidencia-delictiva (accessed 16 April 2021).

Shank, M. and Schirch, L. (2008) Strategic arts-based peacebuilding. *Peace and Change* 33 (2), 217–242.

Solano, J. (2014) Mexico arrests gangster who allegedly conspired with cops to kill 43 students. *Business Insider*, 18 October. https://www.businessinsider.com/mexico-arrests-gangster-who-allegedly-conspired-with-cops-to-kill-43-students-2014-10?r=US&IR=T (accessed 23 May 2021).

Sommer, D. (2014) *The Work of Art in the World*. Duke University Press.

Statista (2022) Ranking of the most dangerous cities in the world in 2022, by murder rate per 100,000 inhabitants. https://www.statista.com/statistics/243797/ranking-of-the-most-dangerous-cities-in-the-world-by-murder-rate-per-capita/ (accessed 2 June 2023).

Tovar, P. (2015) Una reflexión sobre la violencia y la construcción de paz desde el teatro y el arte. *Universitas Humanística* 80, 347–369.

UNESCO (2021) International day to end impunity for crimes against journalists. Commemorations and anniversaries. https://en.unesco.org/commemorations/endimpunityday (accessed 29 July 2024).

United Nations Peacebuilding (2020) United Nations Community engagement guidelines on peacebuilding and sustaining peace. https://www.un.org/peacebuilding/sites/www.un.org.peacebuilding/files/documents/un_community-engagement_guidelines.august_2020.pdf (accessed 19 March 2021).

Vulliamy, E. (2013) Medellín, Colombia: Reinventing the world's most dangerous city. *The Guardian*, 9 June. https://www.theguardian.com/world/2013/jun/09/Medellín-colombia-worlds-most-dangerous-city (accessed August 2021).

Ware, A., Ware, V. and Kelly, L. (2022) Everyday peace as a community development approach. In J. Eversley, S. Gormally and A. Kilmurray (eds) *Peacebuilding, Conflict and Community Development* (pp. 25–39). Policy Press.

Yamin, P., Lahlou, S., Ortega, S. and Sáenz, A. (2021) The power of narratives in social norm interventions: A study of the civic culture interventions of Antanas Mockus in Bogotá, Colombia. *Center for Social Norms and Behavioral Dynamics Working Paper Series*. http://dx.doi.org/10.2139/ssrn.3978846 (accessed January 2022).

Part 2

Popular Arts and Everyday Culture Meet Gender-Based Violence

6 Popular Arts as Communication Tools for the Eradication of Gender-Based Violence and Child Marriage in Ghana

Adwoa Sikayena Amankwah, Hasiyatu Abubakari and Abigail Opoku Mensah

Introduction

According to the United Nations International Children's Emergency Fund (UNICEF, 2021: 9), in Ghana, about 20% of adolescent girls have experienced some kind of gender-based violence, more specifically sexual violence, including rape and coercion, while about 14% of adolescent girls (i.e. aged between 14 and 19 years) have become mothers and some are currently pregnant with their first child. Girls who are pregnant and living in rural areas represent close to twice that percentage figure. The alarming rate of adolescent pregnancies in rural Ghana, and specifically in the Upper East Region, has become a problem that requires immediate intervention. In 2020, 6533 teenage pregnancies were recorded in the Upper East Region among girls aged 10–14, representing an increase from 103 in 2019 to 142 in 2020. According to the Sexual and Reproductive Health and Rights (SRHR) Network in the Upper East Region, poverty and the effects of the COVID-19 pandemic, among other things, have fuelled high rates of unintended teenage pregnancies and child marriages in the region (myjoyonline.com, 2021).

This chapter describes a study set in Ghana. Appearing to support the above statistics, the singer in the study identifies that many children in Kusaal-speaking communities aged between 10 and 18 years get pregnant and are mostly given out in marriage by their parents – a revelation which raises serious concerns. Chapter 9 of this book, 'Promoting Women's Participation in Social Transformation Through Popular Arts in Kusaal-Speaking Communities in Ghana', by the same authors, discusses other aspects of the same study. That study addressed three research questions (see Chapter 9), but the present chapter addresses only the third: How can local popular culture be deployed as tools of effective communication to enable social transformation, specifically, to eradicate child marriage and enhance the education of girls and women?

The subsequent section gives background information on the Kusaal language and its people, discusses the popular culture and exposes the reader to the traditional concept of marriage among the Kusaas. A review of related literature on the subject matter then follows. By deploying uses and gratifications theory, the study attempts to explain the motivations and gratifications behind the practice of child marriage. This is followed by a section presenting the methodology and data collection. The study results are presented largely as excerpts from interviews conducted with participants to solicit their views. Based on the results of the interviews, major themes are derived to form the concept of the lyrics of the *googi* performance (song). The discussion section analyses results of the interviews and the themes of the song, and then the chapter concludes.

Background: The Kusaas and the Kusaal Language

While Kusaal is the name of the language, the speakers refer to themselves as Kusaas (in the plural) and Kusaa (singular). The traditional homeland or areas within which Kusaal is spoken in the Upper East Region

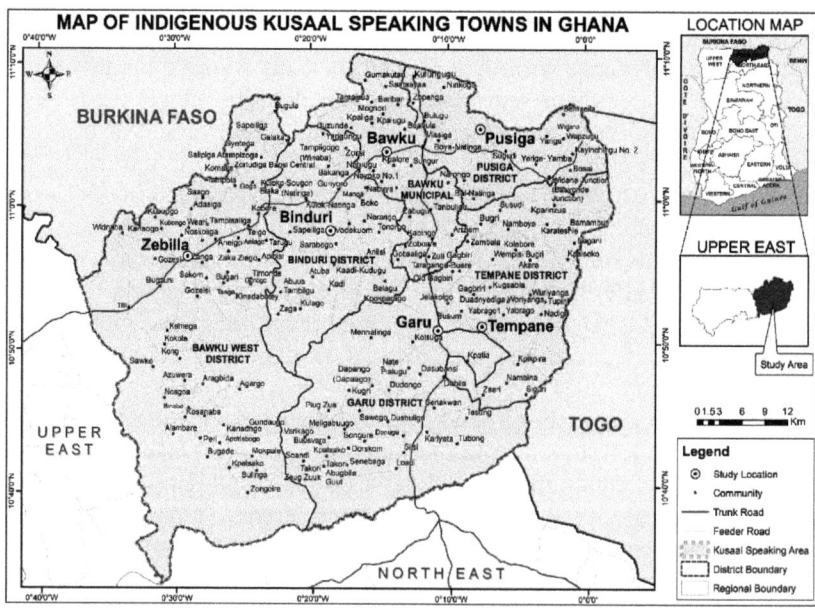

Figure 6.1 Map of the Kusaug (Abubakari, 2022)

of Ghana is referred to as Kusaug (Abubakari & Musah, 2024). Kusaal is mainly spoken in Bawku, Garu, Tempani, Pusiga, Zebilla and Binduri. Bawku serves as the major town of the Kusaas. The Pusiga-Polimakom and Binduri districts emerged from the Bawku Municipality while the Tempane district emerged from what was previously called the Garu-Tempene district. The map in Figure 6.1 shows the six district capitals of the study area.

Across the West African sub-regions, it is estimated that there are over 2 million people who use Kusaal as their native language (Abubakari & Musah, 2024). Information obtained from the Ghana Statistical Service (GSS) based on the 2010 population and housing census indicates that there are 534,681 speakers of Kusaal in the various regions and districts of Ghana (Abubakari *et al.*, n.d.). With a total population of 24,658,823 (GSS, 2012, 2016), the Kusaas constituted approximately 2.2% of the population of Ghana as of 2010. Other sources give different estimates (Abubakari, 2018). While *Ethnologue* (Simons & Fenning, 2017) estimates there are around 420,000 Kusaas in Ghana, Bodomo (2020) gives a figure of around 500,000 Kusaas across Ghana. Abubakari and Musah (2024), for their part, indicate that Ghana houses only about a quarter of the population of Kusaas, while the rest are scattered across West Africa and the diaspora.

Popular culture

The plethora of definitions of popular culture that have generated much debate in the literature (Parker, 2011) do not fall within the scope of the present chapter, which instead seeks to untangle how popular culture can be used creatively to foster social transformation. Popular culture for social transformation is here referred to as the use of local songs, folktales and docudrama, among other cultural artefacts, which are loved and enjoyed by the community from which they originate, for the purposes of education leading to social change. It is often deployed by researchers and local artists as a tool to transform archaic cultural practices that have commonly outlived their usefulness and have become sources of conflicts, including gender-based violence, in the communities within which they function.

Thus, through the vehicle of popular arts, information on the common beliefs, values and lifestyles of the people are crafted into messages and are communicated through local media such as music. In the present context, these messages are geared towards fostering social transformation by educating the local population to desist from engaging in the practice of early marriage. There is a blend of value and belief systems in addition to intangible cultural artefacts in the forms of music, narratives and drama, among others, employed to drum home messages intended to promote peace and harmony for the growth of society. The aesthetic and diversionary gratifications offered by popular culture, touching on the known, loved and appreciated cultural artefacts, makes local people identify themselves with the tools – songs, folktales and others – because inherent in them are the messages of transformation that have been communicated in acceptable formats. A *googi* performance is a local musical performance that is enjoyed by all categories of people in Kusaug. It is performed on occasions like festivals, funerals, and enskinment of chiefs and queen mothers, among other events. *Googi* performers serve as the mouthpiece of the community and have 'a poetic licence' that gives them the liberty to touch on very important sociocultural issues and criticise people in authority (see Abubakari *et al.*, 2021).

Child marriage among the Kusaas and overview of the literature

Marriage before the age of 18 is widespread in communities in both northern and southern Ghana and is an acceptable sociocultural norm among several ethnic groups in the country, with the Kusaas being no exception (Abass-Abaah, 2024; Ahosi *et al.*, 2019). Abass-Abaah (2024), with data from the Toende-speaking area of Kusaug, discusses the twin institutions of courtship and marriage among the Kusaas. In his study, he examines marriage under Ghanaian law, forms of marriage among the Kusaas and the traditional system of marriage in Kusuag. Central to our discussion are the forms of marriage in Kusuag. Abass-Abaah outlines six traditional forms of marriages acceptable in Kusaa tradition: monogamy; polygamy; affinal polygamy, whereby the co-wives come from different families and communities; and sororal polygamy, where the man is allowed to marry the sister of his wife or her other relatives when the wife is still alive (this commonly happens when a wife apparently 'fails' to deliver a male child/heir for her husband). Male children among the Kusaas, unlike girls, who will be 'married off', are assets for economic reasons; they assist on the farm, herd the cattle and sheep, handle the less laborious job of tending the fowl as well as mending the family building in the dry season. Another type of acceptable marriage among the Kusaas is a levirate marriage – whereby a brother to the deceased can marry the widow. More relevant to this work is child marriage, referred to as 'Poa Suork'. Abass-Abaah explains that Kusaa tradition permits child marriage, though he is quick to add that the practice has waned due to the abuse of the system and the misconception of the practice by external observers. Current surveys (GSS, 2018: 269–275) have consistently pointed to the Upper East Region as one of the regions with the highest incidence of child marriage. It must, however, be emphasised that the Upper East Region is home not only to the Kusaas: it also has speakers of Gurenɛ, Nankani, Kasem, Talni, Nabit, Buli and Bisah, among others. Thus, the survey results do not necessarily refer only to cases observed among speakers of Kusaal. Abass-Abaah further indicates that child marriage among the Kusaas is either for religious reasons or in appreciation of a long-standing friendship between two families or as a reward for the exceptional performance of a son-in-law.

Women who are unable to have children after more than two years of marriage are believed to be under spiritual attacks which require the intervention of a diviner. According to Abass-Abaah, a shrine priest is consulted in such instances and the child to be born is promised as a bond child or *dabit* to the shrine. Male children who are born under such circumstances are required to offer sacrifices to the deity throughout their lives, while girls are given in marriage to the priest from birth and may move to live in their new home from the age of 10. They are then made to marry the priest once they reach puberty. Similarly, when a woman suffers neonatal deaths and consults a priest for assistance, if a girl is born, she is taken to the shrine and married to the priest or any member of his family. In all these instances, the girl has no right to fully consensual marriage.

Another aspect of child marriage, described by Abass-Abaah (2024), is when a girl is given as a 'trophy' to a son-in-law who outperforms other in-laws in shows of generosity during a relative's funeral ceremony. As part of the Kusaa traditional customs, all sons-in-law play a significant role by competing with one another at the funeral of an in-law, when on the seventh night of the funeral they are all made to show their wealth. Abass-Abaah explains that each son-in-law is asked to provide the best rams he has tethered to be inspected, and the fattest and biggest among them is selected. The next stage of the competition is a parade of special baskets of balls of millet pap known as TZ (*sa'ab*) heaped into a special cone, from which a winner is selected. The third and final stage is the heaping of fermented millet (*kpaya*), a raw material for brewing *pito* (a local soft drink), into baskets by the sons-in-law, with their wives decked in velvet cloth. The women heap the commodity so high that people standing at one end cannot see those on the opposite side. The son-in-law who wins at the funeral is presented with a young girl as his wife, amid jubilation, music and dance. Abass-Abaah concludes that these are the expected gratifications that lead to the contracting of child marriages. He adds, however, that the child is treated with dignity and is groomed by a chaperon till the age of 17, a year below the legally stipulated age when she could marry.

This study observes that the cultural practice of early marriage has outlived its uses and gratifications and is currently abused, leading to rising cases of teenage pregnancies and other gender-based forms of violence in the study communities.

Theoretical Framework

The study employs the uses and gratifications (U&G) approach, which originated from Lasswell's (1948) linear model of communication, premised on 'who says what through which medium and with what effect?'. In 1974, Katz, Blumler and Gurevitch conceptualised the U&G approach to include: (1) the social and psychological origins of (2) needs, which generate (3) expectations of (4) the mass media and other sources, which lead to (5) differential patterns of media exposure, resulting in (6) need gratifications and (7) other consequences, perhaps mostly unintended ones (Katz *et al.*, 1974; see also Papacharissi, 2009: 138).

Scholars (Ancu & Cozma, 2009: 569; McLeod & Becker, 1981; Rubin, 2009: 148) have expanded the theory by citing five basic assumptions that underpin the U&G approach, as follows. First, the purpose and motivations of individuals propel their communication behaviour. Second, people are relatively active in that they are aware of their media or popular culture needs and they can select the medium and content to consume. In effect, people can rationalise their reasons for using the media: in the present context, popular arts. Third, social and psychological characteristics of individuals, structure of society, groups within it, existing relationships and personal involvement influence communication behaviour and effects. Fourth, various media compete with each other (functional alternatives) to be selected, attended to and used. Finally, interpersonal effects are more influential than media effects.

U&G theory was applied in this study because motivations for the use of popular art by Kusaas people result in communication behaviour that is likely to cause behavioural change and cultural transformation over time. Second, sociopsychological characteristics of individuals involved in producing and using popular arts are likely to influence communication behaviour in relation to other functional alternatives. Third, activity deriving from individuals' rational and purposeful selection, exposure and consumption of *googi* songs is a component of the gratification expected to be derived from it; therefore, individuals are likely to choose particular popular arts, such as *googi* performances communicated through the oral interpersonal mode, based on their needs and expectations of enlightenment on the child marriage phenomenon, which is likely to cause social transformation over time. This is because these needs culminate as motives for their consumption as well as gratifications, subsequently leading to changes from the practice of child marriage for social-transformational purposes. Thus, the study argues that the purposeful communication of messages on the hazards of child marriage is likely to trigger awareness and abhorrence of the practice over time, leading to a process of behavioural change and social transformation.

The theory of change is also adapted for the study because developmental challenges tend to be very complex and are mainly caused by different sets of factors making it necessary for a framework to be drawn to guide all stakeholders in their endeavour for change. It highlights what works and what does not work in solving the identified developmental challenges and helps to identify various stakeholders who may be relevant to meeting the objectives of the project and, in this case, in the project communities. Thus, the research questions were developed from the results of a pilot study to reflect the understanding of the relevant stakeholders in a way that would support continuous learning and improvement, leading to change in behaviour with regard to child marriage and related practices.

In the case of this project, the theory facilitates understanding of the rationale for child marriage among the communities. If this is culturally rooted, then the theory of change must start from the baseline analysis of the context and issues. Doing this will help in identifying the exact stages at which the change should occur among key stakeholders in the various communities, though this is a desired long-term change. According to Grantcraft (2006), the change requires a wider view of desired results that have to be carefully probed at each step in what may be a long and complex process even after the dissemination of results.

Methodology

This study was qualitative. Semi-structured interviews explored how popular culture can be deployed to eradicate child marriage and, subsequently, a *googi* musical performance was used to educate people about gender-based violence (GBV) and child marriage together with teenage pregnancy as well as the superior alternatives offered by traditional education. The study's 24 participants were queen mothers, opinion leaders and victims of child marriage from the six Kusaal communities. The purpose of the interviews was to find out how the Kusaas frame the GBV narrative on child marriage, the uses and gratifications of popular culture, such as songs and folktales, and how popular culture can be communicated effectively to eradicate child marriage and other GBV-related incidents.

All 24 interviews were transcribed from Kusaal to the English language in Word documents, and the first and second author read and reread these excerpts to familiarise themselves with the transcribed data. During this immersion stage, notes were taken to produce a list of ideas. Second, this list of ideas was used to generate initial codes from the data. The data were coded to generate the research questions. Coding was manually done by using highlighters to 'indicate potential patterns' (Braun & Clark, 2006: 89). A list of codes was then produced. Third, the different codes were sorted into potential themes. For example, codes sharing similar meanings were grouped and were given a common name or term to differentiate one group of codes from another. At the fourth stage, the researchers met to discuss the initial themes they had each identified. The researchers reviewed these initially identified themes together to ensure that each theme reflected the objectives and theoretical underpinnings of the study. Lastly, some rich, thick excerpts from the data were included in the write-up of the report to boost the credibility of the study's findings (Miles & Huberman, 1994).

The lyrics of the song were derived conceptually from the interview results and also translated and transcribed from Kusaal to English using the same process of content analysis as used for the interviews. The results of the interviews then formed the basis for an educational *googi* musical performance (song) and a docudrama on early marriage and teenage pregnancy performed by Alembood Akidaug Akologo with her Winpang *googi* team at Yakote in Bawku and Winimi in Zebila, respectively. This song was performed on 5 August 2022 and commissioned by a team working on the project Promoting Women's Participation in Social Transformation Through Popular Arts in Kusaal-Speaking Communities in Ghana, with sponsorship from the University of Glasgow's Culture for Sustainable and Inclusive Peace Network Plus, in collaboration with the Institute of African Studies, University of Ghana.

Abubakari *et al.* (2021) posit that *googi* is a type of performance which is loved and enjoyed by children, adults, males and females. It is a kind of social leveller during the performance in which everyone, young and old, can participate in dancing and singing. It resonates very well with the people, and it is one major means used for communicating important social issues. Following Abubakari *et al.* (2021) and Ali and Bodomo (2021), the song is transcribed and translated into English. This approach gives non-speakers of Kusaal a full understanding of the message. The following section presents results from the study interviews.

Results

The results were framed around the research objectives and questions. The series of sub-questions asked during the interviews are considered in Chapter 9; this chapter focuses on the third research question, regarding popular arts as tools for the eradication of child marriage and GBV, that is, how popular culture in the form of songs, proverbs and folktales could be used to promote social change among women and girls in the study areas. It also sought information from the participants on how the problem of child marriage could be mitigated. The question stemmed from the presumption that people are often emotionally attached to their culture. Therefore, when the same culture is used as a channel for transformational change, it will have greater impact.

The participants were asked how songs and folktales could be used as a medium of communication in reducing child marriage. The responses from the participants indicated that children and adults are attracted to songs and so when the dangers of child marriage are channelled through songs and folktales, people become more receptive to the advice offered.

Participants Abuosi and Asibi contended that if the song is full of moral lessons that teach about the dangers of child marriage, it will attract many people to listen to it and that will help more than the pieces of advice, because the children like listening to songs more than advice.

Similarly, participants Asibi, Abuosi, Alamisi and Apuasan intimated that songs in their local dialect are easily assimilated; therefore, if the songs are converted and become downloadable, people can download or copy the lyrics onto their phones and listen to the songs. They can also be played on radio stations for people to listen to them.

Giving further explanation of the importance of songs in reducing child marriage, participant Awinpang commented:

> The benefits are derived from the explanations of the songs. This one explains how to take proper care of your girl-children and also explains how people get into child marriages. Those who were not aware that child marriage was bad and how to avoid it got to know it through the song.

Similarly, talking about the use of songs and folktales in reducing child marriage, Asibi stressed that:

> They should be inculcated in our social gatherings like funerals, festivals, and especially during cultural activities in our schools. They can also be communicated through the media such as radio stations.

Furthermore, participant Alamisi sang a song during the interview, which when translated meant that the woman did not prepare well before coming to marry, she did not know how to manage her home and they have to send her back to her own family. In the case of child marriage, when you are forced to marry someone that you do not like and you are not patient, you could also misbehave so that they dismiss you to go back to your parents. Highlighting the implication or lessons from the song, participant Alamisi stated that the song has been:

> able to educate people to know that forcing girl-children to marry men they are not interested in was bad and that when they learnt that could lead to broken marriages, some stopped doing it.

Narrating lessons learnt from folktales and songs which have enlightened her on why child marriage should be stopped, after recounting the lyrics in one of the local songs, participant Awinpang stated that:

> I think this song helped me because it made me see the difference in the lifestyles of those who took proper care of the children and those who did not. Those who took proper care of their children are now enjoying it because their children are now in big positions and are now taking care of them as well, while the others did not get this opportunity. It also enables me to know that when my daughter is going to school, I should get money for her on a daily basis so that she won't demand money from elsewhere, which can lead them to bad situations such as sleeping with men they are not married to.

The participants were also asked about how songs and folktales could be communicated to achieve peace and transformation and recommend reducing child marriage. The participants alluded to the intervention of non-governmental organisations (NGOs) and the government to initiate educational programmes aimed at eradicating child marriage in order to bring transformational change. Participants Awinpang, Azumah, Atibil and Abuosi indicated that with proper investment in girl-child education, numbers of early unexpected pregnancies would be reduced. Similarly, through quality education, many of the traditional people would be enlightened and such enlightenment would invariably be transformed into social change.

Participant Awinpang made a specific recommendation:

> Every girl-child should resist child marriage and rather take their studies and other skill-training seriously. This is because if you marry without any work, you will suffer greatly in the marriage. So, if you are a student or an apprentice, you should make sure that you complete your schooling or the training before you get married.

Seconding the positions of other participants, participants Awinpang and Atibil contended that such resistance as recommended by participant Awinpang could be fruitful only when the girl is well educated. Such education would empower the girl to stand up for her rights, protect her interests and aspire to greater things in life. As indicated above, the results of the interviews were used to conceptualise the theme of the *googi* musical performance and a docudrama on child marriage among the Kusaas.[1] These edutainments were intended to influence local people to take actions that will lead to peaceful transformation and coexistence by eliminating the culture of early marriage and teenage pregnancies. The composer of the *googi* performance crafted her message on central themes to encourage people to eschew cultural practices such as child marriage and teenage pregnancies and to encourage parents, youth and traditional leaders to ensure that formal education is promoted in all the communities. The script for the docudrama also focused on the negative repercussions of early marriage, on the health of the teenager and on the need for formal education.

Main Themes of *Googi* Performance and Docudrama on Child Marriage and Teenage Pregnancy in Kusaug

Abubakari *et al.* (n.d.) argue that the fight to achieve the United Nations' Sustainable Development Goal 5, on gender equality, by 2030, is more of a mirage if extra effort is not made in rural communities in Ghana. This comes on the back of recent observations through this study on the alarming rate of early marriages and teenage pregnancies in rural

Kusaal-speaking communities in Ghana's Upper East Region. The *googi* performance on child marriage, as well on the docudrama on the same theme, reveal the harrowing effects on the lives of young rural girls in the name of culture and traditional norms. In the docudrama, we see a clash between the old and new generations, where the latter call for the abolition of early marriages while the former insist it is a cultural practice that cannot be abandoned.

> Son: Dad...! Marriage is for the mature! I don't agree to this! She is a schoolgirl and has not gone anywhere yet.
> Abodib (father): It is normal in our culture that when an in-law performs well at your father's funeral, he may be given an additional young girl to marry and that was what happened, and Asinim was given out.

These popular performances, the *googi* performance and docudrama, seek to educate local people to embrace formal education for peaceful coexistence, and socioeconomic and sociocultural advancement of the people. Both performances focus on the cultural, social, economic and health implications of early marriage and teenage pregnancies. The discussion below partly follows the argument made in Abubakari *et al.* (n.d.) regarding the central themes of the *googi* performance.

Child marriage as a traditional cultural norm

Both the docudrama and *googi* performance identify culture and traditional norms as the main propeller of child marriage. It is culturally accepted for a girl to be betrothed to a man at an early age. She might drop out of school if the man approaches the family to honour their obligation of fulfilling the betrothal arrangement.

In the docudrama, we see the father of the teenage girl saying:

> Abodib: Thank you, my good friend! You may be right, but it is not our fault. She has already been betrothed. It is normal in our tradition to do that.

From the beginning of the song on child marriage, the performer indicates that it is an appeal for a review of the cultural norm that allows betrothal and early marriage. This is illustrated in the lines below (also see Abubakari *et al.*, n.d.):

(1) Mmm! Ghana dima oo eeeh! apʋ bi' ka nɔk pʋʋg laa   Mmm! My fellow Ghanaians, haven't you heard about early marriage?

(2)	Du'adiba ya daa pʊ baŋ bɛɛ	Parents! Didn't you know about it?
(3)	Ya daa zi' ye gbaʊŋ malisaa	Didn't you know that education is good?
(4)	Ka yɛl ye buudi tʊʊma eeh! Anɔk biigi tisɛ ka o pʊ bi naae yee! Ayoo	And gave girls away to early marriage because of culture
(137)	Sakur yɛla mɔn'oe nidibnɛ	Education is now important to people
(138)	Ka madam Hasiya paana	That is why Madam Hasiya is here
(139)	O paanɛ Yakuta	In the Yakut community
(140)	Yakut na'aba Adelwin tɛŋ oo!	And before the chief of Yakut, Adelwin
(141)	Ka m kaasi buol Nayok na'ab	She is calling on Nayok's chief
(142)	Ka kaasi buol Zabug na'ab oo	She is calling on Zabug's chief
(143)	O bɔɔd ye ya sʊŋ o yaa	She needs help
(144)	O bɔɔd ye sʊŋ kat pu'a-ɛlig tisib oo	She wants you to help eradicate early marriage

Both the song and the docudrama highlight culture as the main root of early marriage and the need to seek formal education. The young generation are represented in the 'son' to promote the need to abandon aspects of the local culture that need to be reviewed in the face of current global situations.

The chorus of the song gives assurance that the people did not know the detrimental effect of early marriage and teenage pregnancy, and that they have received some enlightenment about it. To this effect they accept that early marriage and teenage pregnancy should be eradicated since they are not good practices. This is illustrated in the song lines below:

(14)	Nannana ti yʊ'ʊm baŋyaa	We didn't know but now we know
(15)	Nannana ti yʊ'ʊm baŋyaa apʊ bi' ka nɔk pʊʊgaa	Now we know teenage pregnancy is not good
(16)	Nannana ti yʊ'ʊm baŋyaa	Now, we know

Health implications of early marriage and teenage pregnancy

The two popular cultural performances also highlight the health implications that commonly arise due to teenage pregnancy, which is fuelled by early marriage. The *googi* performer shares the message that health practitioners in the community have been advocating for the need to educate children, adding that teenagers suffer various complications when they get pregnant. Abubakari *et al.* (n.d.) mention some leading health problems often observed with teenage pregnancies: pre-birth complications, stillbirths, fistula, sexually transmitted diseases and even death. The following are excerpts from the song (also in Abubakari *et al.*, n.d.):

(23)	Biig nɔk puug ka pu paae yuum biiga; Ka kɛŋ ka li an namisug	A teenager who becomes pregnant always suffers
(31)	Laafi tuntunib la pa'al ye yaa	Health workers have advised that
(32)	Ya kɛl ka biis la woo kɛŋ sakur yee	All children should be educated
(33)	Ba ya'a baŋɛɛ li na suŋi tii	If they are educated it would help us
(34)	Ya ya'a zan'asɛɛ ti kpɛn gɛɛndii, nannana ti yu'um baŋyaa	If they are not, all of us would continue to suffer
(35)	Apubi' ka nɔk puug laa nannana ti yu'um baŋyaa	We didn't know about [the consequences of] early marriage but now we know
(79)	Ya kɛl ka ba baŋ gbauŋɔɔ	Let them [girls] be educated
(80)	Ba ya'a baŋ gbauŋɔ li na suŋi ba	It will help them if they are educated
(81)	Kilim tika li na suŋi ba yee!	If they become teachers, it would help them
(82)	Ba ya'a kilm du'ata li na suŋi ba yee!	If they become doctors, it would help them
(83)	Ka kilm MP li na suŋi ba yee!	If they become Members of Parliament, it would help them

The docudrama propagates the following message on the health risks that a teenage mother is likely to face:

Friend: Asinim got married at age 14, oooh. And anytime she got pregnant she suffered and is still suffering, battling with complications.

In addition to the lines above, a 'community man' adds the following, intending to caution the people that early marriage is illegal and that teenage pregnancy comes with its own health complications:

Community man: Please listen to me, Mr Abodib. You've arranged your daughter's marriage but is she old enough to be married? She is only 13 years old! Are you aware of the complications that accompany child marriage? Don't you know that child marriage is illegal in Ghana? Abodib, don't you know that a girl can't be married if she is under 18 years of age? Girls less than 18 are not ready to be wives and mothers. Their health can be jeopardised by having children too young. What is more, it is illegal and a punishable offence.

Poverty as both cause and result of early marriage and teenage pregnancy in Kusaug

Abubakari *et al.* (n.d.) also identify poverty as a leading cause of early marriage and teenage pregnancy. It is important that just as poverty propels parents to give out their daughters at a very early age in marriage in exchange for a dowry of four cows, so early marriage and teenage pregnancy place young parents into a vicious cycle of poverty. Thus, the *googi* song shows that endemic poverty becomes cyclic. A girl gets married off due to poverty; she goes and her husband is unable to take care of her. She returns and becomes a burden to her poor parents. The woman often becomes the main victim of poverty and its associating suffering (Abubakari *et al.*, n.d.).

(71)	Biig ya'a paae ka pʋ nyɛ di; O ya'a lɛm paae ka pʋ nyɛ sɔn'	When a teenager gets married and doesn't get to eat or wear,
(72)	Bikanna yʋ'ʋ yaanɛ o ma nɛɛ	she becomes a burden on her mother.
(160)	Ka o ma giligi gʋn'ʋŋ ka mɔr o paana; O paana nyɛt ki'ibʋ yaanɛ; O nyɛt zambaad yaanɛ dʋgʋda; Sankanna li namis o nɛ	After the mother sent her around and couldn't find the man who is responsible for the pregnancy, taking care of her alone including what she will eat and wear becomes difficult.
(161)	Apʋ bi' ka nɔk pʋʋga	Teenage pregnancy

In the docudrama, the theme of poverty is expressed when Abambood, the mother of the teenage victim of early marriage, says:

> Abambood: For me, I will say let us allow him to marry her. You and I have nothing and cannot support her education; neither are we sure she can complete her vocation.

In the final scene of the drama, the teenage mother indeed appears very poor, a replica of her mother's status.

Discussion: Cultural Motivations for Child Marriage and Popular Art as a Tool for its Mitigation

The results revealed that child marriage and teenage pregnancy are prevalent in rural Kusaal-speaking communities in Ghana. Some of the children are given away for marriage as early as 15 to 16 years of age. The results further revealed that traditional customs, such as giving the first girl to a male native doctor for marriage, and socioeconomic conditions, such as poverty, parental and family coercion, are the cultural motivations that contribute to child marriage.

The results on giving first-born girls to traditional priests are consistent with the observation of Abass-Abaah (2024), who contends that when a woman is unable to give birth after some years in marriage, a shrine priest is consulted and promised that a child will be brought and affiliated to his shrine, who will thus become a bondage *dabit* child. A child who is conceived in such circumstances, if it is a boy, is required to offer sacrifices to the deity throughout his life and, in the case of a girl, she is given in marriage to the priest from birth and may move to live in her new home from the age of 10. She may marry the priest once she reaches puberty, when she is given to the children of the priest for marriage. Similarly, when a woman suffers neonatal deaths and consults a priest for assistance, any girl who is born with the assistance of the priest is taken to the shrine and married to the priest or a member of his family. In all these instances, the girl has no right to free and full consent. This practice was confirmed by one of the participants, who intimated that she was taken away for marriage at the age of five and later given to the grandson of the traditional priest.

This finding regarding coercion and unexpected teenage pregnancy forcing children into marriage is consistent with statistics. In 2020 about 6533 teenage pregnancies were recorded in the Upper East Region of Ghana among girls aged 10–14, representing a 38% increase from 2019 (Ghana Health Service, 2020). The statistics are confirmed by the number of participants who indicated that they got pregnant at the age of 16 or 17 years and were forced to get married against their wishes.

The results further revealed that forms of popular culture like songs, folktales and proverbs can contain messages which fuel gender-based violence and child marriage. However, most of the songs and folktales as well as docudramas give lessons about the negative effects of child marriage. Most of the participants indicated that they were attracted to these songs, most especially when sung in their local dialects. The results pointed to the fact that songs and folktales are important transformational tools that could be used to empower adults and children to understand the need to indulge in practices that will reduce and eradicate teenage pregnancies and avert the possibility of child marriage.

Conclusions

The exploitation of traditional norms by some families tends to reinforce gender-based violence against young girls, such as teenage pregnancies and child marriage. Notwithstanding the emergence of pockets of resistance to the practice among the younger generation, child marriage, largely a result of teenage pregnancies, persists in some parts of the project communities. To mitigate these practices, the project deployed popular art, such as docudramas, folktales and songs in the local dialect, as tools for social transformation and empowerment of young girls and women to ensure social cohesion and build peace in the families and communities. The project has implications for both policy and practice. In terms of policy, the adoption of popular art such as music, folktales and docudrama as tools for social resistance offer diversionary, entertainment and educational gratifications, which suggest superior functional alternatives to the material gifts parents and guardians of child marriage victims receive from the perpetrators. Furthermore, the framing of messages of change in the local language to be disseminated by opinion leaders fosters acceptance and ownership by local people. It is at this point that change begins to happen to complement government and other stakeholders' endeavours to eradicate child marriage.

Acknowledgement

This project has been funded by CUSP (Culture for Sustainable and Inclusive Peace Network Plus). CUSP is funded by UK Research and Innovation (UKRI) as part of the UK government's Global Challenges Research Fund (GCRF) and its support is gratefully acknowledged.

Note

(1) The docudrama was added to supplement the *googi*, and is considered further in Chapter 9. Both the *googi* song and the docudrama on child marriage among the Kusaas are available online at https://iascusp.org/audio-media (accessed 5 July 2024).

References

Abass-Abaah, A.J. (2024) Courtship and marriage. In H. Abubakari, A. Musah, A. Apusiga and J. Atibila (eds) *The Kusaas: An Indigenous Perspective* (pp. 84–105). Digibooks.

Abubakari, H. (2018) Aspects of Kusaal grammar: The syntax–information structure interface. PhD thesis, African Studies Department, University of Vienna.

Abubakari, H. (2022) The grammar of the Kusaal language of Ghana. Unpublished manuscript, Institute of African Studies, University of Ghana.

Abubakari, H. and Musah, A. (2024) The Kusaal language. In H. Abubakari, A. Musah, A. Apusiga and J. Atibila (eds) *The Kusaas: An Indigenous Perspective* (pp. 63–83). Digibooks.

Abubakari, H., Assem, S.I. and Amankwah, A.S. (2021) Framing of Covid-19 safety protocols in Kusaal musical health communication: Language and literary analysis. *Language and Communication* 81, 64–80.

Abubakari, H., Amankwah, S.A. and Opoku, M.A. (n.d.) Effective communication through popular culture for social transformation: A rhetorical analysis of a *googi* performance on child marriage among the Kusaas of Ghana. Unpublished manuscript, Institute of African Studies, University of Ghana.

Ahosi, B., Fuseini, K., Nai, D., Goldson, E., Owusu, S., Ndifuna, I., Humes, I. and Tapsoba, I.P. (2019) Child marriage in Ghana: Evidence from a multi-method study. *BMC Women's Health* 19, 126.

Ali, M. and Bodomo A. (eds) (2021) *Yɛ´ Gorógoró Yaa: Dagaare Folktales in Parallel Texts.* LIT Verlag.
Ancu, M. and Cozma, R. (2009) MySpace politics: Uses and gratifications of befriending candidates. *Journal of Broadcasting and Electronic Media* 53 (4), 567–583.
Bodomo, A. (2020) Mabia: Its etymological genesis, geographical spread, and some salient genetic features. In A. Bodomo, H. Abubakari and S.I. Alhassan (eds) *Handbook of Mabia Languages of West Africa* (pp. 5–34). Galda Verlag.
Braun, V. and Clark, V. (2006) Using thematic analysis in psychology. *Qualitative Research in Psychology* 3, 77–101. https://doi.org/10.1191/1478088706qp063oa.
Ghana Health Service (2020) *Adolescent Health Service Policy and Strategy, 2016–2020.* https://www.afro.who.int/publications/adolescent-health-service-policy-and-strategy-2016-2020 (accessed 15 March 2023).
Grantcraft (2006) Mapping change: Using a theory of change to guide planning and evaluation. https://learningforfunders.candid.org/wp-content/uploads/sites/2/2018/12/theory_change.pdf (accessed 17 February 2023).
GSS (Ghana Statistical Service) (2012) *2010 Population and Housing Census: Summary of Final Results.* Ghana Statistical Service. https://statsghana.gov.gh/gssmain/storage/img/marqueeupdater/Census2010_Summary_report_of_final_results.pdf (accessed 20 February 2023).
GSS (2016) *2010 Population and Housing Census: Population of Kusaas by District.* Ghana Statistical Service. https://statsghana.gov.gh/gssmain/fileUpload/pressrelease/2010_PHC_ National_Analytical_Report.pdf (accessed 14 March 2023).
GSS (2018) *Multiple Indicator Cluster Survey (MICS2017/18).* Ghana Statistical Service. https://statsghana.gov.gh/gssmain/fileUpload/pressrelease/MICS%20SFR%20final_compressed.pdf (accessed 20 February 2023).
GSS, Ghana Health Service and ICF (2018) *Ghana Maternal Health Survey 2017.* GSS, GHS and ICF. https://dhsprogram.com/pubs/pdf/FR340/FR340.pdf (accessed 13 March 2023).
Katz, E., Blumler, J.G. and Gurevitch, M. (1974) Utilisation of mass communication by the individual. In E. Katz and J.G. Blumler (eds) *The Uses of Mass Communication: Current Perspectives on Gratifications Research* (pp. 19–32). Sage.
Lasswell, H. (1948) The structure and function of communications in society. In L. Bryson (ed.) *The Communication of Ideas* (pp. 37–51). Harper and Row.
McLeod, J. and Becker, L. (1981) The uses and gratifications approach. In D. Nimmo and K. Sanders (eds) *Handbook of Political Communication* (pp. 67–100). Sage.
Miles, M. and Huberman, M. (1994) *Qualitative Data Analysis.* Sage.
Myjoyonline.com (2021) Teenage pregnancy surge as Upper East Region records 6,533 cases. *My Joy Online*, 18 May. https://www.myjoyonline.com/teenage-pregnancy-surge-as-upper-east-region-records-6533-cases/ (accessed 4 April 2022).
Papacharissi, Z. (2009) Uses and gratifications. In D. Stacks and W. Salwen (eds) *An Integrated Approach to Communication Theory and Research* (pp. 137–152). Routledge.
Parker, N.H. (2011) Toward a definition of popular culture. *History and Theory* 50, 147–170.
Rubin, A.M. (2009) The uses and gratifications perspective on media effects. In J. Oliver and M.B. Bryant (eds) *Media Effects: Advances in Theory and Research* (pp. 165–184). Routledge.
Simons, G.F. and Fenning, C.D. (eds) (2017) *Ethnologue. Languages of the World* (20th edn). SIL International. https://www.ethnologue.com/language/kus (accessed 5 July 2022).
UNICEF (2021) Situation of adolescents report. https://www.unicef.org/ghana/media/4101/file (accessed 22 April 2022).

7 Resilient Palestinian Women Facing Gender-Based Conflict in the Gaza Strip

Mahmoud O. Jalambo, Nazmi Al-Masri, Somaya M. Sayma and Azza Al-Sahhar

Introduction and Background

Gender-based violence (GBV) is a widespread conflict that affects individuals, groups, societies and states with significant negative social and economic impacts. It is a global pandemic that affects one in three women, with the majority of female murders committed by intimate partners. Furthermore, 35% of women worldwide have experienced physical and/or sexual violence from intimate partners or non-partner sexual violence, while 7% of women have been sexually assaulted by someone other than a partner (Baldi, 2018; Fulu & Heise, 2015; Michau et al., 2015; World Bank, 2019). Violence against women (VAW), which, UN Women (2024a), constitutes misuse and/or abuse of power, is the main cause of GBV.

GBV is an ongoing conflict in the Occupied Palestinian Territory but is not adequately reported. The Gaza Community Mental Health Programme (GCMHP) reported 2536 cases in 2020 of psychological, physical, sexual or verbal conflict, with 51% of the cases being against women and girls. Many Palestinian women do not report conflict or violence committed against them for sociocultural reasons, such as the stigma in such a conservative society; therefore, the actual number could be higher. Palestinian women face discrimination and gender-based inequalities in various aspects of life, despite enjoying certain rights in fields such as education, health and social and economic status. GBV is a significant problem in the Occupied Palestinian Territory, with women experiencing violence due to gendered laws, traditional practices and the violence of the Israeli occupation. Palestinian women have been suffering from the practices of the occupation since 1948, including exposure to killing and arrest, violation of basic rights such as residence, housing and movement, and denial of access to services like health, education and social security.

Palestinian women have been subjected to unnecessary death since 1948, either directly (e.g. by the Israeli occupation) or indirectly (e.g. because they were prevented from travelling abroad for medical treatment). In 2014, 510 women were killed during the 51-day aggression by Israeli occupation forces in Gaza, which represents 22% of the total 2322 Palestinians killed. Furthermore, Abu al-Khair (2018) reported that the occupation authorities arrested 53 Palestinian women and girls, including children, and subjected them to numerous violations. The study concludes that the increasing number of restrictions imposed by the Israeli occupation on the movement of Palestinians have impeded the access of Palestinian women to their schools and universities and restricted their access to medical care and other daily activities. It also illustrates that the Israeli occupation forces violate Palestinian women's right to life by killing or injuring them (Abu al-Khair, 2018; Palestinian Ministry of Health, 2015). The Israeli occupation has subjected the Palestinian people in general and Palestinian women in particular to precarious socioeconomic and political conditions (Baldi, 2018; Women's Center for Legal and Social Counselling, 2019). UN Women (2024b) reported that in the first six months of the Israeli aggression on Gaza since 9 October 2023, over 10,000 women have been killed.

Disabled Palestinians are more vulnerable to violence due to their dependence on others and lack of resources. A 2019 study by the United Nations Population Fund (UNFPA) found that disabled Palestinian women are marginalised due to societal structure, discrimination and gender. The frequent Israeli aggression in Gaza had increased the disability prevalence rate to 6.8% by 2017, with females with disabilities being more vulnerable to violence. The arbitrary practices of the Israeli occupation authorities have been linked to the suffering of women, as they are either directly exposed to violence or are members of a family that suffer the consequences. The inter-Palestinian political division has also oppressed Palestinian women, causing challenges such as poverty, unemployment, displacement and limited access to health services (Culture and Free Thought Association, 2012; Fuqaha, 2018; Independent Commission for Human Rights, 2022; UNFPA, 2019).

In this chapter, we use the term 'gender-based conflict' (GBC) to encompass a wide range of conflicts, including but not limited to violence, discrimination and inequalities, that Palestinian women face in their daily lives. While GBV refers specifically to acts of violence targeting individuals based on their gender, GBC encompasses a broader spectrum of gender-related challenges, including socioeconomic disparities, cultural norms and political factors that contribute to the marginalisation and oppression of women. Throughout the chapter, we emphasise the interconnectedness of GBC and GBV, highlighting how gender-based conflicts often manifest as acts of violence against women but also extend to various forms of discrimination and inequality prevalent in Palestinian society. By exploring the root causes and contextual factors underlying GBC, we aim to provide a comprehensive understanding of the multifaceted challenges faced by Palestinian women.

The GBCs experienced by Palestinian women were confirmed by a report of the United Nations (2019) which revealed that a multi-impact burden falls on Palestinian women owing to the blockade imposed on the Gaza Strip in addition to the drawback of the inter-Palestinian division. The report illustrates a significant rise in unemployment rates among Palestinian women, especially among educated young women, which reached 78.3% in the second quarter of 2018. The report notes the sharp contrast between the high levels of educational attainment among women and the escalating levels of unemployment among the same group. Recent statistics from the Gaza Community Mental Health Programme (GCMHP) reveal the impact of the GBC. GCMHP provides clinical, social, research and other services to improve Palestinian community mental health and to advocate for human rights. Its free telephone counselling services received 2553 calls in 2020, with 51% made by women and girls. Most callers (78%) reported psychological suffering, while the types of abuse reported were physical (27%), verbal (16%), sexual (11%) and neglect (7%). The causes of abuse were mainly family members (48%) and husbands (41%), with a small percentage (8%) attributed to external abusers and 3% to collective violence (Gaza Community Mental Health Programme, 2021).

The inter-Palestinian political division has led to an increase in murders committed because of so-called family honour prioritised by some Palestinian cultural traditions. As in other traditional societies, a family's honour in Palestinian society is often reflected in the virtue of its women, in that whatever the woman's behaviour is, it could affect the dignity of her family. Modesty and chastity among women are key values. In 2018 and 2017, 28 and 18 females, respectively, were documented to have died in Gaza and the West Bank due to mysterious causes that indicate the possibility of being motivated by so-called family honour, according to the Independent Commission for Human Rights. The political inter-division has also disrupted the Legislative Council's role in protecting Palestinian women legally. Despite the decline in violence in Palestinian society in recent years, a survey conducted by the Palestinian Central Bureau of Statistics (PCBS) in 2019 revealed high and dangerous levels of violence (PCBS, 2022). The survey found that more than one out of every four women (27%) within the family had been exposed to some form of violence by their husband, with 18% experiencing physical violence, 57% subjected to psychological violence and 9% experiencing sexual violence. Additionally, during the 11-day aggression against Gaza in May 2021, at least 39 Palestinian women and around 67 children (more than 50% of them girls) were killed.

The previous studies conducted in the regional and local sphere indicate that women in conflict and crisis areas, or those subordinated to traditional societal culture, occupy the weakest position and suffer the most. In the Palestinian context, the Israeli occupation and 15-year Gaza Strip siege have negatively impacted women's lives and all aspects of family life, leading to serious problems. The repercussions of the occupation are reflected in all aspects of life in Palestine, including women's rights.

The context of this study is the Gaza Strip, a tiny strip of land of 365 km², home to more than 2 million Palestinians, making it one of the most densely populated areas in the world (PCBS, 2018). The ongoing blockade imposed by the Israeli occupation forces on the Gaza Strip since 2006 makes it a place threatened by difficult socioeconomic and cultural conditions, including limited (individual) human mobility, and a limited flow of basic goods and raw materials, in addition to the difficult political situation due to the repeated Israeli attacks that increase the Palestinian suffering. As a result, the Palestinian women in Gaza have been suffering from the trauma of war, socioeconomic marginalisation and internal political conflicts (Fassetta *et al.*, 2020).

Accordingly, this study investigates the GBC that Palestinian females most commonly and frequently face within the context of the Gaza Strip. It thereby contributes to determining the priorities to be taken into consideration when planning future interventions to improve the conditions of Palestinian women in the Gaza Strip. In addition, the study reflects on the past experiences of some women who suffered from GBC but succeeded to transform such conflicts to prevent the oppression of women and girls and mitigate their suffering. This chapter answers the following three questions:

(1) What are the GBCs that Palestinian women encounter in the Gaza Strip?
(2) What are the most common GBCs that Palestinian women encounter in the Gaza Strip?
(3) How do Palestinian women transform the GBCs in the Gaza Strip into success stories?

This chapter next presents an overview of the methodology, encompassing research design, data collection methods and tools for both quantitative and qualitative data. Subsequently, it presents and discusses quantitative results. Qualitative data analysis follows, unveiling themes and patterns derived from interviews. Concluding the chapter, a summary of findings is provided, with implications for practice and policy, accompanied by practical recommendations for future research directions.

Methodology

This study adopted a qualitative approach to collect data directly from a limited purposeful sample to understand the topic under investigation. This approach allows participants to express their experiences, thoughts and ideas freely and in greater depth, which is necessary to explain the current situation of Palestinian women in the context of the Gaza Strip.

The study relied on three-session focus group discussions and three semi-structured individual interviews with a purposeful sample of women participants representing various governmental institutions and NGOs concerned with advocating and supporting women's rights in the Gaza Strip – all of whom have senior administrative and managerial positions in these institutions. The number of participants in the first focus group was 22 (19 females and three males), while the number of those who filled out the online checklist and attended the second session was 13 (12 females and one male). Next, four female success stories were collected from the motivated participants in the third focus group discussion. A further three interviewees then took part in the semi-structured individual interviews (one female and two males).

The focus group discussion and semi-structured interviews were implemented as the main sources for data collection. The first focus group session aimed to collect details of all the possible GBCs that Palestinian women face in the Gaza Strip, and the second named the most common GBCs among a list prepared based on the results of the first. It is worth mentioning that the researchers also designed an online checklist to ask the participants to tick the top GBCs that they felt require urgent intervention from the concerned parties and any other endeavours, bearing in mind that there was a chance to classify the listed GBCs over five domains within the Palestinian context – namely, religious, political, socioeconomic, legal and cultural. The third focus group aimed to collect the inspiring stories of the resilient Palestinian women facing GBC in the Gaza Strip. Finally, the semi-structured interviews afforded a deeper understanding of the collected data from the three focus group discussions to verify the results.

The study meets the ethical standards set by generic research ethics, and all the participants were informed of the reasons behind inviting them to participate in this study, as well as informing them that the study is part of an AHRC-funded project, Culture for Sustainable and Inclusive Peace Network Plus (CUSP N+).

Results

Answering the first and second research questions: Identifying and ranking gender-based conflicts

Two focus group discussions were held on Zoom with the participants from the leading associations for women's rights and advocacy in the Gaza Strip. In the first, the 22 participants discussed the first research question: What are the GBCs that Palestinian women encounter in the Gaza Strip? They listed 48 GBCs (see Tables 7.1 and 7.2). The second focus group had 13 participants, who were purposefully selected from the heads and employees in various official institutions working in the field of women's rights and advocacy in the Gaza Strip due to their resourceful experience in the field of the study. They were asked to fill out an online checklist, which was designed, based on the results of the first focus group, to identify the top 14 GBCs that Palestinian women face in the Gaza Strip (see Table 7.1). These findings were then summarised to reveal the most common GBCs that Palestinian women encounter in the Gaza Strip. Tables 7.1 and 7.2 reflect how varied and overlapping those challenges and conflicts are, since the same conflict can fall under more than one domain, such as religious, political, socioeconomic, legal and cultural.

The participants of the focus group discussed the 14 most common GBCs, especially the nature and impact of each conflict. The coded excerpts were then thematically sorted, as discussed below.

Violence

The results of this study are consistent with many previous studies, such as Al-Somali *et al.* (2019) and Al-Hadidi and Saad (2016), which found that women suffer discrimination due to a society's culture, as manifested through the traditional distribution of roles and restrictions imposed on women carrying out their work and tasks. The current investigation found that cases of GBV against women have increased in recent years, as confirmed by the results of the 2019 survey conducted by the Palestinian Central Bureau of Statistics. One participant, AS, adds, 'Palestinian women in the Gaza Strip are exposed to all forms of physical, verbal and psycho-social violence'. The specificity of violence against women in the Gaza Strip is caused by multiple sources of violence, such as the Israeli siege of the Gaza Strip over many years, thereby causing poverty and economic problems, in addition to the prevalent sociocultural barriers. Another participant, AT, clarifies that 'There is no violence above the violence of the occupation because the occupation is the main cause of all problems that the Palestinian society suffers from'.

Likewise, participant HY highlights the impact of the Israeli occupation on Palestinian women: 'The Palestinian women suffer from political violence caused by the occupation, as they are killed, detained and lose shelter, and consequently the loss of sustainable livelihoods'.

AS adds, 'Occupation violence does not directly affect women' but includes all Palestinian people because the occupation is killing, arresting and displacing Palestinians, threatening the life of Palestinian society. AS reiterates that 'Women are exposed to more violence during political tension because they are women, and they are always the weakest'.

In addition, the deteriorating economic conditions in the Gaza Strip affect the quality of life, which results in an increased incidence of poverty and a low standard of services. In this context, participant QA confirms that 'Women are always the victims and are the ones who pay the price', adding that 'violence against women has increased in the Gaza Strip due

Table 7.1 The top 14 forms of GBC among Palestinian women as identified by the first focus group and then ranked by the second focus group

Rank	Form of GBC
1	Denying the divorced Palestinian woman custody of her children
2	Violence in all its forms (psychological – verbal – physical) and the covering up of this violence
3	Depriving women of independent financial assets
4	Discrimination within the Palestinian family between boys and girls in privileges such as expenses and educational opportunities
5	Denying a woman the freedom to choose her spouse and forcing Palestinian girls to marry or not
6	The rejection of the Palestinian community of the idea of widowed or divorced women being the family providers
7	The use of unfair power by the male guardian, such as a father or brother, to deprive women of their basic rights such as the right to education or choosing the university specialization that they want
8	The culture of early marriage for girls (women under the age of 18) and the existence of laws that allow early marriage
9	Inequality of working women in the domestic and social treatment and the work environment
10	The low level of representation of women in decision-making positions, and, where women are present, the assignment of women to some weak tasks due to the stereotyping of women in Palestinian society
11	The weak awareness among the Palestinian women of their rights and duties
12	Food insecurity for women and their families is compounded when a woman is the breadwinner for the family
13	Forcing Palestinian women to work in inappropriate conditions (violence in the workplace)
14	The reluctance of affected Palestinian women to join heuristic programmes

to the deteriorating economic situation, and that has been evident due to the increase of cases contacting our psychological support programmes'. Participant NH supports this point by declaring 'Women suffer more in situations of poverty and low standards of living'.

There is another factor that increases women's suffering due to GBV, which is some Palestinian traditions and customs; as participant AT confirms, 'Women suffer from verbal, psychological and physical violence because of some society's traditional culture and its negative views towards women'. This negative culture in society appears in multiple forms, as society criticises the abused women approaching institutions to seek their help; as participant HY states: 'The abused woman faces psychological pressures because she cannot go to the specialist institutions for fear of stigma'. Participant SB explains the reasons behind this:

- Family problems, especially violence against women, are a sensitive (social) issue and they are not disclosed in many cases.

Table 7.2 The other forms of GBC among Palestinian women identified by the first focus group

Forms of GBC
Weak participation in the crisis and disaster recovery process (Women are under enormous pressure to support family members through the recovery process, but women need all the support available to be able to overcome the crisis recovery phase.)
Difficulty for women to travel to obtain higher education opportunities
The traditional stereotypical view of Palestinian women
Depriving women of their inheritance
Palestinian women are exposed to various psychological disorders, pressures and problems
Women suffer from chronic diseases such as cancer, anaemia and other health problems
Cyberbullying
The impact of the COVID-19 pandemic on Palestinian women (where the private education sector including kindergartens and private schools is the most severely affected sector, especially as the majority of those institutions are led by women)
Neglecting the privacy of women in crises and quarantine centres
Depriving a woman of her salary and forcibly handing power of attorney to her husband
Minimizing the role of women to only a reproductive role (delivering babies)
Having multiple roles (mother, wife, daughter, sister, worker) and thus a multiplicity of tasks
Palestinian society's negative view of divorced women
Palestinian women fear receiving psychological treatment owing to their belief that their husbands may take advantage of this as a conviction in the courts
Feeling the stigma of being a female
Preventing women from proceeding with their higher education (MA and PhD)
Palestinian women lack of modern skills (IT and soft skills)
Girls' reluctance to enrol in modern applied disciplines when studying in universities
Begging and its impacts on Palestinian women
Decreasing the wages for women compared to those for men
Low participation of women in the workforce
High unemployment rates among women
The lack of projects and programmes that work on the economic empowerment of women
The marginalisation of qualified women and their exclusion from senior leadership positions
Restriction of women's freedom of movement due to the closure of the border crossings
Women are more affected by political crises, such as the Great Marches of the Return
The lack of a unified reference for feminist work
Blackout of violence and crimes against women
The deactivated laws relating to women and some family protection laws
Women's poor access to justice
The inability of Palestinian law to protect women from domestic violence against them
The absence of the Legislative Council's role in issuing laws to confront emerging issues facing women
The absence of articles in Palestinian law that support the right of a divorced woman to the custody of her children when she wants
Electronic blackmail

- The abused woman faces psychological pressure because she cannot go to specialist institutions for fear of stigma.
- Family problems, especially violence against women, are a sensitive issue which is kept hidden in many cases.

It is anticipated, as participant HS confirms, that 'The figures for cases of violence against women in the Gaza Strip do not give real statistics because there are a large number of cases that cannot reach support and protection institutions'. From participant QA's point of view, this causes an increase in cases of violence in the Gaza Strip because 'Violence is practised against women in light of the silence of society and the silence of the victim as well'. Even on social media, girls suffer from violence in the form of cyberbullying. Participant NH clarifies: 'A girl suffers from cyberbullying when she identifies herself on social media as someone who is exposed to harassment and hurt'.

These results were verified and validated by the results of the three individual interviews. Participant ON mentions that, in the Gaza Strip, women hold a higher status than women in other Arab countries across several levels and positions; for example, in the field of education, there is no illiteracy due to gender and, consequently, females represent the majority of university students, reaching more than 60% in most local universities. The interviewee added that women can serve society in several sectors, and that can be proven by the existence of female employees in both governmental jobs and private sector jobs. However, participant ON adds that this does not mean that there are no GBCs. In other words, there is still some derogation of Palestinian women's abilities and intelligence, which hurts their work and society in general.

Furthermore, participant QO illustrates with statistics that the COVID-19 era saw increased levels of violence because staying at home was problematic for both husbands and wives. The interviewee explains that for some men staying at home exposes them to economic crises as they cannot afford food for their families due to the obligatory lockdown coming after a prolonged siege. The same interviewee added that early marriage is another issue, attributed mainly to economic factors as fathers cannot afford the cost of a decent living and education for their daughters, and therefore marriage is seen as a solution to get rid of this burden. Moreover, COVID-19 led to celibacy among young people who were not able to afford the expense of marriage and establishing a family in a stable and peaceful home environment.

Negative discrimination against women

The study shows that women suffer from negative discrimination in various sectors, including employment and education. One of the participants, AS, claims, 'The participation of women in the labour force in the Gaza Strip is very low, reaching no more than 20%, and it is very low compared to the participation of women in other countries in the world'. This reflects the existence of negative discrimination in the Gaza Strip towards women specifically. Participant AS explains: 'The problems facing women and girls in the Gaza Strip are that there is a noticeable increase in their enrolment in education and obtaining qualifications, but this has not been positively reflected in the opportunities they get in the field of work'. This, according to participant AT, has led to 'an increase in the level of unemployment among women, as the level of unemployment in the Gaza Strip has reached 69% in general, and unemployment has reached 88% among women in particular, which is considered to be one of the highest [rates] in the world'. Participant AT adds, 'In some cases, discrimination is practised against women by preferring men over women in competition over job opportunities so that employers do not have to bear the cost of women's special circumstances'.

Regarding the distribution of work, as participant OS explains, 'The division of work between the male and female is still traditional; women are the primary caregivers and men hold senior leadership positions'. Participant AS stresses the fact that women are poorer: 'The poverty rate is higher in families headed by women compared to families headed by men'.

On the political side, women suffer exclusion and marginalisation simply because they are women; according to participant OS, 'Women are present in political movements, but at the very lowest level, and when women reach higher positions and decision-making positions, they face strong opposition'. Another interviewee confirms that 'Women are excluded from sensitive committees and decision-making in political work, although they are seen as decoration and used to show that the party supports women's participation in political work'. Following the negative experiences of women in political work, some of them withdraw and do not continue in politics; according to participant HY, 'Some women have left political work due to the feeling they experience when they work with men in such political positions. I mean that women are marginalised in political positions in the presence of men.'

The broad distinction is also evident in the field of university specialisation, as participant NH states: 'The parents do not respect a female student's university preferences and desires and push her towards theoretical disciplines because, from their point of view, this is more appropriate for females'. Participant NH adds, 'They [parents] consider applied majors such as medicine, engineering and technology primarily appropriate for male students'.

Discrimination is not limited to these fields. Discrimination is practised in its worst form in the case of divorce, whereby a divorced woman suffers from negative societal perceptions while a divorced man does not receive the same opprobrium. Participant NH indicates that 'a divorced woman is treated as inferior, which makes her feel stigmatised, while a man does not feel these feelings at all because the society does not look at him as it looks at women'. Participant AS attributes the problems resulting from negative discrimination against women to the culture (negative traditions and inherited perception) of Palestinian society, saying, 'The problems facing women are based on unequal gender roles'. Participant HY asserts that 'The culture of Palestinian society consecrates discrimination through dealing with women unfairly and focusing on a specific role for them, which is the reproductive role'. There are other general reasons that drive the policy of discrimination deeper into Palestinian society; participant AQ states, 'Broadly speaking, Palestinian society does not accept the presence of women in leadership positions, nor does it accept the feminist movement'. On the other hand, feminist movements bear the responsibility for this continuing discrimination because, in AQ's view, 'the feminist movement is disjointed and disunited'.

The results of the interviews confirm and validate the results of the focus group discussions, in which participant ON attributed the GBCs faced by Palestinian women in the Gaza Strip to the Israeli occupation in the first instance, then secondly to Palestinian customs and traditions, and thirdly to legal illiteracy. This is confirmed by participant ET, who mentions that legal illiteracy is a big problem in Palestinian society, and therefore women are ignorant of their rights. Legal illiteracy is not linked to women's educational qualifications, as sometimes females with bachelor's degrees or master's graduates are still not aware of their rights and access to justice.

Participant ON highlights that the stigma of divorce is rooted in Palestinian society and, accordingly, divorced women suffer more than other women in the Gaza Strip. In Palestine, neither men nor women accept divorced women; therefore, almost no mother would accept her son marrying a divorced woman. The interviewee explains that neglecting the rights of divorced women raises the unanswered question, 'Who will financially support her?'. In other words, the Ministry of Social Affairs cannot cover the costs of all divorced women, the number of whom is increasing due to ongoing economic crises (high unemployment rate, low salaries and people not receiving 40–50% of their salaries regularly) in almost all key sectors in Gaza for more than 15 years.

In the economic sphere, participant ON reveals that there is no room for women in the field of business within the Palestinian context, especially in the Gaza Strip. The interviewee clarifies either that men deny the right of women to practise some economic activities and run their own businesses, or that women themselves have isolated themselves from this field. The latter could be due to them being convinced that they cannot compete with men in trade and business; it could also be due to the reduced freedom of mobility, as well as the social and political restrictions imposed on Palestinians.

Deprivation of rights

Women in the Gaza Strip lack easy and free access to their rights, a lack that has been recognised clearly by both Islamic and humanitarian law; however, the main problem, according to participant AA, is that 'Palestinian society abides by customs and traditions more than it does under the law'. Among the examples of rights that women struggle to obtain or are denied entirely is the right to reach senior leadership positions within the governmental and private sectors, as indicated by participant AS: 'No matter how scientifically (academically and culturally) advanced women are, they cannot reach senior leadership positions such as the presidency of a state, a prime minister, or represent the state abroad'. Additionally, women lack independent financial security; as participant NH mentions, 'Palestinian women face the problem of exercising their free disposition because their husbands control their property or salary'. Moreover, women in the Gaza Strip suffer from the continued deprivation of their inheritance, although Islamic Sharia and state law have approved and supported their rights clearly in this regard. It is worth mentioning that, as participant SB explains, 'According to statistics, many women do not have full inheritance rights, even if the court rules in favour of her; sometimes there is no execution because women fear a conflict with their relatives'. At the same time, increasing numbers of divorced and widowed Palestinian women in Gaza (resulting from the context of conflict and protracted crises) suffer from being deprived of custody of their children. As explained by participant AA: 'Divorced or widowed women are deprived of the right to custody of their children, and the problem is that there are no laws protecting the right of mothers to have custody of their children'.

In addition, participant NH states that 'Girls are forced to get married at an early age, thus depriving them of educational opportunities, and are forced to marry someone they do not want'. Participant HY attributes the reasons for the existence of discrimination to 'The negative customs and traditions [that] still prevail in society despite noticeable development in education levels for all groups in society'. Moreover, participant TN considers that one of the most important causes of this problem is that 'Palestinian law does not provide for the effective follow-up of law enforcement', while participant AQ criticises how 'Palestinian law is not unified, as there are special laws in Gaza and various laws in the West Bank that occurred owing to the political division between the Gaza Strip and the West Bank'. Participant TN adds that the problem could be that 'Women themselves do not have a legal culture and no longer know what their rights are and how to access them'.

Moreover, the results of the individual interviews verify the results of the focus group discussions. Interviewee ON, for example, states that there is a considerable percentage of employed women whose husbands control their salaries. ON adds that this is a fact and reality, and even unmarried female employees are exposed to this violence since some fathers are in control of their monthly salaries. In this regard, it is worth mentioning that Islam approves of independent financial responsibility for women, as does the civil law; however, in reality, there is no independent financial responsibility.

Another interviewee summarises that GBC is a serious issue caused by psychological pressures resulting from the Israeli occupation and the economic situation.

Transforming gender-based conflicts into success stories

The aspects of conflict that Palestinian women encounter in the Gaza Strip involve various overlapping social, cultural, economic, psychological, political and legal grounds. To answer the third question of the current investigation, 'How do Palestinian women transform gender-based conflicts in the Gaza Strip into success stories?', the third focus group was conducted on 6 June 2020 with four women selected from among those who participated in the first and the second focus group sessions of this study. The four women were chosen to represent success stories achieved by Palestinian women in the Gaza Strip when facing GBCs. They encountered different conflicts represented by the stereotypical view of women in Palestinian society, the practice of all forms of violence against women and the denial of women's rights to education. Thus, this part of the study contains the ways and means used by these women to surmount the challenges, bearing in mind that they are leaders and heads of women's institutions. These success stories were classified according to the type of conflict and challenges they belong to, as follows.

Women and the struggle for roles

Broadly speaking, Palestinian society considers the primary role of a woman to be that of the housewife, responsible for household chores and raising children. This requires a lot of time and effort, which does not allow women to think about competing for any academic or professional achievements. Therefore, can Palestinian women, living in the Gaza Strip, achieve success despite these burdens, namely the struggle of performing roles in light of harsh external conditions and deep-rooted social barriers that confine women to the narrow circle of the home? Participant TA tries to answer this question in the following story she has lived and narrated:

> I got married at an early age after I finished high school in 1998. Our Palestinian society in the Gaza Strip at that time did not pay much attention to females' education … having 10 children was never an obstacle to my will to succeed, and despite my great preoccupation with taking care of my large family and my 10 children, I always dreamed of completing my higher education. The time came when I achieved my dream in 1998

and the whole story started when I studied law, and again the burden of my large family did not prevent me from eagerly studying. My dreams did not end with a bachelor's degree; I also got my master's and PhD in law, during which I travelled to study at Cairo University in Egypt. Then, I leaped into the field of work by establishing my own legal office, and I was the first woman in the Gaza Strip to work in her own legal office. After that, I worked in governmental institutions until I reached a high leadership position, where I currently work as a counsellor for the General Personnel Bureau, and I hold the position of consultant for many community institutions that defend women's rights.

Depriving women of their right to education and self-realisation

Despite the quantitative and qualitative improvements in the educational system in Palestine at present, women in the Gaza Strip have suffered from negative discrimination and deprivation of educational opportunities, due to the traditional view that prevailed at the time when the world of women was confined to the home, as the perception of the primary role of women was to deliver children. That was illustrated by another success story, which participant ET experienced:

> I graduated from high school with distinction, and I dreamed of going to university like the rest of my classmates and I aspired to achieve something special in society. My first shock was being denied, by my family, to be allowed to proceed with my university education under the pretext that the woman's place is the home. Accordingly, I got married afterwards and gave birth; so my suffering increased, as I lived in a marginalised area in the Gaza Strip in which people believe women should not leave their homes except for the most urgent need. However, I kept my dream to learn and contribute to making a change in society to support women's rights, especially their right to education, work and self-realisation. Therefore, I joined the university, years later. I studied for my BA in journalism and media, then completed an MA in crisis management, while I also worked in the field of community services, believing in my future vision of working in women's institutions to contribute through raising awareness to change the reality of Palestinian women and develop their abilities to reach the rights that they have been denied. Then, I moved to work in governmental institutions and I reached high positions of influence and communication, and through my position, I began to exert efforts and influence to change some traditional mentalities that still exist in our society to change their views of women. I endeavour to raise the decision-makers' awareness towards recognising that women possess great capabilities and skills that qualify them to be active members in the development of society.

Women and their family members exposed to abuse by the Israeli occupation

The Israeli occupation's use of military force in Palestine, and the Gaza Strip in particular, has led to the killing, injury, imprisonment and displacement of many members of the Palestinian community. The Palestinian woman suffers directly from the Israeli occupation as it attacks her directly or indirectly by attacking her family members, which may cause her to lose her husband or children through killing or arrest. The loss of the main breadwinner (i.e. the man) is the reason many women are forced to take over the role of breadwinner for their families, on top of the psychological hurt and painful impact of losing a husband, or father, or son. Some of these women become alienated and introverted; some resort to relief institutions to obtain support for their families and others turn to paid work. It is worth mentioning that the percentage of families living below the poverty line has increased, and additional burdens and responsibilities have increased for the women caring for their families, bearing in mind that families headed by the mother are among the poorest. In this context, participant AA tells her story:

> I am the wife of a martyr and the mother of a martyr, and my husband was a detainee in the occupation prisons before he was assassinated, where he spent eight years in prison. My experience as a detainee's wife meant I became closely acquainted with the conditions of women who had lost their husbands, and I felt empathy for their social, economic and psychological suffering, and when my husband was martyred and then my eldest son, my suffering increased as well as my burdens because I have a large family that needs care. However, I was not occupied with my own suffering at that time, but with the similar sufferings of other Palestinian women; so, I decided to establish an association to protect and care for the wives and mothers of the detainees and the martyrs, and I named this association 'The Bright Candles'. Through the association, I was able to provide psychological, social and legal support and assistance to a large number of these women, because, unfortunately, the woman who loses her husband in our society loses protection, since society considers the husband's presence as protection. With these givens, it was necessary to organise psychological support and community rehabilitation programmes for these women so that they became capable of protecting themselves and managing their lives and their families independently and confidently. One of the greatest accomplishments I have achieved is lobbying the Legislative Council to pass a law protecting the right of the wife who loses her husband to retain her right to custody of her children for life.

Exposure to violence in all its forms

Palestinian women suffer from a double burden of violence: that is, the violence of the Israeli occupation and the violence of the local community. Accordingly, Palestinian women are exposed to various forms of violence, including social, psychological, family and verbal violence, but the number of specialist centres that provide protection and support services to those women is still limited. This is due to the political and economic situation in Palestine, and the Gaza Strip in particular. The protection of women and girls from GBV faces a challenge owing to the absence of laws that protect women from violence or a lack of commitment to them in practice, as well as the traditional culture, which attaches stigma to battered women and prevents them from complaining or reporting the problem. The following story illustrates the success of one Palestinian woman in transforming herself from a victim of domestic violence to a leader in the field of supporting and protecting women who suffer from GBV in the Gaza Strip.

> Fifteen years from the present time, I was experiencing a harsh life, as I was a victim of domestic violence in a society that refuses and denounces a woman that confronts those who violate her and contacts an external party to ask for help, but I challenged these circumstances and contacted an institution for the protection and support of battered women, and I still remember to this today the head of that institution encouraging me and telling me, 'One day you will be a worthy woman'. Furthermore, I challenged the circumstances again and completed my university education, before joining one of the institutions that support women, especially in the field of protecting women from GBV. I am currently the director of the support and counselling unit in this institution, a community activist and the head of other committees in the community that work to defend and protect women's rights. I am very happy and proud that I was a victim and then a survivor of violence, and that I have now become a person in charge of aiding Palestinian women. I feel that the reason for my success in my work is that I lived the experience that many women in society suffer from.

Discussion

The results obtained from the questionnaire and individual and focus group discussions reflect that Palestinian women in the Gaza Strip face distinct problems due to the illegitimate measures of the Israeli occupation authorities, inter-Palestinian political divisions, and sociocultural conflicts in their local community. The interviewees revealed that there are certain commonalities in the problems facing Palestinian women in the West Bank, the Gaza Strip and the Palestinian diaspora, but there is also specificity for each region. They also clarified that Palestinian women live in conflict because of the Israeli occupation and blockade, and suffer political, economic and social hardships; this is why women are depressed and stressed.

The results of this study are consistent with the results of some previous studies, such as Shara and Tarawneh (2019), Sideris (2000) and Fuqaha (2018), which indicate that the level of GBV increases within conflict zones. In this regard, participant QO explains that the women in Gazan society are those affected the most negatively by this pressure. Even though some women are responsible for spending on the family, some men in those families remain convinced that they are the ones with the power to control family income. Accordingly, the man is the one who takes the pressure off the women and children in his family.

The GBCs exist in Palestinian society because it is a society governed by customs and traditions rather than Islamic rules and regulations. Participant ON asserts that, 'We do not have a correct understanding of religion.... The culture of our children is not from religion but rather customs and traditions.... Our religious culture is weak'.

The results of the focus group discussion as well as the individual interviews confirm the Israeli occupation is the main cause of the suffering of Palestinian women. ON highlights that the occupation forces are aware of the essential role Palestinian women play in society, and therefore women have been attacked to corrupt and destroy the values and ethics of Palestinian life. On the other hand, the male-dominated Palestinian society threatens the rights of Palestinian women, especially if the man has no religious conscience. ON explains that in conservative Palestinian society, the majority of men have no other way of dealing with wives but by beating and shouting. Participant ET asserts that the oppression of women in Palestinian society is an extension of the culture of their parents and grandparents, who used to look down on females.

In conclusion, the four success stories of Palestinian women above depended on common means of survival and transforming the conflict they faced into an opportunity to live with dignity:

- turning to education to build women's capabilities and improve their economic and social realities;
- self-reliance and belief in the ability of women to change;
- establishing societal institutions that raise awareness of women's rights, defending and protecting them.

Conclusion and Recommendations

This chapter addresses a critical gap in the understanding of GBV within the unique context of the Gaza Strip. While various studies have explored the negative impact of GBV on women and their societies, limited attention has been given to the Gaza Strip, which is characterised by prolonged conflict and crises. The chapter aims to provide much-needed evidence and insights into the types of GBV faced by Palestinian women in this specific context. Additionally, the current investigation delves into the underlying causes of the most prevalent forms of GBV in Palestinian society. Furthermore, the chapter documents the transformative stories of women who have overcome oppression to lead associations advocating for women's rights and empowerment. The findings reveal that Palestinian women in the Gaza Strip experience diverse forms of GBV, including violence, discrimination and deprivation of rights. This specificity is attributed to the complex conflicts stemming from the Israeli occupation, economic challenges and cultural factors. While societal norms and sensitivities often hinder addressing these issues, Palestinian women exhibit resilience in the face of adversity. Despite the challenges posed by the Israeli occupation and cultural norms, Palestinian women's success stories underscore their ability to effect change and challenge societal paradigms through determination and activism.

The recommendations provided by the authors of the chapter aim to address the issue of resilient Palestinian women facing GBV in the Gaza Strip. Each recommendation focuses on a different aspect of the problem, and collectively they aim to create a more just and equitable society for women in Gaza. Thus, the researchers recommend the following to provide a comprehensive plan for addressing GBV in Palestine, offering practical strategies to create positive change and empower women:

- *Activating the role of Palestinian civil society organisations.* Recognising the influential role of civil society organisations, it is crucial to empower these entities to advocate for women's rights in Palestine. These organisations can facilitate workshops, training sessions and awareness campaigns specifically focused on addressing GBV. By offering resources, legal aid and safe spaces, these organisations can assist survivors in breaking free from the cycle of violence. Additionally, they can engage in lobbying efforts to influence policy changes that protect women's rights and promote gender equality.
- *Investigating the root causes of GBV.* To effectively combat GBV, a comprehensive understanding of its root causes is essential. Conducting research to identify the most prevalent forms of GBV among Palestinian women in the Gaza context will shed light on the underlying factors. This information can then inform the development of targeted interventions and policies that address these specific issues. By addressing the core reasons behind GBV, lasting solutions can be implemented to prevent its occurrence.
- *Comprehensive protection of Palestinian women.* Acknowledging the multifaceted impacts of GBV, there is a need to establish comprehensive protection mechanisms for Palestinian women. This entails providing legal frameworks that ensure the prosecution of perpetrators, offering psychological and medical support for survivors, promoting economic empowerment through skill-building and job opportunities, and creating cultural shifts that reject violence against women. By addressing the various dimensions of GBV, holistic protection strategies can be developed.
- *Launching inclusive awareness programmes.* Raising awareness of GBV among all segments of Palestinian society is vital. Educational programmes and awareness campaigns can target both men and

women, highlighting the causes and consequences of GBV. These initiatives can foster a culture of respect, gender equality and empathy. By dismantling harmful stereotypes and promoting open discussions, these programmes contribute to changing societal attitudes and reducing the acceptance of violence against women.
- *Utilising culture and the arts for advocacy.* Culture and the arts possess a unique power to convey powerful messages and ignite social change. Incorporating narratives of Palestinian women who have experienced GBV within the broader context of political, economic and social conflicts can create a deeper understanding of their struggles. This approach can increase empathy, raise awareness and challenge societal norms that perpetuate violence against women.
- *Embedding awareness in education.* Education is a cornerstone for shaping values and attitudes. Incorporating human rights education and discussions around GBV and discrimination into school curricula can foster a sense of responsibility and respect from an early age. By teaching children and young people about healthy relationships, gender equality and the consequences of GBV, a new generation can be nurtured to reject violence and advocate for women's rights.

References

Abu al-Khair, I. (2018) *Violations of the Israeli Occupation against Palestinian Women in 2017*. Women for Palestine Center for Studies and Research.

Al-Hadidi, N. and Saad, N. (2016) Saudi women and entrepreneurship: Successes and challenges. *Faculty of Education Journal* 64 (4), 332–362.

Al-Somali, S., Al-Jafri, H. and Zaki, K. (2019) Challenges facing academic women to obtain leadership positions in the public higher education sector. An applied study on King Abdulaziz University in Jeddah. *Dar Al-Samat for Studies and Research* 8 (9).

Baldi, G. (2018) Between patriarchy and occupation: Violence against women in the occupied Palestinian Territories. In G.M. Piccinelli, I. Kherkheulidze and A. Borroni (eds) *Reconsidering Gender-Based Violence and Other Forms of Violence Against Women: Comparative Analysis in the Light of the Istanbul Convention* (pp. 247–295). Libellula Edizioni.

Culture and Free Thought Association (2012) *Violence against Palestinian Women as a result of the Israeli Occupation of the Gaza Strip*. CFTA.

Fassetta, G., Imperiale, M.G., Aldegheri, E. and Al-Masri, N. (2020) The role of stories in the design of an online language course: Ethical considerations on cross-border collaboration between the UK and the Gaza Strip. *Language and Intercultural Communication* 20 (2), 181–192. https://doi.org.10.1080/14708477.2020.1722145.

Fulu, E. and Heise, L. (2015) State of the field of research on violence against women and girls. *What Works to Prevent Violence against Women and Girls Evidence*, Paper 1. What Works to Prevent Violence.

Fuqaha, N. (2018) *Palestinian Women, Occupation, Patriarchy and Gender Relations: Case Studies in Area C and the Old City of Hebron*. UN Women.

Gaza Community Mental Health Programme (2021) Snapshot 2020 [blog post]. https://www.gcmhp.ps/publications/1 (accessed 20 February 2021).

Independent Commission for Human Rights (ICHR) (2022) *The Status of Human Rights in Palestine: Executive Summary* (28th Annual Report). https://www.ichr.ps/en/reports(accessed 23 July 2024).

Michau, L., Horn, J., Bank, A., Dutt, M. and Zimmerman, C. (2015) Prevention of violence against women and girls: Lessons from practice. *Lancet* 385, 1672–1684.

Palestinian Ministry of Health (2015) *The Zionist Aggression on the Gaza Strip in 2014.* Palestinian Ministry of Health.

PCBS (Palestinian Central Bureau of Statistics) (2018) Labour Force Survey: (July–September, 2018) Round, (Q3/2018). Press Report on the Labour Force Survey Results. Ramallah – Palestine. https://www.pcbs.gov.ps/portals/_pcbs/PressRelease/Press_En_8-11-2018-LF-en.pdf(accessed 23 July 2024).

PCBS (2020) Violence Survey in the Palestinian Society, 2019. https://www.pcbs.gov.ps/PCBS-Metadata-en-v5.2/index.php/catalog/719 (accessed 23 July 2024).

Shara, S. and Tarawneh, M. (2019) Gender-based violence against Syrian refugee women outside refugee camps in Jordan, Al-Manara. *Journal for Research and Studies.*

Sideris, T. (2000) *Gender, Culture, and Trauma: Mozambican Women Share Experiences of War Dislocation and Survival.* Lola Press.

United Nations (2019) Women in Palestine: Evidence of violence, staggering levels of unemployment and underrepresentation in decision-making. https://news.un.org/ar/story/2019/05/1033191 (accessed 20 January 2021).

UN Women (2024a) FAQs: Types of violence against women and girls. https://www.unwomen.org/en/what-we-do/ending-violence-against-women/faqs/types-of-violence (accessed 23 July 2024).

UN Women (2024b) Facts and figures: Women and girls during the war in Gaza. *UN Women*, 16 April. https://www.unwomen.org/en/news-stories/feature-story/2023/10/facts-and-figures-women-and-girls-during-the-war-in-gaza (accessed 5 July 2024).

UNFPA (2019) Women and girls with disabilities: Needs of survivors of gender-based violence and services offered to them. https://palestine.unfpa.org/sites/default/files/pub-pdf/Women%20and%20Girls%20with%20Disabilities_0.PDF (accessed 5 July 2024).

Women's Center for Legal Aid and Counselling (2019) *The Status of Palestinian Women and Legal Protection Mechanisms.* WCLAC.

World Bank (2019) Gender-based violence (violence against women and girls). https://www.worldbank.org/en/topic/socialsustainability/brief/violence-against-women-and-girls (accessed 5 July 2024).

8 Popular Culture and Gender-Based Violence in an Evolving COVID-19 Context in Zimbabwe

Manase Kudzai Chiweshe, Sandra Bhatasara and Gareth James

Introduction

This chapter examines the intersection of popular culture and gender-based violence (GBV) in Zimbabwe. While both men and women experience interpersonal violence, women and girls are more likely to experience repeated and severe forms of abuse, including sexual violence (Garcia-Moreno et al., 2012), and it is estimated that GBV affects one in three women globally (World Bank, 2019). In Zimbabwe, 43% of women aged 15–49 report experience of physical or sexual violence by an intimate partner (Zimbabwe National Statistics Agency & UNICEF, 2019: 56). More recent reports suggest that GBV intensified in Zimbabwe during the COVID-19 pandemic, perhaps because the isolation caused by national lockdowns made it harder for victims to escape abuse or access support (ZimFact, 2020).

It is also likely that the consumption of some types of popular culture increased during this time, as people were confined to their homes. Kidd et al. (2017: 284) define popular culture as 'widely shared images, ideas, and objects ... produced by the institutions of mass media'. This includes television, film, literature, fashion and advertisements. In this study, we focus specifically on locally produced songs, music videos and increasingly popular skits (short, funny plays that make a joke of something). These types of media are said to reflect and shape the everyday lives and experiences of ordinary people (Barber, 2018; Kidd et al., 2017). While we acknowledge the potential significance of transnational popular culture or 'Western' influences on local artistic expression, a full examination of these is beyond the scope of this chapter (instead, see Chari, 2009).

This chapter contributes to a greater understanding of how popular culture normalises experiences of GBV in Zimbabwe. Our interest in popular culture as a fertile ground for GBV stems from previous research undertaken by two of this chapter's authors, Chiweshe and Bhatasara (2013), in which they argue that hegemonic masculinities (see Connell & Messerschmidt, 2005) and misogyny are celebrated and venerated while the perceived inferiority of women is recreated and reinforced in Zimbabwe's popular music genres (including urban grooves, sungura, dancehall, reggae, gospel and house). Over 10 years on, the genre of Zimdancehall has exploded and is now the most famous music genre in Zimbabwe (Kanengoni, 2018). Over the same period, the use of social media has increased, and skits have become increasingly popular because they can be shared easily online and quickly 'go viral'.

Our aim is therefore to revisit the problem of GBV against the backdrop of COVID-19 lockdowns and to examine the extent to which these new iterations of popular culture (i.e. Zimdancehall and skits) continue to promote and normalise GBV. We also set out to explore the extent to which popular culture could be used as a vehicle for promoting counter-narratives and creating safe spaces for women and girls. While our focus is primarily on the plight of women and girls, we also find that online platforms that create safe spaces for non-heterosexual people, which have received little attention in research to date (save Mateveke, 2022), are becoming an important part of the popular cultural landscape in Zimbabwe.

The chapter is divided into four main sections. First, we present a brief review of the literature, which shows that contemporary Zimbabwean urban music has been characterised by sexist, misogynistic and violent lyrics. Second, we discuss our research design and methods of data collection and analysis. The study described here focused on Harare, the epicentre of music production in Zimbabwe, and used a combination of content analysis, key informant interviews and cyber ethnography to generate new insights into the intersection of popular culture and GBV. Third, we present our findings, which show that music genres such as Zimdancehall continue to celebrate hegemonic masculinities while denigrating women. However, we also find evidence of counter-narratives, and safe spaces being used to raise awareness of and combat GBV, misogyny and homophobia. In the final section, we discuss our findings in the context of COVID-19 and make some recommendations on how popular culture might be used to combat GBV as part of the post-COVID recovery in Zimbabwe. Readers should note that the chapter contains examples of explicit and potentially offensive language.

Gender, Sex and Violence in Zimbabwean Popular Culture

There is a growing body of literature on how women (and, to a lesser extent, men) are portrayed in popular culture in Zimbabwe. Representations of women and gender in contemporary urban music is a particular focal point. Writing at the height of the urban grooves period and before the rise in popularity of Zimdancehall, Chari (2008: 98) states that 'Women, particularly young women, are a staple subject of male-produced urban grooves music'. Chari's analysis of the lyrics of five male urban grooves musical groups (Maskiri, aka Alishias Musimbe; EXQ; Nasty Trix; Stunner; and Extra Large) shows that women are regularly 'presented as "playthings" under the control of men or simply as sex objects', and that they are often confined to 'traditional, less powerful and stereotypical roles [which] trivialises and minimises the contribution of women in society' (2008: 98). In another paper, Chari (2009) argues that the popularity of such narratives can be traced, at least in part, to the glamorisation of violence in some Western popular music by the likes of Eminem, Tupac and 50 Cent. Mate (2012: 124) also notes that the language used in urban grooves to objectify and subjugate women is often set against the 'affirmative and positive' language used to describe men. While these respective contributions are among the first to examine representations of gender in urban grooves music in Zimbabwe, subsequent studies reaffirm these findings by revealing a persistent pattern of sexism and misogyny in the lyrics of contemporary urban music throughout the 2010s (Kufakurinani et al., 2018; Mabuto & Saidi, 2018; Sibanda & Nkala, 2020).

Sex and violence intersect and feature prominently in Zimbabwean contemporary urban music. Again, with reference to urban grooves in particular, Chari (2008: 101) writes:

> There is a significant amount of representation of women as victims of various forms of violence. The levels of violence vary from subtle emotional violence to outright physical subjugation. Psychological male-produced violence within urban grooves music includes verbal abuse, sexist remarks and misogynistic attitudes, while physical violence ranges from references to grabbing or clutching, rape, sex dance and simulated rape.

Kufakurinani et al. (2018: 81) argue that Zimdancehall also 'normalises violence against women' and that 'Some of the songs of Zimdancehall seem to condone if not legitimise domestic violence against women' (2018: 89). Violence against women features in the music of both male and female artists, and some female musicians, such as Lady Squanda, peddle violence against men (Kufakurinani & Mwatwara, 2017: 43–44). However, women undoubtedly remain the primary targets and feature more often as victims of (sexual) violence at the hands of men. Mangeya (2022: 361–362) asserts that the discourse of Zimdancehall constructs sexual intercourse between a man and a woman as a 'bedroom match' during which 'the man has to totally dominate the woman and emerge as the winner'. Within this discourse, the penis is constructed as a weapon for use in dominating and disciplining a woman. Zimdancehall is thus described as a 'phallocentric discourse that advances not only the infliction of pain on the woman but the physiological domination through the wearing out of the vagina' (Mangeya, 2022: 374). From this perspective, Zimdancehall may be considered a form of GBV.

Contemporary urban music lyrics, Chari (2008: 99) writes, thus 'promote patriarchal hegemonic cultural narratives that transfer power from women to men' and that power, in turn, 'gives licence to men to trample on the rights of women through sexual exploitation, sexual abuse, violence and marginalisation since women are constructed as subservient to men'. Marufu (2014, cited in Mabuto & Saidi, 2018: 64), for example, draws a connection between Zimdancehall and the exploitation of teenage girls by older men in bars and wider society. Other studies also draw on news stories for contemporary examples of GBV to demonstrate that the promotion of patriarchal hegemonic cultural narratives in popular music encourages predatory and sexually aggressive behaviour in men. Tivenga (2018: 118), for example, highlights street-level harassment and 'body policing' whereby young women are condemned for wearing mini-skirts, resulting in incidents of women being stripped naked in public. The negative consequences of toxic masculinities are also evident in the high levels of sexually risky behaviours among men who put themselves and their partners at risk of HIV infection (Shoko, 2012: 91, cited in Mangeya, 2022). These forms of GBV are further fuelled and licensed by influencers like Andrew Tate and, in Zimbabwe, Shadaya Knight – a social media personality who has gained popularity for his anti-feminist views.

However, there is also some evidence to suggest that some urban musicians are beginning to counter narratives of GBV. Chiweshe and Bhatasara (2013: 167) contend that popular music can create space for female musicians actively 'to protest and carve out space to create and perform their identities'. Viriri (2014) identifies two female musicians – Edith Katiji and Sandra Ndebele – as 'game changers' because they were unwilling to be seen as victims, instead performing their musical styles and identities. There are also examples of male artists at least attempting to offer counter-narratives. For instance, Ureke and Washaya (2016) find that some songs by male artists Sniper Storm and Winky D challenge GBV, the sexual abuse of children and the misuse of drugs. Similarly, Ncube and Chipfupa (2017: 117) examine the song lyrics of two male artists, Outspoken and Synik, concluding that 'instead of perpetuating this misogynistic culture characteristic of rap and hip-hop, they drastically break away from this continuum. The two artists acknowledge women as integral to the wellbeing of society and the nation at large'. Sibanda and Nkala (2020) examine Clement Magwaza's lyrics and find that the artist challenges gender stereotypes by encouraging men to publicly express their affection for their spouse or partner and refrain from having multiple wives. Finally, Chireshe (2022) examines the lyrics of Oliver Mtukudzi's songs, some of which portray men as remorseful and humble, which is counter to narratives of hegemonic masculinity, while elsewhere he condemns spousal abuse. However, the extent to which these examples evidence the emergence of an established counter-narrative to the sexist, misogynistic and violent content that dominates popular genres such as Zimdancehall has been questioned (Chiweshe & Bhatasara, 2013: 167).

There is some suggestion within this literature that popular music genres merely reflect Zimbabwean society and lived experiences (Kufakurinani *et al.*, 2018; Parwaringira & Mpofu, 2021a). Drawing on an interview with long-time famous *sungura* musician Alick Macheso, in which he states that 'A musician is just a social commentator', Chaya (2015: 55) asserts that 'society is the problem as musicians are merely reflecting what they see and hear from the society'. However, this assertion seems remarkably naïve given that popular music is well established as 'an important carrier and transmitter' of cultural and social ideas (Chiweshe & Bhatasara, 2013: 167). Indeed, as Mabuto and Saidi assert, 'hegemonic masculinities prescribed by societal norms, values and the traditional Zimbabwean culture easily find expression *and promotion* through this type of music' (2018: 66; emphasis added). Several studies suggest that lyrics of popular songs not only reflect lived experience but also shape it (Chari, 2008; Chiweshe & Bhatasara, 2013; Mabuto & Saidi, 2018; Parwaringira & Mpofu, 2021b). While this line of argument is convincing, it is also more challenging to demonstrate; therefore, further research may be needed to establish more firmly the influence of popular music on action and behaviour.

Methodology

We adopted a qualitative research approach to generate a more nuanced understanding of the intersection between popular culture and GBV in Zimbabwe. Berg (2009) notes that qualitative research seeks to answer questions by examining various social settings and the individuals who inhabit them. Kumar (1999) asserts that the primary focus of qualitative research is to understand, explore, discover and clarify people's situations, feelings, perceptions, attitudes, values, beliefs and experiences. This approach allowed us to examine popular art as a performance and a portrayal of everyday life. We used three qualitative methods simultaneously: content analysis, cyber ethnography and key informant interviews.

We undertook a content analysis of popular songs and skits. The sampling of songs and skits followed a stepwise process. First, we identified the most popular Zimdancehall songs and skits of the previous six years based on radio chat shows, streaming numbers (i.e. YouTube views), radio airplay and general popularity in Zimbabwe. We also purposively sampled songs and videos popular with youths which do not get airplay due to vulgar content. Such pieces are popular on the streets and often used on social media platforms, including TikTok and Instagram Challenges. We chose to focus on the past six years (three years before and after the onset of the COVID-19 pandemic) to ensure a sample of recent songs which currently have an impact on communities. This resulted in a sample of 40 songs and 20 skits.

For social media spaces, we utilised cyber ethnography focusing on popular pages and websites in Zimbabwe, such as Zimcelebs, Bustop TV, Pachopisa, and the pages of social influencers and personalities such as Comic Pastor, Mai TT and Madam Boss. The authors used their own existing social media accounts to passively observe content and conversations on these pages across platforms such as Facebook, Twitter and Instagram over three months. According to Black (2016: 105), cyber ethnography refers to the collection of research data by using online participant observation, online focus groups, social media sites, chats, Skype and YouTube. With the rising popularity and expansion of the internet, online platforms have become a feature of social interaction. As a result, people now have an online habitat that was accentuated during the COVID-19 lockdowns. This method therefore enabled us to examine both the extent to which these platforms normalise GBV and how that is reflected in online communications. The data (particularly those pertaining to public figures and organisational accounts) can be considered to be in the public domain and no personal data pertaining to site users was collected or is reported here. The authors also refrained from interacting with site users or contributing to online discussions.

Finally, we conducted interviews with 20 key informants: the representatives of four civil society organisations, three academics, three music artists, a radio disc jockey, two policymakers, three actors and four producers. Again, informants were purposively sampled. The interviews enabled a nuanced understanding of how critical stakeholders involved in the production and dissemination of popular culture understand the problem of GBV within the sector and the extent to which the cultural products they produce exacerbate the problem.

We undertook a thematic analysis of the resulting data, which is a method for identifying, analysing and reporting patterns and themes within the data (Terry *et al.*, 2017). Our approach involved coding qualitative data to identify themes or patterns in the lyrics, melodic phrases and language used in interviews, online communications and songs. We employed the following steps: organised and prepared the data for analysis; read all the collected data; coded all the collected data; used the coding process to generate a description of the setting or people, as well as categories or themes for analysis; interpreted the results; and, finally, developed a qualitative narrative based on our interpretation of the results. We summarise our findings in the next section.

Findings and Discussion: Popular Culture as a Vehicle for Normalising and Combating GBV

Our findings are presented in two parts. First, we look at the evidence supporting the argument that popular culture continues to normalise, if not explicitly promote, GBV in contemporary Zimbabwe. This is evident in the explicit and vulgar lyrics of many Zimdancehall songs. Second, we point to evidence of popular culture being used to promote counter-narratives and provide safe spaces for women and girls. We go on to suggest that these attempts to reappropriate popular culture as a vehicle for combating GBV may hold lessons for policymakers and practitioners seeking to reverse the upward trend in GBV since the onset of the COVID-19 pandemic.

Normalising GBV by denigrating and sexualising women

A majority of the songs and music videos we examined display misogynistic expressions and movements that show women in a negative light. Misogyny in this research refers to the objectification, exploitation, or victimisation of women in song lyrics, videos, skits and other popular media (Weitzer & Kubrin, 2009). The themes we identified in our data include specific references to women as 'whores', 'witches' and 'weak', as well as the explicit commodification of women, and the sexualisation and shaming of their bodies. Drawing on the evidence from our research, we assert that these representations of women serve to normalise GBV in Zimbabwe.

Several of the media outputs we examined portrayed women as sexually indiscriminate. In the song 'Unoda Zvinhu' ('You Want Things'), Zimdancehall artist Maggikal portrays a girl as promiscuous. The song builds into a narrative that women love money and will have multiple relationships for money. Even in songs that try to portray a good message, there is still the use of tropes that women love men with money. Comic Pastor, in the song 'Tsamwa' ('Get Angry'), narrates how he was being turned down by a girl who wanted married men with cars and money. The accompanying music video conveys a long-held belief that girls will regret it when the poor boy 'makes it'. A Zim hip hop artist, Holy Ten, has a tendency to refer to women as 'whores'. In a 'love song' titled 'Mwana Ndakubirai' ('I Have Stolen your Daughter') he sings 'I am gonna sideline mawhores angu' ('I am going to sideline my whores'), and in another 'paUZ pane mawhores' ('there are whores at the University of Zimbabwe').

Women are also often portrayed as evil or cruel people who use men and leave them with broken hearts. In this characterisation, popular art paints women as witches, and in this space their primary purpose is to harm innocent men whose only crime is to love them. For example, urban grooves musician Kae Chaps, in the song 'Juzi' ('Jersey'), sings, 'wakandirakidza kuti zveshuwa uri mwana waEve' ('you showed me that you are Eve's daughter'). The biblical reference to Eve is intended to evoke the creation myth of Abrahamic religions which tells of Eve's role in the 'Fall of Man' in which she and Adam are cursed by God for eating the forbidden fruit and expelled from the Garden of Eden. In this myth, Eve is often and unfairly portrayed as beguiling Adam on behalf of the Devil. The same singer, in the song 'Gehenna' ('Hell') sings, 'Way too jealous, waisada kundiona with anybody when you were fucking with everybody. I know what you did so ukuenda kugehena' ('Way too jealous, you never wanted to see me with anybody when you were fucking everybody. I know what you did so you are going to Hell'). Here, again, women are portrayed as promiscuous and therefore on the path to Hell – a place reserved for evildoers.

The portrayal of women as the weaker sex is also prevalent in popular music. This is based on a historical patriarchal order that promotes the ideal of strong men protecting vulnerable women (Wood, 2019). Listening to radio programmes for this research, we found that such sentiments are often expressed by DJs and callers on phone-in programmes. These attitudes tend to reinforce and normalise toxic masculinity, which has a negative impact on men, women and the rest of society (Wikström, 2019). This toxic masculinity is evident in songs by the likes of Jah Prayzah. In a song dedicated to the Zimbabwe male football team, 'Fambai Nebhora' ('Move with the Ball'), Jah Prayzah sings, 'tovanzvenga sevarandakadzi' ('we dribble them like women slaves') and also 'tovapfekedza pitikoti, mapitikoti' ('we make them wear petticoats'). Jah Prayzah faced a backlash from some women's organisations over these lyrics because of how they demean women as weak and useless. Chiweshe (2014) has shown that within football fandom spaces, misogynistic songs and phrases are prevalent.

The commodification of women is also evident in lyrics that reduce women to property that men often use to show their success to other men. In the song 'Chii Chimwe Tikurakidzei?' ('What Else Can We Offer You?'), Uncle Epatan sings about success as the accumulation of wealth in the form of money, houses, planes, cars, guns and also women. Viewing women as property is problematic because it promotes the view that men can or should control, discipline and abuse women without facing any consequences. As owners, men are entitled to treat their property however they see fit. In a radio interview, a female musician, Sandra Ndebele, spoke about her own experience of exploitation as a young artist (Ndlovu, 2022). A female actress we spoke to also told us that sexual exploitation is 'prevalent in the arts industry. People are embarrassed to talk about those issues, but it is happening'. These insights highlight the challenges faced by young women who get into the entertainment industry.

In Zimbabwe, these attitudes towards women are reflected in (and perhaps shaped by) the representations discussed above as well as the overt sexualisation of women in popular music. Qounfuzed's lyrics and music video for the song '9ine' speak to the hypersexualisation of women in popular culture. The video shows lurid sexual dances by girls talking to the song's lyrics that celebrate this type of dancing. In the song, Qounfuzed sings:

chiuno chake kunge propeller	your waist dancing like a propeller
vasingagone huyai muzokopera	those who cannot dance like this, come and copy
ndokumbirawo kukochekera	can you please allow me to connect with your body
besu rako richiwombera	Your buttocks clapping [in the video, it shows naked buttocks dancing in a clapping manner]
ndine skiri randiri kuda kuyedza	I want to try a skill [sexual innuendo] on you
wakandigarira uchinderedza	while you are sitting on me and gyrating your back

Another artist, Uncle Epatan, sings 'bata chimwana icho, chine mhata' ('grab that girl with the big ass') and, in another song, 'garo rinobatwa ipapo ipapo' ('we hold ass without delay'). In these songs, women are reduced to sexual objects. The sexual gyrating of women's buttocks is used to attract views, as in Baba Harare's song 'Generator' and Enzo Ishall's 'Magate' ('Calabashes'). Some of these songs have landed artists in trouble with the law, including Tawanda Mumanyi (aka Seh Calaz), who was fined by a judge for contravening the Censorship and Entertainment Control Act with a song called 'Kurova Hohwa' (*hohwa* translates as 'mushroom' but is also a euphemism for sex in this song) (see Rupapa, 2018).

Ideal types of beauty are used to categorise female bodies as desirable and undesirable. In Zimdancehall, the former are often described as *pombi* or *kanyama last* (both colloquial ways of saying beautiful woman), *akabatana* (shapely), *simbi* (precious metal) and, in the recent past, *mutumba* (drum). Conversely, undesirable bodies are described as *tsitobone, shatrisha, kahuma* (all informal ways of saying someone is ugly). For example, Zimdancehall artist Mad Viper, in the song 'Zvandinotemba' ('What I Trust'), targets a female artist, Kadijah, with derogatory lyrics about her weight and complexion. These ideal types also shape access to the industry and often lead to discrimination against talented women because of their size or looks (Lin & Yeh, 2009). One of the actors interviewed confirmed this: 'When it comes to women getting opportunities, your looks can play an important part. If you are considered overweight or not sexually desirable by the standards of those in charge, you will not get the opportunity.' Our analysis of online communications also highlighted how audiences comment negatively on the looks and perceived beauty of the artists. Often this has led to anecdotal reports of women bleaching their skin to meet the desirable or ideal standard of *kayellow bone* (light-skinned women). In Baba Harare's song 'Yellow Bone' the central message is that 'yellow bone ndere mbinga, slay queen ndere mhene' ('light-skinned women are for wealthy men'). Enzo Ishall, in 'Bhiza' ('Horse'), describes a woman as being shaped like a horse and stating horses need a rider. As we have demonstrated, many artists favour such descriptions laced with sexual innuendo that tend to reduce women to sexual objects.

Some female artists in Zimbabwe have participated in and propagated the sexualisation of women through their own music and videos. There is some debate as to whether this is a form of internalised sexism or, as Mitchner (2019) argues, a way of gaining control and asserting power by means of subversion (also see Chiweshe & Bhatasara, 2018).

Overall, however, we assert that these pejorative representations of women serve to normalise GBV in Zimbabwe. For example, Shinsoman, in the song 'Mukadzi Nzenza' ('Loose Woman'), berates a woman who is 'lazy', 'dirty' and 'promiscuous'. These are given as justifications for the use of physical violence against a wife. Another artist, Bazooker, sings, 'ndine mababe akawanda mamwe acho ndongomitisa, amwe acho kutomamisa, mamwe acho ndongoitisa, mamwe macondom ndinoshandisa…' ('I have many girls, some of them I impregnate, others I beat, others I use, others like condoms I use them too…'). These are examples of lyrics that praise men for their ill-treatment of women. Weitzer and Kubrin (2009: 15) write:

> In these lyrics, it is a badge of honour for men to abuse women verbally and physically. Men win respect from other men when they act like 'players,' 'pimps,' and exploiters of women – financially, sexually, and emotionally.

Combating GBV with counter-narratives and safe spaces

However, popular culture is not only a vehicle for normalising GBV; it has also been used to promote an end to physical violence, especially intimate-partner violence. This was evident during the COVID-19 lockdowns, when levels of intimate partner violence increased. Various popular art forms designed to educate people on the evils of physical violence and promote support services to victims were released and widely viewed during the lockdown periods. One key informant, a producer of popular online media content, told us:

> We understand that for those who were staying with the perpetrators at home, especially during the first 21 days of lockdown, it was hectic. Before the lockdown at least people would go out to work and come back home at the end of the day and just go to sleep as they were tired. But during the

lockdown, people were always together and indoors. So we had to, one, do more content so that people could watch when they were relaxing; two, with that content, we were informing people that if [GBV] were to happen to them, there were safe houses available.

The same content producer aired skits during the COVID-19 lockdowns to provide support and information for survivors of rape. The producer stated that 'Based on the statistics from the Adult Rape Clinic, we understand that since the launch of our informative skits, the cases of rape victims seeking help at the clinic has increased'.

Musicians were also tackling GBV in music popular at this time. Ammara Brown, for example, in the song 'Tichichema' ('Crying'), sings, 'Soon you'll be pulling on my hair (Why...) You beat me; Saying you're sorry then you need me; (Why...) You hit me'. In the same song, she also highlights two critical dimensions of intimate-partner violence, in particular, how it affects children ('He's just a boy; How is he meant to drown the noise; You raise your voice, Hell in our home') and the role of alcohol in fuelling violent acts ('It's past midnight; You are walking in to start a fight; This is your life; Day in and out drinking all night'). Bazooker, in the song 'Bodo', sings, 'Kana bodo, ehe mukadzi haarohwe; Ngaavhaire achiti ini handirohwe' ('no, no, no, you should never beat up your wife. Let her feel proud that her husband does not beat her'). Seh Calaz, a Zimdancehall artist who has many songs that denigrate women, nevertheless has released music that denounces intimate-partner violence. For example, in the song 'Usamurove' ('Do Not Beat Her'), he sings:

babe rangu harisi reku boxer	my partner is not for boxing
haufe wakandiona ndichimu forcer	you will never see me forcing her
vanhu ava havana kusimba	women are not strong
havadi kurwiswa chavanoda kudiwa	they do not want to fight, but love
kana une wako usamushushe	if you have yours, do not trouble her
paatadza usamurove, tauriranai; gadzirisanai	when she is wrong, do not beat her, speak, and resolve the issue

Other songs focus on physical violence in intimate-partner relationships but have some problematic messaging. One example is Felly Nandi, who also utilised music as an art form to raise awareness of GBV during the lockdown period. However, in her song 'Mangoromera', she tries to locate the problem of male violence away from individual actions and towards some evil spirits.

BlacPerl, an urban music artist, has provided insights into violence in other public spaces. In her song 'Dai Maiziva' ('If You Knew'), she sheds light on the violence that happens to women in public areas, especially those deemed to be dressed 'inappropriately'. She sings, 'Vamwe vachidamburwa hembe [some are getting their clothes torn from their bodies] and the next thing/Society blames that on her dressing'. There are multiple documented examples of women stripped naked in Harare's central business district for dressing in a culturally inappropriate way (see e.g. Mwando, 2015). Such violence is meant to control women's dress in public spaces, and the victim is often blamed for the violence perpetrated against her. Wikström (2019: 29) concludes:

> through street harassment, men objectify femininity and any non-normative expression of gender or sexuality…. Society rationalises their behaviour as an aspect of their 'masculine entitlement'. From an early age, these intrusions are dismissed as 'boys' behaviour', and are not considered a valid form of harm.

BlacPerl's song also highlights multiple layers of systemic violence against women, including physical violence, income insecurity, under-representation in positions of power, and the lived experience of girls who cannot attend school for lack of sanitary pads. These may seem like disparate issues, but they stem from a problematic androcentric culture.

Several arts-related initiatives have focused on GBV. One such initiative is the Love Should Not Hurt campaign, implemented by Population Solutions for Health (PSH) with support from the Embassy of Sweden. The unique nature of this initiative is the use of music as part of the programmatic activities to promote anti-GBV messages. In 2020, the programme utilised creatives such as Winky D, Ammara Brown, Holy Ten, Seh Calaz and Roki to produce a collection of songs. Although Winky D's back catalogue includes songs that glamorise GBV and toxic masculinity, one of the most popular songs in the Love Should Not Hurt campaign, 'Rudo Harurove' ('Love Does Not Beat You Up'), outlines the critical message that intimate spaces must be loving and not violent. At the programme's first launch, Winky D noted, 'I'm in solidarity with the survivors of GBV. I want to assure them they will not walk alone as long as my music plays' (Mukucha, 2021). The programme has also included artists being involved in community outreach activities. For example, Freeman performed at a Love Should Not Hurt soccer and netball tournament in Bindura. Kumbirai Chatora, PSH social marketing director, in describing the campaign, said that:

> We want to create a movement of men against Gender-Based Violence. We collaborate with artists who have created jingles on Love Should Not Hurt. During our research, we noted that men use violence to discipline their wives as a form of love. We are reframing that to say love should not hurt. In the heat of the moment, we encourage men to step back, take a deep breath and walk away. (Gwarisa, 2022)

Some of the informants we spoke to collaborated on this and similar campaigns. In 2022, the Love Should Not Hurt campaign programme produced another collaborative song against intimate-partner violence featuring Winky D, Freeman, Ammara Brown, Holy Ten, Sandra Ndebele and Hwabaraty. The chorus echoes, 'ukaona ruchirova haruzi rudo nekuti rudo harurove' ('if it involves beatings, then it is not love because love should not involve beating'). The programme has also utilised comedians such as Vharazipi to produce skits that promote a message of love, and shame for men who beat up their wives. Another project is the No to GBV Riddim (a Jamaican slang pronunciation of the English word 'rhythm'), which included female artists such as Dvyne, Ninja Lipsy, Pauline, Nina Grande, Colleta, Daruler, Lady Bee, Faceless, Tytania, Kadjah and Empress Massina. The songs explore different forms of GBV experienced by women, especially in intimate-partner relationships. In addition, they showcase an essential message against GBV through the voices of women musicians. For example, in one of the songs, Lady Bee urges women to stand up for their rights.

The censorship of GBV-promoting content in popular culture is not a priority in Zimbabwe. In music, both artists and DJs admitted that there were not enough editorial guidelines, censorship or regulation of content and language. For example, a DJ can create a playlist with all the 'right' songs, and they pass through the editor, excluding those with vulgar, sexist and derogatory language, but when on air they can be spontaneous. This is how songs that promote GBV end up being played on air. Nonetheless, some awareness has started to emerge, as noted by one radio DJ:

> To a certain extent, artists of today are trying. If you check the videos and look at our music icons like Tuku singing 'Tozeza Baba' ['We Are Afraid of Father'], they portray violence as bad. Songs like 'BP Yangu Yakwira' ['My Blood Pressure Has Shot Up], to mention just a few, you will find that gender-based violence issues are there. Right now, I think due to some organisations that are fighting gender-based violence, you will see that our musicians are getting endorsements from those organisations, and their lyrics are written as per the organisation's request. The organisations then fund everything. Some artists compose their music to lure those organisations to sponsor their work. So, you will find that with every theme an artist pursues, they will write something along those lines.

EXQ and Freeman, for example, have a song that challenges gendered assumptions and provides an alternative view of a 'good wife'. Despite references to *nzenza* (loose women), they go against the grain and claim they love their *nzenza*. In the song 'Nzenza', they sing, 'varume ndakaitoida nzenza iyoyo, ndoraramira nzenza iyoyo, ndiyo inoita ndigo senza iyoyo chero mukati nzenza' ('guys, I love that loose woman. I live for that loose woman. She is the one I work for even if you call her loose'). At the song's end, EXQ concludes, 'Let's love our women; let us not harass our women. Let us not call our women names'.

In our research, we found the lack of funding was a key barrier to promoting more progressive narratives. Artists, be they in the music or film industries, need more resources to make ends meet. Instead of putting their creative efforts into combating societal issues like GBV, they tend to focus on what sells and what can entertain. One key informant, a human rights activist, noted:

> [Raising awareness of GBV] is something we have been exploring, but it is also underfunded. If you look at the arts industry, it is more about passion. There is no funding, but artists do it only as a passion. So, the needed support is more financial, and we cannot give it or provide it.

National broadcasters represent another barrier because they are intimately connected with national politics, particularly the ruling party's politics. Hence broadcasters are perceived as impenetrable bureaucracies and moral guardians. One respondent, a policy advocate at a civil society organisation, described national broadcasters as 'difficult to work with' because of the 'bureaucracies' and their 'heavily politicised' processes and structures, adding that 'They seem to lack the authority to make their own decisions'. It is, therefore, difficult for those who want to promote specific content on the harmful effects of GBV to do so via the mainstream media. Those who want to avoid political confrontation or who do not subscribe to a particular moral or patriarchal order will therefore seek to create or occupy safe spaces away from more popular outlets, potentially limiting the impact of their work. Nevertheless, these spaces are an important arena for challenging patriarchal, misogynistic and homophobic cultural norms and narratives.

In our research we explored some of these online spaces where creatives are promoting the acceptance of 'non-normative' expressions of gender, as well as non-heterosexual orientations and identities in Zimbabwe. Speaking about LGTBQI+ artists, the same policy advocate quoted above told us:

> We have seen those who engage in painting and now with technology, a lot of them also are engaging in some skits. Some of them even throw a line or two about sexuality and in some way, they are also advocating their own rights and trying to raise awareness for LGBTI people.

The popularity of some LGBTQI+ actors and comedians in Zimbabwe, at least in the online environment, has shown how entertainment can be critical in advancing acceptance of 'non-normative' expressions of gender and sexual diversity. The most popular social influencer during and beyond the COVID-19 lockdowns is Tatelicious, whose live performances have attracted thousands of online viewers and followers. She is a transwoman who has fully transitioned, and her popularity has been influential in combating social stigma against trans persons. Another popular act is Mai Vee/Mhosva TV, whose sexuality has generated immense debate online; yet, the content from this creator has broadly been accepted in Zimbabwe.

Bustop TV has used its platform to promote stories and documentaries that highlight the experiences of homosexuals in Zimbabwe and avoid the use of negative stereotypes in the skits it broadcasts. Several respondents stated that these media are beginning to make inroads in terms of promoting greater awareness of GBV and tolerance of 'non-normative' expressions of gender and sexual identity. As the policy advocate quoted above put it:

> Definitely [progress is being made], for example, when Bus Stop TV made that clip around tolerance and diversity ... we received many calls from around the country ... [it] has managed to create awareness for the general population; but also, our membership grew because of that advertisement.

And the same respondent also told us:

> The good thing about art is it makes a very difficult conversation easier to discuss in some way. It reveals issues that people are not comfortable talking [about] one on one, but at least it kind of pokes there for one to think, to reflect and also, in some way, they also implement policy review.

There have thus been attempts to combat GBV, as well as to encourage acceptance of diverse sexual orientations and identities, through popular art and media in Zimbabwe. These attempts include nationwide campaigns driven by non-governmental organisations and featuring popular urban musicians, as well as attempts to create safe spaces for women, girls and non-heterosexual people. However, these new forms of popular music and art are still emerging and their impact in terms of shifting the societal and cultural dial has been limited.

Conclusions and Recommendations: Harnessing Popular Culture to Combat GBV in a Post-COVID Recovery Context

In this chapter, we have shown how popular culture is used to produce, reproduce and reinforce various forms of GBV, while celebrating toxic masculinities and misogyny. The discourse of Zimdancehall, for example, often serves to re-create and reinforce the patriarchal order and its associated practices around acceptable roles of women, appropriate forms of beauty, ideal manhood and masculinity, and violence as a way of disciplining women into submission. While it is difficult to establish a causal connection between these discourses and the observed increase in intimate-partner violence during and since the COVID-19 lockdowns, it is reasonable to suggest that the increased consumption of popular media played some part by normalising GBV.

The government of Zimbabwe has attempted to address the problem, including through section 56 of the constitution, which provides a framework for the protection and promotion of the rights of women and men, girls and boys in Zimbabwe. Zimbabwe's constitution also recognises the equality of all persons and explicitly outlaws discrimination on the grounds of sex or gender. Other measures include criminal codes, the Zimbabwe Republic Police's specialised 'victim friendly units' and the Zimbabwe Gender Commission. The Ministry of Women Affairs, Gender and Community Development also works with civil society and various UN agencies to tackle GBV (Moyo-Nyede, 2022). Additionally, the Data Protection Act 2021 aims to protect people from harm online. There have also been debates about banning or censoring genres like Zimdancehall (Chihora, 2016: 49; Parwaringira & Mpofu, 2021a).

While censorship may be part of the answer, a more convincing solution might be to harness the power of music to transmit counter-hegemonic perspectives. Indeed, the creation of alternative spaces for expression and resistance through song has been a constant feature of the musical landscape from the colonial era (Hancock-Barnett, 2012) and throughout the post-independence years (Ncube & Chipfupa, 2017). It is our assertion therefore that popular culture has the potential to foster cultures of sustainable peace as part of the post-COVID recovery in Zimbabwe, and we have worked with a local Zimbabwean female artist and music producer to create a music video using the findings from this research which makes an active contribution towards realising this goal.[1]

Our research, building on existing evidence, highlights new counter-narratives in contemporary urban music and the creation of safe spaces online for women, girls and non-heterosexuals, but these are not yet a part of the mainstream. More research is needed to examine further the persistence of hegemonic masculinities, including on: the influences of transnational popular culture and especially the toxicity of social media influences like Andrew Tate and Shadaya Knight, to which we have only alluded; the extent to which popular culture can truly be said to shape actions and behaviours; and the specific impact that counter-narratives are having in terms of tackling GBV in Zimbabwe. These remaining gaps notwithstanding, we draw on our experiences, existing literature and the findings from this research to make the following seven recommendations for policy and the industry:

- *Build capacity and advocacy in the arts sector.* There is a need for a clear action plan that engages the creative sector and builds capacity among key actors (including creatives, producers and radio stations) to understand and appreciate the problem of GBV. This could be achieved through training targeted at prominent decision-makers in the sector, who might then champion change in how women are treated, represented and celebrated in popular culture. There are good examples within the industry from which others could learn, including approaches to training and advocacy in established civil society organisations.

- *Invest in positive storytelling in the arts.* There is a need to counter the notion that controversial creations, especially those that are sexual in nature, are the only way to become successful. As one music producer told us, 'I think it's every artist's responsibility that whatever message they deliver to their audiences, it's a message that preaches positivity, it's a message that preaches peace, it's a message that teaches social values, rather than just to entertain people'. Such change requires investment so that artists can still make a living out of progressive messaging in their art. Public and third sector organisations could commission artists to produce materials for use in community engagement programmes, thus providing them with access to paying clientele.
- *Encourage male artists to act as agents of change.* Attitudes and behaviours that may lead to GBV begin to develop at a very young age (Chari, 2008: 109). Male Zimdancehall and Zim hip hop artists, especially, should be encouraged to use their influence among the youth to help shape attitudes and behaviours before ideas about gender roles and norms become established. One of the male artists we spoke to agreed: 'as artists ... we have to speak as often as we can. Each and every artist has an obligation to do this because it is affecting our communities, it is affecting our society, it is affecting our country. So, if each and every artist finds it in their heart that they have to speak about this, you'll find that the whole nation will hear about this ... and people will start practising caution when it comes to gender-based violence.'
- *Tackle sextortion and sexual abuse in the arts sector.* Policymakers need to provide concrete frameworks, both social and legal, that focus on combating sextortion. The limited nature of national policy and legal frameworks on sextortion dissuades victims/survivors from exposing perpetrators. There is a lack of accessible, safe, confidential and gender-sensitive reporting mechanisms to support survivors, especially in an arts sector that relies on close personal relationships to get work. We therefore recommend a gender policy in the arts sector that has a clear reporting structure which ensures anonymity and also provides a transparent investigative process. As one representative from an arts-focused parastatal organisation put it: '[an involving sextortion or sexual abuse is] something that the sector should not tolerate, it's something that should be reported as and when it happens. So that appropriate measures are taken and such culprits should not be allowed or given the space to practise because the arts sector should be a safe environment.'

- *Increase the standing of women in the arts sector.* One way to do this is to increase the numbers of women who occupy decision-making roles within the sector through the use of quota systems. We argue that a male gaze in these vital positions tends to entrench specific patriarchal practices and gender norms. Increasing gender diversity at the top of the sector could help to ensure a wide variety of voices influence the production process of popular arts and thus the ways in which women and men are depicted. We recommend equal-share representation in senior roles such as general directors, managers, artistic directors, curators and editors.
- *Collect gender-disaggregated data in the arts sector.* There is a lack of readily available data on gender participation and experiences in the arts sector in Zimbabwe. These data are essential to build informed policy frameworks and monitor progress towards gender equality and inclusivity in the sector. Data are also required to track the production of artistic products by gender, and to analyse audience trends and how they are influenced by various processes such as access to social media, television, radio stations and other platforms. Understanding these dynamics will assist in formulating more gender-responsive policies.
- *Provide enhanced protections against online abuse.* During the COVID-19 lockdowns, social media replaced most forms of social interaction, including various live performances by famous artists. These platforms sometimes exposed people to new forms of harm online. The government of Zimbabwe, in December 2021, gazetted the Data Protection Act, which has some progressive clauses targeting online abuse, including cyberbullying, revenge porn and child pornography. However, it is still unclear how the law will be implemented, including reporting mechanisms for those who suffer online abuse. The government must do more to educate the public on the provisions and protections of the Act. In addition, there is a need to engage social media companies to ensure that they provide more protection on their platforms against abuse.

It is our assertion that these measures could go some way towards raising awareness of the harms caused by GBV, and perhaps could even begin to reverse the upward trend in GBV and intimate-partner violence since the onset of the COVID-19 pandemic through the more regular transmission of counter-hegemonic perspectives. As one radio DJ reasoned, some people might listen to a song and think 'it's just one of those many other songs' and they will not change their behaviours, whereas others 'will hear the message in the song, just like you will find others who will hear the word of God and change ... because, as I understand music, it has free entry into one's soul; it can influence someone to make good decisions'.

Note

(1) The music video can be viewed at https://www.youtube.com/watch?v=XGJ1ofYHsi8 (accessed 5 July 2024).

References

Barber, K. (2018) *History of African Popular Culture*. Cambridge University Press.

Berg, B. (2009) *Qualitative Research. Methods for the Social Sciences*. Allyn & Bacon.

Black, M. (2016) Cyber ethnography: A critical tool for the Department of Defense? *Comparative Strategy* 35 (2), 103–113.

Chari, T. (2008) Representation of women in male-produced 'urban grooves' music in Zimbabwe. *Journal of Music Research in Africa* 5 (1), 92–110.

Chari, T. (2009) Ethical challenges facing Zimbabwean media in the context of the Internet. *Global Media Journal – African Edition* 3 (1), 46–79.

Chaya, V. (2015) Rethinking music and gender: Of Alick Macheso and Lady Squanda music. Dissertation, Midlands State University.

Chihora, T. (2016) The use of vulgar lyrics by Zimdancehall artists in some of their songs: A survey carried out in Gweru, Midlands, Zimbabwe. Dissertation, Midlands State University.

Chireshe, E. (2022) Championing marital harmony through music: An examination of four selected songs by Oliver Mtukudzi. In M. Nyakudya, B. Chinouriri, P. Matveke and E. Chitando (eds) *The Cultural and Artistic Legacy of Oliver Mtukudzi: Using Language for Social Justice* (pp. 155–168). Palgrave Macmillan.

Chiweshe, M.K. (2014) One of the boys: Female fans' responses to the masculine and phallocentric nature of football stadiums in Zimbabwe. *Critical African Studies* 6 (2–3), 211–222.

Chiweshe, M.K. and Bhatasara, S. (2013) 'Ndezve Varume Izvi': Hegemonic masculinities and misogyny in popular music in Zimbabwe. *Africa Media Review* 21 (1–2), 151–170.

Chiweshe, M.K and Bhatasara, S. (2018) Performing manhood in Zimdancehall: Music as patriarchised space. In L. Gimenez and M.T. Vambe (eds) *Performing Zimbabwe: A Transdisciplinary Study of Zimbabwean Music* (pp. 253–275). University of KZN Press.

Connell, R.W. and Messerschmidt, J.W. (2005) Hegemonic masculinity: Rethinking the concept. *Gender and Society* 19 (6), 829–859.

Garcia-Moreno, C., Guedes, A. and Knerr, W. (2012) *Understanding and Addressing Violence Against Women: Intimate Partner Violence*. World Health Organization, online publication. https://apps.who.int/iris/bitstream/handle/10665/77432/WHO_RHR_12.36_eng.pdf (accessed 16 January 2023).

Gwarisa, M. (2022) 'Love Shouldn't Hurt campaign movement grows in the grasslands'. *Health Times*, 15 April. https://healthtimes.co.zw/2022/04/15/love-shouldnt-hurt-campaign-movement-grows-in-the-grassroots/ (accessed 19 August 2023).

Hancock-Barnett, C. (2012) Colonial resettlement and cultural resistance: The mbira music of Zimbabwe. *Social and Cultural Geography* 13, 11–27.

Kanengoni, T. (2018) Music genre of Zim Dancehall captures sound, spirit of urban life in Zimbabwe. *Global Press Journal*, 14 February. https://globalpressjournal.com/africa/zimbabwe/music-genre-zim-dancehall-captures-sound-spirit-urban-life-zimbabwe/ (accessed 16 January 2023).

Kidd, D., Kim, J. and Turner, A. (2017) Popular culture. In K. Korgen (ed.) *The Cambridge Book of Sociology: Specialty and Interdisciplinary Studies* (pp. 284–292). Cambridge University Press.

Kufakurinani, U. and Mwatwara, W. (2017) Zimdancehall and the peace crisis in Zimbabwe. *African Conflict and Peacebuilding Review* 17 (1), 33–50.

Kufakurinani, U., Nyakudya, M. and Chinouriri, B. (2018) 'Wakachipa Kunge Bhero': Gender and the portrayal of women in selected Zimdancehall songs. In B. Chinouriri, U. Kufakurinani and M. Nyakudya (eds) *Victors, Victims and Villains: Women in Musical Arts in Zimbabwe – Past and Present* (pp. 80–97). University of Zimbabwe Publishers (UZP).

Kumar, R. (1999) *Research Methodology: A Step-by-Step Guide for Beginners*. Sage Publications.

Lin, C-L. and Yeh, J-T. (2009) Comparing society's awareness of women: Media-portrayed idealised images and physical attractiveness. *Journal of Business Ethics* 90 (1), 61–79.

Mabuto, K. and Saidi, U. (2018) Locating the nihilistic culture within Zimdancehall in contemporary Zimbabwe. *Dande Journal of Social Sciences and Communication* 2 (2), 57–74.

Mangeya, H. (2022) Zimdancehall music as rules of sexual engagement. In A. Salawu and I.A. Fadipe (eds) *Indigenous African Popular Music* (Vol. 2, pp. 361–377). Palgrave Macmillan.

Mate, R. (2012) Youth lyrics, street language and the politics of age: Contextualising the youth questions in the third chimurenga in Zimbabwe. *Journal of Southern African Studies* 38 (1), 107–127.

Mateveke, P. (2022) Zimbabwean popular cultural expressions of alternative sexual identities. *Journal of African Cultural Studies* 34 (1), 32–47.

Mitchner, B. (2019) When misogyny sells: Empowerment, authenticity and female sexuality in today's music'. *Alice*, 5 November. https://alice.ua.edu/when-misogyny-sells-empowerment-authenticity-and-female-sexuality-in-todays-music (accessed 19 August 2023).

Moyo-Nyede, S. (2022) Zimbabweans see gender-based violence as most important women's-rights issues to address. *Afrobarometer*, 3 October, Dispatch No. 557. https://www.afrobarometer.org/publication/ad557-zimbabweans-see-gender-based-violence-as-most-important-womens-rights-issue-to-address (accessed 16 January 2023).

Mukucha, J. (2021) PHS launches Love Shouldn't Hurt campaign. *Spiked Media*. https://spikedmedia.co.zw/psh-launches-love-shouldnt-hurt-campaign/ (accessed 19 August 2023).

Mwando, M. (2015) Jail for Zimbabwe men who publicly stripped woman hoped to deter sex pests. *Reuters: World News*, 27 March. https://www.reuters.com/article/uk-zimbabwe-women-idUKKBN0MN22E20150327 (accessed 19 August 2023).

Ncube, G. and Chipfupa, D. (2017) Outspoken cynics? Rethinking the social consciousness of rap and hip-hop music in Zimbabwe. *Journal of Music Research in Africa* 14 (1), 103–122.

Ndlovu, B. (2022) Sandra Ndebele show interview ... 'I was sold to sexual suitors without my knowledge'. *Sunday News*, 27 November. https://www.sundaynews.co.zw/sandra-ndebele-show-interview-i-was-sold-to-sexual-suitors-without-my-knowledge/ (accessed 19 August 2023).

Parwaringira, B. and Mpofu, P. (2021a) Appreciating vulgarity in raw Zimdancehall music as an expression of truth. *African Identities* 21 (2), 227–245.

Parwaringira, B. and Mpofu, P. (2021b) In pursuit of recognition and the expression of power? Making sense of vulgarity in Zimdancehall. *Journal of Music Research in Africa* 17 (2), 18–39.

Rupapa, T. (2018) Zimdancehall singer fined over lewd lyrics. *The Herald*, 11 May. https://www.herald.co.zw/zimdancehall-singer-fined-over-lewd-lyrics/ (accessed 19 August 2023).

Sibanda, N. and Nkala, N. (2020) A gendered discourse analysis of Clement Magwaza's Istambo Sami song text. *Music and Arts in Action* 7 (2), 16–29.

Terry, G., Hayfield, N., Clarke, V. and Braun, V. (2017) Thematic analysis. In C. Willig and W. Stainton-Rogers (eds) *The Sage Book of Qualitative Research in Psychology* (pp. 17–37). Sage Publications.

Tivenga, D.R. (2018) Zimbabwe urban grooves music and the interconnections between youth identities and celebrity culture. PhD thesis, Free State University.

Ureke, O. and Washaya, Y. (2016) Social commentary, subaltern voices and the alternative medium of Zimdancehall music: Unpacking the music of Winky D and Sniper Storm. *Journal of Music Research in Africa* 13 (1), 68–88.

Viriri, A. (2014) Female participation in the post-independence Zimbabwean popular music industry: A case study of Edith Katiji (Weutonga) and Sandra Ndebele. MA dissertation, University of the Witwatersrand.

Weitzer, R. and Kubrin, C.E. (2009) Misogyny in rap music: A content analysis of prevalence and meanings. *Men and Masculinities* 12 (1), 3–29.

Wikström, M.C. (2019) Gendered bodies and power dynamics: The relation between toxic masculinity and sexual harassment. *Granite Journal: A Postgraduate Interdisciplinary Journal* 3 (2), 28–33.

Wood, H.J. (2019) Gender inequality: The problem of harmful, patriarchal, traditional and cultural gender practices in the church. *HTS Theological Studies* 75 (1), 1–8.

World Bank (2019) Gender-based violence (violence against women and girls. https://www.worldbank.org/en/topic/socialsustainability/brief/violence-against-women-and-girls (accessed 5 July 2024).

ZimFact (2020) Factsheet: Domestic violence during coronavirus lockdown. *ZimFact*, 24 April. https://zimfact.org/factsheet-domestic-violence-during-coronavirus-lockdown/ (accessed 16 January 2023).

Zimbabwe National Statistics Agency and UNICEF (2019) *Zimbabwe Multiple Indicator Cluster Survey 2019: Snapshots of Key Findings*. ZIMSTAT and UNICEF. https://www.unicef.org/zimbabwe/media/2511/file/Zimbabwe%202019%20MICS%20Snapshots%20of%20Key%20Findings%202020.pdf.pdf (accessed 16 January 2023).

9 Promoting Women's Participation in Social Transformation Through Popular Arts in Kusaal-Speaking Communities in Ghana

Hasiyatu Abubakari, Adwoa Sikayena Amankwah and Abigail Opoku Mensah

Introduction

On a daily basis, women and young girls in Ghana suffer from different forms of gender-based violence (GBV) (physical, sexual, psychological, economic and social violence, harassment and forced confinement, among others) (Global Database of Violence Against Women, 2007; GSS, 2016a). This becomes even more alarming when mention is made of rural communities, where practices such as child marriage, teenage pregnancies and female genital mutilation are considered acceptable cultural norms. According to the District Health Information Management System (DHIMS) of the Ghana Health Service (see Myjoyonline.com, 2021), in 2020, a total of 6533 teenage pregnancies were recorded in the Upper East Region of Ghana among girls aged 10 to 14. It further states that teenage pregnancy in the region has increased from 103 in 2019 to 142 in 2020, a figure which represents a 38% increase (Myjoyonline.com, 2021). According to the Sexual and Reproductive Health and Rights (SRHR) Network in the Upper East Region, poverty and the COVID-19 pandemic, among other things, fuelled high rates of unintended teenage pregnancies and child marriages in the region (myjoyonline.com, 2021). GBV, such as teenage pregnancy and child marriage, is still rife in Kusaal-speaking communities located in the Upper East Region of Ghana, which is the least urbanised region of Ghana, with over 79% of the population classified as rural. Kusaal communities make up a population of 24,658,823 (GSS, 2012, 2016b). The region has long seasons of drought, poor road networks, a lack of potable water and electricity, a lack of school buildings (with classes given under trees, for example) and only one government hospital (GSS, 2012). Notwithstanding these challenges, research on the Kusaal language is gradually gaining attention in the literature (Abubakari, 2018; Eddyshaw, 2019; Musah, 2018; among others).

However, there is an emerging generation of young, educated people who have begun questioning and resisting practices such as child marriage, teenage pregnancy and sexual, physical and psychological abuse. Thus, the project described in the present chapter – 'Promoting Women's Participation in Social Transformation through Popular Arts in Kusaal-Speaking Communities in Ghana' – was intended to empower women and girls to speak out as well as pursue education and/or training aimed at making them economically self-sustaining, in line with the United Nations' Sustainable Development Goal (SDG) 16. This chapter discusses the overall project, while the complementary Chapter 6 focuses on how popular arts can be deployed as effective tools of communication to stamp out GBV. Overall, the project's aim was to explore and analyse GBV practices, particularly child marriage and related issues like teenage pregnancy, and verbal and sexual abuse in rural Kusaal-speaking communities. It investigated how popular culture – songs, docudramas, folktales, proverbs among other intangible cultural artefacts – could be leveraged to fight GBV. The activities included:

(1) training for field assistants on project ethics and safeguarding;
(2) field trips to six Kusaal-speaking communities to gather interview data;
(3) partnership with a local artist, Fati Osman (a singer), and a local film producer, Winimi Productions, to produce a song and a docudrama (a short video) to create awareness and educate people about GBV.

The main intended outcome was to educate, empower and promote women's participation in peacebuilding and social transformation.

Data were gathered from the six district capitals of the Kusaal-speaking communities (Zebilla, Bawku, Garu, Tempani, Pusiga and Binduri) in the Upper East Region of Ghana. Through interviews, locals were asked how GBV concepts are framed by the indigenous people. The project was intended to deploy an appropriate short local film or docudrama and a song as tools to mitigate the GBV-related practices. By using a website, Northern Television Station in Tamale and Max Empire (a local radio station), as well as local community-based artists, the productions were made available and accessible to the rural communities, so that women and children could be educated and empowered to resist GBV-related practices. This strategy will complement efforts such as hotlines and safe spaces created by the government, the Ministry of Gender, Women and Children, and non-governmental organisations (NGOs) to mitigate these practices in Ghana. These aims and objectives align with the main aim of the Culture for Sustainable and Inclusive Peace Network Plus (CUSP N+) of enhancing the popular arts and arts of rural communities in ways that promote women's and girls' participation in peacebuilding and social transformation. The specific objectives were:

(1) to explore how local popular arts frame GBV-related issues among the Kusaasi people;
(2) to examine the uses of popular arts and 'gratifications' by the local people;
(3) to enlighten, educate and empower women and girls to engender social transformation.

The results will arm NGOs, local media, peer mentors, artists and opinion leaders (particularly women and girls) with information on how to frame useful and gratifying popular arts so they become reference points for the identification and transformation of GBV-related social conflicts, coercion and injustice.

Three research questions guided this project:

(1) How do local popular arts in Kusaal-speaking communities frame the GBV narrative on child marriage?
(2) What uses do local people have for their popular culture and what gratifications do they derive from it?
(3) How can local popular culture be deployed as tools of effective communication to enable social transformation, specifically, to eradicate child marriage and enhance the education of girls and women?

Scant information exists in the literature on how GBV-related narratives about child marriage are framed through folklores and other oral literary genres among the Kusaas people of Ghana. These questions highlight the research problems, and the answers will equip stakeholders with alternative tools of resistance against GBV practices.

Methodology and Design

Data collection and research activities

The project adopted a purely participatory and interpretivist qualitative approach. With the support of translators, interviews and selected folktales, songs and a docudrama were transcribed and translated from Kusaal to the English language for documentary analysis. Furthermore, open-ended, semi-structured interviews were conducted with selected people in each community. Each interview session lasted no more than 45 minutes, and interviews were conducted at the preferred location of the study's participants.

Data analysis

The first stage of the analysis comprised literary and linguistic analysis of translated folklore, and the second stage involved thematic analysis of semi-structured open-ended interviews with the target group and partners such as the local artists. Using the transcribed and translated folktales, docudrama and songs, we analysed the ways speakers and artists deploy language, linguistics and literary techniques to communicate GBV-related issues in order to evoke adherence or resistance by the local people to the culturally accepted norms of early child marriage. It was observed that literary devices such as euphemism, imagery, anaphora, repetition and contrast as well as linguistic tools such as rhetorical questions, sentence variation and sentence structure, among others, facilitate understanding of cultural narratives and help rural people to identify with the themes of the selected popular cultural performances. In the second stage of the analysis, the interviews with chiefs, queen mothers, opinion leaders, victims of GBV and selected educated youth were analysed using thematic content analysis covering GBV-related themes. The results of the thematic and literary analysis were then deployed using change theory to develop manuscripts to assist the production of local songs, short films and docudramas against GBV to create awareness and empower victims to resist GBV-related practices like child marriage. This will go a long way to resolve the many conflicts within households and families which result from child marriage, as well as sexual and verbal abuse and teenage pregnancies.

Furthermore, by employing the uses and gratifications theory of communication as the framing approach, together with the change theory for the management and processes of content development, the production and communication of local popular media such as songs and docudramas were also investigated to determine the methods and motivations that influence producers and artists to frame GBV-related issues. Furthermore, through interviews, the project examined how the target group uses these cultural artefacts and the gratifications they derive from them. It is expected that the project outcomes will bring change, even though these desired changes may not be seen immediately but in the long term.

Pilot study

The town of Assin Fosu in the Assin Municipality of the Central Region was purposively selected for the pilot testing of the study instruments (described below) because the Central Region has similar characteristics to the project communities selected for inclusion in the study. Villages and small towns within the Assin municipality are purported to have a high incidence of child/early marriage among other types of GBV. The main aim of pre-testing the instruments was to ensure that interview participants understood the questions and that the items were relevant.

Development and pre-testing of research instruments

Based on the aims and objectives of the study, research instruments were developed around the following variables – framing of GBV and popular art, cultural and linguistic tools, utility and gratifications, popular arts and communication, popular culture, education and social transformation. The instruments were administered in the pilot phase to the selected community. The pre-test examined the following items:

(1) Sociocultural context of GBV.
(2) What are the circumstances (cultural/social/moral) that lead to GBV-related practices in your community?
(3) Which specific incident(s) of GBV have you suffered from?
(4) What challenges are you faced with as a result of GBV?
(5) How popular arts frame GBV.
(6) How do local popular arts in Bamahu frame the GBV narrative on child marriage in your community?
(7) What themes do the popular arts (songs, proverbs, docudramas) in your community cover?
(8) How do local popular arts frame the GBV narrative on child marriage in your community?
(9) What cultural and linguistic tools can be deployed to resist the GBV narratives in popular arts?
(10) Uses of and gratifications from popular arts.
(11) What do you use your popular arts for?
(12) What gratifications (benefits/satisfaction) do you obtain from your popular arts?
(13) How do popular arts influence your personal/family values?
(14) Framing of popular arts on GBV for education and social transformation.
(15) How can local popular arts be communicated effectively so they are understood by both males and females?
(16) How can local popular arts be communicated so they are owned by both males and females?
(17) How can local popular arts be communicated effectively to promote change in GBV-related practices?
(18) How can local popular arts be communicated so as to build peace and ensure social transformation in your community? (Ask opinion leaders and artists.)

Answers to the questions informed the finalisation of the research instruments before they were administered in the field for the main study.

Sampling

Through purposive sampling, four people were selected for inclusion in the sample in each district, as follows: one chief or one queen mother or their representative; an educated elderly woman or opinion leader who was a native of the town, averse to the practice of child marriage and willing to partner with this project to support young girls to resist child marriage in culturally constructive ways; an educated young person; and a child-marriage victim (aged 10–19).

Findings

Preliminary findings of the document review

As part of preparatory work carried out from 2 August 2021, the investigators extensively studied documents related to GBV and popular arts from the global perspective, through the continental, to national policies, and organisational and regional information.

Documents perused included the section of the OECD's Social Institutions and Gender Index publication on Ghana (OECD Development Centre, 2019), policies such as the National Gender Policy (see below) and other GBV-related materials published by both academics and gender-based NGOs. The national entity tasked to advance women's holistic welfare in Ghana is the Ministry of Gender, Children and Social Protection (previously the Ministry of Women and Children Affairs). The Ministry is mandated to 'ensure compliance with international protocols, conventions and treaties in relation to children, gender and social protection' (OECD Development Centre, 2019: 1).

In 1998, the government instituted the Domestic Violence and Victim Support Unit (DOVVSU), within the Ghana Police Service, which is mandated to respond to and enforce legislation that addresses issues involving gender, women and children, and which responds to sexual and gender-based violence and child abuse and provides child protection. The Unit also responds to the need for protection of all vulnerable persons from abuse and investigates allegations of sexual and gender-based violence (CEDAW, 2014).

In May 2015, the government of Ghana published a National Gender Policy, which seeks to mainstream gender equality in development processes through targeted interventions and improvements to the legal, social, political, cultural and economic conditions of Ghanaians, particularly women, girls and children. The five main policy commitments in the document are: (1) to improve women's rights and access to justice; (2) to improve women's empowerment and livelihoods; (3) to improve targeted accountable governance structures and women's leadership and participation; (4) to improve women's economic justice; and (5) to improve gender roles and relations. The Ministry of Gender, Children and Social Protection is tasked with operationalising this policy through a strategic implementation plan, which makes the protocols and guidelines to be followed by the relevant ministries clear (Government of Ghana, 2015).

Regarding forced and child marriages, the relevant legislation includes the Children's Act, 1998 and the Criminal Code, 1960. The Children's Act provides for legislative protections against forced and child marriage by defining a child as someone under the age of 18 and setting the minimum age that one can be married at 18 too (article 14). Article 14 goes on to state that no one can force a child to be betrothed, to be the subject of a dowry transaction or to be married (Parliament of the Republic of Ghana, 1998). The Criminal Code also prohibits compulsion in marriage, by making void a marriage that is the result of 'a female [being] compelled to marry another person by duress' (section 100). Section 109 criminalises the act of forcing someone into a marriage, and someone found guilty of that offence will be charged with a misdemeanour (Parliament of the Republic of Ghana, 1960). Despite these legislative protections, there are still reports that girls and boys as young as 16 have been married with the consent of their parents (Girls Not Brides, 2017, in OECD Development Centre, 2019).

The 2014 'shadow report' from the Committee on the Elimination of Discrimination Against Women (CEDAW, 2014) mentions the customary practice of 'marriage of elopement' that occurs in the northern parts of Ghana, where women are forced to marry their abductors. In 2014, the Ministry of Gender, Children and Social Protection created an Ending Child Marriage Unit, which, with the support of civil society and NGOs, directly intervenes in communities. Under the purview of the Ministry, the Advisory Committee on Ending Child Marriage was established to provide the Unit with technical expertise and guidance on appropriate interventions (Ministry of Gender, Children and Social Protection, 2016). These changes helped to build towards the 2016 launch of the 2017–2026 National Strategic Framework for Ending Child Marriage in Ghana. Ending early marriage remains a priority for Ghana, and the Ministry's *Framework* report notes that pregnant child brides are less likely to receive proper medical care than adult women, which increases the chances of both maternal and foetal mortality (Ministry of Gender, Children and Social Protection, 2016).

A 2016 government study on domestic violence in Ghana revealed that women are largely blamed for the violence they experience (GSS, 2016a). In its concluding observations on the combined sixth and seventh periodic reports of Ghana, CEDAW stated it had deep concerns about 'the persistence of adverse cultural norms, practices and traditions, in addition to patriarchal attitudes and deep-rooted stereotypes regarding the roles and responsibilities of women and men in the family and in society, which contribute to the persistence of violence against women and harmful practices' (CEDAW, 2014).

The Domestic Violence Act, 2007 is the overarching piece of legislation that addresses domestic violence in Ghana (Global Database on Violence Against Women, 2007). The law provides specific provisions for the investigation of allegations and the prosecution and punishment of perpetrators. The definition of domestic violence in the Act covers physical, sexual, psychological, economic and social violence as well as harassment and forced confinement, and deprivation of access to food, water, clothing and shelter (by former partners and within the family). A 2016 national study highlighted the main challenges and characteristics of domestic violence in Ghana. Age, class and a range of socioeconomic factors were named as key determinants of domestic violence, including education levels, asset levels, tensions over property, money, unemployment, poverty and economic shocks (GSS, 2016a). The study found that the most common forms of domestic violence experienced by women were economic violence followed by social then psychological, physical and then sexual (Domestic Violence Study, 2016). However, not all respondents agreed with what was understood to be violence in the study. For some respondents, some of what was described as violence was seen by them to be coping mechanisms, accepted social norms and ways of resolving conflict (Domestic Violence Study, 2016). The study reiterated that harmful social norms and attitudes underpin and normalise domestic violence. Many instances of domestic violence may go unreported and even unrecognised; moreover, they may be denied by people not wanting to report 'private' matters and out of fear of not being believed (Domestic Violence Study, 2016).

Thus, this is the situation report in terms of GBV in the country. The present project's desktop study revealed a number of limitations, including the following:

- The National Gender Policy does not address the direct and indirect forms of discrimination against women and verbal and bodily harassment of women accruing to indecent assault.
- Female genital mutilation, although on the decline in Ghana, is also not addressed in the National Gender Policy.
- Other relevant literature indicated the lack of provision of safe spaces and helplines for victims of GBV.
- The literature does not address the issue of participatory and inclusive actions to mitigate GBV at the community levels using popular arts such as local films and docudramas as well as relevant indigenous music.

In terms of dissemination of results after the study, the following were executed. Firstly, the song and the docudrama that were produced were aired and telecast using local media houses. The song was added to the playlist at Max Empire, a local radio station, to be aired until the station stops operating. The local artist also performs the song during social events and other gatherings. Queen mothers and influential women have also pledged to champion the campaign against GBV in their communities long after the project ends.

Secondly, the findings were also developed into research papers for publication in social science/cultural-based journals such as *Language and Communication* (indexed in Elsevier's Scopus database) to inform scholarship and encourage further research on using arts and culture as tools for GBV resistance, peacebuilding and social transformation. They will also be presented at a relevant international conference to enlighten the global research community.

Finally, the outcomes will be measured against the aims and objectives of the project.

Limitations

The limitations for the study primarily concern the risks and limitations of the framework used, based on the applied methodology of social science and the qualitative methods of linguistic and thematic analysis. However, this limitation was offset by the expected depth of the rich information that would be derived, which was non-existent in previous quantitative surveys.

To offset these limitations, we propose the investment of more resources (finance and time) in the field so as to get more representative results, notwithstanding that qualitative studies do not aim at generalisability but specificity. However, considering the enormity of this challenge at the national level and in some sections of the continent and in Asia, we recommend future studies to enlarge the scope of this study to include other regions in Ghana as well as other countries, for a comparative analysis of the situation in order for this canker to be tackled in a holistic way.

Notwithstanding the provision of funds by CUSP, based on submission of reports per the agreed time lines, the partner university's pre-financing is very challenging, to say the least.

Major findings

The major findings of the project from the interview data captured are presented in Table 9.1. The findings on the folktales, songs and docudrama corroborate the testimonies of the participants captured in Table 9.1.

Analysis and Discussion of the Interviews

This section presents data analysis from various interviews conducted within the study settings. The analyses were based on the research objectives and questions. A series of sub-questions were asked during the interview, and some of the responses are quoted in the analysis for clarity and full understanding.

Research question 1: How does popular local culture in Kusaal communities frame the GBV narrative on child marriage?

The first research question sought to explore how local culture within Kusaal-speaking communities contributes to GBV within the context of child marriage. The overriding reason for this question was that the GBV narrative on child marriage within sub-Saharan Africa stems from local culture, beliefs and practices. When interviewed about their ages when they got married, most of the participants indicated that they got married before attaining the age of 18. This was corroborated by participants Awinpang, Atiewin, Awinimi, Azumah, Apuasan, Awimbun, Alamisi and Atini. Awinpang, Atiewin and Alamisi were either 15 or 16 years old.

When asked about the role of local culture in terms of the prevalence of child marriage, the participants revealed that, although child marriage is gradually reducing, parents sometimes force their children into marriage. Awinpang, Atiewin, Awinimi, Apuasan, Awimbun, Awinzua and Asibi claim that, but for their parents, they would not have married at an early age.

In addition to parents being key initiators of child marriage, responses from the participants revealed that traditional customs and culture play a significant role. For instance, Apuasan and Atini indicated that a girl could be betrothed to a particular family. In this case, culture allows that any male child in the betrothed family who finds the girl attractive can marry her. Apuasan continued that, in some instances, young girls who are brought to a man's house by his wife as house-help are also given out for marriage. This narrative was corroborated by Atini.

Similarly, many of the participants cited early unexpected pregnancy as a cultural basis for child marriage, rather than suffering the shame and humiliation of carrying a baby out of wedlock. According to Atiewin, Azumah, Apuasan, Anapua, Awinzua and Asibi, the narrative points to the situation where poverty leads young girls under 18 years to have sexual relations with adults. These adults appear to help the young girls financially and end up impregnating them. Responses from the participants revealed that, when these young girls get impregnated, they are forced into getting married to the adult. Specifically, Apuasan said: 'I was learning a trade and mistakenly got pregnant and was asked to marry and I got married.' Similarly, Anapua said: 'Okay, I was in my father's house and got pregnant and ought to marry the guy and I married him. So, it was the pregnancy that made me marry.' The responses from Atini and Asibi indicated that they voluntarily got married, aged 16 and 17, respectively. The conversation with these participants indicated that they did not see anything wrong with getting married at that early age. That is, this practice had become embedded within their cultural norms.

Citing another cultural issue, Alamisi narrated an age-old custom which requires that young girls are given out in marriage to a traditional

Table 9.1 Findings from the interviews with Kusaal-speaking participants in Ghana

Question	Responses by interviewees	Number/ frequency	Percentage
Theme 1: Sociocultural context of early marriage			
Briefly describe how you got married	I was given out to marriage at a young age because my parents needed help	8	38.1%
	I got pregnant and was asked/force to marry the guy	7	33.33%
At what age did you marry?	Below 18	16	76.19%
In your opinion what do you think about child marriage?	Not a good practice	18	85.71%
	Good practice if the man can take care of the girl. It reduces the burden on the girl's parents	3	14.29%
Who are the key people who influence or implement child marriage?	Parents	21	100%
Are there any challenges you faced as a result?	Yes. Lose respect, no proper education, maltreatment	19	90.48%
Are there any benefits associated with child marriage?	No benefits	18	85.71%
	Some benefits	3	14.29%
Theme 2: How popular arts frame early marriage			
Do you know of any songs/docudramas/folktales that talk about early/child marriage	No	15	71.43%
What are they?	N/A	N/A	N/A
What message do the songs/docudramas/folktales that talk about early/child marriage give you on early marriage?	N/A	N/A	N/A
How popular are the songs/docudramas and folktales?	N/A	N/A	N/A
Theme 3: Uses and gratification of popular arts for change			
What do you use the songs for?	For festivals and other cultural occasions	19	90.48%
What benefits do you obtain by using the songs?	They give lessons	11	52.38%
How do the songs influence your personal family values?	It helps me to know the importance of waiting to grow before marriage.	6	28.57%
What recommendation would you make to minimise early/child marriage?	Girls should be educated, advocacy on radio, television and social media	21	100%
Theme 4: Framing of popular arts on early marriage for education and social transformation			
What attracts you to songs/docudramas/folktales about early marriage?	The message in the songs	18	85.71%
How can songs/docudramas/folktales on early marriage be used to achieve peace and social transformation?	It should be infused in songs so people can get on their phones, play on radios, upload on social media and on televisions	19	90.48%

priest or any relative of a herbalist (native doctor). She indicated that, when married women find it difficult to get pregnant, they seek help to enable them to conceive from the traditional priest or herbalist. The cultural practice is that when the traditional priest or herbalist is able to help a married woman to give birth, the first girl is given out for marriage during infancy. Alamisi further revealed that she was given out from her father's house at the age of five years. The herbalist came to take her away at the age of five and she married the grandson of the herbalist when she was 15 years old.

Awinpang, Asibi, Ayepoka, Awinpang, Azumah, Apuasan, Alamisi, Awinzua and Atini indicated that child marriage results in the young girls being maltreated by their husbands. This is usually because the young girls do not love the men to whom they are either forced to marry or are betrothed to. The participants further indicated that child marriage results in situations where the young girls, because they have less experience, are unable to take proper care of their babies.

Azumah, Apuasan, Anapua and Alamisi indicated that child marriage curtails some of the freedoms and liberties of the child. They indicated that child marriage denies a young girl of the opportunity to learn a meaningful trade or successfully complete formal education. Anapua said: 'I was in primary 4 when I got married and stopped schooling. It is worrying me because I don't have work today because I married [as a] child.'

Apuasan had this to say about the challenges that child marriage brings:

> Oh, when you are in your father's house, you have your liberty to go and do all that you want but if you are in your husband's house, you can't do that because you don't have your freedom. Child marriage is difficult. There is also stigmatisation in child marriage. I couldn't continue learning a trade because my colleagues were always teasing and making mockery of me that I was a married woman.

When asked about whether there are any benefits associated with child marriage, the data revealed mixed reactions. While some indicated that child marriage has no benefit to the young girls, others gave reasons to justify the practice, saying that, to some extent, it is beneficial. The participants who alluded to benefits in child marriage indicated that, due to poverty, some parents are unable to cater for their children; therefore, as means of getting money and other forms of compensation, they give a daughter out for marriage. Ayepoka indicated that if the man is capable of taking good care of the girl, then it is beneficial since it also reduces pressure on parents. Asibi had this to say:

> The only benefit I know is that if the husband can take care of you, it eases the burdens of your parents. This is because many child marriages are linked to poverty. So, when your parents are poor and cannot take care of you, it's better they give you out to someone who can take care of you.

Apuasan also indicated that child marriage is good because, otherwise, girls in their late teens often get pregnant before marriage. Most often, it is difficult to get men to take responsibility for the pregnancy, hence creating a burden for family members. Therefore, if girls are given out for marriage at an early age, it reduces the tendency for girls to get pregnant out of wedlock.

Research question 2: What uses do local people have for their popular culture and what gratifications do they derive from it?

Research question 2 sought to examine how the use of popular culture contributes to child marriage. Specifically, it examined how messages in songs, proverbs, folktales and docudramas talk about marriage.

Concerning songs and folktales, many of the participants indicated that they have neither heard nor remember any proverbs or songs that promote child marriage, but a small few indicated that they have heard songs and folktales that implicitly promote it: Asibi, Ayepoka and Awinimi. For instance, when asked if they have heard of any song or folktales that talk about child marriage, Asibi said, 'Yes, I know a short folktale that says girls (wives) should be patient and stay with their husbands'. Ayepoka said, 'Yes, I know this popular song that says a wife-to-be does not disrespect her mother-in-law-to-be. The song promotes tolerance and respect between the to-be wife and the family of the groom'. The implication is that although most of the participants did not readily have songs and folktales in their minds that promote child marriage, the responses from these few showed that some songs, proverbs and folktales do present child marriage as something normal. Concerning docudrama and videos, the participants indicated that although they have seen some that talk about child marriage, the message in them does not promote child marriage but, rather, discourages it.

Research question 3: How can local popular culture be deployed as tools of effective communication to enable social transformation?

The third research question asked how popular culture in the form of songs, proverbs and folktales could be used to promote social change among women and girls in the study areas, specifically, to eradicate child marriage and enhance the education of girls and women. It also sought information from the participants on how the problem of child marriage could be mitigated. The question stemmed from the presumption that people are mostly glued to their culture. Therefore, when the same culture is used as a channel for transformational change, it will have greater impact. The results in relation to this question are presented in detail in Chapter 6, on how popular arts can be used as communication tools for the eradication of gender-based violence and child marriage in Ghana.

Results and Discussion of Feedback from the Interviewees

Results

The results of feedback from the interviewees indicate that child marriage has a cultural correlation as it is perceived as a better alternative than being pregnant out of wedlock or outside the context of marriage. The typical contractual age for the phenomenon ranges from 15 to 18 years. Notwithstanding the cultural, social and economic gratifications of child marriage, the study finds that the cost incurred in behaviour in terms of societal transformation and the development of girls far outweighs the present perceived material and social benefits. This is attested to in the literature as well as from the testimonies of the victims. The voices of the queen mothers and male opinion leaders who were interviewed also lend credence to the demerits of the practice and to the need for the local populations to desist from it.

The framing of the docudrama speaks very loudly on scenarios that generate situations leading to child marriage as well as the outcomes of such marriages in the long term, although there could be perceived short-term material benefits. This popular art form portends a viable tool for dissemination in the areas under study and other Kusaal-speaking areas for strategic cultural resistance that can lead to social transformation aimed at building strong social institutions such as families and non-formal educational efforts.

Folktales are great sources of entertainment for the people, though there is dwindling interest in this genre among the youth. The need to revitalise and rekindle interest in folkloric entertainment need not be overemphasised. The people admit that the moral lessons in folktales help them identify taboos and live according to the bye-laws of their community. Thus, it is recommended that folktales and other forms of popular culture – songs, docudrama, among others – be created to serve as channels for educating rural people on the need to abandon cultural practices, such as child marriage, that have outlived their significance and are now being abused to the detriment of women and girls. The people should be encouraged to re-narrate and reinvent folktales that reflect current situations and address current societal problems for peaceful sociocultural transformation.

In respect of the songs, the project's singer calls on all traditional leaders, parents and the youth to resist the culture of early marriage and embrace education for the sociocultural and socioeconomic transformation of the people. The *googi* performance on early marriage is crafted using several rhetorical devices that are verbally communicated to help advance the themes of the song through persuasion (see Chapter 6). The performer employs alliteration, metaphors, ideophones, repetition and repetition with variation (among others) as instruments to make the piece very memorable and, above all, entertaining.

The study revealed that early marriage, teenage pregnancies and other GBV-related practices can be curbed by employing popular culture to manage and sustain peace, especially in instances where women and girls are the most vulnerable. Unwholesome cultural practices that have outlived their usefulness and impede progress should be addressed, irrespective of their perceived uses and gratifications. To do this, local people should be offered better, functional alternatives, such as education, so that they personally embrace the need for change without being made to feel offended. One sure approach to this is through the use of music, folktales and other cultural artefacts, such as *googi* performances.

Discussion

The project revealed that child marriage is still prevalent among the Kusaal-speaking communities in Ghana. Some of the children are given away for marriage as early as 15 or 16 years of age. The findings further revealed that traditional customs, like giving the first girl to a male native doctor for marriage, as well as poverty, parental and family coercion, are the culturally based practices that contribute to child marriage.

Betrothal of first-born female children to shrine priests as spouses or offering male children as bondmen for shrines

The findings on giving away the first daughter to the traditional priest are consistent with that of Abass-Abaah (2024). The latter author intimated that when a woman is unable to give birth for some years after marriage, a shrine priest is consulted and promised a child to be brought and affiliated to his shrine, thus becoming a bondage *dabit* child. A child who is conceived in such a situation, if a boy, is required to offer sacrifices to the deity throughout his life, and in the case of a girl, she is given in marriage to the priest from birth and may move to live in her new home from the age of 10. She may marry the priest after puberty or be given to his siblings or children for marriage. Similarly, if a woman who suffers neonatal deaths consults a priest for assistance, a girl born with the assistance of the priest is taken to the shrine and married to the priest or any member of his family. In all these cases, the girl has no right to free and full consent. This practice was confirmed by one of the participants, who intimated that she was taken away for marriage aged five and later given to a grandson of the traditional priest.

Unplanned teenage pregnancy as a contributory factor to child marriage

The finding on coercion, and unexpected teenage pregnancy, which force children into marriages is consistent with previous studies. For instance, according to the United Nations International Children's Emergency Fund (UNICEF, 2021), 20% of adolescent girls reported having experienced sexual violence such as rape and coercion within the past 12 months, while 14% of adolescent girls aged 14–19 years have had a live birth or are currently pregnant with their first child; the percentage of girls in rural areas aged 14–19 years who are pregnant is twice that of families in urban settlements. It is further shown that the proportion of girls who get pregnant is higher among families in lowest wealth quintile of households. The statistics are confirmed by the number of participants who indicated that they got pregnant at a younger age (16 or 17 years) and were forced to get married against their wishes. They also happen to come from families with very low income.

Role of popular songs, folktales and docudramas as tools of social resistance to child marriage

The findings further revealed that some forms of popular culture, like songs and dramas, though few in number, contain messages which fuel gender-based violence about child marriage. However, the large majority of the songs and folktales, as well as docudramas, give lessons about the dangers of child marriage. Most of the respondents indicated that they were attracted to these songs, most especially when sung in their local dialects. The findings pointed to the idea that art, drama and songs are important transformational tools that could be used in empowering adults and children to understand the need to indulge in practices that will reduce teenage pregnancies and avert the possibility of child marriage, which is sometimes a consequence of teenage pregnancy.

Analysis of the folktales, songs and docudramas indicate the prevalence of GBV (particularly, teenage pregnancy and child marriage) in the selected communities. The folktales are 'reflections' of the culture and tradition of the people and show how rules of acceptable behaviours serve as a window to their perception and world views. Regarding marriage and courtship, it was revealed that the types of marriages practised by the Kusaas are reflective of the types of marriages expressed in their folktales. In trying to identify causes of child marriage and teenage pregnancies in Kusaug and to verify whether there were links with certain cultural practices, the folktales on marriage and the discussion of these by community members revealed that age is not a major factor in deciding when a girl can be married or betrothed. Child marriage is a customary practice and indigenous rural people see it as very normal. This leads to the assertion that the increase in the numbers of teenage pregnancies in rural Kusaal-speaking communities could have a bearing on the practice of child marriage.

The project also found that folktales are great sources of entertainment, though there is dwindling interest in this genre among the youth. The need to revitalise and rekindle interest in folkloric entertainment among the Kusaas is apparent because folktales serve an one of the intangible cultural assets of the people, from which their oral history, traditions and indigenous knowledge systems, among other things, can be traced. The people admit that the moral lessons in folktales help them identify taboos and live according to the bye-laws of their community. Thus, it is recommended that folktales and other forms of popular culture – songs and docudramas, among others – are created to serve as channels for educating rural people on important sociocultural practices while discouraging practices such as teenage pregnancy and child marriage.

Notwithstanding the uses and gratifications to be derived by stakeholders through child marriage, the lyrics of the *googi* performance produced by this project emphasise that the detriments associated with child marriage are so grave that the practice is not worth the risk. The effects of teenage pregnancies, as indicated earlier, and as advocated in the lyrics of the song through the advice of health professionals, can be offset through purposeful communication, as done through the *googi* performance. The song further highlighted the need for education to bring about the needed behavioural change over time. The performer, Alembood Akidago, highlights some key issues by tracing the root causes of early marriage and teenage pregnancies to the culture where girls can be betrothed as soon as they are born and are allowed into marriage before they are 18, with the associated cultural and familial gratifications. However, in spite of these gratifications, she explains that teenage pregnancy poses major health risks and calls on everyone to help fight the menace. She further explains that early marriage and teenage pregnancy are major causes of poverty in the region. The teenage girls are often unemployed and if they get impregnated by a man who refuses responsibility, then they become a burden on their parents, who may themselves not be meaningfully employed.

Use of mass media as complementary tools to popular arts in fighting child marriage

The findings revealed that the use of mass communication, television, radio and social media as educational resources could reduce child marriage, a finding supported by Morrell *et al.* (2012). These authors contend that an increase in efforts at communication for social and behavioural change in schools, communities and through both national and social media directed at adolescent girls and boys, families and adult men (especially targeting rural areas and poor households) could further reduce the rate of adolescent pregnancies and address the issue of older men using their position of power for the sexual coercion of adolescent girls and child marriage.

Conclusion and Recommendations

The project concludes that popular art, such as folktales, docudramas and songs, should be adapted as popular tools to disseminate information regarding child marriage and teenage pregnancy. This is because the mode of translation in terms of the context and the language are both culturally accepted. Indigenous people are comfortable with the communality that the transmission of folktales, docudramas and songs bring to them as well as a sense of shared values and belongingness. These constitute some of the pillars of an enduring traditional society.

Songs, docudramas and folktales about child marriage and teenage pregnancy, aptly communicated in Kusaal, is likely to engender greater receptivity among the local people, because these popular art forms are vehicles of cultural transmission that they are familiar and comfortable with. Aligned with uses and gratifications theory, feedback from the interview participants indicated the superior long-term cultural and social gratifications they derived from the songs, folktales and docudramas compared to the short-term gains of child marriage such as material wealth, and the fleeting security of having a home, husband and acceptance in the community. The framing of the lyrics of songs, the textual and audio-visual content of docudramas as well as the strong cultural references to mythical folktales could provide an irresistible tool for cultural resistance to the practice of child marriage in the face of the superior functional alternatives of education, in the form of self-worth, respect, economic independence and the opportunity for greater social impact and transformation.

Therefore, with the artillery of the songs, folktales and docudrama produced by the investigators and by deploying change theory, the target audience are encouraged to resist the cultural pressures that culminate in child marriage and teenage pregnancy. The study takes cognisance of the fact that change takes time. However, the strength of this change begins with education about the phenomenon, thereby creating awareness of the negative consequences of child marriage and engendering a sense of responsibility among all stakeholders, particularly the parents and guardians of the victims and potential victims, to desist from the practice and aspire to better lives for their daughters. By deploying widely used media – namely, radio stations such as Dastek, Max FM and Ghana Television – the message of change would impact many more people beyond those in the six project communities.

In sum, the study indicates an unfolding of a process of change based on gratifications that go beyond the scope of this project. The findings of the project are unique, very practical and relevant for adoption by communities in Ghana and other African countries, where the practice of child marriage is rife. The literature on mitigation of GBV and child marriage in Ghana does not have the participatory elements and foci of this project – namely, popular arts of songs, folktales and docudramas. In effect, this project fills a gap in the literature that can be harnessed practically to make the mitigation efforts of both government and relevant stakeholders more effective. Thus, it needs to be replicated and extended to other communities and countries on a wider scale through a larger project.

The project recommends the adoption of the unique popular art forms, namely songs, folktales and docudramas. The strategic participation of queen mothers and opinion leaders in this project have addressed a gap in the literature on GBV and child marriage mitigation efforts by government and other stakeholders in Ghana. Thus, future intra- and inter-country projects could adapt this. Furthermore, the tools for social resistance to child marriage and teenage pregnancy need to be familiar and accepted popular arts, such as songs and docudramas, as they offer diversionary entertainment and educational gratifications and so are accepted and owned by the target populations. Additionally, the vehicle for transmission of cultural resistance to child marriage needs to be in the local language. This is because language connotes a sense of identity and belongingness. Hence, when the message of change is framed using the local language, it is more likely to be accepted. Moreover, the role-models used in cultural change communication need to be respected local people, such as queen mothers and opinion leaders, as they have the voice, authenticity and ability to engender trust in the local people, as the queen mothers testify to the superior functional alternatives of education and concomitant benefits of economic independence, professional careers, respect and provision of a robust space through popular arts for girls and women to transform society. Opinion leaders need to be equipped to continue educating young girls and parents on the phenomenon of child marriage as well as the superior functional alternatives and gratification to be derived by desisting from the practice. Additionally, a select group of young girls or victims needs to be equipped with skills training and education to enable them to earn decent livelihoods. Finally, it is recommended that the Institute of African Studies at the University of Ghana continues this collaboration with CUSP on a wider scale that has more potential to impact the entire country, particularly in communities where child marriage thrives.

References

Abass-Abaah, A.J. (2024) Courtship and marriage. In H. Abubakari, A. Musah, A. Apusiga and J. Atibila (eds) *The Kusaas: An Indigenous Perspective*. Digibooks.

Abubakari, H. (2018) Aspects of Kusaal grammar: The syntax–information structure interface. PhD thesis, African Studies Department, University of Vienna.

Ahosi, B., Fuseini, K., Nai, D., Goldson, E., Owusu, S., Ndifuna, I., Humes, I. and Tapsoba, I.P. (2019) Child marriage in Ghana: Evidence from a multi-method study. *BMC Women's Health* 19, 126.

CEDAW (Committee on the Elimination of Discrimination Against Women) (2014) Concluding observations on the combined sixth and seventh periodic reports of Ghana, adopted by the Committee at its fifty-ninth session. https://digitallibrary.un.org/record/790982?ln=en (accessed 20 October 2022).

Eddyshaw, D. (2019) A grammar of Kusaal: Agolle dialect. https://www.academia.edu/30678520/A_grammar_of_Kusaal (accessed 20 October 2022).

Girls Not Brides (2017) Why it happens. https://www.girlsnotbrides.org/about-child-marriage/why-child-marriage-happens (accessed 12 February 2023).

Global Database on Violence Against Women (2007) Domestic Violence Act 2007 (Act 732). https://evaw-global-database.unwomen.org/en/countries/africa/ghana/2007/domestic-violence-act-2007-act-732 (accessed 11 September 2023).

Government of Ghana (2015) *National Gender Policy: Mainstreaming Gender Equality and Women's Empowerment into Ghana's Development Efforts*. Ministry of Gender, Children and Social Protection https://www.mogcsp.gov.gh/mdocs-posts/national-gender-policy/ (accessed 25 October 2022).

GSS (Ghana Statistical Service) (2012) 2010 Population and Housing Census: Summary of Final Results. GSS. https://statsghana.gov.gh/gssmain/storage/img/marqueeupdater/Census2010_Summary_report_of_final_results.pdf (accessed 20 February 2023).

GSS (2016a) Domestic Violence in Ghana: Incidence, Attitudes, Determinants and Consequences. GSS. http://www.statsghana.gov.gh/docfiles/ publications/DV_Ghana_Report_FINAL.pdf (accessed 20 October 2022).

GSS (2016b) 2010 Population and Housing Census: Population of Kusaas by District. GSS. https://statsghana.gov.gh/gssmain/fileUpload/pressrelease/2010_PHC_National_Analytical_Report.pdf (accessed 14 March 2023).

Ministry of Gender, Children and Social Protection (2016) *National Strategic Framework on Ending Child Marriage in Ghana 2017–2026*. Ministry of Gender, Children and Social Protection. https://www.girlsnotbrides.org/documents/637/2017-2026-National-Strategic-Framework-on-ECM-in-Ghana.pdf (accessed 20 October 2022).

Morrell, R., Jewkes, R. and Lindegger, G. (2012) Hegemonic masculinity/masculinities in South Africa: Culture, power, and gender politics. *Men and Masculinities* 15 (1), 11–30. https://doi.org/10.1177/1097184X12438001.

Musah, A.A. (2018) *A Grammar of Kusaal: A Mabia (Gur) Language of Northern Ghana*. Peter Lang.

Myjoyonline.com (2021) Teenage pregnancy surge as Upper East Region records 6,533 cases. *My Joy Online*, 18 May. https://www.myjoyonline.com/teenage-pregnancy-surge-as-upper-east-region-records-6533-cases/ (accessed 4 April 2022).

OECD Development Centre (2019) *Gender, Institutions and Development* (2019 edn). OECD International Development Statistics (database). https://doi.org/10.1787/ba5dbd30-en (accessed 14 March 2023).

Parliament of the Republic of Ghana (1960) Criminal Code, 1960 (Act 29). https://www.ilo.org/dyn/natlex/docs/ELECTRONIC/88530/101255/F575989920/GHA88530.pdf (accessed 11 September 2023).

Parliament of the Republic of Ghana (1998) Children's Act, 1998 (Act 560). https://ir.parliament.gh/handle/123456789/1772 (accessed 20 October 2022).

UNICEF (2021) *Situation of Adolescents Report*. UNICEF. https://www.unicef.org/ghana/media/4101/file (accessed 22 April 2022).

Part 3

Reflexivity, Dilemmas and Safeguarding with Grassroots Organisations

10 Decolonial Praxes: Metaphors, Mediation and Writing in Motion

Rocío Elizabeth Muñoz Santamaría and Carlos Eduardo Arias Galindo

Introduction

IBBY México, also known as Asociación para Leer, Escuchar, Escribir y Recrear A.C., is a non-governmental association committed to fostering meaningful reading experiences that promote individual and collective development. In 2021, a collaborative project was initiated with the Culture for Sustainable and Inclusive Peace Network Plus (CUSP N+, University of Glasgow) and CRIM-UNAM (Center for Multidisciplinary Research, National Autonomous University of Mexico). The project aimed to identify organisations or groups engaging in arts-based initiatives for gender equality and transformative peace. The first phase, led by CRIM-UNAM, supported groups through basic training and funding, ethically examining art's role in conflict transformation.

Under the guidance of IBBY México, the second phase involved the selection of cultural collectives (referred in the following as *colectivas* in a metaphorical sense laden with political implications, to highlight their language and the active presence and action in managing safe cultural spaces, a role predominantly undertaken by women). These *colectivas* are dedicated to countering violence and nurturing social peace as well as harnessing expertise in reading, storytelling and narrative to empower interpretation, communication and shaping. The collaborative reading space fosters democratic engagement, cultural participation and dialogical practices aligned with respect, inclusivity and empathy. Community reading acts as a catalyst for transformation, enriching experiences and dismantling gender and sexuality stereotypes.

This project strengthened regional collectives and artistic groups, resonating in Mexico and Latin America, addressing colonial legacies, financial realities and oppressive dynamics. Also, the project engaged with children through the use of children's and young adult books, and with communities by creating safe spaces for reading and using interventions for dialogue and understanding, fostering proposals that reshape perspectives for futures within a culture of peace.

The second phase aimed to build social peace through reading and art-led interventions, working along with the *colectivas* frameworks, such as dialogue-based workshops for knowledge exchange on violence/injustice topics, and curating documents and experiences as reference for political and social decisions or research. These approaches, including consultation and community channels, seek to contribute to welfare promotion through cultural work by *colectivas* and IBBY México positively affecting migrant groups, those with limited online access or precarious employment, and domestic violence victims, and highlighting their impact.

Praxes as a Methodological Approach

The CUSP N+ in Mexico was conceived as a qualitative, participatory and dialogue-driven study rooted in participatory observation by community groups. These groups explored mutual interests like gender-based violence, migration and systemic violence, guided by the educational philosophy of Paulo Freire. Additionally, a social intervention framework created spaces for peace through books, reading and collective listening. Inclusive reappropriation of technology was also considered due to the digital shift prompted by the onset of the COVID-19 pandemic.

Initial research activities included assessing sociodemographic profiles, monitoring logs, baseline and final interviews about the significance of books, exploring cultural sectors, and reading as a tool for peace, while collaborative curation collected data for a website repository.

These research activities employed a methodology based on IBBY México's 'theory of change', which is as follows:

> If large sectors of the population conceive reading as a vital, recreational, daily, necessary and reflective experience; If there is sufficient production and a growing demand for accessible reading materials adapted to different profiles and contexts of the population; If there is a daily practice of community reading that gives rise to dialogue and collective reflection; and *if* each of the country's municipalities, town halls and localities has a library or space with adequate and accessible infrastructure for the exercise of reading; *then* people have access to meaningful reading experiences that favour their individual and community development.

Aligned with the above, IBBY México outlined three pivotal action themes as objectives:

- **Conceptual.** This involved collaborating with *colectivas*, focusing on violence, aiming to positively influence conflict transformation and peacebuilding. Rooted in IBBY México's theoretical and conceptual

framework, the hypothesis posits that individuals engaged in meaningful reading experiences demonstrate personal, communal and social development. This is assessed through factors like reading comprehension, reflections on the significance of reading and the availability of communal and public reading spaces.
- *Operational.* To gauge the qualitative impact of reading spaces on peacebuilding, the initiative employs a diagnostic approach and follow-up context evaluation. These evaluations are executed through planned activities on virtual platforms like Zoom, as well as physical locations where *colectivas* operate. These locations encompass areas of high migration, vulnerable urban zones, places of incarceration, indigenous children and youth, individuals with disabilities and those affected by gender-based violence.
- *Political.* To underscore the role, political significance and relevance of advocacy in involving cultural actors in the act of reading, an informational baseline will be developed to illustrate the social impact of reading in various contexts of violence.

In addition to these objectives, two research questions were formulated to provide insights into the contextual background of Mexico, the institutions involved and the project's development. These questions also seek to explore how the initiative contributes to bridging knowledge gaps, aligning with the CUSP methodology:

- What is the purpose of reading and its role in peacemaking, particularly its involvement in conflict resolution within the contexts of migration, jails and schools?
- How does the book function in these contexts? This encompasses its potential as a catalyst for social change, its role in producing inclusive, intercultural, autonomous reading and writing materials, community-based reading and writing activities, and the creation of communal spaces.

These research questions explored reading's peacemaking purpose and the book's role in contexts of change, intercultural materials and communal spaces. Dissemination aimed to raise awareness and encourage alliances at local and global levels, ensuring sustainability, and a foundation in decolonial praxes and pluriversality by Catherine Walsh (2019) underscored the project's ethos. As she highlights, decolonial praxis 'is the sowing and growing that give root to praxis; a sowing and growing that herald life in an era of violence-death-war, and that give cause to decoloniality as a process, practice, project, and praxis of radically "other" thinking, feeling, sensing, being, knowing, doing, and living' (Walsh, 2019: 11). This ethos resonates throughout the initiative.

The information about the participating *colectivas* is sequentially presented below, listed according to geographical locations and the projects proposed by them:[1]

Chiapas
- Colectivo viajeros is an initiative established to provide migrants in San Cristóbal de las Casas with an educational alternative; this initiative offers recreational learning centred around reading.
- Colectivo Leyendo y pedaleando is an initiative that aims to redefine spaces occupied by migrants, commonly referred to as *cuarterías*, through workshops on reading intervention and the reclaiming of public spaces.

Morelos
- Colectiva Vivas nos queremos advocates for improving the quality of life of women belonging to university communities, creating spaces for dialogue and reflection that will draw attention to violence against women.
- Colectiva Pactos violeta has a main goal of creating spaces for reflection and advocacy about the exercise of women's human rights, with an emphasis on the sexual and reproductive rights of women who are currently or have previously experienced gender-based violence.
- El nido colectivo seeks the elimination of gender-based violence through the creation of safe spaces for infants and young children.
- Colectiva Atzihuatil is composed by five artisan women who produce and manage the sales of handmade ecological products for girls, teens and women of reproductive age from the stance of ecofeminism and economic solidarity.
- Colectiva editorial Hermanas en la sombra is the first prison-based publisher in Mexico. It develops its activities working with jailed women, teaching them writing skills that enable them to articulate their identities and experiences.
- Colectivo de profesionistas independientes por la paz (CPIP) is reshaping gender stereotypes for teens through the creation of a safe space that allows for the reappropriation of the body.
- Colectivo Algarabía, through Paulo Freire methodology of community education, mainly, works from the perspective of youth, gender, human rights, childhood and interculturality.

Tijuana, Baja California
- Colectiva Palabras que acompañan was founded by two reading intermediaries dedicated to fostering community spaces for migrants. Its initiative involves training migrants to facilitate reading interventions, thereby promoting inclusion within migrant communities.

Worth noting, however, not all the *colectivas* on this list could participate. Colectivo viajeros, Pactos violeta, El nido colectivo, Colectiva Atzihuatilm and CPIP decided not to take part in the second phase of the project. As a result, four new *colectivas* were integrated into the collaborative effort. These are listed below, again according to their respective geographical locations and the projects proposed by each.

Acapulco, Guerrero
- Colectiva Letras con Perspectiva has as one of its main goals to offer other women a stereotype-free space for discussion and the presentation of their ideas in all areas of public life, while never forgetting the political dimension of the private.

Ciudad de México, CDMX
- Taller Sentir – Naturaleza. In this initiative, stop-motion animation is employed as a pedagogical tool to assist childhood communities or those working with them in telling collective stories about the concept of symbiosis.

Estado de México
- Minuscula, Literatura en Breve is a journal initiative of short literature that publishes young authors. Its aim is to provide workshops for utilising micro-fiction, poetry and chronicles to express stories of violence.

La Paz, Baja California Sur
- Casa Alfaque is an initiative which enables a community space that encompasses projects and cultural activities centred around five core pillars: imagery, text, embodiment, nourishment and mobility.

After selecting collectives to ensure inclusive participation, a diary format was devised for the coordinators (the chapter authors) with the primary purpose of maintaining a comprehensive record of various project-related meetings, agreements, significant dates and pertinent information aimed at refining the project's strategies and objectives. It is worth noting that the initial analysis section, conducted by one of the coordinators, draws heavily upon these records, with her sharing insights derived from them.

The diary template was crafted such that each member of the *colectivas* recorded uniform foundational details prior to documenting their unique observations and captivating insights. This strategy acknowledges the diversity in members' priorities and their varying levels of importance, highlighting how multiple perspectives enhance daily operations. The template adhered to the following structure: meeting title, date, subject, participants, key discussion points, initiator of each issue, consensus achieved, established deadlines, upcoming meeting date and expected participants.

The CUSP N+ in Mexico was primarily led by two coordinators, each of them working from different contexts and backgrounds. The observations and considerations regarding the development, implementation and environment of the project naturally varied between the two coordinators due to their distinct contexts and backgrounds. While their approaches may have differed, they operated within the same overarching framework, ensuring alignment with the project's objectives.

We have chosen in this chapter to present our perspectives separately, as the coordinators, to highlight the diverse range of themes and issues that emerged. By doing so, we aim to provide a comprehensive understanding of the multifaceted nature of the impact of the CUSP N+ project in Mexico and the complexities inherent in its implementation.

Exploring Intersectional Realities

The following analysis is authored by Rocío. Within it, she explores various intersectional realities, encompassing topics such as injustice, oppression, language, colonial realities, postcolonial legacies, marginalisation, pluriversality, peacebuilding and hegemonies. These themes are examined through the lens of Rocío's experiences and the dynamics shared with the different individuals and ecosystems involved in the project.

Hegemonic financial realities

The financing of cultural collectives by hegemonic entities, such as globalist elites from the Global North and state institutions, raises significant questions about the motives behind such support and its impact on marginalised communities. As Gramsci mentioned in the *Prison Notebooks* (1991), 'The essential activity of the ruling groups is the organisation of consensus, and the more fully these groups succeed in establishing themselves as the dominant hegemony, the more they will succeed in presenting their own conception of the world, their own philosophy, their own religion, as "natural"' (Gramsci, 1991: 328). Understanding these dynamics and critically evaluating the constraints of this assistance are crucial to prevent inadvertently bolstering prevailing power structures and marginalising non-hegemonic experiences and knowledge.

Hegemonies' motivations for supporting cultural collectives can vary. While some may genuinely seek to promote cultural diversity and empower marginalised groups, it is essential to approach these motives critically. As Nigerian writer and activist Chimamanda Ngozi Adichie (2009: para. 9) warns, 'The single story creates stereotypes, and the problem with stereotypes is not that they are untrue, but that they are incomplete'. Therefore, we must question whether hegemonic financing aims to amplify diverse voices or merely serves as tokenistic gestures that perpetuate unequal power dynamics.

The implications of hegemonic financing for cultural collectives should be examined in terms of its potential to reinforce existing power structures. Mexican-American writer and scholar Gloria Anzaldúa (1987: 25) emphasises the recognition of power dynamics, stating, 'The struggle is inner: Chicano, indio, American Indian, mojado, mexicano, immigrant Latino, Anglo in power, working class Anglo, Black, Asian – our psyches resemble the border towns and are populated by the same people'. This highlights the interconnectedness of power dynamics and the need to consider how hegemonic financing might inadvertently reinforce unequal power distribution within cultural collectives, marginalising – even more – certain groups.

Economic considerations are important in recognising the diverse economic realities of Global South countries and any other context. For example, in Mexico, economic challenges and inequalities affect the viability of cultural collectives and their initiatives. Nobel laureate Amartya Sen (1999) underscores the importance of economic development rooted in cultural freedoms and diversity. Similarly, economic factors in other Global South countries, like Bangladesh and Nigeria, shape the opportunities and resources available to cultural collectives. Nigerian playwright Wole Soyinka (1986: 20) highlights the link between economics and culture, stating, 'A people without a culture are easily eliminated'. This underscores the importance of considering economic factors to understand the conditions under which cultural collectives operate.

Cultural dynamics play a pivotal role in shaping the context for cultural collectives. Each country possesses unique cultural heritage, traditions and artistic expressions that influence culture. Overlooking these dynamics, hegemonic entities may inadvertently undermine the authenticity and relevance of cultural collectives' initiatives. Valuing and respecting cultural diversity within communities are vital to ensure that the provided support aligns with local cultural values and aspirations.

Moreover, financial and tax considerations are essential when analysing the impact of hegemonic financing on cultural collectives. Financial sustainability is crucial for their long-term success, and tax regulations significantly affect their resource access and operational efficacy. Hegemonic entities in the Global North that provide financial support to cultural collectives in the Global South must account for specific financial and tax dynamics in countries where cultural collectives operate. Mishandling these aspects can lead to victimisation or revictimisation of their activities from their state institutions.

In the case of the CUSP N+ project, certain *colectivas* chose not to participate in the second phase due to political stances against assuming fiscal responsibilities under a negligent government that continuously undermines its citizens. The new fiscal policies in Mexico exacerbate fiscal burdens on individuals with low earnings or belonging to minority groups, making the bureaucratic process of registering with fiscal institutions a cumbersome one. This process can become a tool used by the state to target individuals lacking the power or means to respond to fiscal requirements with the same level of proficiency as those who have the resources to navigate the system in their favour. Moreover, the current government discourse fosters a climate of distrust around civil associations and other groups working with highly vulnerable communities and/or minorities. This contributes to a sense of unjust persecution, particularly when considering that the revenue generated from their activities is minimal at best. Furthermore, a significant portion of the work performed by these *colectivas* is voluntary, with many members holding multiple jobs to sustain their projects. Therefore, adopting the country's fiscal measures to access resources further intensifies the precariousness of their activities, so much so that they decided to forego financial support before confronting the tax system in Mexico and its implications.

Finally, regarding the Global North, the funds allocated by the University of Glasgow for the project arrived months after the collectives had completed all their activities. The ongoing request for their active and willing participation by the CUSP N+ team, despite the delayed or belated receipt of funds, heightened the feelings within the *colectivas* of frustration, unfairness, disrespect and distrust.

Injustice and oppressive realities

Examining the interconnectedness of racial, gender and economic injustices and the power dynamics that perpetuate systemic inequalities is of paramount importance. Indian author Arundhati Roy (2006: 1) addresses the power dynamics perpetuating gender injustices, arguing, 'There's really no such thing as the "voiceless". There are only the deliberately silenced, or the preferably unheard'. Roy's assertion highlights the suppression of women's voices and experiences, perpetuating gender inequalities and hindering progress towards gender equity.

Bangladeshi economist Muhammad Yunus (2007: 87) emphasises the systemic nature of economic injustices, stating, 'Poverty is not created by poor people. It is created by the system we have built, the institutions we have designed, and the concepts we have formulated'. Yunus elucidates how economic injustices stem from structural inequalities and the unequal distribution of resources.

The interconnectedness of injustices is eloquently captured by Black feminist writer and activist Audre Lorde (1984: 133), who asserts, 'There is no such thing as a single-issue struggle because we do not live single-issue lives'. Lorde's assertion underscores the need to address multiple forms of oppression simultaneously, recognising that individuals' experiences are shaped by the intersections of various injustices.

Oppression in Global South countries is deeply rooted in historical contexts and the legacies of colonisation. These oppressive realities have profoundly impacted marginalised communities, shaping their access to resources and opportunities. As Mexican-American writer and scholar Gloria Anzaldúa (1987: 215) illuminates, 'The struggle is inner: Chicana, Latina, mestiza, Indian in the mind, Mexican on the skin, but on both accounts oppressed'. Anzaldúa's words exemplify the intersectionality of oppression and the intricate experiences faced by individuals in Global South countries.

In the Mexican context, historical oppression of indigenous communities has enduring effects on their socioeconomic conditions. The legacy of colonialism, marked by exploitative practices and marginalisation of indigenous populations, continues to influence the realities confronting these communities. Anzaldúa (1987: 220) emphasises this, stating, 'We are a blending of cultures, a mestizaje of blood, a mestizaje of cultures'. This underscores the significance of recognising the pluriversity within societies in Global South countries and the importance of cultural collectives in reclaiming and preserving diverse identities.

The *colectivas* engaged in projects under the guidance of the CUSP N+ methodology hail from diverse contexts and have been working on community projects for quite some time, and during the project's midpoint conversations emerged concerning the methodology delivered through the CUSP N+ platform. The *colectivas* expressed the view that receiving workshops without opportunities to share their experiences with the other members of the project was colonial. They, rightfully, perceived themselves as being treated as passive recipients of information, and found little space for active engagement within the programme's dynamic as it was stated. The *colectivas* observed and knew that they held the most experience in terms of peacebuilding in their spaces, particularly given their work within hostile environments. Thus, receiving workshops where their experiences and knowledge were not actively considered became another facet of hostile dynamics in which they felt entangled.

Meetings addressing these concerns were crucial, as the *colectivas* exhibited and shared signs of discontent that were clearly communicated, not only through limited participation. Addressing their concerns was essential, not only for the project's full development but also for our commitment to working horizontally and fostering a community of research and support. This open dialogue was vital to actively align the project's values, visions and objectives with theirs.

Colonial realities – History and language

The colonial era has left an indelible mark on the cultural, economic and political fabric of Global South countries. The imposition of foreign rule and resource exploitation has spawned profound disparities and inequalities. Kenyan writer Ngũgĩ Wa Thiong'o (1986: 23) contends that the colonial system estranged the colonised from their own culture and that of the metropolis, engendering a sense of cultural orphanhood. This disconnection from cultural roots impedes the formation of a coherent collective identity.

Decolonisation endeavours have aimed to confront these colonial legacies and restore agency to marginalised communities. Yet the complexities of decolonisation should not be underestimated. It entails reimagining institutions, reclaiming indigenous knowledge systems and challenging existing power structures. The impact of decolonisation on collective memory is pivotal, as it moulds the narratives and historical understanding of marginalised groups. As Anzaldúa (1987: 233) aptly phrases it, 'So, if you want to really hurt me, talk badly about my language'. Language becomes a battleground for resistance, embodying cultural heritage and functioning as a conduit for identity reclamation and resistance against oppressive systems. Language is where the identity of the people is located, for language is not what human beings have, but what human beings are (Mignolo, 2011: 139)

Language occupies a pivotal role in power dynamics and the marginalisation of communities. Linguistic discrimination fortifies inequities, ostracising marginalised groups from opportunities and social interaction. Anzaldúa (1987: 33) underscores language's significance in asserting one's identity, observing, 'We needed a language with which we could communicate with ourselves, a secret language'. This underscores the significance of language revitalisation efforts aiming to reclaim marginalised languages and to empower communities.

Language revitalisation does not solely safeguard linguistic diversity but also fosters cultural pride and belonging. It furnishes platforms for marginalised communities to oppose oppressive systems and reclaim their voices. As Anzaldúa (1987: 33) eloquently phrases it, 'I change myself, I change the world'. This encapsulates language's transformative potential and the agency it confers in challenging oppression and shaping social realities.

By acknowledging the realities of oppression, colonial legacies and language dynamics, we recognise their significance. This refers to the intentional use of collective memory and historical narratives to shape political agendas and societal dynamics. It encompasses manipulating the recollection of past events to sway public opinion, validate certain actions or advance specific ideological viewpoints. Memory politics frequently involves selective remembering or forgetting of events to further specific interests, and it plays a role in crafting national identities, justifying policies and influencing intergroup relations.

In light of the aforementioned, another significant barrier for the *colectivas* was the issue of language. Many of the meetings and materials were in English, with the materials they generated aiming primarily to share their outcomes in this language and constantly respond to a hegemonic language before their very own language and community: another colonial practice. Thus, in the present context, the names of their projects as well as the designations given to them are in Spanish, carry importance as a research community, serving as a form of protest and seeking linguistic justice regarding cultural production in spaces where the common language is not hegemonic.

In the following section, the aforementioned structural violence is confronted through the project's collective efforts. This exploration delves into two key themes: pluriversity and memory politics. Through this exploration of pluriversity and memory politics, I strive to unearth alternative perspectives of accompanying *colectivas* in their pursuit of justice, equity and transformative change. By embracing pluriversity, we challenge monolithic forms of knowledge and recognise the validity of diverse epistemologies. Memory politics, in turn, guides in critically examining dominant historical narratives and engaging in a process of reclamation. Together, these themes form a dynamic framework that positions *colectivas* as agents of change in the struggle against structural violence.

Memory politics – Contesting historical narratives

Memory politics are pivotal in shaping the collective comprehension of history, often reflecting the perspectives of the powerful while sidelining alternative viewpoints (Thapar, 1999). The construction of historical narratives holds intrinsic political implications, influencing societal perceptions and power dynamics.

Within the Global South, memory politics illuminate the struggles of marginalised communities against colonialism and oppression. In Mexico, for example, the memory of the Mexican Revolution and indigenous resistance movements underscores the nation's collective identity (Poniatowska, 2014). Cultural collectives amplify these narratives, providing platforms for marginalised individuals to share experiences, preserving oral histories and confronting erasure (Adichie, 2013). As marginalised voices challenge dominant narratives, cultural collectives foster inclusivity and accuracy in historical understanding.

In the Mexican context, cultural collectives such as the Zapatistas and Taller de Gráfica Popular (TGP) have been memory politics protagonists. The Zapatistas challenge dominant narratives, advocating indigenous rights and autonomy. Similarly, the TGP employs art to critique social injustices in post-revolutionary Mexico (Smith, 2002).

Amid these contestations, cultural collectives pave the way for peace-making through culture and arts, resisting the pervasive violence that traverses their communities. By engaging with pluriversality, a concept that emphasises the coexistence of diverse cultural perspectives and knowledge systems (Mignolo, 2000), cultural collectives disrupt oppressive structures and contribute to peacebuilding efforts. Pluriversity recognises that various cultural worldviews and knowledge are equally valid and valuable, challenging the dominance of a single perspective.

Through our roles as coordinators within a research community, our focus was on maintaining active participation and fostering horizontal communication. One early challenge we encountered alongside the *colectivas* was the issue of taxation. Considering the context of structural violence, many *colectivas* hesitated to register due to new fiscal policies and a sense of persecution. To address this, dialogues were established between them and the administrative personnel of IBBY México. These conversations aimed to provide guidance and address concerns, ensuring informed decisions on participation throughout. The conversations also helped us to recognise that there were structural issues beyond our collective reach.

Regarding the development of the workshops as initially planned, a shift occurred based on the feedback from the *colectivas*. In response to their dissatisfaction with being seen as passive recipients, they proposed presenting their practices and expertise to one another. This approach strengthened communication, encouraged collaboration and birthed joint projects. This process enriched the network's ethos, extending beyond the CUSP N+ programme. An integral outcome was a collaborative article (Galindo *et al.*, 2023) discussing epistemic injustices witnessed by different members of the *colectivas*.

Lastly, concerning language, as previously mentioned, we kept their project names in Spanish. In the Ghana CUSP N+ meeting, projects were also presented in Spanish, the language of their work. This decision was a form of protest against linguistic hegemony. However, I would like to outline that Spanish is also a European colonial language. The imposition of Spanish, along with other European colonial languages, was integral to the colonial project, as it facilitated the subjugation and inferiorisation of the colonised (Fanon, 1963). Those who did not conform to the linguistic norms dictated by the colonisers were often marginalised and deemed uncivilised, perpetuating a narrative of cultural and linguistic hegemony (Sibanda, 2021). The resistance against naming the projects in English while maintaining Spanish names reflects a nuanced understanding of decoloniality. While Spanish is indeed a colonial language, the choice to retain Spanish names can be interpreted as a strategic move to disrupt colonial power dynamics and assert agency within the constraints of a colonial legacy (Sibanda, 2021). It signifies a reclaiming of linguistic space and a refusal to adhere to linguistic norms imposed by colonial structures. Despite promoting pluriversity, peace and knowledge-sharing, the prevailing discourse still has colonial undertones, favouring a language associated with linguistic hegemony rather than the communities generating knowledge. So, this is an effort of reclaiming linguistic autonomy within a context shaped by colonial legacies.

Finally, speaking about my personal experience, this project has been truly enriching. I have consistently been learning and questioning myself and my own practices. There has not been a single day when I have not admired the collective effort and dedication of everyone involved in the project, mostly the work of the *colectivas*, which has enabled and made possible different practices towards peacebuilding, not only through this initiative. However, the pressure to balance the demands of a project such as CUSP N+ and maintaining a horizontal and equitable relationship with the *colectivas* was huge. At times, it felt as if I were the sole person managing decisions between two sides when the ideal was that we all were communicating on the same page and on the same level. This is another important lesson for me, about being a more active participant who fosters space of communication, instead of being just a mediator.

Decolonial Praxes: Metaphors, Narratives and Knowledge Praxes Through the Mediation of Reading

This section, authored by Carlos, the other coordinator, discusses the topic of reading, metaphors and their significance in the development of the project and the communities it impacts.

When we talk about knowledge, culture and community in the context of promoting reading, the concept of a mediator is often used. The mediator is a person who engages with the community and, through dialogue and facilitation, serves as an agent to support the community's initiatives. It is common for mediators to present themselves as advocates for horizontal relationships, active listening and collaboration. However, in practice, these principles, which appear to guide the mediator's ethics, are not easy to achieve. Even when it seems they have been achieved, you often realise that the achievement is nuanced and applies to only a portion of the community. This is because mediation involves not only facilitating participatory dialogue but also engaging with the community's hierarchy and established roles, managing them along with the community's processes and the required components such as economic resources, educational materials and cultural and technological resources, as well as collaboration with other institutions. In my experience, each community or working collective I have collaborated with has had a leadership figure. In the case of indigenous communities, particularly, there is an operational leader and a spiritual leader, who are usually elders, and their advice determines the decisions.

First and foremost, it is important to clarify that the metaphor is not limited to its linguistic and poetic use. Different authors have explored its implications in the construction of branches of knowledge in cell biology or embryology (Haraway, 2004; Reynolds, 2019). The use of metaphor has also been explored in literary technology to explain technical objects and construct knowledge, from the laboratory to scientific articles (Latour &

Woolgar, 2013; Shapin & Shaffer, 2005), in the design and innovation of science and technology (Simondon, 2007) and in the conception of the body itself and its relationship with the environment (Caracciolo, 2012). However, I believe that the aforementioned examples focus on the constructivist benefits and the amalgamation of different knowledge through abductive processes. As mentioned later, metaphors not only highlight and conceal similarities but can also highlight and conceal important differences because their normalised use establishes meanings that may no longer refer to something concrete.

In summary, this section explores the implications of metaphor in the practice of cultural management, based on personal experiences as a designer of projects and content that promote community appropriation of science and technology.

This discussion draws on my experience as a designer, manager and workshop facilitator in various projects aimed at fostering community engagement with scientific, technological and artistic knowledge through the mediation of reading and various artistic and cultural practices that stem from it. Primarily, these activities have taken place within the methodological framework used by both the private assistance institution (IAP) 'Leer Nos Incluye a Todos' and the civil association Asociación para Leer, Escuchar, Escribir y Recrear A.C., also known as IBBY México (International Board on Books for Young People – Mexico).

According to IBBY México, a reading space is an initiative that seeks to bring the library experience to communities that do not have access to a school or public library. This space has a reading mediator who accompanies and guides children, their families and the community in the reading and borrowing process. The main objective of a reading space is to foster reading from an early age, promoting interaction among people, families and the community around reading, reflection, storytelling and the relationship with texts and authors.

In these spaces, the figure of the mediator is essential.

> Mediators are individuals who have the ability to narrate their own experiences, express their feelings, pay attention to what others say, and take it into account. They show an interest in learning to express their own thoughts and listen to others. They are convinced that there is no single absolute truth, understanding that truths are provisional constructions we create to respond to the reality as we know it but are constantly evolving. They are open to the world, to diverse opinions, and to learning. They are individuals who have the ability to see others (children, youth, adults, and the elderly) as beings who know, feel, prefer, yearn, and need. They are readers who read for themselves or want to read for themselves because they know or suspect the wonders that reading holds. (IBBY México, *Manual for the Installation and Implementation of a Reading Space*. Copyright. No year specified)

Metaphor in the narrative construction of knowledge

In their book *Metaphors We Live By*, Lakoff and Johnson (2008) position 'metaphor' as part of our conceptual system, rather than being exclusively an element of poetic language. The authors draw inspiration from Piaget's psychological tradition, as well as the ecological psychology developed by J.J. Gibson and J. Jenkins, and the anthropology of Claude Levi-Strauss and Bronisław Malinowski. Considering metaphor as part of a conceptual system implies that it has systematicity and functions as a cognitive mechanism that allows us to understand and experience something generally abstract through another, usually more concrete, domain.

Lakoff and Johnson (2008) argue that our basic bodily experiences, such as having a body, moving in space and sensorially perceiving the world, influence how we conceptualise and understand abstract concepts. Through embodied metaphor, we apply conceptual structures related to our bodies to abstract or metaphorical domains. In fact, constructing arguments about the world is conceptually a metaphor, as statements like 'I demolished his argument' or 'He attacked my argument' reflect a cultural aspect of how we talk about what we know. The systematicity of constructing metaphors involves highlighting similarities or hiding them. Since linguistic expressions have meaning in themselves and are polysemic in that each person attributes different meanings to them, discussions often generate conflicts, due to the lack of consensus on the meaning of a concept. However, there is cultural coherence in how we use metaphors, to the extent that they have relationships and orientations that the authors illustrate with examples such as 'wake up' and 'I'm down', which are related to states of health or physical positions that lead us to consider basic things like 'up is good and down is bad'.

But if the construction of the world is metaphorical, how can science explain objective truths if it uses metaphors in its discourse, considering that, 'after all, metaphor involves using words typically attributed to one kind of thing to describe another thing, and the result, in general terms, is a statement that is literally false' (Reynolds, 2019: 1)? Reynolds talks about the use and implications of metaphors in the construction of scientific knowledge, especially in the realm of explanation. The author situates this topic within the discussion that differentiates between the context of discovery and the context of justification. In the context of discovery, metaphor has been considered to have virtues in providing a heuristic value that allows us to intuitively approach scientific discoveries. However, the goal of discussing the value of metaphor in scientific explanation is to discern its cognitive role in justifying the theories we develop. In this sense, metaphor serves a dual function, as it not only establishes a comparison between two instances but also refers to intentionality and the standpoint from which the discourse is constructed.

Metaphor can also be found in the narrative construction of knowledge. However, important questions arise. How can science offer objective explanations if its discourse is based on metaphors? How does the use of metaphors affect knowledge construction and the creation of ignorance? Can metaphors imply epistemic violence? Donna Haraway is an example of a philosopher who combines cultural studies with the production and circulation of knowledge. She uses metaphors as a means of analysis and support in her 1976 work *Crystals, Fabrics, and Fields*. Drawing on Kuhn's concept of a paradigm, which itself is a metaphor, she describes how changes in scientific progress involve a complete system of assumptions, values and techniques. This system includes shared symbolic generalisations, the belief in the appropriateness of particular models, values regarding prediction in explanation, and examples or concrete solutions used in the literature and important for education. Donna Haraway (2004) explores the construction of knowledge fields in biology, such as the Club of Theoretical Biology formed at the University of Cambridge in the 1930s or the 'crystallographic turn' that drew attention to molecular biology. Why? Because both moments in biology represent different ways of communicating and representing results, or, in other words, representing a narrative of the world. In Haraway's terms, this happened when different metaphorical bodies were conceived, which directly affected the visual culture of what was expected to be seen and how it was represented for communication purposes.

Metaphors, in this sense, shape narrative modes of knowledge communication. Going beyond examples in biology but keeping the focus on ways of life, Donna Haraway (2020) extends these narrative theories and metaphors into more political realms, such as the bodies that produce knowledge (embodied knowledge validation), the narratives under which the knowledge produced in a geographical terrain is situated (situated knowledge) and her development of the proposal of SF. SF stands for string figures, but also for speculative fiction, the author inviting us to imagine and speculate fictions, to create narratives together that lead us to weave new forms of knowledge, but also of affection, and thereby move from speculation and fiction to establishing concrete processes.

The proposal of storytelling is taken to the point of writing fictions about possible worlds that reflect better ways of living. The act of fiction here lies in inclusively and representatively including modes of life and bodies that have not been represented, that are discriminated against, and it is the practice of epistemic justice to seek solutions through fictions that can become reality. Although Haraway does not speak in terms of cultural or literary mediation, her proposal implies ways to transmediate different spaces where knowledge is produced, approaches to unravel the metaphors, narratives and images that shape the culture of scientific practices, and situates storytelling as a way to share empathetic practices of knowledge. It is not uncommon for Haraway to be used in Mexico by different groups that promote community actions through art, science and technology, based on reading her works and constructing methodologies. For specific examples, one can refer to the projects run by Arte Ciencia y Tecnología (ACT) at the National Autonomous University of Mexico (UNAM) and the seminar on technological rewrites at the same institution. Additionally, there is the book *Cyborgs in Latin America* (Brown, 2010).

The supports are relevant, and it seems appropriate to conclude this reflection on metaphors in the construction of knowledge by speculating on the role of the book and its mediation in the present day, amid the diversity of digital media communication. The hypertextual metaphor of social appropriation of knowledge raises the question: how can different scientific communication media and the narratives to which they adhere in different formats contribute to or detract from the processes of social appropriation of knowledge?

We live in a world where there is more and more information, and less and less meaning, according to Baudrillard's theory of simulacrum and culture (Baudrillard, 1988). French philosopher Jean Baudrillard contends that modern society has evolved into a 'society of the spectacle', where appearance and image hold greater significance than truth. One of the key ideas in Baudrillard's philosophy is hyper-reality. Hyper-reality is the state in which images, symbols and representations appear to be more accurate than reality itself. In other words, the reality we directly encounter is less appealing and powerful than the representations we see in the media, advertisements, movies and so on. As people become incapable of discerning between the real world and fiction, hyper-reality generates a sense of alienation and disorientation in society. According to Baudrillard (Baudrillard *et al.*, 1978), the result of technology and consumer culture is a society that increasingly relies on images and representations to understand the external world. Simulacra are used to replace reality and create the appearance of what reality should be. For example, advertisements depicting happy and successful individuals are used to give the impression that this is the case, even when it may not be true in real life.

In *This Craft of Verse* (1967–1968), Jorge Luis Borges observes, 'If we consult a good etymological dictionary (I'm thinking of my old and unknown friend, Dr. Skeat), and look up a word, I am certain that somewhere we will find a hidden metaphor' (Borges, 2000: 22). In this work, he proceeds to elucidate the significance of words such as 'moon' in various languages. Borges emphasises how each language gives rise to unique poetic interpretations, carrying cultural implications for diverse societies. Consequently, the concept that every word conceals a concealed metaphor itself functions as a metaphor. When viewed through the lens of the philosophy of science, this notion raises intriguing points.

Firstly, metaphors are fundamental in the construction and communication of knowledge, whether in the form of scientific narratives or in the social appropriation of knowledge. Metaphors allow us to understand abstract concepts by relating them to more familiar and concrete experiences and concepts.

Secondly, the diversity of communication media and narratives across different platforms can both contribute to and detract from the processes of social appropriation of knowledge. On the one hand, different media and narratives can expand access to knowledge, reach diverse audiences and facilitate understanding through various forms of presentation. On the other hand, there is also a risk that overexposure to images and media representations may lead to a hyper-reality, where appearances and images are more valued than truth or reality. In this sense, it is important to maintain critical thinking and be aware of how media can influence our perception and understanding of knowledge.

Lastly, Borges's quote about every word being a hidden metaphor highlights the richness and complexity of language and how words can have multiple meanings and connotations in different cultural contexts. This reminds us that the metaphors and words we use in the construction of knowledge are not neutral but are imbued with cultural meanings and values. It is important to be aware of this and consider how metaphors and language can influence our understanding and representation of the world. Some of these ideas can be summarised in the following points:

- Everyday usage of a concept can either conceal or highlight the similarities and differences in understanding its meaning.
- It is through the cultural practice of a concept within a community, locality or guild that a word acquires its meaning.
- The multiplicity of meanings behind a word often goes unnoticed and sometimes obscures relevant issues, as is the case with the concept of 'the social'.

Returning to Baudrillard, from Ward's interpretation (1994), 'the masses' as a signifier no longer corresponds to an object in the world. It is complicated to refer to the masses as a civil society, a culture, 'the people', a class, or as a reservoir for revolution or social action. Every reference and, with it, every associated meaning has been levelled. With this levelling comes the 'implosion' of the social signifier. The social has become empty. Baudrillard (1988: 177) writes:

> It is by the simulation of a conventional, restricted perspective field, where the premises and consequences of any act or event are calculable, that a political credibility can be maintained (including, of course, 'objective' analysis, struggle, etc.). But, if the entire cycle of an act or event is envisaged in a system where linear continuity and dialectical polarity no longer exist, in a field, unhinged by simulation, then all determination evaporates, every act terminates at the end of the cycle having benefited everyone and been scattered in all directions.

As Ward (1994) argues, information technologies have effectively obliterated the notion of the social as a distinct and recognisable principle of reality, reducing it to a formless and indistinguishable mass, and utilising it accordingly.

Bringing Baudrillard's theory into the discussion is important because in the current context, the practice of reading mediation is not detached from digital media platforms, nor is it detached from its political relevance in promoting the agency of children, the practice of imagination, and narrative, which cannot be separated from knowledge and culture, as they are validated through the practices that people engage in as a community.

Baudrillard shows us a different approach to metaphors and their use in mass media. Like Haraway, he knows that the visual imagination influences how we conceive, for example, climate change, violence against women, migrants and the environment. But unlike Haraway, he knows that the media promote spectacle and simulation because the media have a logic that does not correspond to the practices that take place in the community.

In the case of promoting reading, I am very familiar with the culture of TikTok and the now-called 'booktokers'. The content that usually has the greatest impact is characterised by being brief, using trends in filters and music, effective descriptions, and hashtags that sometimes have no relation to the content but help mark a presence in the recommendation algorithm. Without going into details about the various content focused on books that encompass all nuances, I emphasise that there is a condition influenced by the digital medium, regardless of the content, in which the creator-mediator of reading must delve into and adapt to its production logic.

This issue can lead us to validate the practice of promotion in terms of views, likes or follows, rather than the effort to construct critical or affective materials or to seek interactions more closely related to community values. In this situation, it is worth keeping in mind Donna Haraway's approaches to technology and storytelling, as well as situated practices with face-to-face interactions. Otherwise, we run the risk of falling into cultural simulation practices in which we would be knowingly communicating a form of knowledge largely sustained by the digital medium and its production logics, rather than concrete meanings.

Experiences of mediation and writing in motion

Following Michèle Petit (2015), reading begins in the body, a premise that aligns with what Lakoff and Johnson (2008) suggest and also with Roland Barthes in *The Pleasure of the Text* (1973), in which he delves into the sensory and metaphorical aspects of reading and how readers use language to describe their reading experiences. When I started listening to people talk about their readings, I was soon struck by the abundance of oral metaphors: 'I read until I was no longer thirsty', 'I devoured it all', 'I savoured it', 'it was like a treat', 'what delight, what delight', 'I want to try everything', 'there are those who raid the refrigerator, I raid the library', 'if you don't read, you die, it nourishes life'.

It's an old story. Michel Melot recalls that 'in most myths about the origin of writing, the letters had to be absorbed. And the learning of the Torah was done with a tile smeared with honey that the child would lick' (Michel Melot, 2006, as cited in Petit, 2015: 161).

To these examples, I can add other common ones, such as craving a good book or movie or references like 'sweet words' or 'bitter endings'. I do not mean to say that this is a particular phenomenon that happens only when sharing our experiences and desires regarding stories. But the fact that stories and books are part of a social event that we construct through a language linked to the sensation and act of hunger/eating leads me to suggest that our conception of books and stories is as deep, technically and cognitively, as our culture of cooking and the relationships we have with food and the act of eating. Eating is vital, a book is not, but the act of narrating and reading with the body is, because that is the foundation of being social. So much so that our entire system of life is governed by meta-narratives such as the state, money, normality, science and so on.

Given the fact that reading inhabits the body and, therefore, the body itself inscribes it in its world, it is relevant to discuss the book as a device that largely manages to transmediate spaces and experiences. Children's and young adult literature is a hybrid of literature that, at its core, carries the concern of telling a good story or an effective poem, but is always linked to aspects of childhood and youth. This means addressing adverse or positive situations in a way that allows the reader to empathise with the world of children and young people. It is not a simple act, as children's and young adult literature is not about moralising, giving lessons, narrating childish situations or using youthful characters. It is about offering the world to children through a book.

I remember being on the children's and young adult reading committee of IBBY México a few years ago, defending the selection of a picture book that deals with divorce. My arguments were based on the sensitivity with which the author explained how, in a divorce, children can perceive the figure of the mother or father as a monster, and it is the child who can mediate. At the end of my arguments, the thesis with which I concluded was 'this book is very good for explaining divorce'.

Among the several committee members, I was made acutely aware that it was not a 'good' children's and young adult book because it was functionalist. They explained that it carried prejudices and certain injustices of representation. For example, why should a book burden the responsibility of divorce on the children? Furthermore, why should divorce be a story in itself for a child? It would be better to present it as one of the situations that a character faces and transforms within a story that has connotative meanings in its prose. As I mentioned above, it is about giving the world a narrative that can be unravelled, constructed by the reader in relation to their experiences, situating themselves in their body and the place they inhabit.

A genre that serves as an example of the case I mentioned is 'coming-of-age literature', that is, narratives that follow the classic hero's journey scheme. I now remember *Krabat*, a novel written by Ottfried Preußler (1971) and based on a traditional legend of the Sorbian people in present-day Germany. Set in the 17th century, it tells the story of a young man who becomes an apprentice of the dark arts, but along the way there are situations that force him to make decisions whose consequences transform him into a completely different person. *Krabat*, which won the Hans Christian Andersen Award, plays with metaphors from the world of sorcery to construct a personal meaning with the reader's experiences, as someone who has surely faced similar tropes in a coming-of-age story: curiosity about a new world, a desire for adventure, fears, encounters with friends, mentors and adversity, decisions and transformations that, at the end of the day, when they conclude, give way to new stages where we are others, or other characters, if we want to continue with the metaphor of initiation.

Escritura en movimiento – 'Writing in motion'

Zacualpan is a community located in Ometepec, Guerrero, Mexico. At a certain point in 2021, I had the opportunity to be in contact with the project Escritura en movimiento, an initiative developed by the IBBY México association in collaboration with the Alberto Bailleres Foundation. The project aimed to create community reading spaces that focused on the act of dialogue as an exercise of liberation through the imagination that emerges from reading.

During the project, we visited the bilingual Basque school in Quiroga, Zacualpan. On this trip, there were three of us: two project coordinators responsible for community dialogue, content design, collaboration strategies and teaching; and one person dedicated solely to audio-visual documentation, who, like us, interacted actively with the community members. Our visit lasted two days.

On the first day, we were welcomed with an academic gathering that included school administrators accountable to the Ministry of Education in Mexico. The students arrived dressed in traditional community attire and were accompanied by a band formed by former students. Initially, we felt a certain embarrassment, thinking that the welcoming gesture was for us. However, we soon realised that it was not us who were being welcomed but rather what we brought with us: boxes with over 250 books, including novels, graphic novels, stories, poetry, picture books and illustrated books from various genres such as science, technology, fantasy and history.

The selection of books took into account the thematic requests of the community, such as gender, environment and violence.

I am aware that the selection of a collection may seem contradictory in relation to the anti-functional idea I mentioned earlier about children's and young adult literature. However, this activity is important to avoid bringing topics that do not generate interest in the community and, therefore, cannot relate to their territory and social experiences. During our visit, one of the books we worked intensively with was *In Their Shoes*, a picture book that illustrates how a child experiences their family, social and school environment with a father who dresses as a woman. The book approaches the perspective that it is the social environment that seems to have a problem with the father's choices, problems that translate into prejudices from the people in the child's community. These prejudices reach the point where the father decides to change their appearance to avoid 'disrupting' their child's environment, who until then seemed to understand that there is a 'problem' with their father that they had not noticed.

We presented the book to 25 teachers, and during the reading, various reactions emerged: laughter, seriousness, murmurs and many nods of approval or empathy. Some teachers spoke about how strange it might be to dress as a woman and mentioned that one particular teacher wanted to take the book home. At that moment, taking advantage of the laughter, one of the project coordinators asked, 'And if they want to take it home, what's wrong with that?'. To which someone responded, 'It's because they want to dress like that at home'. The laughter continued, and I responded by suggesting that women's clothing is often of better quality, more comfortable and offers more variety, and it can also reflect how we feel in certain moments, just like any other garment. The conversation took different turns, covering what makes a garment 'for' men or women, whether it is the colour, shape or perhaps ourselves as a community and our openness to other forms of expression.

My summary of that beautiful and nuanced dialogue, which was enriched by gestures, voice inflections and other sounds, does not capture the diversity of emotions, but it is a way to bring it from Zacualpan to a document on the computer. My community anecdote is an attempt to illustrate how, through reading, a process was generated in which the individuals present gradually reflected themselves in their comments, gestures and sounds regarding the content of the book. Some shared their own experiences, while others provided important information to eliminate prejudices.

The story of what a child experiences in the book with a father who dresses as a woman was transmitted and transformed during the dialogue. It moved from the pages and their illustrations to my mouth as I read it aloud. Then it was received by the ears and eyes of the teachers, who ultimately saw themselves reflected individually and collectively, which materialised in their questions and comments. Some shared their experiences, while others shared important information to eliminate prejudices. The story acquired a new meaning as it related to what they experience in school and in their private lives. It achieved a meaning that is as personal as it is shared.

Can we say that this whole process transformed space? Is what was once just a simple classroom with books now something more? To some extent, yes, because the relationships among the people present were transformed, at least temporarily. We all had a common reference point: the story that was told and the diverse opinions, observations and perceptions about its content.

Indeed, I dare say that the mediation of reading, beyond acting as an intermediary between different tools such as the book, the body, the illustration or the voice, becomes a transmedia process when it harnesses the possibilities to create spaces that reproduce new ways of linking experiences across different media and methodologies.

Transmediation is achieved when mediation constructs a space in which all the agencies and media involved, from the reading environment to the world as a whole, become visible. This process transforms the reading experience into something deeper and more meaningful, and literature becomes a powerful tool for exploring and understanding the diversity of experiences and perspectives that exist in our society.

Conclusions

As we conclude this chapter, we find ourselves immersed in a comprehensive exploration that takes us through a diverse spectrum of themes encompassing decolonial praxes, metaphor, narrative construction, knowledge communication, community engagement and the pivotal role of reading mediation. Our journey through these concepts has illuminated the intricate tapestry of complexities that shape the way we navigate horizontality and active participation, particularly within the context of the CUSP N+ project in Mexico.

Being coordinators with distinct backgrounds, the dissection of intersectional realities – such as hegemonic financial dynamics, injustice and oppression, and colonial legacies – has unveiled the multifaceted challenges that cultural collectives in the Global South face.

Our examination of hegemonic financial realities has underscored the necessity of scrutinising the motivations underlying the financing of cultural collectives. While some support genuinely aims to accompany marginalised groups, we must be wary of tokenistic gestures that perpetuate unequal power dynamics. Economic considerations have shone a light on the imperative of comprehending the economic challenges inherent in Global South countries like Mexico, and their influence on the viability of cultural collectives.

The interconnected nature of injustice and oppressive realities resonates strongly with us. Racial, gender and economic injustices interweave to perpetuate systemic inequalities, prompting us to recognise the importance of addressing multiple forms of oppression simultaneously. We have been reminded that individual experiences are shaped at the crossroads of various injustices. The profound legacy of colonialism and historical oppression continues to cast its shadow on marginalised communities. Here, the reclamation of cultural heritage and identities through cultural collectives stands as a beacon of empowerment.

As we explore colonial realities and language dynamics, the lasting impact of colonialism on cultural, economic and political dimensions becomes evident. Language emerges as a potent tool for challenging oppression and reclaiming identities. Memory politics, as emphasised in this chapter, shape historical narratives, contest dominant perspectives and foster inclusivity. Through cultural collectives, marginalised voices are amplified and the battle against erasure is fiercely waged.

We have journeyed alongside as coordinators, witnessing efforts to address challenges like taxation concerns and passive participation. The commitment of all the individuals and collectives involved to open dialogues and collaborative approaches has been a testament to the importance of maintaining a horizontal relationship while championing pluriversity and equity.

While writing this, we find ourselves standing at the crossroads of recognition and action. The imperative to acknowledge and confront structural violence while sharing, listening, learning with and of these *colectivas* to challenge oppressive systems reverberates with significance, recognising their pivotal role as agents of change, steering us towards justice, equity and transformative shifts within our society.

All the above helped us to comprehend that our reading mediation journey is not merely a voyage through pages; it is a catalyst for shared experiences, transformative dialogues and the cultivation of a society that thrives on inclusivity and informed understanding. As we embrace the multifaceted realm of mediation, we recognise that each concept we have encountered within this project is a thread intricately woven into the fabric of our evolving understanding of the world. The insights we have gleaned here bolster us to engage thoughtfully, mediate meaningfully and contribute fervently to the ever-evolving tapestry of knowledge and communal growth.

Note

(1) Sharing information about the projects and initiatives of the *colectivas*, even in a brief mention, is crucial because they are at the core of the project. Despite not being explicitly named in the subsequent sections of the chapter, acknowledging their presence is essential as they are integral throughout.

References

Adichie, C.N. (2009) The danger of a single story. *TED*, July. https://www.ted.com/talks/chimamanda_ngozi_adichie_the_danger_of_a_single_story (accessed 10 July 2024).
Adichie, C. N. (2013) *Americanah*. Alfred A. Knopf.
Anzaldúa, G. (1987) *Borderlands/La Frontera: The New Mestiza*. Aunt Lute Books.
Barthes, R. (1973) *Le plaisir du texte* [The Pleasure of the Text]. Éditions due Seuil.
Baudrillard, J. (1983) *Simulations*. Columbia University Press.
Baudrillard, J. (1988) *Selected Writings* (ed. M. Poster). Stanford University Press.
Baudrillard, J., Vicens, A. and Rovira, P. (1978) *Cultura y Simulacro* [Culture and Simulacrum]. Kairós.
Borges, J.L. (2000) *This Craft of Verse*. Harvard University Press.
Brown, J.A. (2010) *Cyborgs in Latin America*. Springer Nature.
Caracciolo, M. (2012) Narrative, meaning, interpretation: An enactivist approach. *Phenomenology and the Cognitive Sciences* 11 (3), 367–384.
Fanon, F. (1963) *The Wretched of the Earth* (trans. C. Farrington). Grove Press.
Galindo, C.E.A., Cantú Mendívil, M., Fernández Sevilla, A., Flores Ortega, M., Muñoz Santamaría, R.E., Pico Birzuela, P., Renteria Cervantes, B.D. and Suárez Balleza, D. (2023) Promoting peace: Colectivas, art, and cultural injustice in Mexico. *Language and Intercultural Communication* 23 (6), 542–558. https://doi.org/10.1080/14708477.2023.2255163.
Gramsci, A. (1991) *Selections from the Prison Notebooks* (ed. and trans. Q. Hoare and G. Nowell Smith). Lawrence Wishart.
Haraway, D.J. (2004) *Crystals, Fabrics, and Fields: Metaphors That Shape Embryos*. North Atlantic Books.
Haraway, D.J. (2020) *Seguir con el problema: Generar parentesco en el Chthuluceno* [Staying with the Trouble: Generating Kinship in the Chthulucene]. Consonni.
Lakoff, G. and Johnson, M. (2008) *Metaphors We Live By*. University of Chicago Press.
Latour, B. (2021) *Pandora's Hope: Essays on the Reality of Science Studies*. Editorial Gedisa.
Latour, B. and Woolgar, S. (2013) *Laboratory Life: The Construction of Scientific Facts*. Princeton University Press.
Lorde, A. (1984) *Sister Outsider: Essays and Speeches*. Crossing Press.
Melot, M. (2006) *Livre*. L'œil neuf Editions.
Mignolo, W.D. (2000) *Local Histories/Global Designs: Coloniality, Subaltern Knowledges, and Border Thinking*. Princeton University Press.
Mignolo, W.D. (2011) Geopolitics of sensing and knowing: On (de)coloniality, border thinking and epistemic disobedience. *Postcolonial Studies* 14 (3), 273–283.
Petit, M. (2015) *Leer El Mundo: Experiencias Actuales de Transmisión Cultural* [Reading the World: Current Experiences of Cultural Transmission]. Fondo de Cultura Económica.
Poniatowska, E. (2014) *The Heart of the Art of Being Mexican*. Penguin Random House.
Preussler, O. (1971) *Krabat y el Molino del Diablo*. IGUANA.
Reynolds, A.S. (2019) *The Third Lens: Metaphor and the Creation of Modern Cell Biology*. University of Chicago Press.
Roy, A. (2006) *The Ordinary Person's Guide To Empire*. Penguin Books India.
Sen, A. (1999) *Development as Freedom*. Oxford University Press.
Shapin, S. and Schaffer, S. (2005) *Leviathan and the Air Pump: Hobbes, Boyle, and the Experimental Life*. Universidad Nacional de Quilmes.
Sibanda, B. (2021) Language as being in the politics of Ngũgĩ wa Thiong'o. In M. Steyn and W. Mpofu (eds) *Decolonising the Human: Reflections from Africa on Difference and Oppression* (pp. 143–163). Wits University Press.
Simondon, G. (2007) *El Modo de Existencia de los Objetos Técnicos* [The Mode of Existence of Technical Objects]. Prometeo Libros Editorial.
Smith, E. (2002) Print politics: The Taller de Gráfica Popular and the Mexican political

print. In A. Kaplan and S.L. Kleinberg (eds) *Between History and Literature: Selected Essays of Erich Auerbach* (pp. 329–352). Verso.

Soyinka, W. (1986) *Myth, Literature, and the African World.* Cambridge University Press.

Thapar, R. (1999) *The Historian and Her Craft.* Orient Blackswan.

Wa Thiong'o, N. (1986) *Decolonising the Mind: The Politics of Language in African Literature.* James Currey.

Walsh, C. (2019) Decolonial praxis: Sowing existence – Life in times of dehumanities. Keynote talk presented to the IX Congress of the International Academy of Practical Theology, São Leopoldo, Brazil, 5 April. *International Academy of Practical Theology Conference Series* 2 (2021), 4–12.

Ward, S.C. (1994) In the shadow of the deconstructed metanarratives: Baudrillard, Latour, and the end of realist epistemology. *History of the Human Sciences* 7 (4), 73–94.

Yunus, M. (2007) *Creating a World Without Poverty: Social Business and the Future of Capitalism.* PublicAffairs.

11 Contextualising Safeguarding in International Development Research: Requirements and Challenges

Maria Grazia Imperiale, Giovanna Fassetta and Fatma Abubaker

Introduction

Safeguarding has been a high priority in the UK for many years, especially following the uncovering of cases of exploitation by staff in large charities. In 2018, safeguarding became an international matter and was spotlighted when senior staff at Oxfam were accused of sexual exploitation in Haiti, where the charity was working to provide relief to earthquake victims (BBC News, 2018). Issues of bullying and harassment within other eminent humanitarian and development organisations also came to light (Daoust & Dyvik, 2022; Orr et al., 2019). These scandals were the start of a discussion around power imbalances in international development and the risks these pose to people in vulnerable situations who may be easily exploited. A consequence of this was a demand for safeguarding principles and procedures to be put in place in all work that relates to international development and/or involves minors, including publicly funded research with partners based in lower- and middle-income countries (LMICs).

The Culture for Sustainable and Inclusive Peace (CUSP) Network Plus is a large, £2 million project funded for four years (2019–2023) through the Global Challenges Research Fund (GCRF) of UK Research and Innovation (UKRI, a government non-departmental body that is a main provider of such public funding), which is set up to support research to address challenges faced by LMICs. The CUSP project is a network led by the University of Glasgow, with partners in Palestine, Morocco, Mexico, Ghana and Zimbabwe, which works on strengthening the United Nations' Sustainable Development Goals 5 and 16, looking at conflict that has its roots in gender inequalities and ways to strengthen artistic and cultural institutions so that they can be hubs for conflict transformation.

As with every project funded by the UKRI, and as per University of Glasgow policy, CUSP had to develop a safeguarding policy and had to treat the issue of safeguarding with extreme care and sensitivity. The CUSP Network follows a decentralised approach. Similarly, to many research projects led by UK universities in partnership with Global South institutions and organisations, CUSP relies on co-investigators and local researchers based in each partner country. The co-investigators and researchers work with local partners and organisations/institutions to carry out the research and to monitor and assess the project on an ongoing basis. The principal investigator and project coordinator are the 'nodes' that connect and draw together the research carried out by local partners in each country.

With reference to safeguarding, this also means 'decentralising' safeguarding procedures and practices. The common safeguarding policy needs to be applied by the partners in each country and this brings with it some challenges, not only in terms of practical implementation and operationalisation but, most importantly, in relation to the conceptualisation of safeguarding as a decentralised matter and a way to contribute to the prevention/ of tensions and conflicts, at both personal and institutional/ organisational levels. This requires reflection on the ways in which this can be done effectively while, at the same time, avoiding the imposition of Western assumptions and approaches. While trying to navigate 'safeguarding' within CUSP, we came across several conundrums, to which we did not find easy and straightforward answers.

This chapter unpacks the main dilemmas we encountered, as we believe that the process of reflection and the discussions that led to the conundrums are crucial aspects of ethical research. Even if the conundrums do not have an easy solution, we think that awareness of the complexities and ongoing reflections on their potential challenges and impact are all crucial to ensure that safeguarding does not become another set of boxes to tick and then forget about but, rather, a truly collaborative effort to ensure the safety and wellbeing of everyone involved in research and, in particular, of those who are more at risk of abuse or harm because of their characteristics (age, gender, ability, etc.).

In this chapter, the first conundrum we reflect on concerns the opacity of the concept of safeguarding. There is no univocal definition, and even though there are principles around which safeguarding policies can be developed, these are subject to institutions' and organisations' policies and procedures. Secondly, we propose a reflection on the relation between vulnerability and safeguarding, as vulnerability is a contested concept and how we use it can have an impact on our understanding of safeguarding and expose tensions between individual responsibility and the ideologies and structures that allow exploitation and harm to take place. Thirdly, we look at the possibility of decentralising safeguarding in research and of ensuring it is appropriate to a range of different contexts. Even though we all work within decolonial paradigms, we acknowledge that, even within a collaborative project such as CUSP, we were not entirely able to decentralise and 'decolonise' safeguarding. We then summarise these issues in the final section, where we present our reflections. We cannot draw conclusions, but we suggest that having an open and candid debate on these questions is crucial to ensuring effective and respectful safeguarding.

First Conundrum: The Opacity of Safeguarding

Until now, there has been no univocal definition of safeguarding, and different organisations and institutions apply their own definitions of the term (Orr *et al.*, 2019). However, they present similar characteristics that are usually based on government documents that set out frameworks to which local authorities need to refer in order to protect people at risk. The concept of 'opacity' as defined by philosopher Edouard Glissant is useful here for framing our discussion. Glissant (1997) proposes the 'right to opacity' for everyone; the idea of opacity challenges the assumption that everyone and everything should be clear and transparent, and, rather, argues that we should embrace the complexity, incomprehensibility and uniqueness of the 'other'. A clear sign of the complexity of the idea of safeguarding is the opacity of its operationalisation, which indicates that – while ostensibly straightforward – it can mean different things to different people at different points in time and space.

For example, safeguarding in England and Wales is grounded in the Care Act 2014, which came into force in April 2015. Scotland refers to the Adult Support and Protection (Scotland) Act 2007, while Northern Ireland uses Adult Safeguarding Prevention and Protection in Partnership framework, published in July 2015. The Care Act 2014 in England and Wales superseded all previous documents that aimed to protect 'vulnerable adults' or 'adults at risk' (Johnson & Boland, 2019). Albeit slightly different, all these policies share some commonalities in the way safeguarding is defined. They highlight the challenges of creating a safe environment, where everyone is protected, respected and valued; they stress the need to ensure that organisations and institutions are ready to act in order to prevent harm; and they note that safeguarding is everyone's responsibility, that it is a collective responsibility, which should become part of organisations' and institutions' day-to-day activities.

It is important to note that the focus of most definitions is not only on protection from abuse and harm but also on promoting welfare and wellbeing. Safeguarding is therefore not only about reacting to what is happening or has happened in the past but is also about preventing harm and promoting and enabling structures to support and strengthen individuals' wellbeing for the future.

By way of an example, the statutory guidance for the Care Act defines adult safeguarding as follows:

Safeguarding means protecting an adult's right to live in safety, free from abuse and neglect. It is about people and organisations working together to prevent and stop both the risks and experience of abuse or neglect, while at the same time making sure that the adult's wellbeing is promoted including, where appropriate, having regard to their views, wishes, feelings and beliefs in deciding on any action. This must recognise that adults sometimes have complex interpersonal relationships and may be ambivalent, unclear or unrealistic about their personal circumstances.

Organisations should always promote the adult's wellbeing in their safeguarding arrangements. People have complex lives and being safe is only one of the things they want for themselves. Professionals should work with the adult to establish what being safe means to them and how that can be best achieved. (UK Government, 2014b: paras 14.7, 14.8)

In the context of research, following the major concerns in international development and humanitarian aid briefly explained in the introduction to this chapter, in October 2018 leading members of the UK Collaborative on Development Research (UKCDR) issued a joint statement confirming an intensified focus and commitment to safeguarding in international development research (Orr et al., 2019; UKCDR, 2018). International development research refers to all research funded by UK leading funders that aims to achieve social or economic benefits in LMICs. As a result of this statement, research was commissioned: (a) to scope existing evidence and guidance on safeguarding, including drafting principles for safeguarding in international research, through an evidence review (see Orr et al., 2019); and (b) to validate those guiding principles through international consultation (UKCDR, 2020a, 2020b).

The UKCDR defines safeguarding as preventing and addressing:

any sexual exploitation, abuse or harassment of research participants, communities and research staff, plus any forms of violence, exploitation and abuse ... such as bullying, psychological abuse and physical violence. (UKCDR, 2020a: 2)

The evidence review conducted by Orr *et al.* (2019) notes that this definition of safeguarding is broader than usual definitions, since it goes beyond 'do no harm' to include the so-called 'bystander' concerns, which comprises researchers who become aware of issues outside of their research activities. This definition also includes bullying within the workplace, which was not covered by other definitions of safeguarding.

Orr *et al.* (2019) conducted a review and collected responses through questionnaires and interviews with relevant stakeholders to evidence ways in which safeguarding is understood and operationalised in international development research. The authors found that the shift in the definition to include bystanders and bullying had caused uncertainty in some organisations around the scope of safeguarding. For example, even within the

UK, researchers interviewed during the study reported that safeguarding was vague and confusing, and that existing safeguarding policies were not drafted with this broader definition in mind, which caused even more uncertainty (Orr *et al.*, 2019: 28). The review notes that there is no shared understanding of safeguarding in research, nor of what processes it entails. Orr *et al.* also point out that the term 'safeguarding' until very recently has been predominantly used in the UK, and that this poses challenges in terms of adopting and adapting safeguarding within international research projects.

The UKCDR's definition, however, does not address wellbeing explicitly. This instead has become the focus of other institutions' safeguarding policies. By way of example, Education Scotland (2021: 3) uses the following definition:

> [Safeguarding] is a much wider concept than child protection and refers to promoting the welfare of children, young people and protected adults. It encompasses protecting from maltreatment, preventing impairment of their health or development, ensuring that they are growing up in circumstances consistent with the provision of safe and effective care, and taking action to enable all children, young people and protected adults have the best outcomes.

NHS England (n.d., para. 1) defines safeguarding as follows:

> Safeguarding means protecting a citizen's health, wellbeing and human rights; enabling them to live free from harm, abuse and neglect. It is an integral part of providing high-quality health care. Safeguarding children, young people and adults is a collective responsibility.

As can be seen, both definitions focus on wellbeing and welfare and the main thrust is ensuring that safeguarding goes beyond the prevention of harm to encompass a duty by institutions to providing everyone with the best possible opportunities to live safely and healthily and to ensure they can enjoy their human rights. In the past, safeguarding was considered mainly for 'vulnerable adults' and children, and it focused – and still does – on people who, because of issues they face, need additional care and support, or on people who experience, or are at risk of experiencing, abuse and harm and cannot protect themselves. However, if safeguarding is about promoting wellbeing and human rights, then it applies to all individuals and not only to people at risk, as can be seen in the extracts from Education Scotland and NHS England. It is nevertheless important to consider that some people may be more at risk than others – for example, due to illness, communication difficulties or additional needs, as these people may indeed be particularly at risk of suffering abuse and neglect. However, the broader conceptualisation of safeguarding which we highlighted above means to amplify the scope of safeguarding itself.

Within CUSP, safeguarding applies to people who are at risk of 'abuse and harm'. In CUSP safeguarding policy, abuse and harm are defined as:

> an act of oppression and injustice, exploitation and manipulation of power by those in a position of authority. Abuse and harm can be inflicted directly or can be caused by the failure to act to protect an individual from others. Abuse and harm are not restricted to any socioeconomic group, gender or culture. (CUSP, 2020: 3)

It is important to note that, here, abuse and harm might be the result not only of mistreatment but also of inaction and omission. Abuse and harm can be intentionally inflicted or can be a consequence of the failure to act to protect and ensure someone else's wellbeing. They can also be unintentional: for example, adults who puts themselves at risk because the right support is not in place, which may result in neglect or self-neglect.

Abuse and harm are often inflicted by people who abuse a position of trust and power to take advantage of those they are meant to support and who are in dependent positions (UK Government, 2023). Such acts of abuse and harm can be inflicted by anyone – a professional carer, a relative, a social worker, a volunteer, or a stranger – and often happen within victim's home. Many forms of abuse are criminal offences and should, therefore, be treated as such. It is important to note that acts of abuse can be repeated or be one-off and can affect one or more people.

Abuse and harm can take many forms, some more obvious than others. The Care and Support Statutory Guidance (UK Government, 2023) identifies 10 types of abuse and harm:

- physical abuse;
- domestic violence or abuse;
- sexual abuse;
- psychological or emotional abuse;
- financial or material abuse;
- modern slavery;
- discriminatory abuse;
- organisational or institutional abuse;
- neglect or acts of omission;
- self-neglect.

This list is not exhaustive, as forms of harm and abuse can vary. Physical abuse may include: assault, hitting, slapping, suffocating or deliberately making someone ill, misuse of medication, physical punishment and rough handling.

Domestic violence or abuse is defined by the UK government in the same document as 'any incident or pattern of incidents of controlling, coercive or threatening behaviour' between those who are or have been intimate partners or family members. It may include honour-based violence, forced marriage and genital mutilation. Evidence from the UK charity SafeLives (2020) shows that domestic violence and abuse increased worldwide after the onset of the COVID-19 pandemic.

Sexual abuse includes rape, attempted rape or sexual assault, indecent exposure and inappropriate touch anywhere, non-consensual sexual penetration or attempted penetration, sexual harassment, sexual photographs or forced use of pornography, or the witnessing of sexual acts.

Psychological or emotional abuse includes deprivation of contact, humiliation, blaming, controlling, intimidation, coercion, harassment, threats of harm or abandonment, verbal abuse, cyber-bullying, isolation, removing mobility or communication aids, or intentionally leaving someone unattended when they need assistance.

Financial or material abuse includes fraud, theft and coercion in relation to an adult's financial affairs or arrangements.

Modern slavery includes slavery, human trafficking, forced labour, coercive enforcement of individuals into a life of abuse, servitude and inhumane treatment. Modern slavery is an international crime that often involves organised crime groups across different countries.

Discriminatory abuse involves discriminating against someone because of protected characteristics, which are age, disability, race, gender, sex, religion, sexual orientation, marriage and civil partnership, pregnancy and maternity. Within the UK, the Equality Act 2010 provides a legal framework to tackle these types of abuse and discrimination (UK Government, 2010).

Organisational abuse encompasses poor practice within an organisation or institution, or care settings. It includes neglect or poor professional practice as a result of the structures and processes in place within an organisation. In a report on gender-based violence in Morocco developed by CUSP's partner organisation Racines, the authors identified and presented cases of how institutions can be a source of abuse against women, for example, by humiliating women reporting rape, or not providing facilities for women (e.g. toilets within schools), thus effectively excluding them (Racines, 2021).

Neglect or acts of omission include ignoring a person's medical, physical and emotional care needs, failure to provide adequate services, failure to provide for a person's basic needs (such as food, heating or medication as prescribed) and failure to ensure privacy and dignity.

Finally, self-neglect includes lack of self-care that may threaten personal health and safety, self-harm, failure or inability to seek help as appropriate.

Although this list is quite comprehensive, it is still not exhaustive, and abuse and harm may vary across different contexts, which can pose an issue when it comes to 'decentralising' safeguarding in international research, something that will be discussed in more depth as part of the third conundrum.

Summarising this first conundrum on the opacity of safeguarding, we can note that safeguarding is a concept that does not have a single definition, that is applicable in an increasingly broad range of contexts, including a range of situations that refer not just to the identification or prevention of situations of abuse and harm but also to the need to ensure welfare and wellbeing. While safeguarding is still a concern for people who are more at risk of abuse and harm, it is also increasingly inclusive of everyone, regardless of their characteristics. Although the lack of a clear definition of safeguarding can be problematic, especially in terms of clarity for those who engage with it, we recognise that in a multi-relational and ever-evolving world, we can accept the 'opacity' (Glissant, 1997) of a particular concept. This allows for different ways of understanding the world and challenges the rationality of the Enlightenment and its claim to universal truths, as well as the Western emphasis on the individual dimension of safety and wellbeing.

First conundrum: points for reflection and discussion

- What are the pros and cons of a definition of safeguarding that is not neatly defined for organisations and institutions that work in international development contexts, including in research?
- To what extent does the broadening of the definition of safeguarding to include ensuring the wellbeing and welfare of everyone involved in international development contexts help to protect those involved in research?
- Who should be responsible for ensuring this?
- Can a more specific and clear-cut definition of safeguarding and a more restricted list of potential risks and individuals/groups lead to concerns and/or harm being missed, or would this make safeguarding more effective?

Second Conundrum: Vulnerability and Safeguarding

In many safeguarding policy documents, we can still read that safeguarding applies to children and those who are identified as 'vulnerable adults'. In fact, in recent documents, the term 'adult at risk' is preferred, since vulnerability is considered a contested term.

The word 'vulnerability' comes from Latin, *vulnerare*. That is a verb that means 'to hurt', 'to damage', 'to offend', but also 'to break a principle'. In Late Latin this term was used also in the sense of 'to break a law'. The adjective *vulnerabile* then followed, meaning something that 'can be broken, hurt, or damaged'. From the adjective *vulnerabile* comes the English 'vulnerable'. It is interesting to know that vulnerability as an analytical concept emerged in environmental science in the 1990s in relation to the effects of natural or economic disasters on human beings. It was only later that it was used in other fields, for example in health, social care and policymaking (Virokannas *et al.*, 2020). The term was used before then, but it was only in the 1990s that it became an analytical concept.

Different authors have written about the concept of vulnerability. The scholar Elina Virokannas and her colleagues reviewed 86 academic journal articles that used this concept. They found that the term was often used in a 'self-evident manner, referring to certain people or groups' (Virokannas *et al.*, 2020: 335). They noted that many of the articles they reviewed presented a critique of the term 'vulnerable'. However, they hardly ever found a satisfactory definition of this term, and concluded that 'definitions of who is seen as vulnerable and for what reasons vary enormously' (Virokannas *et al.*, 2020: 328).

The main critiques of the term 'vulnerable' argue that it can deny the agency and voice of those perceived as vulnerable and, perhaps even more importantly, it may lead those responsible for preventing vulnerability – for example, the state – to be overlooked (e.g. Koch, 2015; Mishra, 2014; Szupinski Quiroga *et al.*, 2014). In other words, if we label people as vulnerable, the structures and institutions responsible for their welfare may not be held accountable for preventing harm or for supporting those in need. The consequence of this is that vulnerability is seen as an intrinsic condition of individuals rather than the result of specific ideologies or determined by structural imbalances.

On the other hand, there are other scholars, especially philosophers, who talk about a universal human condition of vulnerability and argue that we are all vulnerable but that this is denied for some groups who see themselves as 'invulnerable' on ideological grounds. For example, Fineman (2010: 267) writes that human vulnerability 'arises from our embodiment, which carries with it the imminent or ever-present possibility of harm, injury, and misfortune' and that vulnerability is both universal and particular. Similarly, Nussbaum (2004: 17) argues that vulnerability is a common trait of humanity, and she calls for 'a society of citizens who admit that they are needy and vulnerable, and who discard the grandiose demands for omnipotence and completeness that have been at the heart of so much human misery'. Butler (2020: 46) discusses vulnerability as a potential condition of all human beings, as we are all, at some point during our lives, in a condition of dependency, and

> to be dependent implies vulnerability: one is vulnerable to the social structure upon which one depends, so if the structure fails, one is exposed to a precarious condition. If that is so, we are not talking about my vulnerability or yours, but rather a feature of relation that binds us to one another and to the larger structures and institutions upon which we depend for the continuation of life.

Thus, for Butler, vulnerability is the consequence of our immanent dependency and is relational, since we rely on other people, objects and institutions for our lives and, when these disappear, are withdrawn or fall apart, we are all rendered 'vulnerable to being dispossessed, abandoned, or exposed in ways that may well prove unlivable' (Butler, 2020: 46).

What philosophers like Fineman, Nussbaum and Butler have in common is that they argue that vulnerability is a state shared by all human beings, as we are all 'vulnerable' at some point in our life, for example as a new-born baby, an elderly person, when we fall ill or when we need medical assistance (Nussbaum, 2004). Denying this state of vulnerability is an ideological position, one that ascribes dependency to some individuals or groups who are perceived as weaker or in some way deficient and thus responsible for their own failure and deserving of the consequences (Butler, 2020). The relational dimension of vulnerability is, then, key to unpacking the relationships between individuals and society to understand the social processes that generate vulnerability, and we should therefore acknowledge the responsibility that the state carries towards its citizens to alleviate the causes and consequences of vulnerability. While there is no harm in admitting that we are needy and thus being vulnerable is part of being human (Nussbaum, 2004), we also need to act to reduce the causes and consequences of vulnerability, as well as demanding that the state and its institutions are held responsible for ensuring that their citizens are not made vulnerable.

Latouche (2023) reflects on the politicisation of the term vulnerability by discussing vulnerability-focused humanitarian programmes in Greece and how policies that ostensibly were put in place to protect 'vulnerable' groups were used to harden border control. In that context, women needed to perform gendered stereotypes of 'vulnerability' at the border in Greece in order to be transferred to the mainland. Despite this, after receiving international protection, migrant 'vulnerable' women are then forced to leave their flats, and Latouche (2023: 179) argues for the need to 're-politicise vulnerability', conceptualising it as a 'long-term, intersectional precarity'. Butler et al. (2016: 4) call for a reconceptualisation of vulnerability as one of the conditions of the very possibility of resistance and to challenge the association between vulnerability and passivity/inaction as well as the dismantling of 'masculinist fantasies of sovereign mastery' that drive this association.

Featherstone and Gupta (2017) draw on qualitative research they conducted in England with families who had been involved with the child protection system and recommend that we frame child protection and its system within a broader understanding of social justice, one that is underpinned by the capability approach (CA) (Nussbaum, 2004; Sen, 1999). The authors reflect on the fact that the CA is a normative framework developed to assess wellbeing and social arrangements. It considers wellbeing in relation to the opportunities (capabilities) to transform what we are able to be and to do into achieved outcomes (i.e. functionings). The CA has found application in different academic fields, including economics, education, philosophy and human development and, importantly, it has influenced broader public policy areas. Central to Featherstone and Gupta's argument is how the CA can be used to identify the structural basis of poverty – which affects certain capabilities and may even lead to some people being entirely deprived of them. As the authors note:

> The CA provides a framework for poverty analysis that avoids the dichotomy of only focusing on material deprivation or individual factors at the expense of structural inequality, and includes an interconnecting of different levels of analysis (micro and macro, individual and context, means and ends) that contribute to our understanding of the relationship between structure and agency. (Featherstone & Gupta, 2017: 189)

Regarding the term 'child protection' within an English context, the authors refer to 'the laws, policies and practices relating to children deemed to be at risk or likely to be at risk of abuse and neglect' (Featherstone & Gupta, 2017: 184). They also explain that the term 'child protection', in the English context, refers mainly to protecting children from harm that is predominantly caused within the domestic walls, that is, maltreatment at the hands of parents or guardians. Originally, the focus of the child protection system in England was not only the protection of children but also a 'constructing [of a] balance between supporting families and protecting children' (Featherstone & Gupta, 2017: 185); that is, child protection also incorporated some features of family services, and thus greater recognition of the structural dimensions of safeguarding. Currently in England, after a child protection investigation, if a child is judged to be suffering or likely to be suffering 'significant harm', there are two options: (1) the child is removed from home; or (2) the child can remain in the care of parents/guardians but is placed on a child protection plan.

During the period from 2009–2010 to 2014–2015 in England there was an increase of 79.4% in child protection investigations, and a 40% increase in the number of children placed on a child protection plan, with neglect as the most common cause for this, followed by emotional abuse (Featherstone & Gupta, 2017). Neglect has often been associated with poverty, which has a direct impact on the material resources that parents or guardians can provide to children. It has also an indirect impact, caused by the considerable stress that living on a very low income can create. And yet, at least in relation to the English context,

> consideration of the impact of poverty and inequality is either absent and or actively discouraged. [...] The construction of neglect is one of a problem whereby children need to be rescued from rather than one that their parents can be supported to address. (Featherstone & Gupta, 2017: 189–190)

This brings us back to the previous discussion on the political dimensions of the concept of vulnerability and how this has increasingly become an individual problem that denies the crucial social and structural aspects of safeguarding.

Poverty and neglect, Featherstone and Gupta (2017) note, should be addressed through providing additional family support and not by way of stigmatising or even 'dehumanising' families. Studies investigating the perspectives of parents found that the nature of the contemporary child protection system 'stigmatises and blames parents, leading them to feel dehumanised and unheard – that is, depriving them of dignity' (Featherstone & Gupta, 2017: 192–193). While considering child protection as the priority of the child protection system, Featherstone and Gupta argue for a broader understanding of structural inequalities and of social justice within public policies, and especially within the child protection system. They stress the need for also considering parents' capabilities, so that the whole system may strengthen child protection and human flourishing. The authors conclude their chapter by outlining specific policy recommendations at the national and local level – underpinned by the following argument:

> What is required is a paradigm shift from a narrow focus on risk and to one that fundamentally aims to promote the wellbeing of children and their families. The CA offers a theoretical framework for the development of policies and practices to support such a paradigm shift aimed at promoting social justice and human flourishing. Parental difficulties would not be ignored, and there will be a need for the state to take protective action in circumstances of significant harm to a child, but this would be in the context of the provision of supportive state services aimed at reducing the deleterious effects of poverty and other forms of inequality on children and their parents. (Featherstone & Gupta, 2017: 195)

Summarising this second conundrum regarding the concept of vulnerability and the tensions between the individual and social dimensions of vulnerability and – consequently – of safeguarding, we note that vulnerability is a highly politicised term. Discussions by philosophers such as Nussbaum or Butler converge in identifying vulnerability as a trait that is common to all human beings, as we are all dependent on other humans but also on objects and structures and even the environment for our survival. The withdrawal or breakdown of support is what makes people at risk, but this is denied by ideologies that see vulnerability as the trait of weaker individuals or groups. The CA can be a framework that recognises the need for structural support so that everyone is given the opportunity to enjoy capabilities that are essential to living a life of dignity and to develop capabilities into actual 'functionings'. This requires institutional and social forms of support as it recognises that, without appropriate forms of support, individuals and groups may be denied their capabilities.

Second conundrum: Points for reflection and discussion

- If we say that people are vulnerable, are we denying their voice and agency?
- How can safeguarding enhance people's voice and agency?
- Can we actually use safeguarding to do that?
- As safeguarding relies on the concept of vulnerability, how can we ensure that, while providing protection for all, safeguarding also frames vulnerability as a result of structural failures and of specific ideologies?
- Are there specific conditions that make people/groups vulnerable?
- If so, what can we do about it through safeguarding?
- To what extent are safeguarding principles designed to protect institutions such as universities?
- Could the CA become a framework around which safeguarding policies can be effectively structured?

Third Conundrum: Contextualising Safeguarding in Research

Nussbaum's CA has been developed with a specific focus on ensuring that, while universal, the central capabilities she puts forward are also constructed in conversation with scholars and activists from across the globe. Charusheela (2009: 1136) notes that,

> in her search for a non-ethnocentric universalism, Nussbaum asks whether there exists an approach that is both robust enough to provide universal ethics, yet flexible enough to ensure that we avoid the racism, ethnocentrism, orientalism and paternalism of discredited universalisms.

Despite the clear attempt to avoid developing a framework that relies on Western onto-epistemological assumptions, the CA has been critiqued from a postcolonial perspective, with the argument that, while broad enough to be widely applicable, the analysis of social interactions and structures it relies on is nevertheless one that takes as granted Western understandings (Charusheela, 2009).

The balance between ensuring that everyone around the globe is guaranteed the same opportunities to live a life of dignity, regardless of who they are or where they live, and ensuring that these capabilities are fine-tuned to take into account local onto-epistemological specificities as well as traditions and practices, is not a simple one to find. Several safeguarding policies make references to United Nations (UN) conventions, including the Universal Declaration of Human Rights, which was proclaimed by the UN General Assembly in Paris on 10 December 1948. Rising from the grief and sorrow of the Second World War,

> [t]he Universal Declaration envisaged a world in which every man, woman and child lives free from hunger and is protected from oppression, violence and discrimination, with benefits of housing, health care, education and opportunity. This encapsulates the global culture of human rights that we strive towards and should therefore be a unifying rather than a divisive force within and among all cultures. (Pillay, 2019)

However, the universality of human rights from which the Declaration emanates is sometimes questioned, mainly on grounds of coloniality and 'cultural relativism'. In their critical analyses of human rights discourses and the coloniality of human rights, Mignolo (2009) and Spivak (2011) challenge the notion of 'the human' who speaks for human rights. This includes Eurocentric scholars who promote universal notions of the 'human being' without questioning – or acknowledging – coloniality and the constructed nature of the 'human', which has, historically, excluded entire groups and which still creates divisions between those who are fully humans and those whose lives are 'ungrievable' (Butler, 2009).

While the conundrum discussed above is true for all safeguarding in international development, it is perhaps even more crucial for those engaged in research that is carried out in partnership with organisations and institutions in LMICs. Traditionally, there was an expectation that, compared with international development projects, research would be less hands-on, as researchers would limit themselves to observing, documenting or 'extracting' data from participants to increase knowledge of particular issues. While the boundaries between international development work and international research were never clearly defined, in recent years they have become even more blurred. This is largely a result of the demand that academic research demonstrates measurable 'impact', a criterion that is increasingly central to the allocation of funding. This also carries the expectation that research will address challenges that are highlighted by LMIC partners, and that it will be conducted as much as possible through collaborative work. At the same time, international development agencies may carry out research to inform their work, ensure it responds to locally identified needs, and evaluate and evidence progress (Orr *et al.*, 2019).

The emphasis on collaboration and co-production of research to ensure sustainable, long-term impact means that UK higher education institutes (HEIs) are increasingly 'devolving' research to co-investigators and researchers in LMICs, sometimes – albeit not exclusively – based at local HEIs, as is the case for the CUSP Network Plus. This further complicates safeguarding policies and reporting structures, as

> reliance on local fieldworkers can [...] limit researchers' oversight and control of research strategies, and thus of safeguarding processes and practices. This might occur if local fieldworkers develop strategies without fully explaining them or engage in some deception of participants about

the nature of research. This, combined with embedded financial and power disparities, raises important questions about the extent to which responsibility and accountability can be transferred to local research assistants. (Orr *et al.*, 2019: 16)

As well as creating challenges for the transposition of research principles, policies and practices between different contexts, research on some particularly difficult topics, such as gender violence, can carry greater risks for local researchers if they report it. The risk of vicarious or secondary traumatisation is a further possibility that local researchers may experience when investigating sensitive topics, leading to risks for their wellbeing.

The work by Orr *et al.* (2019) highlights the challenges that can arise from a disjuncture between the expectations of safeguarding and the role of research staff on the ground (whether local or from Global North institutions) – in particular, junior staff – in dealing with safeguarding issues: specifically, knowing where the boundaries of safeguarding lie, and to what extent (local), researchers can be expected to carry responsibility for reporting what occurs in the broader community in which the research is grounded. Being aware of reporting procedures and of ways to avoid backlash for the victims or the researchers themselves can also be difficult to manage in situations that can be characterised by unequal power relations, lack of clear reporting structures for what can be complex and unpredictable situations, and by interpersonal or institutional dynamics about which researchers may not be fully aware. While, of course, ensuring wellbeing and safety is paramount, the risk of endangering victims or whistle-blowers must be fully taken into account by safeguarding policies. To ensure effective safeguarding and to challenge structural inequalities, agencies and researchers could work to empower the people they work with to know their rights; engage with local feminist and LGBT groups; and challenge the racialised, gendered and colonial structures which create fertile ground for exploitation and harm on an ongoing basis (Daoust & Dyvik, 2022).

In an earlier article, Daoust and Dyvik (2020) point to how safeguarding policies are almost invariably drawn up by Global North organisations and make references to 'local' concerns, practices and understandings only as a way to contextualise procedures and implementation. However, the expertise that informs the safeguarding policies usually lies with the Western partner, an expertise that the contextualisation in local practices only aims to confirm. This is often the case also for research, where Global South partners are called to 'translate' and implement safeguarding policies, but never to design them in the first place. This disparity rests on the assumption that organisations/institutions of the Global North are the ones that hold universally applicable knowledge and expertise, while the 'local' partners hold only 'local' knowledge. Quoting Berenstain (2016), the authors stress how the demands for Global South partners to translate and 'contextualise' safeguarding policies created by Global North partners can amount to 'epistemic exploitation' – that is, the exploitation of knowledge – as those in positions of privilege demand that those who are marginalised do the work of contextualising while dismissing their knowledge and/or excluding them from the 'realm of recognized knowledge creators' (Daoust & Dyvik, 2020: 97).

The development of international ethics guidance documents for the Global South often highlights concerns regarding representation and diversity in academic scholarship. These guidelines primarily reflect concerns of the Global North, while voices from the Global South are often absent, leading to epistemic injustice, as emphasised by Pratt and de Vries (2023). This injustice is closely linked to enquiries into epistemic freedom, as articulated by Ndlovu-Gatsheni (2021) and Santos (2014), who advocate for cognitive justice and the recognition of diverse methods of understanding. Silencing the epistemologies and experiences of populations from the Global South reinforces cognitive injustice and coloniality of knowledge, as Tosam (2018) points out, perpetuating inequalities in valued knowledge production.

The absence of epistemic justice can result in what Ndlovu-Gatsheni (2018) terms 'epistemic violence', which must be considered in the development of safeguarding principles for international development research. Pratt and de Vries (2023) propose addressing epistemic justice through three layers: who produces ethical knowledge, which theories and concepts are applied, and whose voices are incorporated. They suggest avenues for achieving greater epistemic justice and decolonisation, including understanding the problem through context-specific research, fostering dialogue between North and South, and implementing structural changes in ethics funding, education, evaluation and publication. Ultimately, understanding the asymmetrical power relations and moving towards generating anti-/de-colonial knowledge may lead to achieving 'epistemic freedom' (Ndlovu-Gatsheni, 2018; Landström, 2024), allowing researchers to give voice to marginalised perspectives and overcome epistemic violence in international research (Mertens *et al.*, 2022).

In addressing the complexities of conducting research in international settings, we acknowledge the intersection of these challenges with safeguarding concerns. Researchers from the Global North can play a crucial role in fostering ethical, equitable and inclusive international research practices by critically examining their epistemic positions and politics. This may involve amplifying the voices of marginalised communities in the Global South through dialogue, knowledge exchange and the use of decolonising methodologies to ensure a fair and respectful approach to global knowledge production. Additionally, adherence to ethical principles of justice, equity and inclusion necessitates transparency in research processes, awareness of biases and genuine engagement with and fair distribution of benefits to local communities.

A further consideration is the importance of adequate training and of guidance on safeguarding in research. Basic training should be available to all researchers, and not only to those who deal with human participants, since safeguarding is also about the workplace (Orr *et al.*, 2019). Moreover, the lack of training and of guidance affects certain groups more than others. Orr *et al.* (2019: 5) found that 'women, junior researchers, and local fieldworkers are more likely to be at risk of harassment by fellow researchers and/or risks posed by challenging research contexts, topics, relationships'. In addition, unequal power relations are always present in research, and this may hinder partners in LMICs. Importantly, Orr *et al.* (2019: 5–6) report that:

> Discussions about safeguarding with partner organisations should be conducted in the spirit of two-way learning and capacity building, rather than imposed as a set of requirements, with honest acknowledgment of policy requirements that must be met. Agreed codes of conduct can clarify expectations of working relationships.

Summarising this third conundrum regarding the challenges of contextualising safeguarding in international research, we have highlighted concerns about the way in which safeguarding policies and procedures in research are currently a request that Western institutions put on LMIC partners. We have discussed how they may take on universal points but also the difficult balance between universality and imposition of Western perspectives. In doing so, we have discussed the researchers' epistemic responsibilities in cross-cultural research projects. We have questioned whether LMIC partners can contribute to shape safeguarding policies, as most research projects do not last long enough for them to be discussed and decided in a truly collaborative and informed way. We also noted that in this way safeguarding policies may end up overlooking the concerns, experiences and expertise that are available in LMICs that are involved in international projects, and further entrench power imbalances.

Third conundrum: Points for reflection and discussion

- Do you think safeguarding principles can be universal, or should each cultural context decide which safeguarding principles are relevant to that specific context?
- To what extent do you feel that safeguarding is imposing Western concerns onto LMIC partners?
- Whose responsibility is it to ensure that safeguarding is adhered to and what may be the challenges for local researchers and referents?
- What are the tensions between ensuring that safeguarding is fully localised and externalising accountability to partners who are often on much lower salaries and more precarious contracts than their counterparts in Western institutions?

- How can safeguarding become part of researchers' reflections on and questions about epistemic locations and politics and the ways in which these interact with the knowledge systems of the people and communities they work with?
- How could local practices of conflict resolution be embedded as part of safeguarding policies as a way to ensure capacity building and reciprocal learning in a sustainable way?

Final Reflections and Unsatisfying Conclusions

In this chapter we discussed: the concept of safeguarding and the challenges of clearly defining what this concept refers to and whom it is for; the origins and *raison d'être* of safeguarding in international development research; different understandings of vulnerability as a common human trait or as a disempowering attribute assigned to specific individuals and groups; and the way in which safeguarding may further entrench views of abuse and harm of people in vulnerable circumstances as perpetrated by 'rogue' individuals rather than as part of broader patterns embedded in inequality and power imbalances that need to be tackled at social and systemic levels. We also discussed the possibility of using the CA as a framework for safeguarding that can be adapted to different circumstances, and the challenges in ensuring that safeguarding does not become another requirement put on LMIC partners by Western institutions but, rather, is adapted to contextual understandings, approaches and practices.

For all the main points mentioned above, we have attempted to describe the challenges that are posed by the lack of clear definitions and agreed criteria; the ever-expanding remit of safeguarding policies; the lack of time in international research to effectively and collaboratively discuss these policies; the tensions between universality and locality; and the challenges inherent in requiring LMIC research staff to become responsible for the implementation and monitoring of policies. We have not tried to solve these challenges but, rather, have conceptualised them as three main conundrums relating to the following: the opacity of safeguarding; vulnerability and safeguarding; and contextualising safeguarding in international research. For each of these conundrums we have offered a rationale of the main points of discussion and contestation, as well as a set of questions that may be useful for researchers involved in international research projects in collaboration with LMICs to engage with when thinking about safeguarding policies.

Rather than offering definite answers – which we do not have – we think that the asking of questions and the collective looking for an answer may be the most important part of the process of designing safeguarding policies that do not pretend to offer easy, off-the-peg solutions. We believe that effective change starts from the acknowledgement of difficulties and conundrums as a way to work out ways to minimise them.

With this in mind, we argue that by tackling safeguarding concerns in international development research and examining the challenges outlined in this chapter, we have provided perspectives on how addressing these concerns could contribute, to some extent, to the promotion of sustainable peace, particularly at the micro-level. Safeguarding in international research fosters ethical behaviour, empowers communities and encourages collaboration, all essential components for sustainable peace. By involving communities in the research process and prioritising the welfare and rights of all stakeholders, safeguarding contributes to creating more environments conducive to peaceful coexistence and development. This fosters trust, respect, empowerment and inclusive participation, essential for fostering peaceful and prosperous communities.

References

BBC News (2018) Oxfam Haiti allegations: How the scandal unfolded. *BBC News*, 21 February. https://www.bbc.com/news/uk-43112200 (accessed 10 July 2024).

Butler, J. (2009) *Frames of War: When Is Life Grievable?* Verso.

Butler, J. (2020) *The Force of Nonviolence*. Verso.

Butler, J., Gambetti, Z. and Sabsay, L. (eds) (2016) *Vulnerability in Resistance*. Duke University Press.

Charusheela, S. (2009) Social analysis and the capabilities approach: A limit to Martha Nussbaum's universalist ethics. *Cambridge Journal of Economics* 33, 1135–1152.

CUSP (Culture for Sustainable and Inclusive Peace Network+) (2020) CUSP safeguarding policy. https://www.cuspnetwork.org/network-plus/safeguarding/ (accessed 23 August 2023).

Daoust, G. and Dyvik, S. (2020) Knowing safeguarding: The geopolitics of knowledge production in the humanitarian and development sector. *Geoforum* 112, 96–99.

Daoust, G. and Dyvik, S.L. (2022) Reconceptualizing vulnerability and safeguarding in the humanitarian and development sector. *Social Politics* 29 (1), 355–378.

Education Scotland (2021) Child protection and safeguarding policy. https://education.gov.scot/media/dkxhqhwz/child-protection-and-safeguarding-policy-es-feb21.pdf (accessed 23 August 2023).

Featherstone, B. and Gupta, A. (2017) The capability approach: What can it offer child protection policy and practice in England? In H. Otto, M. Walker and H. Ziegler (eds) *Capability-Promoting Policies: Enhancing Individual and Social Development* (pp. 183–200). Policy Press Scholarship.

Fineman, M.A. (2010) The vulnerable subject and the responsive state. *Emory Law Journal* 60 (2), 251–275. https://ssrn.com/abstract = 1694740.

Glissant, E. (1997) *Poetics of Relation* (trans. B. Wing). University of Michigan Press (original work published 1990).

Johnson, K. and Boland, B. (2019) Adult safeguarding under the Care Act 2014. *BJPsych Bulletin* 43 (1), 38–42. https://doi.org/10.1192/bjb.2018.71 (accessed 11 July 2024).

Koch, E. (2015) Protracted displacement in Georgia: Structural vulnerability and 'existing not living'. *Human Organization* 74 (2), 135–143. https://doi.org/10.17730/0018-7259-74.2.13.

Landström, K. (2024) On epistemic freedom and epistemic injustice. *Inquiry*, 1–24. https://doi.org/10.1080/0020174X.2024.2323561.

Latouche, A. (2023) Repoliticising gendered vulnerability: The blind spots of vulnerability-focused humanitarian programmes in Greece. In A. Miranda and A. Pérez-Caramés (eds) *Migration Patterns Across the Mediterranean* (pp. 179–194). Edward Elgar. https://doi.org/10.4337/9781800887350.

Mertens, C., Perazzone, S. and Mwambari, D. (2022) Fatal misconceptions: Colonial durabilities, violence and epistemicide in Africa's Great Lakes region. *Critical African Studies* 14 (1), 2–18. https://doi.org/10.1080/21681392.2022.2059901.

Mignolo, W. (2009) Who speaks for the 'human' in human rights? *Human Rights in Latin American and Iberian Cultures* 5 (1), 7–24.

Mishra, A.K. (2014) Safety net measures for unorganised workers in India: Critical gaps and challenges. *Social Change* 44 (2), 179–203. https://doi.org/10.1177/0049085714526278.

Ndlovu-Gatsheni, S.J. (2018) *Epistemic Freedom in Africa: Deprovincialization and Decolonization*. Routledge.

Ndlovu-Gatsheni, S.J. (2021) Epistemic injustice. In F.J. Carrillo and G. Koch (eds) *Knowledge for the Anthropocene* (pp. 167–177). Edward Elgar. https://doi.org/10.4337/9781800884298.00026.

NHS England (n.d.) About NHS England safeguarding. https://www.england.nhs.uk/safeguarding/about (accessed 11 July 2024).

Nussbaum, M. (2004) *Hiding from Humanity: Disgust, Shame, and the Law*. Princeton University Press.

Nussbaum, M. (2011) *Creating Capabilities*. Harvard University Press.

Orr, D., Daoust G., Dyvik, S.L., Puhan, S. and Boddy, J. (2019) *Safeguarding in an International Development Context*. Collaborative on Development Research. https://www.ukcdr.org.uk/news-article/ukcdr-publishes-draft-briefing-paper-and-evidence-review-on-safeguarding-in-international-development-research/ (accessed 23 August 2023).

Pillay, N. (2019) Are human rights universal? *UN Chronicle*. https://www.un.org/en/chronicle/article/are-human-rights-universal (accessed 11 July 2024).

Pratt, B. and de Vries, J. (2023) Where is knowledge from the global South? An account of epistemic justice for a global bioethics. *Journal of Medical Ethics* 49, 325–334.

Racines (2021) Gender-based violence in Morocco. https://www.racines-aisbl.org/en/base_documentaire/gender-based-violence-morocco/ (accessed 23 August 2023).

SafeLives (2020) Impact report 2020–21. https://safelives.org.uk/sites/default/files/resources/SafeLives_Impact%20Report%202020%E2%80%9321_Digital_A-compressed.pdf (accessed 23 August 2023).

Santos, S.B. (2014) *Epistemologies of the South: Justice Against Epistemicide*. Paradigm.

Scottish Government (2007) The Adult Support and Protection (Scotland) Act (2007). https://www.gov.scot/publications/adult-support-protection-scotland-act-2007-short-introduction-part-1-act (accessed 23 August 2023).

Sen, A. (1999) *Development as Freedom*. Oxford University Press.

Spivak, G.C. (2011) Righting wrongs. In A.S. Rathore and A. Cistelecan (eds) *Wronging Rights? Philosophical Challenges for Human Rights* (pp. 78–103). Routledge. https://doi.org/10.1215/00382876-103-2-3-523.

Szkupinski Quiroga, S., Medina, D.M. and Glick, J. (2014) In the belly of the beast: Effects of anti-immigration policy on Latino community members. *American Behavioral Scientist* 58 (13), 1723–1742. https://doi.org/10.1177/0002764214537270.

Tosam, M.J. (2018) African perspectives in global bioethics. *Developing World Bioethics* 18 (3), 208–211.

UK Government (2010) Equality Act 2010. https://www.legislation.gov.uk/ukpga/2010/15/contents (accessed 12 July 2024).

UK Government (2014a) Care Act 2014. https://www.legislation.gov.uk/ukpga/2014/23/contents/enacted (accessed 12 July 2024).

UK Government (2014b) Care and support statutory guidance: Using the Care Act. https://www.gov.uk/government/publications/care-act-statutory-guidance/care-and-support-statutory-guidance#safeguarding-1 (accessed 12 July 2024).

UK Government (2015) *Adult Safeguarding: Prevention and Protection in Partnership*. Department of Health. https://www.health-ni.gov.uk/publications/adult-safeguarding-prevention-and-protection-partnership-key-documents (accessed 23 August 2023).

UK Government (2023) Statutory guidance: Care and support statutory guidance. https://www.gov.uk/government/publications/care-act-statutory-guidance/care-and-support-statutory-guidance (accessed 12 July 2024).

UKCDR (2018) Annual report 2018–19. https://www.ukcdr.org.uk/resource/ukcdr-annual-report-2018-19 (accessed 23 August 2023).

UKCDR (2019) Safeguarding in international development research: Briefing paper. https://www.ukcdr.org.uk/resource/safeguarding-in-international-development-research-briefing-paper/ (accessed 23 August 2023).

UKCDR (2020a) Safeguarding in international development research: Report on phase 2 international consultation. https://www.ukcdr.org.uk/wp-content/uploads/2020/04/170420-UKCDR-Safeguarding-Phase-2-International-Consulations-Report.pdf (accessed 23 August 2023).

UKCDR (2020b) Guidance on safeguarding in international development research. https://www.ukcdr.org.uk/resource/guidance-on-safeguarding-in-international-development-research (accessed 23 August 2023).

United Nations (n.d.) Universal Declaration of Human Rights. https://www.un.org/en/about-us/universal-declaration-of-human-rights (accessed 12 July 2024).

Virokannas, E., Liuski, S. and Kuronen, M. (2020) The contested concept of vulnerability – A literature review. *European Journal of Social Work* 23 (2), 327–339. https://doi.org/10.1080/13691457.2018.1508001.

12 Between Success and Failure: Researching with Grassroots Organisations Involved in Conflict Transformation

Julie E. McAdam, Cristina Amescua and Evelyn Arizpe

Introduction

As researchers we spend considerable amounts of our academic time engaged in writing grants, carrying out research and writing it up for academic publication with notions of 'publish or perish' becoming a way of life. This chapter explores our lived experiences as academic researchers working on a project on gender violence and peace, funded by UK Research and Innovation (UKRI), titled Culture for Sustainable and Inclusive Peace Network Plus (CUSP N+), that united teams of researchers and artists across six countries: Mexico, Palestine, Ghana, Zimbabwe, Morocco and the UK. In March 2020 we, the Mexican co-investigators (based in the UK and Mexico), were working our way towards gathering in Ghana to discuss the aims, objectives and intended outcomes of the project, when COVID-19 lockdowns occurred. Like the rest of the world, we had to adapt by moving all our work online, and it was not until over two years later, in October 2022, that we were able to come together physically. In the meantime, we negotiated internet connectivities and time-zone differences and, through virtual meetings and workshops, attempted to use this online space to build a community of enquiry to take forward the aims of the project. In the midst, and on top, of the pandemic, our research funding was brutally cut. Figure 12.1 provides a visual snapshot of the way the project ran, showing the key events and disruptions.

The Mexican team consisted of two co-investigators, one in Scotland (University of Glasgow) and one in Mexico (the National Autonomous University of Mexico, UNAM). The research associates and partners were all located in Mexico; all meetings were conducted via Zoom, generating conversations and memos in Spanish and English. Multilingual meetings

Figure 12.1 Timeline of events from March 2020 to October 2022

became the norm and multiple platforms were used to move between languages (for example, Google Translate). For over a year we planned how to take our shared expertise of how to use picture books in contexts of crisis and empower grassroots collectives (*colectivos*) to make applications for small grants to carry their work forward. In Mexico and Latin America, these collectives work to understand and transform conflict, using arts and culture to move towards social justice for minority groups. '*Colectivas*', the feminine version of the term, is used by some groups of women as a political act against the murder and erasure of women; this tends to promote women's rights, autonomy and empowerment and work against gender violence or violence against children. This is the term we will use throughout the chapter.

Introducing Conflict

One of the first challenges the Mexican team had to face was our own assemblage. We had not worked together as a group, and we each had a slightly different emphasis in our research or our practical focus, even if we all worked with cultural issues. As we will explore in a later section, some of the team members had some work and experiences in common, and some bilateral longstanding relationships, but the articulation of the whole team was yet to be built and consolidated.

Another important challenge that is worth mentioning is that, when we proposed, back in 2019, the core idea of the work that could be done in Mexico, the focus was on working with vulnerable groups (mainly children and immigrants) through literature and picture books to analyse conflict transformation. Nevertheless, when the general CUSP N+ proposal was approved for funding, a fundamental aspect that then became salient was the need to emphasise work against gender-based violence and the empowerment of girls and women through arts-based initiatives. For us, this implied finding and contacting an additional set of grassroots organisations with which only one of the members of our team had connections. In the end, we started building what we hoped to be our community of enquiry in a context characterised by diversity, long-distance interactions (even before COVID-19) and unequally strong–weak pre-existing relations.

We had then to work towards getting to know each other while seeking to communicate concisely what is a very complex and rich project with many branches, specificities, phases, aims and scopes; getting to know the work of all the different grassroots organisations we were aiming to include in the project; and building a common understanding and a common language to orient our endeavours. Then came the pandemic, with its multiple and globally shared challenges: having to live in a constant state of uncertainty and emergency and between health concerns; practical issues on how to face confinement; how to solve economic problems (particularly for those of us who do not have a steady income, which is the case for most of the people working in the *colectivas*, and some of the members of the team at UNAM); and trying to adapt to the virtual world.

After almost a year navigating these complicated currents, the Mexican team, along with all the international teams, was very excited when the CUSP project was officially launched on International Women's Day (8 March 2021), with online announcements being made about the scope and aims of each geographical location. However, three days later, on 11 March, the UK government announced cuts that stopped our work overnight and left us in shock. The UKRI (the national agency that funds science and research) receives funding from the Official Development Assistance (ODA) budget, which the government suddenly reduced from 0.7% to 0.5% of the gross national income (GNI) (UKRI, 2021). These reductions affected the Global Challenges Research Funds (GCRF) for projects like CUSP N+ that sought to address 'global' concerns. Nwako *et al.* (2023) have analysed the impact these cuts have had on multiple project outcomes and clearly critique the harm wrought upon researchers evidenced in 'material, psychological and relational' ways (2023: 65). They hold the UK government and research councils accountable for not living up to their published principle of 'doing no harm'. We entered a period of confusion; our expectations, our targets, our goals and our timelines were gone, and what replaced them was silence, for we knew not what to do or say. Klein (2008) outlines such government tactics as a deliberate way to create an alternative crisis through the production of shock and confusion, taking attention away from the issues under discussion. The UK government, working under the subterfuge of a spending review created by the pandemic, aimed to dismantle our collective work to counter inequality and privilege. We were forced to answer some serious questions regarding the tensions and turmoil caused by the cuts, questions that challenged whether 'equitable research partnerships are possible within the current systems of research governance'(Nwako *et al.*, 2013: 70). This chapter examines how the cuts impacted on our work and relationships with the *colectivas* and provides some suggestions for how to frame future work with grassroots groups, leaving further critique of the UKRI to Alison Phipps in the final chapter of this volume.

Methodology

This was not a chapter that we set out to write; it became possible and necessary only because of the UKRI cuts in the context of global disruption caused by the pandemic. Our methodological approach was not planned; it grew creatively out of our need to reframe our thinking. To explain our approach we draw on Pratt *et al.*'s (2022) term 'methodological bricolage', which allows us to explain our moves or methodological choices as we 'made do' in the immediate aftermath of the cuts; 'utilised the resources at hand' as we listened more carefully to the *colectivas* regarding the impact of the cuts on their ability to trust and work with us; and 'combined these for the new purpose' (Pratt *et al.*, 2022: 219), which we will explain via a series of methodological moves.

Our first move was to look for a framework to help us with our thinking and initially we were drawn to the work of Cummings *et al.* (2023: 8), who reframe epistemic injustice as epistemic justice based on the need to maintain a positive focus that avoids resistance. However, we also wanted to acknowledge the resistance; therefore, we decided to make use of queer thinking and create a Greimas square, a heuristic tool, to interrogate that awkward space where our work seemed to be failing. Our second move was to use our Greimas square (explained in the section below) in an analysis of what would traditionally be known as data. Our third move was to discuss the themes emerging as insights from working in the space of new possibilities opened up by the Greimas square; we also iteratively returned to literature that was in ontological keeping with our overall aims, to discuss our organic ways of making do, getting by and framing our ongoing work. To complete this section, we have included a further discussion of our data, providing insights into how it was generated; how we selected it for analysis; our positionality as researchers/bricoleurs; and how this influenced the creation of data that we would never have anticipated creating at the grant application stage.

Our work and the generation of texts and artefacts

We have referred several times in the chapter to our work and wish to make it clear that we use the term in an Arendtian sense, since she distinguishes between labour and work (Arendt, 1998: 79–80). Labour carries with it the potential to be alienating and oppressive, whereas Arendt's notion of work is connected to building, making and maintaining a world fit for all. As we worked, we drew on the cultural tools and artefacts that surrounded us, paying attention to the way we used existing texts and collectively produced new texts via multiple platforms to communicate, acknowledging the devices and people we called upon to aid translation. Gualandi et al. (2023) find that even with the arts and humanities, the term 'data' permeates the ways we speak and write about our work, and we recognise it as a problematic term. We concur with their work but constantly find ourselves using the term, which reduces the complexity of the material produced within any collaborative process, a word that contributes to further alienation.

Within this context we will refer to our work as the production of multimodal texts and artefacts which can be sorted using the rupture created by the UKRI cuts, falling into sets of material produced before, during and after. In the period before the cuts, we amassed documents and artefacts connected to the overall purpose of the project – strengthening the capacity of the *colectivas* to do their work, facilitated through small grants for each of them. During and just after the cuts, correspondence around our reactions to the turmoil expressed shock and support in favour of reversal. Then there was what we were able to do after the cuts had been restored, though by then trust had been broken. Here we produced letters of apology as a way of acknowledging the violence caused by the cuts and taking responsibility for events. The final set of materials produced relates to the period when we were finally able to meet face to face as a team in Cuernavaca, Mexico, in October 2022. It is these materials that we draw upon to reflect upon our praxis.

Positionality

The positionality of each of the *colectivas* affected the ways we were able to progress, regress and move towards restoration of trust. The partnerships with UNAM, IBBY (the Asociación para Leer, Escuchar, Escribir y Recrear A.C., a non-governmental association that promotes reading) and two of the *colectivas* had been built through previous work on displacement and picture books led by Evelyn, who, as a dual Mexican-British national, has for many years attempted to work with children's literature in both countries. Her aim has been to create connections between researchers and third-sector organisations in both countries, so the CUSP Network seemed to be the ideal way to strengthen some of these links. Although trust was broken, the effects were somewhat mitigated because there were deep and longstanding relationships (and this was also the case with the relationship of the UNAM team with some of the other *colectivas*). The ways of working, however, also raised questions for Evelyn, such as her assuming the role of translator between languages and cultures, which meant, among other responsibilities, trying to convey the nuances of both. The challenges that the cuts presented led to the need to reflect on her linguistic (and academic) privilege and what it means to (self-)assume that 'in between' role, as well as being open to the changes to language and culture over the years, such as new feminist and decolonial forms of speaking.

Julie's position on the project team could be critiqued as being somewhat precarious, as both an outsider to the Mexican context and a learner of Spanish. She was troubled by her lack of connection to the people and places within the project. Writing up her reflections about the work carried out by the *colectivas*, whose working spaces were often in flux, she noted: 'if you know how to be included in one space, you might then know how to be included in another space'. She understood that this applied to herself and that she could draw on previous work in contexts of flux in the Middle East. She reflected on the ways in which Evelyn and Cristina were key to her invitation into this research space, an invitation that was based on trust.

Cristina, like Evelyn, is bilingual and faced some of the already mentioned challenges of being 'in between' and similar reflections on privilege. At the moment of entering CUSP N+, she was also caught up on other big projects that demanded her attention; therefore, she recruited a team of anthropologists with different sets of abilities and specific training, as follows. Edith and Carolina were two members of the team with whom she had been working for several years in the field of intangible cultural heritage. Carolina, on top of her anthropological training, was also an accountant and could work on the administrative aspects of the project, while Edith has a particularly developed ethnographic sensibility, which allows her to build strong relationships wherever she goes. Berenice had just completed her master's degree in anthropology and had a close involvement with local *colectivas* from Morelos, one of which she founded and in which she is one of the main activists. All three of them had important strengths but none of them used English in their work. Team UNAM was completed by Aline, a language teacher and art therapist who was in charge of ensuring the back-and-forth communication of the team with participants from other latitudes. Cristina oversaw the coordination and articulation of all Mexico's team members. But the state of awe and uncertainty mentioned above engendered important and life-changing sandstorms in both her personal and professional contexts. She was supposed to ensure proper communication with her fellow co-investigators, her team and hence with IBBY and the *colectivas*. But she was paralysed. She could not react since all her energy was then directed at juggling the falling parts of her world, and her silence had a profound impact in allowing a feeling of discomfort and distrust to grow both within the coordinating team (Team UNAM, and IBBY) and most of all with the *colectivas*, which experienced this lack of communication and clarity as epistemic and institutional violence towards their already precarious work conditions.

Between success and failure

As our ontological position valued care, love and transformation, we responded to the period of enforced turmoil by drawing on previous work. We were reminded of Halberstam's (2011) arguments that success equates with heteronormativity and that within economies obsessed with wealth, deliverables and measurements, queers are deemed to fail. In a queer world, failing, losing, forgetting, unmaking, unbecoming, not knowing, offer alternative ways of being in this world (Halberstam, 2011: 2). Queers cannot succeed, and so they can view failure as a liberating practice, since it opens up sites of rupture and possibility (Haiven & Khasnabish, 2014: 123).

To open up these spaces we have used a heuristic tool known as a Greimas or semiotic square that explodes the binary, opening up multiple horizons of thought (Haiven & Khasnabish, 2014: 123). Once in this space, we revisit our research material, our correspondence, memos, photographs and memories of the time we worked together and use these as prompts to engage in reflexive thinking about our positionality and praxis as researchers. We use this framework to reframe our methodological approach and present ways of working that move beyond a perpetuation of the epistemic injustices created through engaging in research limited by concepts of success and failure. These ways of working are a step towards 'dismantling the master's house' (Lorde, 2018) while allowing us to keep focused on how to dwell alongside those working outside the academy for transformative change.

Drawing heavily on Haiven and Khasnabish's application of the Greimas square to work with social movements, we explore how its application allows us to explore our context. This approach could be applied to any human endeavour, but here we are using it to explore our ways of working with the Mexican *colectivas*. In Figure 12.2, we explain the expanded square and, when viewing it, we would suggest the viewer starts with the points shown at A, 'Research that flourishes', and at B, 'Research that fails', a simplified view of a binary relationship. What the square allows is the creation of two counter-states, shown at C, a state where the research 'does not flourish', and D, where the research 'does not fail'. Haiven and Khasnabish (2014: 123) advise that research that flourishes is not the same as to not flourish, and research that fails is not the same as

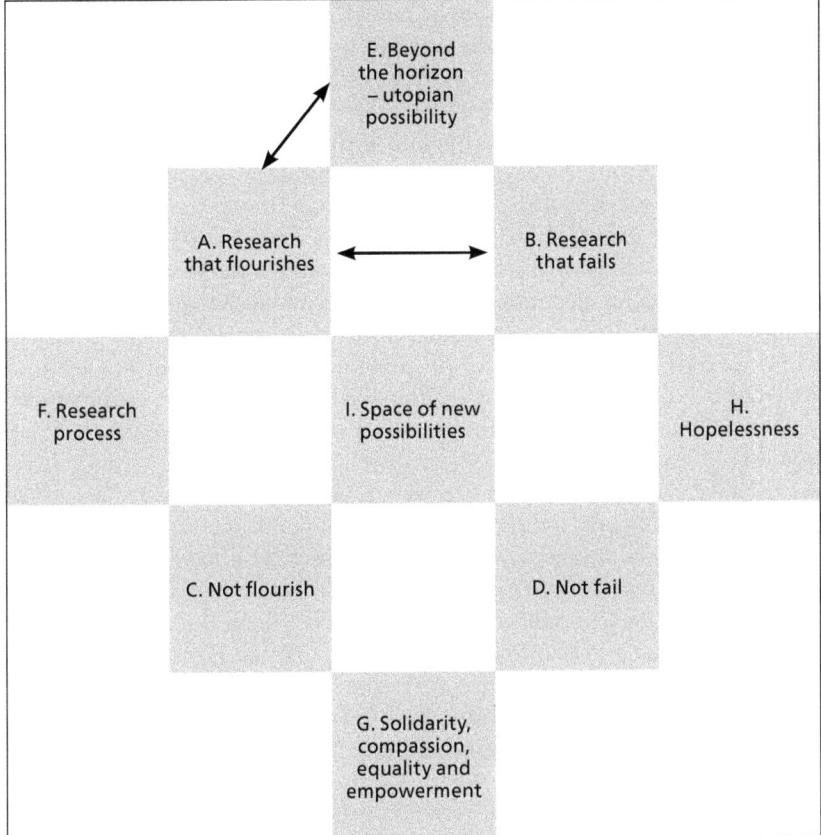

Figure 12.2 Opening up spaces of new possibility using a Greimas square

to not fail. This first expanded square illuminates that when we talk in binaries, we are accounting for only a partial view or understanding of reality, and further expansions of the square will allow further views of what might be possible.

This first expanded square (ABCD) illuminates that when we talk in binaries (AB), we are accounting for only a partial view or understanding of reality and that further expansions (to ABCD and EFGH) of the square will allow further views of what might be possible. In the second expansion (EFGH) and moving upwards, metaphorically aiming for the horizon, we imagine what can be, shown at E, and explained as the utopian possibilities of existing in a space where we have reconstituted our lives without violence. This dimension, even if currently out of sight, is desirable and provides a focus for what can be, a reason for proceeding, dreaming and hoping. Beyond the scope of this chapter, this state, if realised, could feasibly preclude the need for research into peace (Haiven & Khasnabish, 2014: 136), although we would question whether such a state would be sustainable or require continual work.

On the left-hand side, shown at F, we have the normalised research process or project, which must operate within our current society, riddled with instances of violence, oppression and injustice, becoming a process that could be described as tainted. This requires us to ask questions about how our results-driven academic agendas might contribute to the exploitation of all involved. However, if they are understood as processes worth revisiting, considering the conceptual possibilities afforded by E, then they can become more meaningful. Moving towards the right, shown at H, we have named this space 'hopelessness', a space that Haiven and Khasnabish discuss in terms of exploitation and researcher responsibility (2014: 135). This would describe the space we all occupied on first hearing about the UKRI cuts, but it was a space that we had to leave behind, as we were pulled back towards our everyday possibilities at G. This is a space where we can respond pragmatically and prefigure the types of working that overcome the imbalances wrought upon us by hopelessness (H) and the need to be productive (F). Every conceivable link between each of the expanded squares represents a negotiation of ideological tensions between utopian thinking and everyday praxis as we position ourselves to look for creative solutions that are shown at (I), the space of new possibilities.

In the next section, we apply the semiotic square, using it to reflect on our work, thinking through how our images of utopian possibility (E) sustained us, as we worked between the tensions created by working between hopelessness (H) and research productivity (F) to find everyday possibilities (G). These new possibilities foregrounded strategies and ways of being that embrace transformation.

Application of the Greimas square to our work

The next four sub-sections provide our reflections on our collaborative work with the *colectivas* as viewed through the Greimas square. When pertinent, we have added quotes or examples from our texts to illustrate the points being made. These have been anonymised, and we have used pseudonyms that reflect the cultural heritage of the original names used.

Towards utopian possibility

Utopian possibilities exist beyond the horizon, which suggests they are out of reach. However, researchers can use this imaginary space to frame and strategise how they work in the present. To initiate our work, we decided to function as a community of enquiry, drawing on McAdam's (2019) work in this space. This 'community of enquiry' format was designed to safeguard knowledge production as a collaborative cultural activity and acknowledge that we had shared values regarding the potential of using arts, with an emphasis on children's literature and a common aim of wanting to end gender violence (McAdam, 2019: 296). McAdam used storytelling to evoke trust and care among community members, inviting each to share an artefact of value and explain its significance in their lives, and she found that the stories told allowed the community members to engage in acts of mutual care, creating an ethical foundation for all that would follow (McAdam, 2019: 295). We decided to open our initial CUSP N+ meeting by inviting everyone to share an artefact of value. Many of the artefacts brought to the meeting were related to our mothers and grandmothers or instances of the written word.

For example, Evelyn shared the published biography of one of her great-great-grandmothers, who migrated from Ireland to Latin America in the mid-19th century, with a view not so much towards the past, but towards the present and future of women who must find their own paths through a world of tensions between privilege and destitution, between peace and conflict. Julie shared a patchwork quilt made by her mother using fabrics from her childhood. The quilt acted as a metaphor reminding her of the important ways in which women in her family had helped her through personal conflict, 'doing practical things to help you stitch your life back together'. As we shared our stories, we began a process of transformation at our local level, laying down ways of working connected to social relations, decision-making, trust and care. This transformation was not beyond the horizon, existing as a utopian possibility; its existence was brought into being in the present, as we prefigured the type of society we wished to create in the future.

A further source of utopian possibility for the community was provided by picture books. We viewed these as aesthetic and cultural artefacts imbued with transformational power that could trigger a range of creative responses (Arizpe & Styles, 2003; Arizpe et al., 2023). They were instrumental in the work done with reading mediators working in critical contexts of displacement within previous work carried out by the network Children's Literature in Critical Contexts of Displacement (see our website https://www.childslitspaces.com) set up with partners CRIM/UNAM and IBBY Mexico in 2017 and funded by the UK Arts and Humanities Research Counci (AHRC).

Often dismissed as either superficial entertainment or a didactic tool, children's literature can be a powerful vehicle for sharing stories that create safe spaces. By this we mean spaces where respectful dialogue can occur and where topics usually silenced can be discussed, with both sympathy and humour, such as fears and anxieties but also bodily functions such as defecation or menstruation. There are many that deal with conflict through challenging and controversial themes such as bullying, displacement, death and violence; however, these stories can provide counter-narratives to danger and conflict, emphasising positive emotions such as joy and love.

They also prefigure ways of addressing problems, demonstrating home-building, friendships, inter-generational relationships and reciprocity, and thus provide a means to construct and interpret the world, everyday life and also ways of envisioning the future (McAdam *et al.*, 2020: 394). The unique interlocking interaction between words and images offered by picture books invites readers of all ages, cultural backgrounds and literacy levels to experience and share the story, engaging with others and with arts-based practices.

The demands of the research process

The CUSP N+ project functioned as a network (see Figure 12.3) and the work with the *colectivas* had been planned in three phases. The first phase was to create a community of enquiry that would unite participants working within IBBY Mexico and UNAM to collaboratively create workshops that focused on transformation, in terms of how it might play out in children's literature and how we could develop research methods to explore it. In this initial phase we supported mediators to take forward small-scale projects that used texts. We shared these examples via the Children's Literature in Contexts of Displacement website and reflected on how to share our findings with a wider group of *colectivas* in phase 2.

To initiate phase 2, we ran a series of workshops and listened to feedback from the *colectivas* on issues of importance, which were connected to time, resources and clarity of shared aims and ways of working. It was felt that time was never fully costed, and that transformational work undertaken by *colectivas* meant engaging in volunteering, which presented a challenge when activist mediators were engaged in several projects and using their own time. Women with families felt there was a double burden placed on their time to engage in transformational work and often a financial burden as they used their wages from other jobs to supplement activist work. Accessing finances to resource their work also added to the time required, with many of the *colectivas* alluding to tensions created as they negotiated the difference between 'their organic ways of working and having to change what they were doing to align with what funders wanted' (Bertha). Noemy talked of the need to 'reconcile the ethical position of the collective with the institutions that offer funding'. The paperwork required by funders presented challenges in terms of time and because it needed to be written using the language and discourse of the funders. One *colectiva* pointed out that self-funding was often a way to solve this issue, because having to dialogue with the 'people who have the resources, sometimes feels like receiving charity' (Elena). Practical issues were raised, such as what funders expected in terms of the timeline for results, as well as 'the difficulties in documenting the voices and images of those who experience violence' (Beatriz).

The *colectivas* presented us with some serious questions regarding the funding processes we were using in phase 2 (via applications for small

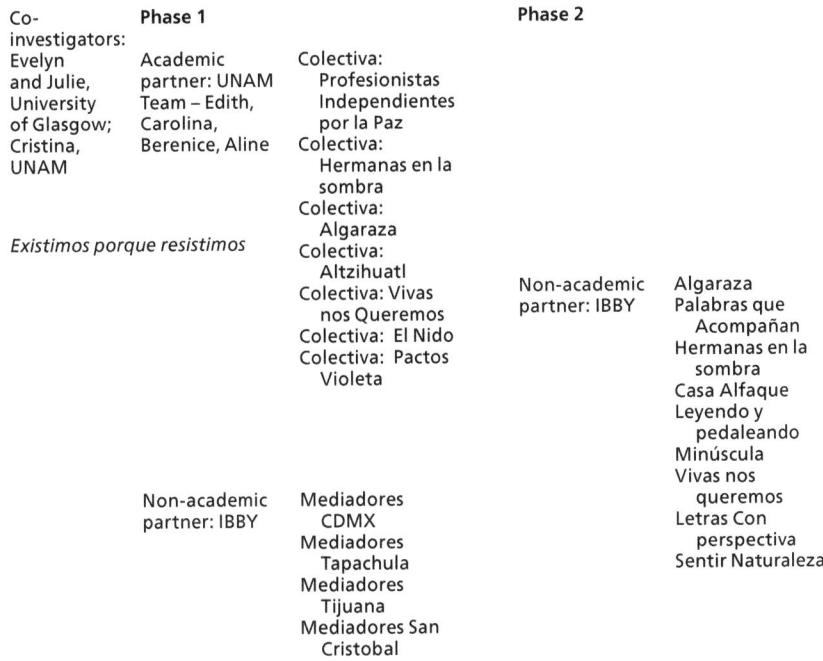

Figure 12.3 Overview of the relationships between the named organisations and the *colectivas*

grants) as well as regarding the ways of documenting and synthesising the outputs of phase 2 in phase 3. At this stage, several *colectivas* made the decision to 'stay off grid' and not get involved in making an application for a small grant. They recognised the 'strength in establishing networks between collectives' (Noemy) but were not prepared to compromise their group's ethics to meet the requirements of the grant applications. Our project processes had been created to model business management systems that operate on logical frameworks, which are ostensibly objective and goal orientated (Økland, 2015: 106). To a degree, they reinforce the systemic violence experienced by marginalised groups caught up in conflict through their requirements to discuss aims, objectives, timing, outputs, impact and sustainability. We may as researchers be able to collaborate and assist in mitigating the excesses of paperwork, but we first need to acknowledge that our adherence to logical frameworks silences those unable or unwilling to participate. One of the *colectivas* expressed a desire for 'further dialogue between both parties' (Hugo) on what it means to write aims and objectives when contexts are shifting. As our thinking entered a space where we were willing to start questioning our intervention as well as the suitability of our intervention, the cuts were announced, and all the work carried out to support the writing of applications for small grants became meaningless – there were no funds.

Hopelessness

The impact of launching our project on International Women's Day on 8 March 2021, followed closely by the announcement on 11 March of the UKRI's cuts to mainly GCRF projects, was beyond our disbelief. Many academics around the world face precarity regarding research funding, but these cuts were unprecedented within the UK's funding landscape. Imperiale and Phipps (2022: 73) responded to the cuts by carrying out a critical metaphor analysis of the ways in which researchers wrote about and discussed the cuts. They found these cuts were discussed in terms of violence, illness and threat, with research positioning itself as connection, health and a journey. The equitable partnerships we had been mindfully building were swept away as we let our partners down, and we entered an uncomfortable period of enforced waiting and silence. Our meetings stopped, the grants were not processed and the *colectivas* expressed their anger at further epistemic violence being imposed upon them.

We do not wish to dwell on this period; it was bleak, troubled and our fight to reverse the cuts was not one that the *colectivas* had time to engage in. Moreover, there was a sense of the unintelligibility of what the cuts meant, how they were going to be implemented and how they would end up affecting the actual work with the *colectivas*. Even if they had been able to articulate with the co-investigators in Glasgow, they didn't know where they could fit in that fight. While they expressed solidarity with us, we broke their trust, and this had to be rebuilt before any work could be recommenced in July 2022. For the first time in our academic lives, we wrote apologies. Evelyn explained that the cuts were 'so unexpected and profound that for the moment they left us paralysed'. Julie wrote about 'confusion and fear' and the ways in which 'undemocratic practices chip away at the ways in which we work to counter inequality and privilege'. We explained that we had joined the protests but the main reason for writing the apologies was to take responsibility for 'doing more in terms of ensuring that communication continued to bring everyone up to date with the facts affecting the entire CUSP project' (Evelyn) and that we needed to do more in terms of 'taking great care not to perpetuate inequality and injustice' (Julie).

Although these apologies paved the way for re-establishing dialogue, only some of the *colectivas* decided to continue with the project, and IBBY opened up the spaces to include new groups with which it started the small-grant proposals. But the apologies also paved the way for greater awareness of the ways in which we needed to be constantly vigilant against causing further instances of epistemic injustice. The next section discusses some of the ways in which we pushed back, alongside the *colectivas*.

Solidarity

As we worked, we organically negotiated and found solutions, often drawing on advice from our colleagues working on the larger CUSP project. Alison Phipps suggests that a reflective stance on researching multilingually can actively begin to chip away at some of the structural inequalities created by current academic practices where partnerships can often reproduce colonial violence (Phipps, 2019). In the context of the CUSP Mexico team, there were tensions between the use of Spanish and English, with translation during meetings and other events taking place either in person or through Zoom chats resulting, for example, in having slides written in English as a *lingua franca* during presentations in Spanish to other country teams by the Mexican team. We had to negotiate the use of language and the move between English and Spanish depending on the context and topic, and often paused to unpick or clarify particular words. In this back and forth between languages there was a concern that meaning could be lost; however, we also learned that meanings could be found or amplified, that a greater sensitivity to body language could be cultivated and that even 'getting the gist' was 'vital' to 'frame and narrate' even that which cannot be known without a language (Phipps, 2019: 43). There was a sense that language was not enough to name the implicit and explicit violence that the *colectivas* were attempting to redress, and therefore we had to resort to symbols and the search for new ways of expressing ourselves.

This also applies to an awareness of the traditional imposition of Spanish and its gendered and rigid forms, which also marginalise Indigenous groups, women and young people. The *colectivas* and the research partners' choice of language was a deliberate attempt to subvert traditional ways of speaking and writing that promoted masculinity. For example, the collective noun for children, *niños*, became *niñes*. Going further still, the feminine collective noun *todas* was used even when men were included in those groups, and perhaps the strongest message was placed in the word *cuerpa*, making the body not masculine (or even neutral, as some would argue), but strongly feminine. *Lenguas* (in English, 'tongues', as parts of the body and also languages) were also part of the discussion of having to learn to use them differently: to name, to protest, to subvert and also to pronounce the unfamiliar. A space was also created for words such as menstruation, violation and abortion. At the same time, we learnt to acknowledge silence.

Many of the *colectivas* used picture books throughout the CUSP N+ project, especially within the small projects run through IBBY with reading mediators. The symbolic significance of books and picture books as ways to begin conversations and generate conversations on key themes with children provided an organic way for our wider group to initiate complex and challenging dialogue about our work. The metaphorical safe space surrounding the picture books and other literary texts allowed us to re-establish connections when the wider project team was finally able to meet in person. For example, one reading mediator used the picture book *¡Estela, grita muy fuerte!* by Isabel Olid and Martina Vanda (published by Fineo, 2008) – a picture book about learning to speak up about/shout against sexual abuse – to introduce the workshops she carried out for young migrant girls (who usually have no intimate spaces in refuges) to speak of their bodies. The project not only attempts to name and push against the violence which even very young girls can be subjected to in a domestic space but also overlaps with the projects of other *colectivas* that resist and speak of female solidarity and safe spaces. The symbolic significance of books and picture books to begin conversations and generate dialogue on key themes was a unifying and healing concept for all involved since we all valued the primacy of storytelling.

Conclusion: Making Space for New Possibilities When Working with *Colectivas*

Project models and funding systems have been established to measure for efficiency, effectiveness, impact, relevance and sustainability (Økland, 2015: 106). Each of these elements prompts the need for a round of further questions; especially when framed through the violent impact of the UKRI cuts. Phipps (2019: 4) asks researchers prepared to work in decolonial ways to consider the many judgements to be made about what to do with our privilege: 'own it; use it; pass it on; pass on it; make space; and many other arts which need a lifetime of struggle, apology, repatriation and some mutual celebration'. Using the expanded dimensions of the Greimas square, we were able to frame our struggles, create apologies, come together and celebrate our work over meals and begin to develop an ontological approach that embraces values of solidarity, compassion, equality and empowerment. These ways of being embrace transformation, but they cannot be captured as strategies and tactics (which could perpetuate epistemic violence); therefore, we conclude this chapter with a set of recommendations phrased as reflective questions that could be used by fellow researchers faced with similar contexts of flux.

The first set of questions is very much focused on nurturing the possibilities that lie ahead (E in Figure 12.2). We suggest that it is vital to spend time probing and developing an understanding of the imagined space one wishes to occupy before commencing a period of work. Sharing and naming the dimensions of the imagined space can help sustain work through challenges. This step should not be confused with goal setting or writing mission statements, for these can be acknowledged in the second set of questions.

- How do you ontologically frame collaborative research?

- What do the group hope to achieve by working collaboratively?
- Would you use arts-based strategies to develop relationships before commencing a research collaboration?
- Would you return to the arts to sustain you throughout the research?

The next set of questions pays attention to the institutional or funding demands made of the research process (F in Figure 12.2), recognising that there are ways to highlight the economic integrity of the work we do. In contexts of precarity, it is vital that we do not contribute further to the precarity of those with whom we collaborate.

- How will you negotiate tensions presented via the research funder in terms of meeting requirements and completing paperwork?
- What costing models will you use to recognise the time and contribution of collaborators?
- Will you avoid terms such as 'in-kind'?

The third set of questions is perhaps the hardest to consider for those used to working within 'funded scenarios', but for many colleagues across the globe these are everyday questions. Moving beyond hopelessness (H in Figure 12.2) to actively seeking alternatives becomes the reality (see Chapter 5 of the present volume, by Arizpe et al.).

- Can moments of tension be discussed in advance?
- Is there space within timelines to plan for the unexpected?
- What plans exist for communication during moments of flux or precarity?
- How can we prepare for 'no more funding' scenarios?

We suggest that in planning research work that can be impactful and sustainable, paying attention to these types of questions ahead of the project will evidence a commitment to solidarity.

- How do we acknowledge our academic and linguistic privilege from the onset?
- What languages will be used across the project?
- How will translation be used? And costed?
- What discussions will take place surrounding the gains and losses of translation?
- What multimodal forms of communication will be used (books, artefacts, dance, singing, quilt-making)?
- How will participants be incorporated into disseminated outputs?

These questions function as our conclusion, for the establishment of solidarity (G in Figure 12.2) is often the reality of our contexts, the day-to-day space where we can push back, prefigure and continue to write and research, so that we can avoid the epistemic injustices wrought by the precarious context created by the UK government. It is to these questions we will return in the preparation of any future work with grassroots organisations.

References

Arendt, H. (1998) *The Human Condition* (2nd edn). University of Chicago Press.

Arizpe, E. and Styles, M. (2003) *Children Reading Pictures: Interpreting Visual Texts*. Taylor and Francis.

Arizpe, E., Noble, K. and Styles, M. (2023) *Children Reading Pictures: New Contexts and Approaches to Picturebooks*. Routledge.

Cummings, S., Dhewa, C., Kemboi, G. and Young, S. (2023) Doing epistemic justice in sustainable development: Applying the philosophical concept of epistemic injustice to the real world. *Sustainable Development* 31 (3), 1–13. https://doi.org/10.1002/sd.2497.

Gualandi, B., Pareschi, L. and Peroni, S. (2023) What do we mean by 'data'? A proposed classification of data types in the arts and humanities. *Journal of Documentation* 79 (7), 51–71.

Haiven, M. and Khasnabish, A. (2014) *The Radical Imagination: Social Movement Research in the Age of Austerity*. Zed Books.

Halberstam, J. (2011) *The Queer Art of Failure*. Duke University Press.

Imperiale, M.G. and Phipps, A. (2022) Cuts destroy, hurt, kill: A critical metaphor analysis of the response of UK academics to the UK overseas aid budget funding cuts. *Journal of Multicultural Discourses* 17 (1), 61–77. https://doi.org/10.1080/17447143.2021.2024838.

Klein, N. (2008) *The Shock Doctrine: The Rise of Disaster Capitalism*. Penguin.

Lorde, A. (2018) *The Master's Tools Will Never Dismantle the Master's House*. Penguin.

McAdam, J.E. (2019) Narratives of change: The role of storytelling, artefacts and children's literature in building communities of inquiry that care. *Cambridge Journal of Education* 49 (3), 293–307. https://doi.org/10.1080 /0305764X.2018.1524001.

McAdam, J.E., Abou-Ghaida, S., Arizpe, E. and Hirsu, L. (2020) Children's literature in critical contexts of displacement: Exploring the value of hope. *Education Sciences* 10 (2), 383–396. https://doi.org/10.3390/educsci10120383.

Nwako, Z., Grieve, T., Mitchell, R., Paulson, J., Saeed, T., Shanks, K. and Wilder, R. (2023) Doing harm: The impact of UK's GCRF cuts on research ethics, partnerships and governance. *Global Social Challenges Journal* 2, 64–85. https://doi.org/10.1332/GJSZ3052.

Økland, A. (2015) Gap analysis for incorporating sustainability in project management. *Procedia Computer Science* 64, 103–109.

Phipps, A. (2019) *Decolonising Multilingualism: Struggles to Decreate*. Multilingual Matters.

Pratt, M.G., Sonenshein, S. and Feldman, M.S. (2022) Moving beyond templates: A bricolage approach to conducting trustworthy qualitative research. *Organisational Research Methods* 25 (2), 211–238.

UKRI (2021) ODA review: Process overview summary. https://www.ukri.org/publications/oda-review-process-overview-summary (accessed 18 September 2023).

13 The Many Twists and Turns in the Pathways to Peace: Reflections on the Bright Sadness of Decolonising and Structuring Cultural Work

Alison Phipps

> Research may not be the intervention that is needed.
> (Tuck & Wayne, 2014: 236)

Introduction

It is very hard to find words sufficient to the task of describing the extent of the failure of the work for peace, of which our own networking project, Culture for Sustainable and Inclusive Peace (CUSP), has been a part.

My newsfeed tells me that today, 23 November 2023, the health authorities in the Gaza Strip, in Palestine, have just recorded over 15,000 deaths. The majority – 67% – are children and women, as confirmed by UN agencies (World Health Organization, 2023). There is a growing fear of unfolding genocide in Gaza, as over 800 scholars of genocide, conflict studies and international law have already termed it (Signatories to Public Statement, 2023). It is only just beginning and by the time this chapter is published that figure is very likely to be much higher. There is little appetite for peace on the part of the Western leaders in the United Nations Security Council even if the General Assembly has shown otherwise, the most powerful being keen to pursue the security objectives of the State of Israel, in this, one of the most violent phases since the founding of Israel and the ensuing 'Nakba' – catastrophe, for the people of Palestine, over 75 years.

Islamophobia has become the organising principle for the world's security politics and at the same time within Islam the freedoms women might enjoy are prescribed. This is strongly documented in the work from Morocco. The security rhetoric of vengeance draws from Christo-Zionist tropes, justifying war and the killing, by Israeli Defence Force, with aid from the USA and the UK, of non-combatant civilians, journalists and humanitarian workers in Gaza. In contexts where the Pentecostal Church has gained greatly in political and sociocultural power – Ghana and Zimbabwe – violence against women and child marriage or forced marriage are leading concerns. In Mexico, Morocco, Zimbabwe, Palestine and Ghana the situation relating to women and gender-based violence has been exacerbated by the lockdowns and emergency legislation passed during the COVID-19 pandemic. Femicide has increased, as evidenced by the contributions from the context of Mexico.

In writing this concluding chapter reflecting on the many twists and turns in pathways to peace, and on the work of the colleagues who have been part of this collective endeavour, I am struck by three things.

(1) There is no shame in defeat, as failure is inevitable in the face of violence, but despair and cynicism are optional. The work of resistance, the advocacy and activism, the creativity and determined searching for possibilities, the refusal of what cannot (yet) serve are all signs of the many ways in which cultural work, especially in the hands of women, has potency. Decolonising is a task for many decades and many workers. Failure and discomfort are part of the task, as demonstrated in Part 1 of this Book.
(2) Intellectual, analytic work is required to find the points of potency and potentiality in the ruins of people's lives and livelihoods. The role of research requires a radical reframing for it to serve the fostering of sustainable peace and conflict transformation. It cannot be narrowly constituted as a neo-liberal agenda for peacebuilding, transferring resources into the hands of cultural brokers, but must be relational, working to decolonise all aspects of the inheritance and find restorative methods and approaches which bring a sense of safety and wellbeing. To invoke the epigraph again: 'Research may not be the intervention that is needed' (Tuck & Wayne, 2014: 236). This said, intellectual work is vital. Without the space to pause, think and wrestle with discomforts and banalities there will not be anything but perpetuation. It may be the starting point rather than the end point and the interventions needed may be ordinary, artful but are often as much about cultural as about political change.
(3) Languages and cultural work are critical to the improvisational work of peace and to what Glissant terms the 'poetics of relation' and the 'poetics of diversity' (Glissant, 2020). Working with poetic relations and diversity all require human beings to improvise with words and improvise with gesture and improvise with things lying around them. They also produce opacity, not transparency. This produces arts and when the aim is peace, safety, protection, wellbeing, then this is the improvisational trajectory. Without the multilingual and creative

resistance and the determined pursuit of possibilities beyond the framing of the funders and the Sustainable Development Goals, none of the beauty that feeds the potency of peace as an idea and a practice would come into being.

Reflecting Back

When devising a programme of research and creating autonomous country-based research hubs with direct financing, the excitement and eagerness of partners and the core team in the UK were palpable. Here was an opportunity not so much to engage in the documentation of 'damage' as Tuck (2008) terms it as instead to see what cultural work, undertaken with, by and also for women and for women's protection, might achieve and show as beauty and resistance. The programme of work began with literature reviews, mapping projects, documentation and narrative research to discover the particular concerns in communities and cultural or women's organisations. The organisations were working variously to provide safe and nurturing spaces for women to find freedom from fear and violence, and the ability to be economically secure without succumbing to various forms of violence.

Some of the organisations jumped straight in with a practice-led approach, devising, improvising, trying things out, organising workshops, discussions of objects, experimenting with 'Theatre of the Oppressed' techniques (Boal, 2000). These are all relative newcomers in the research on conflict transformation, gender-based violence and peacebuilding, but as decolonial praxes they are important as they produce, as the authors of Chapter 5 emphasise, a culture of conviviality. They also allow for error, trial and permission to fail, and build these dimensions from the start into the work. When this is present in many walks of life there is a stronger cultural basis for conflict transformation as there is less of a premium on the need not to fail. However, it is important to stress here that this should not be taken as a universal methodological statement. This is good in the arts, necessary even, but in high-precision fields, like law or medicine or transportation, for instance, accuracy and eradication of error are vital if major social or public conflict is not to be produced.

The research was to allow the identification of key themes for further research and funding for projects which enabled women's concerns to be seen through awareness raising, using cultural and arts-based approaches and educational approaches developed by Freire (1970) and Boal (2000). It also drew on both indigenous and women's approaches to peacebuilding, together with the conflict transformation models developed by Lederach (Lederach, 1995, 2003, 2005; Lederach et al., 2007). Projects were to be opened in each country and small networks would be produced to offer mutual aid and support. Finally, cultural forms would be developed and produced, from dance to short stories, textile art to film and theatre, together with forms of organisation that might be most appropriate to safeguarding women in nascent institutional forms. The award of £2 million was a substantial amount for such an undertaking. There would be the chance to visit each other's projects and learn from the work being done, from the forms resistance and creativity could take, against the odds. Furthermore, it would be possible to look at the importance of cultural work in the arts and in working in contexts of gender-based violence and multiple dimensions of precarity.

In addition, this was not to be work which focused on how terrible the situation was and only told stories of pain and anguish. While this would be part of the work it was clear to all participants that art and cultural work with women survivors and women in education could be ways in which the potency of those on the peripheries (Instituto Maria e João Aleixo, 2017) might be brought to the attention and offer structures for change.

Within less than two months of the set-up phase beginning, the global COVID-19 pandemic radically curtailed our ability to start the project as planned and to follow through on principles of equity which were part of the design. Safeguarding training had to be delivered online, along with all the materials required for training and financing and, as Principal Investigator, I moved from undertaking intellectual leadership to learning about poly-tank installation, mobile signal masts, masks, hand sanitiser, data bundles and money transfers via Western Union, where exchange and taxation rates would be so high that no worker could be paid a living wage. As the administrators of the network we learned directly from our co-investigators as to what would be needed, and duly applied for pots of funds to enable the kinds of antivirus safety protocols to be met in each context. The researchers in each of the countries came together online, as did so many across the world through the early stages of the pandemic. We were greatly guided by the work of our long-term colleagues at the Islamic University of Gaza who had been undertaking work with us for many years online, as a way of mitigating the effects of Israel's blockade and siege (Fassetta *et al.*, 2020). Our online sessions were multilingual and translated and also happy with music, story, research and song. We found that wrapping what would otherwise be highly formal and nervous sessions with cultural elements and the arts brought a calm and joy to the work and to our times together.

The research, much of it desk research or online activities, brought to the surface many concerns, especially with regard to violence against women, domestic violence and femicide through the global COVID-19 pandemic. Calls for research proposals looking at these contexts and the use of cultural artefacts for advocacy, capacity building and conscientisation were developed collectively and on International Women's Day 2021 the network come together with a throng of interested scholars and cultural workers online for the launch of our project and our small grants. It

Figure 13.1 Launch of our project and our small grants. It was a wonderful event with participation of a 'live drawing' artist who documented our work for us and gave a pictorial representation of the processes ahead

was a wonderful event with participation of a 'live drawing' artist who documented our work for us and gave a pictorial representation of the processes ahead.

Three days later, as a number of contributors to this book have noted, the work was cut by 80%, the network and grant call frozen as we digested the news sent to universities in the letter shown in Figure 13.2. This managerial discourse covers up a great deal of violence. The letter is a declaration of harm on all those working in projects funded by the Global Challenge Research Fund and on the universities who had signed the contracts upon

Circular letter

Global Challenges Research Fund (GCRF) QR

To	Heads of English higher education providers
Reference	RE-CL-2021-03
Publication date	11 March 2021
Enquiries to	General queries to globalchallenges@re.ukri.org

Dear Vice-Chancellor or Principal

1. You will have received a letter about ODA project funding from UKRI today. I regret to inform you that as part of wider measures to implement a reduction in Government spend on International Development, BEIS have instructed UKRI and Research England that there will no QR GCRF available for 2021-2022.

2. All HEPs currently in receipt of QR GRCF have already received their final payment of QR GCRF for 2020-21 and will not receive an allocation for the following year. Research England will undertake a standard monitoring exercise, as conducted for previous years, to confirm that the 2020-21 allocation has been spent in line with ODA eligibility rules. This exercise will be conducted at the end of academic year 2020-21.

3. At this point I am afraid that we are unable to make any statement about the likelihood of future QR GCRF allocations.

Yours sincerely

David Sweeney

Executive Chair

Figure 13.2 Letter from the Global Challenges Research Fund (GCRF) confirming funding cuts

award of the funding. The letter severs the contracts of many workers on projects in low- to middle-income countries and cuts short the hopes of many who may have wanted to bid for money. It does so as a political act of violence – cuts – appeasing a right-wing desire in the UK on the part of the government and electorate to take money back from international development, renege on global commitments to overseas development assistance and spend this instead on prison-style detention facilities for those seeking asylum (Wintour, 2023). Receiving the letter, three days after the successful launch, meant I had to return to colleagues with whom I had worked for years building trusted partnerships and tell them there was no future for the project. I also launched a media and political campaign to have the funding returned. This took nine months and was an exhausting process, alongside the 'reprofiling' of the work to see what, if anything, might be possible. It meant working on the project myself as a volunteer and losing most of the funding for the small grants we were to deliver. It meant an inevitable loss of staff who, already on precarious contracts, soon started applying for more securely funded positions.

More importantly, it was not work which could be or was appropriate to ask our partners to lead, from their contexts. Whereas our research model aimed to have the people researching and making art in context lead their work, using methods they felt were most congruent with the violence and research they were addressing, advocacy against the cuts was a solitary affair. It required political understanding of both the funding landscape and the minutiae of UK politics. It required deep political and academic networks and it required an understanding of and experience in campaigning. This was a task which was for the project leader, myself, as I was attempting to communicate to incredulous partners what had befallen us. It required much navigation of the funding decisions and structures in the lead institution to see if we could save the work, and pay our partners, and it required me to work with no time allocation on the project, for over two years. This brought a degree of temporal violence and therefore also physical exhaustion into my own domestic life as well as my work life. What I had planned to do – reading and enabling engagement with the literatures pertinent to the CUSP project – became the work of an academic activist with long experience of the funding mechanisms of UK Research and Innovation (UKRI) and 25 years working in the same institution.

It was top-down work. I was often not in a position to communicate decisions which I knew I would need to work hard to overturn or to change, as to do so would have brought further hopelessness and anger to people waiting and watching. The hierarchy of a professorial position meant this was a legitimate task but it stuck in my throat. The principles of subsidiary, the main ways in which peacebuilding is grassroots, dialogic, participatory, humorous and convivial were unavailable to me. Messages of solidarity on our chats and emails were also full of anger – not at myself – but also of impatience at how long the change was taking.

In order to maintain sanity but also to work in a research mode, Maria Grazia Imperiale, our Research Associate, led an analysis of the discourse used in the many media reports of the cuts to the funding, not least the metaphors used. Together we published an article (Imperiale & Phipps, 2022) which in many ways was something of catharsis but which allowed us to work through our academic freedom and with the new violent materials which were arriving daily. Having something to do during a period of violence and loss, and during a period of active campaigning, that was part of our work, as researchers into applied linguistics, was soothing. It has become one of the important elements in our work whenever crisis strikes, as it does in conflict and peacebuilding contexts regularly. Being able to analyse discourse, to see what the metaphorical and discursive pathways are suggesting, to step back from the immediate scene of conflict and steady thinking allow us to do what Elaine Scarry (2011) calls 'thinking in an emergency'.

Tears and Triumphs

Bit by bit, petitions, questions in Parliament, letters to embassies, by-elections and many articles meant sufficient embarrassment had been sustained for the funding cuts to be reversed, but not without the reversal being grudging and requiring the Principal Investigators to reapply for their funds, or for aspects of the funds. In one surreal moment the following message was received from the funders in email correspondence:

> UKRI then applied the GOOD cost effectiveness multiplier based on the mode score, applying the BEIS value for money methodology.
> Average rubric score x worthwhileness multiplier
> After applying the cost-effectiveness multiplier, the Value for Money score translates to the final score. = 4.

When the funders were asked what the score of 4 was out of, they said this had not yet been determined. This information was met with incredulity, not least following attempts to translate it into the languages in the project.

The return of the funds meant another round of reprofiling and the need to rebuild trust and enthusiasm for the project. Sustainable and inclusive peace needs sustainable and inclusive ways of working and by this point in the project all partners were severely depleted, we might even say burnt out, as was I. There were many Zoom calls in which people were in tears but there was also care and tenacity. The aim of creating a network, where people collaborated across countries, had never had a chance to develop. No one had met face to face, it failed from the outset, but what had been formed was a meshwork, as Ingold (2007) terms it.

> [...] the pathways or trajectories along which improvisatory practice unfolds are not connections, nor do they describe relations between one

thing and another. They are rather lines along which things continually come into being. Thus when I speak of the entanglement of things I mean this literally and precisely: not a network of connections but a meshwork of interwoven lines of growth and movement. (Ingold, 2010: 3)

The important aspect for sustainable peace is that the meshwork is opaque. A network has clear nodes and lines of connection. In the meshwork produced by the impossibility of 'managing' COVID-19 and the cuts, the absolute lack of control possible, as a leader of the research process I had relied entirely on the staff in context to do the work, to know how to do the work and to provide the receipts for the funds received. There was not a lot of room for manoeuvre but within it I had tried to offer reflection and support and largely agree to changes and proposals made by those working in context. At no point did I see myself as an expert in anything other than the mechanisms of funding administration and my own areas of work in languages and intercultural studies, within the context of peacebuilding. But through the struggle to have our funding restored, and through the knowledge of how acutely difficult the cuts had made life for our eager, and hopeful, partners, this was the loneliest of times I have ever experienced in 30 years as an academic.

This latter point was somewhat of a change from a more frustrated, hands-on, desire-to-know-see-and-understand that I had experienced as a principal investigator in a previous project. It was an important change and an aspect which, I was clear, was part of the work of decolonising and allowing for local structuring of cultural work. In many ways I was not 'interested' in the local work and how it was proceeding beyond that it was proceeding, as this meant that the dynamics of resistance and potency could be found locally, used locally, researched locally and presented culturally, locally. My theoretical observations were secondary to ensuring the funds reached the communities, for the research and cultural work they were undertaking. In other words, I also worked to ensure the opacity, not least as I realised after the cuts that maintaining my ignorance was a key to protecting those rendered vulnerable by the cuts.

Every online meeting and seminar of the whole group I would begin in trepidation, not so much suffering from imposter syndrome – I had no doubt at all that I was an imposter in each context, even if I was a welcome guest and long-standing colleague and friend. And at the end of every session, I would marvel at what had been produced, entirely without anything but my administrative assistance and some light offerings of readings, and thoughts and questions. This did not mean that much work was not underway, just because I was not managing the micro or the local; in fact, it meant that the work was entirely owned and produced and understood in context. My role was to see that the work was good, to witness, and to set the different pieces of cultural work produced, and the research, alongside each other and within different frameworks for different bodies. This role, and the one each of the different contexts and their artists and researchers bore to other projects, the attentive listening, the careful questioning and the commendation, was part of the process of conflict transformation and peacebuilding between the network members.

Concluding with Bright Sadness

> The researchers froze because it was a space of spirit.
> (Tawona Sitholé)

As the work we have been contracted to produce draws to an end, the mood is one of bright sadness. Bright sadness is a term from the Orthodox tradition referring to periods of fasting during Lent, before Easter, a term which knows and mediates on the failings of humans, the impossibility of our attempts at sustaining peace. Reading the chapters together, the brightness and the sadness are present throughout. There are joy and tenacity and determination in the use of the arts, folk tales, popular culture, dance, storytelling, in the potency of conscientisation and the liberatory experiences women especially have had during and through the work undertaken. This brightness, or joy in the cultural work made, collectively and thanks to the researchers, is tempered by the sadness, a sadness born of the critical failings in a project funded by a former colonial power, whose overseas development assistance was once generous, even reparatory, and was slashed by 80%, cutting the hope and plans and potency to the quick.

'Quick' as I have stated elsewhere (Phipps, 2007), is an old word for 'life' and especially the life we share between us, what Ingold terms 'the generative capacity of that encompassing field of relations within which forms arise and are held in place' (Ingold, 2010: 3). The 'quick', often lightning-speed reactions to protect or act, but also cut to the quick and made of tears, has characterised the work for those concerned, those violated and abused, excluded and ridiculed by the economic, political, gender-based, social and cultural forces which suggest that a woman's life is not equal to or equally allowed in cultural work, as that of a man.

The generative capacity Ingold speaks of, the field of relations of the work undertaken in this volume represents a space in which forms have arisen and have been held, often tenaciously, in place, by many actors, and by many fractal refusals to collude in structures which demand, or take, or control, or punish. As such, the work is dynamic, improvisational, reactive and tactical, looking for spaces where peace might be possible, analysing the conditions, locally, and then acting when safe, or even risking it when some conditions are favourable but courage is small.

Sustainable peace, then, to me, requires us to be able to suggest that there is something more important than research objectives, however ethical, participatory and well intentioned. The improvisation of peace and sustaining of its potency as idea and as practice may not always need research to be undertaken. Many of the ways in which the cultural work succeeded in its luminosity came from thought in a different mode, thought as Heidegger describes it, as poetic – 'dichterisch wohnet der mensch' (poetically, the human dwells) (Heidegger, 1971: 757). This mode of thought also operates in bright sadness, reflecting back, confessing, knowing the pitfalls and failures and impossibilities but not paralysed by these, as research can be but, rather, ready, enmeshed, generative and able to improvise a peace – a sustainable peace. A peace, bright with sadness. Maybe this is what a sustainable peace is. A peace, bright with the sadness of so much loss and violence, but able to hold, and to weave containers strong enough to sustain the peace and the loss that was and is and is to come.

Figure 13.4 Artwork by a Gazan clinician who prefers to remain anonymous

References

Boal, A. (2000) *Theater of the Oppressed*. Pluto Press.
Fassetta, G., Nazmi, A.M. and Phipps, A. (2020) *Multilingual Online Academic Collaborations as Resistance: Crossing Impassable Borders*. Multilingual Matters.
Freire, P. (1970) *Pedagogy of the Oppressed*. Penguin.
Glissant, É. (2020) *Introduction to a Poetics of Diversity* (trans. C. Britton). Liverpool University Press.
Heidegger, M. (1971) *Poetry, Language, Thought*. Harper Colophon Books.
Imperiale, M.G. and Phipps, A. (2022) Cuts destroy, hurt, kill: A critical metaphor analysis of the response of UK academics to the UK overseas aid budget funding cuts. *Journal of Multicultural Discourses* 17 (1), 61–77. https://doi.org/10.1080/17447143.2021.2024838.
Ingold, T. (2007) *Lines: A Brief History*. Routledge.
Ingold, T. (2010) Bringing things to life: Creative entanglements in a world of materials. *Realities Working Paper 15*. https://eprints.ncrm.ac.uk/id/eprint/1306/1/0510_creative_entanglements.pdf (accessed 15 July 2024).
Instituto Maria e João Aleixo (2017) Manifesto das periferias. *Revista Periferias*. http://revistaperiferias.org/wp-content/uploads/2019/07/periferias-manifesto-2-ingles.pdf (accessed 15 July 2024).
Lederach, J.P. (1995) *Preparing for Peace: Conflict Across Cultures*. Syracuse University Press.
Lederach, J.P. (2003) *Conflict Transformation*. Good Books.
Lederach, J.P. (2005) *The Moral Imagination: The Art and Soul of Peace Building*. Oxford University Press.
Lederach, J.P., Reina, N. and Culbertson, H. (2007) *Reflective Peacebuilding: A Planning, Monitoring, and Learning Toolkit*. University of Notre Dame.
Phipps, A. (2007) *Learning the Arts of Linguistic Survival: Languaging, Tourism, Life*. Channel View Publications.
Signatories to Public Statement (2003) Public statement: Scholars warn of potential genocide in Gaza. *TWAILR*, 15 October. https://twailr.com/public-statement-scholars-warn-of-potential-genocide-in-gaza (accessed 15 July 2024).
Scarry, E. (2011) *Thinking in an Emergency*. W.W. Norton.
Tuck, E. (2008) Suspending damage: A letter to communities. *Harvard Educational Review*, 79 (3), 409–427. https://pages.ucsd.edu/~rfrank/class_web/ES-114A/Week%204/TuckHEdR79-3.pdf (accessed 15 July 2024).
Tuck, E.Y. and Wayne, K. (2014) R-words: Refusing research. In D.W. Paris and T. Maisha (eds) *Humanizing Research: Decolonizing Qualitative Inquiry with Youth and Communities* (pp. 223–247). Sage.
Wintour, P. (2023) Up to a third of overseas aid budget used for housing refugees in UK, MPs report. *Guardian*, 2 March. https://www.theguardian.com/uk-news/2023/mar/02/overseas-aid-budget-uk-select-committee-report-housing-refugees (accessed 15 July 2024).
World Health Organization (2023) Women and newborns bearing the brunt of the conflict in Gaza, UN agencies warn. https://www.who.int/news/item/03-11-2023-women-and-newborns-bearing-the-brunt-of-the-conflict-in-gaza-un-agencies-warn (accessed 15 July 2024).

Index

Note: References are to page numbers: *f* and *t* indicate figures and tables, and 'n' refers to a note.

Abass-Abaah, A.J. 124, 134
Abu al-Khair, I. 139
Abubakari, H. *et al.* 128, 130–131, 134
abuse 232–233
   discriminatory abuse 233
   domestic violence/abuse 232–233
Acapulco, Mexico 106, 205
   continuity and monitoring 114
   'Cultural Community' framework 108
   'drug tourism' 106–107
   El Acapulco que soñamos 99, 115–116
   Escuela de Iniciación Artística 107
   homicide 107
   identity and inclusion 112–113
   investment in infrastructure 110, 111
   mapping cultural and peacebuilding initiatives 99–100
   Ministry of Culture for Guerrero 107
   Municipal Development Plan (2018-2021) 107
   National Institute of Arts 107
   orchestras for children and young people 107
   PRONAPRED programme 107
   recovering community spaces for peacebuilding 96–97
   violence 106, 107
   visibility and networks 113
   'War on Drugs' 97
   conclusion 114–116
   see also tale of two cities: recovering community spaces for peacebuilding in Medellín and Acapulco
Adichie, Chimamanda Ngozi 206
'adult at risk' 234
Adult Safeguarding Prevention and Protection in Partnership (Northern Ireland) 229
Adult Support and Protection (Scotland) Act 2007 229
Africa Disability Protocol (ADP) 75
African Union (AU) 75
Al-Hadidi Saad 16 143
Al-Somali, S. *et al.* 19 143
Alareer, Refaat 3, xxvi–xxviii
Albanese, Francesca: *Anatomy of Genocide* 3
albinism 76
Alcaldía de Medellín 105
Ali, M. 128
Anzaldúa, Gloria 207, 209, 210
Arendt, H. 251, 252
Ash, J. *et al.* 40
Assouli, F. 11

Balmès, José 24
Bang, Hyoeun 98
Barthes, Roland 219–220
Baudrillard, Jean 217, 218, 219
Bazooker 167, 168
Berenstain (2016) 241–242
Berg, B. 162
Berg, L.-A. 1
Bernal, Angelica Lucia Damian 33
between success and failure: grassroots organisations in conflict transformation 248–249
   introducing conflict 249–251
   conclusion: making space for new possibilities when working with *Colectivas* 262–264

between success and failure: grassroots organisations in conflict transformation: methodology 251, 259
application of the Greimas square 256–262, 259
our work/generation of texts and artefacts 252
positionality 252–254
between success and failure 254–256, 255
Bhatasara, S. 159, 161
Black, M. 163
BlacPerl 168–169
Boal, A. 267
Bodomo, A. 128
Boland, B. 229
Bordat, Stephanie Willman 11
Borges, Jorge Luis
This Craft of Verse 217, 218
Brown, Ammara 168, 169, 170
Brown, J.A.: *Cyborgs in Latin America* 217
Burburles, N.C. 55
Bustop TV 172
Butler, J. et al. 235–236, 239, 240

Cabnal, Lorena 36, 40
Calaz, Seh 168, 169
Calderón, Felipe, President of Mexico 97, 106
Cantle, T. 63
capability approach (CA) 236–237
Care Act 2014 (England and Wales) 229–230
Care and Support Statutory Guidance (UK Government) 232
Chari, T. 160, 161
Charusheela, S. 239
Chaya, V. 162
Chiapas 204
child marriage *see* popular arts as communication tools for eradication of gender-based violence/child marriage in Ghana
'child protection' 237
children with disabilities: social conflicts 93–94
Children's Literature in Critical Contexts of Displacement 257
Chipfupa, D. 161
Chireshe, E. 161–162, 165
Chollet, M. 17
coercive enforcement of individuals 233

collaborative cartography 43, 43–48, 45, 444
Colleta 170
Colombia *see* Medellín, Colombia
colonial realities–history and language 209–211
community spaces, reovering and sustaining 108–114
conflict
defined 54
peace and peacebuilding 54–55
resolution 54
conflict transformation: dialogic approach 5, 55–56
see also towards cultures of conflict transformation
contextualising safeguarding in international development research: requirements and challenges 227–229
contextualising safeguarding in research 239–243
opacity of safeguarding 229–234
points for reflection and discussion 243–244
safeguarding, defined 230–231, 232
vulnerability and safeguarding 234–239
final reflections and unsatisfying conclusions 244–245
Corbett, J. 1–2
COVID-19 268 *see also* high school women in the face of violence during the COVID-19 pandemic; popular culture and gender-based violence in Zimbabwe
Cradall 97
Creative Corridors: peace, inclusivity and engagement with persons with disabilities (PwDs) 75–78
social conflicts around children with disabilities 93–94
stories 78–90
from stories to research 90–92
tale of two cities: recovering community spaces for peacebuilding in Medellín and Acapulco 57–94
findings 92–94
concluding remarks 94
CRIM-UNAM (Center for Multidisciplinary Research, National Autonomous University of Mexico) 201

Critical Intercultural Pedagogy for Difficult Times: Conflict, Crisis, and Creativity 1–2
cuerpo-territorio 35–36, 37, 38, 43
Culture for Sustainable and Inclusive Peace Network Plus (CUSP N+) 2–3, 201, 202, 227–228, 232, 248, 250, 252–253
  see also between success and failure: grassroots organisations in conflict transformation
Cummings, S. et al. 251
cyber ethnography 163

Danesh, H.B. 66
Daoust, G. 241, 242
Daruler 170
De Lauretis, Teresa 39
de Vries, J. 242
decolonial praxes: metaphors, mediation and writing in motion 201–202
  Acapulco, Guerrero 205
  Chiapas 204
  Ciudad de México, CDMX 205
  colonial realities–history and language 209–211
  escritura en movimiento - 'writing in motion' 221–223
  Estado de México 205
  experiences of mediation and writing in motion 219–221
  exploring intersectional realities 206–213
  hegemonic financial realities 206–208
  injustice and oppressive realities 208–209
  La Paz, Baja California Sur 205
  memory politics–contesting historical narratives 211–213
  metaphor in the narrative construction of knowledge 215–219
  Morelos 204
  praxes as methodological approach 202–206
  reading 213–214
  Tijuana, Baja California 204–205
  conclusions 223–224
Delice, P.A. 124
dialogue for social transformation 53
discriminatory abuse 233
domestic violence/abuse 232–233
Donoso, J. et al. 107

Dvyne 170
Dyvik, S. 241, 242

Education Scotland 231
Einstein, Albert 52
El Boukhari, Maha 14
emotional abuse 233
Empress Massina 170
Engels, Friedrich 21
  The Origin of the Family … 23
Equality Act 2010 (UK) 233
EXQ 170

Faceless 170
Featherstone, B. 236–238
feminist geography as theoretical and methodological framework 33–40
  collaborative cartography 38
  counter-cartography 38–39
  focus group discussions 37–38
financial abuse 233
Fineman, M.A. 235, 236
forced labour 233
Freeman 170
Freire, P. 53, 56, 57, 63, 64, 68, 202, 267
  Pedagogy of the Oppressed 57
Fuqaha, N. 153

Gadamer, H.G. 56
Galtung, Johan 54, 55, 63
Gaza Community Mental Health Programme (GCMHP) 138, 140
Gaza Strip 2, 140, 141
GCRF *see* Global Challenges Research Fund
gender-based conflict (GBC) 139
  see also Palestinian women facing gender-based conflict in Gaza Strip
gender-based violence (GBV) 5, 31–33, 139, 233
  popular arts 5, 119, 121–122, 174, 179
  see also high school women in the face of violence during the COVID-19 pandemic; popular culture and gender-based violence in Zimbabwe
Ghana *see* popular arts as communication tools for eradication of gender-based violence/child marriage in Ghana; promoting women's participation in social transformation in Ghana
Gill, S. 55

Glissant, Edouard 229, 266
Global Challenges Research Fund (GCRF) 227, 270, 270–271
Global North 4, 241, 242
Global South 3–4, 241–242
Googi performance and docudrama 130–131
  child marriage as traditional cultural norm 131–133
  poverty as cause/result of early marriage/teenage pregnancy 134
  discussion: cultural motivations 134–135
  conclusions 135–136
Gramsci, A. 206
Grande, Nina 170
grassroots organisations *see* between success and failure: grassroots organisations in conflict transformation; between success and failure: grassroots organisations in conflict transformation: methodology
Greimas square: application to our work 256
  demands of the research process 258–260
  hopelessness 260
  solidarity 261–262
  towards utopian possibility 256–258
  conclusion: making space for new possibilities with *Colectivas* 262–264
Gualandi, B. et al. 252
Gupta, A. 236–238, 242
Gwarisa, M. 169

Habermas, J. 56, 68
Haiven, M. 254, 256
Halberstam, J. 254
Hamili, Gisèle 23
Harare, Baba 166, 167
Haraway, Donna 216–217, 219
Hassan II, King of Morocco 9, 14
Heidegger, M. 275
Hiba 63, 65, 68
high school women in the face of violence during the COVID-19 pandemic: spaces of prevention and sisterhood 30–33, 41
  collaborative cartography 43, 43–48, 44, 45, 46
  education 31
  feminist geography as theoretical and methodological framework 33–40
  gender-based violence (GBV) 31–33, 41–48, 44, 45, 46
  mental health 42
  sexual harassment 42
  violence 46, 47–48
  discussion 40–48
  concluding remarks 48–50
Holmes, P. 1–2
Holy Ten 169, 170
human trafficking 233
Hwabaraty 170

I Am You xxvi–xxviii
IBBY México 201, 202–203, 212, 214, 220
Independent Commission for Human Rights 140
Ingold, T. 272–273, 274
integrative theory of peace (ITP) 66, 67
International Convention on the Rights of the Child 20
international development research 230
International Women's Day (2021) 268, 269
intersectional realities 206
  colonial realities–history and language 209–211
  hegemonic financial realities 206–208
  injustice and oppressive realities 208–209
  memory politics–contesting historical narratives 211–213
  intersectional realities: decolonial praxes 213–214
  experiences of mediation and writing in motion 219–223
  metaphor in narrative construction of knowledge 215–219
  conclusions 223–224
introduction 1–5
  1: towards cultures of conflict transformation 5
  2: popular arts and culture meet gender-based violence 5
  3: reflexivity, dilemmas and safeguarding with grassroots organisations 5–6
Ishall, Enzo 166, 167
Islamophobia 265–266
ITP *see* integrative theory of peace

Johnson, K. 229
Johnson, M. 215, 219
Jupp, V. 57

Kadijah 166
Kadjah 170
Kasraoui, S. 11
Katji, Edith 161
Katz, C. et al. 126
Kelly, N.H. 58
Khasnabish, A. 254, 256
Khattabi, Abdelkrim 15
Kidd, D. et al. 158
Klein, N. 251
Knight, H. 58
Knight, Shadaya 161, 173
Kramer, S. 26
Kubrin, C.E. 161
Kufakurinani, U. et al. 160
Kumar, R. 162
Kusaas and the Kusaal language 122, 122–123
   child marriage 124–125
   Googi performance and docudrama 130–134
   methodology 127–128
   overview of literature 124
   popular culture 123–124
   results 128–130
   theoretical framework 125–127

La Paz, Baja California Sur 205
Lady Bee 170
Lakoff, G. 215, 219
Lan, Diana 38, 39
Lasswell, H. 125
Latouche, A. 236
Lederach, J.P. 1, 53, 54, 55, 57–58, 63, 64, 65, 68, 98, 267
Ley General de Acceso de las Mujeres a una Vida libre de Violencia 34–35, 42
Ley Olimpia 34
liberation tactics–echoes of emancipation 24–25
Lipsy, Ninja 170
López Obrador, Andrés Manuel 108
Lorde, A. 208, 254
low- and middle-income countries (LMICs) 2, 227, 230, 240

Mabuto, K. 161, 162
MacGinty, R. 98

Macheso, Alick 162
Mad Viper 166
Magwaza, Clement 161
Mai Vee/Mhosva TV 172
Maiese, M. 55, 66
Mangeya, H. 160–161
Massey, Doreen 33
Mate, R. 160
material abuse 233
McAdam, J.E. et al. 256–257
Medellín, Colombia 101–106
   Casa de la Memoria Museum 105
   continuity and monitoring 114
   cultural actors 102–103, *103*, *104*
   identity and inclusion 111–112
   infrastructure responding to needs of local communities 110–111, *111*
   Lee Kuan Yew World City Prize 96, 101
   Manual de Convivencia Ciudad 105
   mapping cultural and peacebuilding initiatives 99–100
   parques biblioteca 105
   public policy 103–105
   recovering and sustaining community spaces 57–94, 96, 108–114, *109*
   security *102*, 102–103
   UNESCO Learning City 101
   visibility and networks 113
   conclusion 114–116
   see also tale of two cities: recovering community spaces for peacebuilding in Medellín and Acapulco
Melot, Michel 220
Mesquita, André 38
México 3
   Arte Ciencia y Tecnología (ACT) 217
   Ciudad de México, CDMX 205
   Culture for Sustainable and Inclusive Peace Network Plus (CUSP N+) 248
   Estado de México 205
   National Autonomous University of Mexico (UNAM) 32, 36, 217, 248, 250, 252, 253–254
   National Institute of Statistics and Geography (INEGI) 107
   space as a social construct 37
   violence against women 31, 32, 36–38
   see also Acapulco, Mexico
Mignolo, W. 240
Mitchell, G. 55, 66
Mitchner, B. 167

Mockus, Antanas 98–99
modern slavery 233
Monroy, J. 31
Morelos 204
Morocco *see* three Moroccan women's liberation journeys
Mtukudzi, Oiver 161–162
Mukucha, J. 169
Mumanyi, Tawanda 166
Murgue, B. 9–10

Nandi, Felly 168
Ncube, G. 161
Ndebele, Sandra 161, 165, 170
Ndlovu, B. 165
Ndlovu-Gatsheni, S.J. 242
neglect 237
NHS England 231
Niens, U. 55
Niño, N.C. 98
Nkala, N. 161
Nussbaum, M. 235, 236, 239
Nwako, Z. et al. 251

organisational abuse 233
Organization for African Unity (OAU) 75–76
Orr, D. et al. 230–231, 240–241, 243
Outspoken 161

Palestinian Central Bureau of Statistics (PCBS) 53, 140, 143
Palestinian women: facing gender-based conflict in Gaza Strip 53, 138–41
  deprivation of rights 149–150, 151
  exposure to violence in all its forms 152–153
  'gender-based conflict' (GBC) 139, 142–143, 144t, 145
  methodology 141–142
  negative discrimination against women 146–148
  transforming gender-based conflicts into success stories 150–153
  violence 143–146
  women/family members exposed to abuse by Israeli occupation 151–152
  women's struggle for roles 150–151
  results 142–153
  discussion 153–154
  conclusion and recommendations 154–156

Palestinian women: young women's narratives of change 52–54
  dialogue for peacebuilding 52–54
  dialogue for social transformation 53
  participant recruitment 58–59, 59
  research design and recruitment 58–62, 59
  storytelling as strategy for promoting critical dialogue 68–70, 69
  unpacking notions of 'conflict' and 'peace': transformative approach to peacebuilding 54–58
  discussion of findings 62–70, 65f, 66f
  conclusions and lessons learnt 70–72, 71
pathways to peace: reflections 265–267, 269
  reflecting back 267–272
  tears and triumphs 272–274
  concluding with bright sadness 274–275, 275
patriarchal societies 10, 14–15, 16–23
Pauline 170
PCBS *see* Palestinian Central Bureau of Statistics
peacebuilding: discussion of findings 62–63
peacebuilding: research design and recruitment 58
  data analysis 61–62
  data generation 59, 59–61
  participant recruitment 58–59, 59
peacebuilding: transformative approach
  critical dialogue 56–57
  dialogic approach 55–56
  storytelling as form of artistic dialogue 57–58
  what is conflict? 54–55
Peña Nieta, Enrique 107
people with albinism 76
Pepper, M. 98
persons with disabilities (PwDs) *see* Creative Corridors: peace, inclusivity and engagement with persons with disabilities
Petit, Michèle 219
Phipps, Alison 261, 274
Pillay, N. 240
popular arts and everyday culture meet gender-based violence 5, 119, 174
  Palestinian women facing gender-based conflict in Gaza Strip 138–156

popular culture and gender-based violence in Zimbabwe 138–156
popular arts as communication tools for eradication of gender-based violence/child marriage in Ghana 121–122
   background: Kusaas and the Kusaal language 122, 122–125
   child marriage among Kusaas 124–125
   child marriage as traditional cultural norm 131–132
   discussion: cultural motivations and mitigation 134–135
   Googi performance and docudrama 130–134
   health implications of early marriage and teenage pregnancy 132–133
   methodology 127–128
   popular culture 123–124
   poverty as cause/result of early marriage/teenage pregnancy in Kusaug 134
   results 128–130
   theoretical framework 125–127
   conclusions 135–136
popular culture and gender-based violence in Zimbabwe 158–159
   combating GBV with counter-narratives/safe spaces 167–172
   COVID-19 pandemic 158, 163, 168, 175
   findings and discussion 164–172
   gender, sex and violence in Zimbabwean popular culture 159–162
   Love Should Not Hurt campaign 169–170
   methodology 162–163
   No to GBV Riddim 169
   normalising GBV by denigrating/sexualising women 164–167
   Zimdancehall 159, 160–161, 162, 164, 166, 168, 172–173, 174
   conclusions and recommendations 172–176
Popular Solutions for Health (PSH) 169
poverty 134, 237
Pratt, B. 242
Pratt, M.G. et al. 251
Prayzah, Jah 165
Preußler, Ottfried: *Krabat* 221
promoting women's participation in social transformation in Ghana 179–181
   analysis and discussion of interviews 187–191, 189t
   Children's Act (1988) 185
   Committee on the Elimination of Discrimination Against Women (CEDAW) 185
   Criminal Code (1960) 185
   data anaysis 182
   data collection and research activities 181
   development and pre-testing of research instruments 183
   discussion of feedback from interviewees 193–195
   Domestic Violence Act, 2007 185–186
   Domestic Violence and Victim Support Unit (DOVVSU; 1998) 184
   findings 184–187
   gender-based violence (GBV) 179
   limitations 187
   major findings 187, 189t
   methodology and design 181–187
   National Gender Policy (2015) 184, 186
   pilot study 182
   results of feedback from interviewees 192–193
   sampling 183–184
   conclusion/recommendations 195–197
protected characteristics 233
PSH (Popular Solutions for Health) 169
psychological abuse 233
PwDs *see* persons with disabilities

Qounfuzed 165–166

Racines 13, 233
reflexivity, dilemmas and safeguarding with grassroots organisations 5–6
research design and recruitment 58
   data analysis 61–62
   data generation 59–61
   participant recruitment 58–59
Reynolds, A.S. 215
Rocha, H.L. 38, 39
Roki 169
Roy, Arundhati 208
Russelll, G.M. 58

Sadiqi, F. 10, 31
safeguarding *see* contextualising safeguarding in international development research: requirements and challenges
SafeLives 233
Saidi, U. 161, 162
Sánchez Cordero, Olga 31
Santos, M. 34
Santos, S.B. 242
Scarry, Elaine 272
SDGs (Sustainable Development Goals) 75
Sen, Amartya 207
sexual abuse and harassment 42, 233
Shafak, E. 26
Shara, S. 153
Shinsoman 167
Sibanda, N. 161
Sideris, T. 153
sisterhood 34
Sitholé, Tawona 274
slavery 233
Sniper Storm 161
Sommer, Doris 14 98–99
Soyinka, Wole 207
space as a social concept 37
Spanish language 212
Spivak, G. 55, 63
Spivak, G.C. 240
storytelling
  as form of artistic dialogue 57–58
  as strategy for promoting critical dialogue 68–70
Sustainable Development Goals (SDGs) 75
Synik 161

tale of two cities: recovering community spaces for peacebuilding in Medellín and Acapulco 96–98
  Aca En Bici 115
  cultural intervention and everyday peace 98–99
  methodology: mapping cultural and peacebuilding initiatives 99–100
  recovering and sustaining community spaces 108–114
  two cities: Medellín and Acapulco 100–108
  conclusion 114–116

Tanzania: people with albinism 76
Tarawneh, M. 153
Tate, Andrew 161, 173
Tatelicious 171–172
'Theatre of the Oppressed' 15, 267
three Moroccan women's liberation journeys
  2011 constitutional reform 10
  Civil Code 12
  context 9–12, 27n1
  feminist associations 12
  liberation tactics–echoes of emancipation 24–25
  methodology 13–14
  Moudawana (Family Code) 9–10, 20, 23, 27n1
  Three women. Three tempers. Three strategies 14–23
  women's rights 10–12, 27n2
  conclusion 25–27
Three women. Three tempers. Three strategies 14–16
  'It all started at school' – socialisation 16–18
  underage marriage and patriarchy 18–20
  women's domestication 21–23
Tijuana, Baja California 204–205
Tivenga, D.R. 161
Tosam, M.J. 242
towards cultures of conflict transformation 5, 7, 124
  Creative Corridors: peace, inclusivity and engagement with persons with disabilities (PwDs) 57–94
  high school women in the face of violence during the COVID-19 pandemic 30–50
  Palestinian women: young women's narratives of change 52–72
  tale of two cities: recovering community spaces for peace-buildng in Medellín and Acapulco 96–116
  three Moroccan women's liberation journeys 9–27
Tuck, F. 265, 266
Tytania 170

UK Collaborative on Development Research (UKCDR) 230, 231
UK higher education institutes (HEIs) 240

UK Research and Innovation (UKRI) 227–228, 250, 271
  Culture 242
  Global Challenges Research Fund (GCRF) 227
Uncle Epatan 166
underage marriage and patriarchy 18–20
United Nations 140
United Nations Convention on the Rights of Persons with Disability (UNCRPD) 75
United Nations (UN) conventions 239
United Nations International Children's Emergency Fund (UNICEF) 121
United Nations Population Fund (UNPFA) 139
Universal Declaration of Human Rights (1948) 239–240
University of Glasgow 100
unpacking notions of 'conflict' and 'peace': transformative approach to peacebuilding
  critical dialogue for peacebuilding 56–57
  dialogic approach to peacebuilding/ conflict transformation 55–56
  storytelling as form of artistic dialogue 57–58
  what is conflict? 54–55
Ureke, O. 161

Veronese, G. et al. 70
violence against women (VAW) 9, 11, 13, 14, 18–20, 46, 47–48, 138
  Mexico 31, 32, 36–38
Virokannas, Elina 235
virtual space 34
Viviri, A. 161
vulnerability 234–236, 238–239

Wa Thiong'o, Ngũgĩ 210
Walsh, Catherine 203
Ward, S.C. 218, 219
Washaya, Y. 161
Wayne, K. 265, 266
Weitzer, R. 167
WhatsApp 35
Winky D 161, 169, 170

women's domestication 21–23
World Health Organization (WHO) 19

Yunus, Muhammad 208

Zim 174
Zimbabwe
  Constitution 76–77
  Disabled Persons Act (DPA) 76
  persons with disabilities (PwDs) 76–78
  concluding remarks 94
  see also popular culture and gender-based violence in Zimbabwe
Zimbabwe: findings 92–93, *93*
  social conflicts around children with disabilities 93–94
Zimbabwe: from stories to research
  methodological approach to the study 91–92
  research objectives and questions 90–91
Zimbabwe: stories of children born with disability 78
  Chikumi's story 81–83
  Chikunguru's story 83–84
  Chivabvu's story 81
  Gumiguru's story 85
  Gunyana's story 84–85
  Kubvumbi's story 80–81
  Kukadzi' story 79
  Kurume' story 79–80
  Ndira's story 78–79
  Nyamavhuvhu's story 84
Zimbabwe: stories of children's accidents leading to disability
  Matsutso's story 88–89
Zimbabwe: stories of human–wildlife conflict
  Chirimo's story 88
  Mbudzi's story 85–87
  Zvita's story 87–88
Zimbabwe: stories of schools & their mission to empower the differently abled
  Copota School 89–90
  Jairos Jiri School 90
Zimdancehall 174

For Product Safety Concerns and Information please contact our EU Authorised Representative:

Easy Access System Europe

Mustamäe tee 50

10621 Tallinn

Estonia

gpsr.requests@easproject.com